In this engaging book, John Gillies explores Shakespeare's geographic imagination, and discovers an intimate relationship between Renaissance geography and theatre arising from their shared dependence on 'poetic' geographic traditions in which geography is already moralised or alive with human and dramaturgical meaning, pre-eminently the meaning of otherness. Dr Gillies shows that Shakespeare's images of the exotic, the 'barbarous, outlandish and strange', are grounded in concrete historical fact: to be marginalised was not just a matter of social status, but of belonging, quite literally, to the margins of contemporary maps. Through an examination of the icons and emblems of contemporary cartography, Dr Gillies challenges the map-makers' overt intentions, and the attitudes and assumptions that remained below the level of consciousness. His study of map and metaphor raises profound questions about the nature of a map, and of the connections between the semiology of a map and that of the theatre.

D0813711

CAMBRIDGE STUDIES IN RENAISSANCE
LITERATURE AND CULTURE 4

Shakespeare and the geography of difference

Cambridge Studies in Renaissance Literature and Culture

General editor
STEPHEN ORGEL
Jackson Eli Reynolds Professor of Humanities, Stanford University

Editorial board
Anne Barton, *University of Cambridge*
Jonathan Dollimore, *University of Sussex*
Marjorie Garber, *Harvard University*
Jonathan Goldberg, *The Johns Hopkins University*
Nancy Vickers, *University of Southern California*

The last twenty years have seen a broad and vital reinterpretation of the nature of literary texts, a move away from formalism to a sense of literature as an aspect of social, economic, political and cultural history. While the earliest New Historicist work was criticised for a narrow and anecdotal view of history, it also served as an important stimulus for post-structuralist, feminist, Marxist and psychoanalytic work, which in turn has increasingly informed and redirected it. Recent writing on the nature of representation, the historical construction of gender and of the concept of identity itself, on theatre as a political and economic phenomenon and on the ideologies of art generally, reveals the breadth of the field. *Cambridge Studies in Renaissance Literature and Culture* is designed to offer historically oriented studies of Renaissance literature and theatre which make use of the insights afforded by theoretical perspectives. The view of history envisioned is above all a view of our own history, a reading of the Renaissance for and from our own time.

Titles published

Drama and the market in the age of Shakespeare
DOUGLAS BRUSTER, University of Chicago

The Renaissance dialogue: literary dialogue in its social and political contexts, Castiglione to Galileo
VIRGINIA COX, University College London

Spenser's secret career
RICHARD RAMBUSS, Tulane University

Shakespeare and the geography of difference
JOHN GILLIES, La Trobe University

Shakespeare and the geography of difference

John Gillies

Lecturer in Drama, La Trobe University

CAMBRIDGE
UNIVERSITY PRESS

Published by the Press Syndicate of the University of Cambridge
The Pitt Building, Trumpington Street, Cambridge CB2 1RP
40 West 20th Street, New York, NY 10011–4211, USA
10 Stamford Road, Oakleigh, Melbourne 3166, Australia

First published 1994

Printed in Great Britain at the University Press, Cambridge

A catalogue record for this book is available from the British Library

Library of Congress cataloguing in publication data

Gillies, John, 1947–
Shakespeare and the geography of difference / John Gillies.
    p.   cm. – (Cambridge studies in Renaissance literature and culture: 4)
Includes bibliographical references and index.
ISBN 0 521 41719 8 (hardback). ISBN 0 521 45853 6 (paperback)
1. Shakespeare, William, 1564–1616 – Knowledge – Geography.
2. Cartography – History – 16th century.
3. Cartography – History – 17th century.
4. Geography – History – 16th century.
5. Geography – History – 17th century.
6. Geography in literature.   7. Maps in literature.
I. Title.   II. Series.
PR3014.G55 1994
822.3′3 – dc20   93–15562   CIP

ISBN 0 521 41719 8 hardback
ISBN 0 521 45853 6 paperback

CE

For Ali, Sylvia,
and the memory of
my father, Douglas Neil Gillies

Contents

Illustrations

Acknowledgements

More than a few years ago, Stephen Orgel suggested to me that some material I had gathered on *The Tempest* had the makings of a book. This is another book altogether, with a lot more material going in unforeseen directions, but it began with that original suggestion. Much later, when a first and very speculative manuscript landed on Kevin Taylor's desk at Cambridge, I was fortunate to have it directed to Stephen and subsequently edited by him. The finished book owes much to his critical lucidity, the sureness of his compositional judgement, his scholarship and his unfailing generosity. There were, of course, other readers of that first manuscript. In particular, I would like to thank Stephen Prickett, Ian Donaldson, Stephen Greenblatt, Fred Langman, James Brown and Jane Adamson. A conspicuously cross-disciplinary endeavour like this could hardly have prospered without the help of specialists. For anthropological advice, I went to Nicholas Thomas. Ken Johnson and Chris Eade gave advice on historical cartography. My debts to the classicists are legion: to Andrew Farrington and Philip Hardie in particular, also to Bob Barnes and Sol Bastomski. Colin Mayrhoffer, Douglas Kelly and Greg Horsley have assisted with Latin translations. Roger Hilman provided a German translation. For their generous assistance with maps, frontispieces and paintings, I would like to thank Helen King, Jon Mee, Paul Duro and Paul Kaplan. Thanks for general help and suggestions are due to Gino Moliterno, John Bender and my brother Neil Gillies. Thanks to Kevin Taylor, for his patience. For conviviality and discussion, thanks to Rich Pascal, Satendra Nandan, Simon Haines, Glen Lewis and Paul Eggert. Special thanks to Carole Woodrow for inviting me to be dramaturg on her production of *The Merchant of Venice* with The Bell Shakespeare Company, and to John Bell for acting Shylock with rare force and sensitivity. Thanks also to the English Department of the Australian National University, for many things, among them a stipend as scholar in residence. A regret is that I will never be able to show this book to Professor H. W. Piper. I should like to acknowledge a grant towards expenses incurred, from The Australian Academy of the Humanities. For their wisdom and kindness, I owe a deep debt of gratitude to Gary Scholfield, Angela Sands, Eugene Veshner, Tony Wellington and Janet Smith. Thanks to Charlotte for keeping things in perspective. The greatest debt of all – for everything from correcting the final manuscript to giving me courage to jot down the first thoughts – is owed to my wife, Ali.

1 Mapping the Other: Vico, Shakespeare and the geography of difference

> Shakespeare's scenes are almost always laid inside what the ancients called the civilized world, the Christians Christendom, and the geographers Europe. Africa is the centre of interest in Greene's *Orlando*, Asia in Marlowe's *Tamburlaine*, Tunis in Massinger's *Renegado*, the Portuguese Spice and Clove islands of Ternate and Tidore in Beaumont and Fletcher's *Island Princess*; but Europe is Shakespeare's centre, and although things outside intrude now and then, like spectres from another world, his plots, themes, and scenes are almost exclusively European. The only exception is *The Tempest*, which belongs partly to the unsubstantial world of spirits and myths, partly to the New World, but partly, too, to a fragment of Italy transposed onto the New World for a day or two. Although the frontiers of Europe shift from time to time and are not the same in the ancient and modern world, Shakespeare's plants, so to speak, are always rooted in European soil: their environment is invariably European ... Beyond these European limits lay the unknown, or hardly known, wonderland of discovery and romance, where monsters dwelt and miracles were common, and which Shakespeare regarded much as every instinctive geographer regards what lies half within and half without his intellectual horizon ... and as for the east and west Indies – that is to say, nearly all Asia and all America – they were little appendices to his book of life, which book was Europe.[1]

Speculation about Shakespearean 'world views' is no longer as respectable as it was in 1916, when the above account from J. D. Rogers's essay, 'Voyages and Exploration: Geography: Maps', appeared in *Shakespeare's England*. Few scholars today would be persuaded by its view of Shakespeare's 'instinctive' geography. Some would want to dispute the claim that Shakespeare's 'plots, themes, and scenes are almost exclusively European'. Others would take issue with the notion that Shakespeare's imagination of geography is somehow medieval in comparison with that of contemporaries apparently more in touch with the new geography of their age. Most, perhaps, would dispute the sheer scope of Rogers's undertaking – the Johnsonian grandeur of his 'extensive view' of Shakespeare's imaginative geography. Is this sort of project admissible in an era of more sceptical and reflexive 'historicisms', which – presented with a scholarly mental map of a Shakespearean mental map – would want to know whose map and whose mentality is ultimately shown? It is, perhaps, for reasons such as this, that no similarly magisterial survey of Shakespeare's geographic imagination has appeared since Rogers. Neither has a systematic attempt been made to refute the idea that Shakespeare's geographic imagination is 'almost exclusively European'. This is both good and bad: good to the degree that we are weaned away from the habit of shutting texts into 'contexts' which are largely of our own invention; bad to the degree that the question of Shakespeare's geography has tended to urge itself by the back door and to find its answers there. Some years ago I remember hearing the managing director of a prominent Australian mining company cite *The Merchant of Venice* and *Othello* as evidence that Shakespeare disapproved of racially mixed marriages, and would therefore disapprove of the 'multicultural' philosophy of Australia's immigration policy.

In my own teaching, I have found that the large question of Shakespeare's global (as distinct from merely European) geographic imagination is often begged by related questions arising in the course of readings of individual plays. Invariably these plays turn out to be those which, if not actually set 'Beyond these European limits', powerfully urge the question of what Rogers calls 'the unknown, or hardly known, wonderland of discovery or romance, where monsters dwelt and miracles were common'. They are plays in which 'things outside intrude now and then, like spectres from another world' – *things* (images, characters) *like spectres*, which later critics have been in the habit of referring to generically as 'other'.[2]

One important way, then, in which Rogers's project of a Shakespearean geography might be remounted is in connection with Shakespeare's others: Who are they? What do they tell us, either about Shakespeare's construction of 'Europe', or about his construction of its exterior? To what extent is the latter construction 'instinctive'? To what extent is the former properly 'geographic'? Are 'Europe' and its exterior part of the same system of geographic or quasi-geographic ideas? What, if any, are the politics governing the interaction between Europeans and others in Shakespeare? Where would such a politics come from and where does it lead in the context of early modern discourses of race, miscegenation, colonialism and slavery? Is the otherness of Shakespeare's exotics a fact of nature or convention? What is Shakespeare's position on 'miscegenation'?[3] What do Shakespeare's others have in common, and to what discursive heritage – contemporary or traditional, ethnographic or political – do they owe any kinship which they might share? What, if any, is the connection between his imagination of ancient and Renaissance others, and between ancient exoticism and that revealed by the new geography?

A second way in which Shakespeare's extra-European geography might be mapped is through the agency of a Shakespearean figure who is often related to the other. Like the other, this figure is a creature of extremity, a creature of horizons, an explorer of *terra incognita* – of Hamlet's 'undiscovered country from whose bourn / No traveller returns' (3.1.81–2)[4]. Unlike the other, who is generically familiar to us both within and outside Shakespeare studies, there is no generic name for this figure. Hence, I will call him (and her) the 'voyager'. Voyagers may be opposed to others in the way that Prospero is opposed to Caliban, but they may also be allied, as Antony is to Cleopatra. Moreover, just as their alliance contains oppositions, so too do oppositions between voyagers and others contain enigmatic suggestions of a deeper alliance. Thus Prospero is obliged to acknowledge his other ('this thing of darkness') as 'mine' (5.1.278, 279); thus Antonio – so sharply opposed to Shylock at the level of action – is allied with him at a deep and obscure level of symbolic design. Each is a kind of merchant, each is a creature of hubris, each is a rival of Portia, and each is emphatically excluded from the play's community of marriage. Although, therefore, voyagers and others may sometimes oppose each other, their very 'extremity' (their geographic mystery) tends to bring them together in unexpected ways. Thus it is not surprising to find that two of Shakespeare's others are also voyagers: Morocco, who voyages from the ends of the earth for Portia; and Othello, the 'extravagant and wheeling stranger / Of here and everywhere' (1.1.138–9). The word 'extravagant' has a special value in this context. More than simply a spendthrift, it suggests a 'wanderer beyond bounds' by association with the medieval verb *extravagari*. Nor should such errancy be taken in too literal a sense. Desdemona is also a voyager to the degree that her taste for the discourse of voyaging – for what Othello calls his 'traveller's history' (1.3.138) – conjures Othello into imaginative existence.

What is the nature of the geographic imagination mediated by others and voyagers? The mysterious commerce between these two kinds of figure suggests that something rather more than a conventional notion of geography is involved. The geography of these plays is much more than a literal quantity and much more than a backdrop. It is a complex and dynamic imaginative quantity, with a characterological and symbolic agenda. To the extent, for example, that both voyagers and others tend to be creatures of hubris in the original Greek sense of 'overflowing' their bounds, then the exotic geographies that define them will tend to function as a paradigm of their transgressiveness. This will already suggest the poverty of Rogers's procedure of treating Shakespeare's geography independently of the rich nexus of symbolic values which it vehiculates. What we require is a more poetically responsive idea of geography, not just to cope with the poetic vitality which Shakespeare gives it but, more importantly, to elucidate how it actively lends itself to particular kinds of symbolic investment. In what follows, I will suggest that the *imaginative* or poetic dimension of Shakespeare's geographic imagination is not to be understood *sui generis*. Shakespeare is not to be thought of as pressing an inventory of proto-scientific, value-free, morally and mythologically inert geographic ideas into an imaginative existence which is somehow alien to their nature. Just the opposite is true. Shakespeare's geographic imagination is informed by a rich geographic tradition which is already moralised, already inherently 'poetic' in the sense of being alive with human and dramaturgical meaning: specifically, with the meaning of human difference. However, before we begin to look at the geography mediated by the other and the voyager, we need to formulate a more phenomenologically, poetically and historically adequate notion of geography.

1

The idea that geography has a moral or symbolic dimension is hardly new. Rogers himself implies as much about the geographies of medieval Europe and classical China, which is what he is thinking of when he calls Shakespeare an 'instinctive geographer'. Certainly, one has only to read *Mandeville's Travels*, gaze at a medieval world map, or indeed at any *imago mundi* ('world image') formed by a 'traditional' or 'pre-scientific' culture to realise their overwhelmingly human, even sacred, character.[5] Less clear, but no less true, is that European geography, from the sixteenth century to the present (that geographic discourse which we are accustomed to think of as 'scientific') can also be submitted to 'poetic' or phenomenological analysis. Edward Said, for example, has described the Eurocentric discourse of 'Orientalism' from Aeschylus to T. E. Lawrence (and after), while Robert Harbison has spoken of how even modern maps 'sedulously reinforce and protect our sense of where we are are' and operate in a 'semi-religious' capacity as 'our main means of aligning ourselves with something bigger than us'.[6] Non-geographic spaces have also been read as poetic constructions: from a cosmic aspect by Michel Foucault and from a domestic aspect by Gaston Bachelard.[7] There is, then, no shortage of phenomenologically sophisticated ways by which to approach the geographic traditions behind Shakespeare's geographic imagination.

Of all such phenomenologies, however, the notion of 'poetic geography' formulated by the eighteenth-century philosopher, Giambattista Vico, seems most suggestive to our purposes. Briefly, Vico supposes that the archaic image of the Greek *oikumene* – a word which suggestively combines the senses of 'world' and 'house' – predates and prescribes the earliest known formulation of its geography in Herodotus. In other words, the imaginative form of the *oikumene* controls its factual geographic content. Instead, therefore, of supposing that the Greeks formed the image of their world – a world which, in Herodotus, stretches from 'Scythia' in the north to Ethiopia in the south, and from 'Asia' in the east to Gibraltar in the west – from their commerce with that world, Vico supposes that the essential *oikumene* began in Greece itself.[8] In the beginning, then, the Greek image of the 'world' was literally bound by their geographic 'home'. Then, as further geographic knowledge became available, the symbolic architecture of the *oikumene* was simply exported or extrapolated to accommodate it. 'Poetic geography' is accordingly defined as 'the property of human nature that "in describing unknown or distant things, in respect of which they ... have not had the true idea themselves ... men make use of the semblances of things known or near at hand"' (p. 285). What is interesting for our purposes is less Vico's methods – an unashamed mythology of origins supported by an elaborate skein of inferences drawn from fanciful etymologies – than his vision: boldly deconstructing the Enlightenment assumption that the Greeks invented 'geography' essentially in order to understand their world rather than to project it in their own parochial image. Vico, then, is exemplary for our project to the degree that a relatively unproblematised discourse like geography tends to be 'taken for granted' which means being taken in Enlightenment terms.

Vico is exemplary for another reason: his vision of how directly and powerfully the 'poetic' dimension of ancient geography mediates key ideological structures, particularly those which articulate identity and difference. Thus, supposes Vico in a related origin myth, the archaic image of the Latin 'home-world' is itself formed at the most primal stage of social formation: the stage at which a casual grouping of individuals marks itself off from 'the infamous promiscuity of people and things in the bestial state', and so constitutes itself as a society proper. In one sense, this primal geographic and societal drama is to be regarded as belonging to the 'poetic' (which is to say prehistoric) past of ancient societies, but in another sense, that primal drama is always with them, fossilised in the etymology of key geographic terms. The Latin term *terra* (or 'earth') is glossed as follows:

The earth was associated by the theological poets with the guarding of the boundaries, and hence it was called *terra*. This heroic origin the Latins preserved in the word *territorium*, which signifies the district within which the *imperium* is exercised ... the word originated in the fact that the boundaries of those cultivated fields, within which the civil powers later arose, were guarded by Vesta with bloody rites. (p. 274)

Just as the geographic term *terra* is etymologically racked to disclose its roots in the primal terrorism of civilisation, so too geographic myth and symbolism is systematically collapsed into the mythology of the primal city. *Vesta*, for example, the Roman goddess of the sacred hearth-flame, is derived from the Greek *Cybele* (or Earth-mother) 'who wears a crown of towers', from which 'the so-called *orbis terrarum* began to take form, signifying the world of nations, later amplified by cosmographers and called *orbis mundanus* or, in a word, *mundus*, the world of nature' (p. 274). *Orbis* or the bounded 'world' directly recapitulates the sacred drama of the bounded city:

the walls were traced by the founders of the cities with the plough, the moldboard of which, by the origins of language ... must have been called *urbs*, whence the ancient *urbum*, curved. Perhaps *orbis* is from the same origin, so that at first *orbis terrae* must have meant any fence made in this way, so low that Remus jumped over it to be killed by Romulus and thus, as Latin historians narrate, to consecrate with his blood the first walls of Rome. (p. 194)

Thus Vico insistently derives the archaic origins of the 'world' from that of the city. The walls of the city and the borders of its territory are both telescoped into the edges of the ancient map; the personified female body of the city (*Vesta*) is co-extensive with that of the earth (*Cybele*). Inhabited earth and city constantly divide themselves from their opposites. Their thresholds – altars, walls, boundaries, frontiers – threaten transgressors with the sacred violence of sacrifice, law or warfare. The order of city and world is constituted by their violent differentiation from 'the infamous promiscuity of people and things in the bestial state'.

Vico is exemplary not just for devising a 'poetics' of the ancient *imago mundi* but for thinking 'poetic geography' through to the point of requiring a politics or an ethnography or a drama. If the trunk of 'poetic geography' consists in the ability of an archaic world-image to accommodate ever more sophisticated and diverse geographic information, then its root consists in the ceaselessly renewed activity of differentiation. The need to constitute an identity by excluding the other is not just primal, but perennial. With the growth of geographic information and the outward push of imperial borders, come ever more others, renewing the need to differentiate, and perpetuating the need for a symbolic border and ever new rites of exclusion. Notwithstanding the inadmissibility of Vico's accounts of discursive origins, I want to suggest that 'poetic geography' be taken as paradigmatic for any geography which differentiates between an 'us' and a 'them': whether the geographic entities so divided are thought of in terms of the ancient dualism of the 'inhabited earth' versus what Horace calls *terras domibus negata* ('uninhabitable lands'), the Renaissance dualism of the known world versus that class of geographic entity bearing the label '*terra incognita*', or other dualisms such as 'Europe' versus 'the Orient' or 'Christendom' versus 'Paganism'.[9]

2

Vico's importance is in systematically thinking through the *meaning* of geography as an articulation of human perspective, and for suggesting how the most strikingly perspective-affirming conventions of ancient geography – those pertaining to privileged centres and enclosing edges – might be understood in precise 'poetic' or dramaturgical terms. However, to admit his importance as an exemplar is not to accept his mythological fantasies and his etymological methods. The present task, therefore, is to furnish another order of 'proof' of the differential activity of centres and borders in the European geographic tradition, beginning with the historical origins of this tradition in the Hellenic *oikumene*.

Ironically, in view of the prodigality of Vico's myth-making, the extant mythology of the *oikumene* already exemplifies a necessary (and highly Viconian) dialectic of centre and border. One form of this spatial dialectic can be seen in a second-century oration by Aelius Aristides in praise of Athens: 'From every extremity as to a device in the centre of a shield, the signs of Hellas point to this region ... the nation's common hearth'.[10] Another version of the dialectic is revealed by J. P. Vernant's study of the meaning of the mythological relationship between Hestia (goddess of the hearth) and Hermes (god of travellers, the marketplace and boundaries).[11] For Vernant, Hestia 'represents not only the centre of the domestic sphere ... the circular hearth' but also 'the node and starting point of the orientation and arrangement of human space' (p. 128). Hermes, too, is 'associated with man's habitat' and also 'with the terrestrial sphere' (p. 128). But, 'if with Hestia, he inhabits the dwellings of mortals' it is 'in the form of the messenger ... as a traveller from afar ... who is already preparing to depart' (p. 129). Where Hestia represents fixity, Hermes represents 'movement and flow, mutation and transition, contact between foreign elements' (p. 129). Hence is he the god of gateways, boundaries and crossroads. The two gods are, then, complementary:

forever immobile, at the centre of the domestic sphere, Hestia implies, as her complement and her contrast, the swift-footed god who rules the realms of the traveller. To Hestia belongs the world of the interior, the enclosed, the stable, the retreat of the human group within itself; to Hermes, the outside world, opportunity, movement, interchange with others. It could be said that, by virtue of their polarity, the Hermes-Hestia couple represents the tension which is so marked in the archaic conception of space: space requires a centre, a nodal point, with a special value, from which all directions, all different qualitatively, may be channelled and defined; yet at the same time space appears as the medium of movement implying the possibility of transition and passage from any point to another. (p. 130)

While Hermes 'mobilises' space, in contrast to Hestia who 'centres' it, he nevertheless approaches the fixity of Hestia the nearer he approaches the boundary, at which point his movement ceases and he becomes frozen into the *Herm*: the Greek term for a geographical boundary marker.[12] The *Herm* therefore represents the limits of the dynamic Hermetic organisation of space, the point at which movement becomes stasis and randomness of geographic line approaches the geometry of the orbic boundary: what the Ionians referred to as 'the parallelogram of Ephorus' and what William Arthur Heidel generically describes as 'the frame of the ancient Greek maps'.[13]

While the relationship between Hestia and Hermes is fruitfully symbiotic, that between the *oikumene* as a whole and the lands at or beyond its frame is one of utter divorce and difference. Herodotus, who is the first to leave a systematic description of such extreme areas and their peoples, refers to them generically as *eschatia*: end-zones and wastelands.[14] The 'poetry' of the frame controls the discourse of such extremities in two important ways. First, by the logic of exclusion, extreme lands will be constructed as polar opposites of the *oikumene* proper. Second, by the logic of symmetry, all *eschatia* will – in spite of local variations or even glaring antitheses – tend to replicate each other.

The logic of exclusion leads to a generic description of all *eschatia* as the home of *thoma* or 'wonders', a term which fuses the monstrous (in the sense of the physically grotesque) with the marvellous (in the sense of remarkable and precious products such as balm, incense, spices, gold, jewels and drugs). By contrast, *Hellas*, while lacking in *thoma* of either variety, will be plainly superior to the end-zones (particularly those of the frigid north or the torrid south) in its fruitfulness and temperateness. Thus, Herodotus informs us, 'the fairest blessings have been granted to the most distant nations ... whereas in Hellas the seasons have by much the kindest temperature' (3.106).[15] Just as the natural qualities of the *eschatia* differ absolutely from those of *Hellas*, so too the peoples of these regions will represent an extreme (savage, demonic or carnivalesque) inversion of Greek society. Hence, François Hartog finds Herodotean ethnography to be dominated by a rhetoric of 'inversion'.[16] And hence, Edith Hall describes how fifth-century Athenian political mythology and tragedy 'invented' an all-purpose label for non-Hellenes which would simultaneously collapse all their ethnic variety into a single category and assert the absolute 'natural' inferiority of all non-Hellenic peoples to Hellenes.[17] Thus was born the seminal figure of the 'barbarian', an other who would become systematically appropriated by the ethnographic and imperial discourses of Rome and Renaissance Europe. In Athenian tragedy, the formative discursive milieu of the barbarian, the poetry of the *oikumene* becomes both political, in the sense of its intimate relationship to the political mythology of Athens, and truly dramaturgical.[18] For the Athenians, the extreme otherness of barbarians led to their imagery being collapsed into that of mythological Athenian others such as Centaurs and Amazons – who (on account of their femaleness, long hair and flowing robes) came to be elided with the 'Oriental' (and hence effeminate) Persians.[19] Hence the depiction of centauromachies and amazonomachies on the walls of the Parthenon – at the sacred centre of the *Polis* – celebrated in an almost Viconian fashion the violent assertion of Athenian identity over these Athenian versions 'the infamous promiscuity of people and things in the bestial state'.[20] To Aristides, Athens seems the focus of Hellenic culture because, situated 'in the middle of all Hellas . . . it is she alone who purely represents the Hellenes and to the barbarians remains most alien'.[21] The mythology, poetry and drama of the barbarian should not be thought of as coming after the fact of the Hellenic border, but as a vital means of constituting it. Hall observes a similar phenomenon in ancient Egypt and China.[22] World borders tend to be defined as empires form and others are identified.

While the logic of exclusion led to all extreme lands being represented as inversions of *Hellas* (and hence of the Athenian *Polis* which invented the very idea of a Hellenic nation), the same logic led to extreme lands being constructed as mirror images of each other. Thus, according to François Hartog, Herodotus was able to invent an entire ethnography for Scythia (an extreme northerly region of which he knew very little) by systematically inverting everything which he knew about Egypt (an extreme southerly region).[23] Hence where the Egyptians are the most ancient and learned of men, the Scythians are the 'youngest', the most ignorant and the most savage. Where nature in Egypt is dominated by heat, that in Scythia is controlled by cold. Finally, in a purely Viconian geographic extrapolation, the course of the Nile in the south is predicted on the assumption that it will be symmetrical with that of the Ister (or the Danube) in the north.[24] A similar reverence for symmetry leads Herodotus to rank the marvels of India, in extremest Asia, alongside those of Arabia, in extremest Libya (3.104–15).

A version of the 'poetic' tension which we have observed between the centre and the periphery of the *oikumene* is to be found in the Roman *orbis terrarum* or *orbis terrae* (literally, 'the circle of lands'). While the Romans seem to have lacked any mythological equivalent of the subtle spatial dialectic between Hestia and Hermes, they adopted the more aggressive and Viconian Athenian mythologies of geographic difference with a vengeance. Hence, the symbolism of the orbic frame, the essentially *Polis*-centred Athenian mythology of geographic difference, the idea of the barbarian and the Herodotean ethnographic tradition are all writ large in Roman poetic geographic discourse. Unlike the edges of the *oikumene* or of *Hellas*, which (because they were essentially symbolic) are often telescoped together in the mythology of the *oikumene*, the edges of the Roman 'world' have a powerful physical presence. Hence, Gibbon speaks of Augustus's desire to confine the empire 'within those limits which Nature seemed to have placed on its permanent bulwarks and boundaries: the Atlantic Ocean on the west; the Rhine and Danube on the north; the Euphrates on the east; and toward the south, the sandy deserts of Arabia and Africa'.[25] Yet the very self-evidence of these 'permanent bulwarks and boundaries' testifies to a prior need to project a human world (Vico's *orbis terrarum* or 'world of nations') in natural terms (Vico's *orbis mundanus* or 'world of nature'). Ovid relates a Roman proverb: *Gentibus est aliis tellus data limite certo, Romanae spacium est urbis et orbis idem* ('The land of other nations has a fixed boundary: the circuit of Rome is the circuit of the world').[26] What this and similar proverbs suggest is that the Roman *imago mundi* was as much a construction of 'poetry' and rhetoric as of factual geography.[27] In his study of the *orbis terrarum*, J. Oliver Thomson remarks how the Romans actually suppressed their knowledge of extra-imperial regions such as China, in order to preserve the proverbial equivalence of the Empire with the world.[28]

For all their monumental physicality, then, the edges of the Roman world are as mysterious and poetic as those of the *oikumene*. Plutarch observes their fascination for Roman map-makers: 'geographers ... crowd into the edges of their maps parts of the world which they do not know about, adding notes in the margin to the effect, that beyond this lies nothing but the sandy deserts full of wild beasts, unapproachable bogs, Scythian ice, or a frozen sea'.[29] The 'instinct' which led Plutarch's geographers to take poetic licence with precisely those 'parts of the earth which elude their knowledge' also informs the Roman terms for 'boundary': *terminus* and *finis*. *Terminus* could have the sense of 'a concrete object', which insofar as it served to mark a boundary 'was of great importance in law and religion; the man who removed landmarks was accursed'.[30] In this sense it was personified as 'the god of boundaries'.[31] While this sacralisation of the boundary appears to have suggested property boundaries in the first instance, it powerfully suggests civic and world geographic boundaries too. Hence, to transgress these – especially the bounds of Rome or the western boundary of the *orbis terrarum* marked by the mountains of Calpe and Abdylla (the 'Pillars of Hercules') at the Strait of Gibraltar – was to incur all the pollution danger of the man who violates a boundary between fields.[32] *Finis* also suggests the boundary in both a physical and moral sense, as, for example, in Lucan's description of Cato's piety: 'to observe moderation and hold fast to the limit' (*servare modum finemque tenere*).[33] The impiety of Marcus Crassus is conveyed by the historian Paterculus in terms of a conventional wordplay on the simultaneously moral and geographical character of limits. Accordingly, Crassus is one 'who knew no limits (*modum*) and accepted no bounds (*terminum*)'.[34]

The superiority of Rome to the terminal lands is further expressed in a wholesale transformation of Greek geographical ideas into Roman geographical discourse, and indeed, into a repertoire of rhetorical topoi. Rome was *medius mundi locus* ('the centre of the world').[35] Natural historians like Pliny, Pomponius Mela and Gaius Julius Solinus followed the example of Herodotus when reporting on the existence of monsters and marvels in distant lands, while the preference of Italy over such places was commonplace. The topos of the *Laudes Italiae* (the 'praise of Italy') is one of a host of rhetorical formulae in which the climatic and agricultural superiority of Italy is asserted over the wonders of what Virgil (in a notable exercise in the genre) refers to as the ends of the earth.[36] Such a formula blends the Herodotean geographic tradition with a tradition of *temperies* associated with Hippocrates.[37] *Temperies* equated variations in the natural and the human world with differences in climate, and thus was able to derive the moral superiority of *Hellas* over northerly and southerly countries from its superior climate. A formulaic blend of both discourses can be found in an ode by Horace (via which, incidentally, both discourses find their way into Shakespeare's *Titus Andronicus*). In *Integer Vitae* (*Odes*, 1.22), Horace imagines himself securely placed within a temperate region bound by his own farm (a joking periphrasis of Italy and the Roman *orb*) and asserts the 'integrity' of his little world to endure against all extremities (in the imagined form of extreme lands, with intemperate climates, wild beasts and moors with poisoned weapons).

Horace's image of himself as a man of 'upright life' scorning 'the bow and javelin of the moor', suggests how completely the fifth-century Greek invention of 'the barbarian' had passed into Roman discourse. Though the moor was a Roman bogeyman as distinct from a Greek barbarian, the idea of the barbarian was assimilated via the discourses of tragedy (the original formative milieu of the barbarian) and the Athenian *Polis*. In the tragedies of Seneca, the otherness of the barbarian tends to be even more polluting and more demonic than in his Greek sources (Seneca being entirely without the irony which, in Euripides, tends to undermine the Athenian ideological opposition of Greek and barbarian even while affirming it). If tragedy was one source of the Roman idea of the barbarian, Athenian political philosophy was another. Lidia Storoni Mazzolani has described how the Roman idea of empire came to exalt the city of Rome in the way that the Athenian idea of empire had exalted the *Polis*, and how as a consequence Roman political philosophers such as Cicero came to adopt the Aristotelian idea of exotic races as barbarous – ironically at a time when contemporary Greek philosophers were inventing the idea of a 'cosmopolitan' empire based on the world rather than on the city, and an idea of all Roman subjects as 'citizens of the world'.[38] Ultimately, as we shall see, the construction of the barbarian in classical tragedy, and his importance in the imperial ideas of Rome and Athens, ensures his transmission to Shakespeare.

3

In spite, then, of the fact that the *oikumene* and the *orbis terrarum* were not geographically equivalent, the boundaries of each are expressed by idioms which Vico would have recognised as 'poetic' and as mediating a primal drama of identity, difference and transgression. Given the substantial similarity of such a drama in both ancient poetic geographic discourses, how might we characterise it? What is the nature of the transgression and what is the nature of the drama? What is their bearing on the drama of transgression in Shakespeare?

Vico's mythological dramatisations of the power of borders in the archaic imagination of the world find a suggestive echo in the work of modern anthropologists on the symbolism of borders in relation to ideas of pollution, taboo – ultimately, to what Mary Douglas calls 'the idea of society':

The idea of society is a powerful image. It is potent in its own right to control or stir men to action. This image has form; it has external boundaries, margins, internal structure. Its outlines contain power to reward conformity and to repulse attack. There is energy in its margins and unstructured areas. For symbols of society any human experience of structures, margins, or boundaries is ready to hand.[39]

For Douglas, the most suggestive 'human experience of ... margins' is that of the body, a key mediation of 'the idea of society'. Accordingly, she proceeds to discuss the pollution beliefs of traditional cultures pertaining to 'the energy' of the body's 'margins and unstructured areas' (the orifices) not as evidence of the presumed infantilism of those cultures, but as evidence of how any given culture will tend to mirror its construction of social margins in its symbolic construction of the body: 'the mistake is to treat bodily margins in isolation from all other margins' (p. 121). All cultures develop pollution beliefs relating to bodily margins because 'all margins are dangerous' and because 'any structure of ideas is vulnerable at its margins' (p. 121). Fundamental to Douglas's approach to the 'human experience of margins' is the idea that the 'external lines' of a given social system will tend to recapitulate its 'internal structure', and vice versa. By way of example, Douglas considers prohibitions governing the preparation of food in India. The elaborateness and severity of these prohibitions is seen to reflect the caste system rather than a concern for hygiene as such. This is because the food consumed by higher castes is prepared by lower castes, thereby threatening the integrity of the caste system itself, as 'one cannot share the food prepared by people without sharing their nature'.[40] The point is that 'food is not likely to be polluting at all unless the external boundaries of the social system are under pressure' (pp. 126–7).

Like the Indian caste system, the imagined edges of the ancient map would represent a case of 'external boundaries' recapitulating the 'internal lines' of prohibitions governing the body and its orifices. Hence *eschatia* and *termini* tend to be figured as 'wastelands' by Plutarch's geographers: a circumambient zone of 'sandy deserts full of wild beasts, unapproachable bogs, Scythian ice or a frozen sea'. More than just a desert, the margin was *mundi faece repletam*, or 'full of the shit of the world' (in a phrase that Lucan ironically applies to a Rome polluted by the peripheral races which have flocked to her).[41] Such places were not merely 'uninhabited' but 'uninhabitable' (in the active sense of Horace's *terras domibus negata*); their very nature seeming to conspire with the 'infamous promiscuity' of the abortive races (monstrous, savage and barbarous) which possessed them. Hence, in the words of Seneca the Elder, 'all that is primitive and incomplete in nature has retreated to this far refuge'; simply to *be* at the edge is to be abominable: 'if this were not an evil thing, it would not lie at the end of the earth'.[42] The link between monstrosity, margins and sexual 'promiscuity' is far from casual. Mythological edge monsters such as centaurs and harpies are hybrids, or the offspring of literally 'promiscuous' unions between creatures of different kinds. So too are the monsters – animal and human (Sciapods, Monoculi, Blemmyes, etc.) – of the ancient teratological tradition in writers such as Julius Solinus.[43] Serious Renaissance geographers attributed the remarkable prevalence of such creatures in Africa to the interbreeding of different species at desert water-holes.[44] The idea would remain a commonplace well beyond the Renaissance.[45] Amazons, while not physically monstrous, offend against the laws of kind by excluding men and propagating promiscuously outside of marriage.

The sexual promiscuity of legendary races like the Amazons is also attributed to barbarians in general. In Euripides's *Andromache*, Hector's widow finds herself accused of incestuous tendencies by Hermione, the jealous wife of the Spartan general who has taken her as a concubine:

> this is a Greek city.
> And you have the effrontery, you immoral wretch,
> To sleep with the man whose father killed your husband, bear
> Children with the blood of his murderer in their veins!
> You orientals are all alike – incest between
> Father and daughter, brother and sister, mother and son;
> And murder too – the closest family ties outraged,
> And no law to forbid any such crime! You can't
> Import your foreign morals here.[46]

Clearly, the idea that 'Asians' are incestuous is not representative of the play's own ethos (Euripides is ironically sceptical of Hermione's motives). But the very fact that the accusation leaps so readily to the tongue – the fact that it already exists as a rhetorical commonplace – underlines the generic association between barbarians and the most infamous of promiscuities.

Outsider in the city, stranger on the hearth, the barbarian is a transgressor of bounds and a violator of prohibitions: notably the prohibition on incest upon which rests the institution of the family and ultimately that of the state. In *Iphigenia in Aulis*, Agamemnon justifies the 'strange lust' which 'rages with demonic power throughout the Hellene army' as a desire to 'stop Barbarians from raping Hellene wives'.[47] With pathetic dignity, Iphigenia – the daughter who is to be sacrificed to appease the army's 'strange lust' – accepts her death as a guarantee of 'the future safety of Greek wives from barbarous attacks':

> To Hellas, then, I dedicate myself.
> Sacrifice me; take and plunder Troy. For me, your victory
> Shall be children, marriage – for all time my glorious monument.
> Greeks were born to rule barbarians, mother, not barbarians
> To rule Greeks. They are slaves by nature; we have freedom in our
>   blood.

(lines 1398–402)

Again, the 'official' ideology represented by Iphigenia and Agamemnon seems undercut by bitter irony: the only way for the supposedly lustful barbarians to be chastised is for an innocent Greek girl to be sacrificed to the 'strange lust' of the chastising Greeks. But, again, the irony merely testifies to the power of the prior ideological construction of the barbarian. Though the irony may seem overdone to the modern reader, it cannot have seemed so to a contemporary Athenian audience, nor to Aristotle who cites Iphigenia's words as an illustration of his doctrine of 'natural servitude' (*Politics*, 1252b).[48] For Aristotle, the promiscuity of the barbarian is indicated by a failure to distinguish between female and slave ('non-Greeks assign to female and slave exactly the same status') and by a consequent incapacity for marriage (*Politics*, 1252a). By inference barbarians are also incapable of living a civilised existence because Aristotle derives the state from the family and thereby from nature itself (*Politics*, 1252a–1253b). The inability of barbarians to live within the 'natural' institutions of family and state thus makes them unnatural and hence 'slaves by nature'.[49]

The structural nature of the linkage between barbarians (a threat to the 'external lines' of *Hellas*) and incest (a threat to its 'internal structure') implies that the barbarian will be constructed in terms of another sexual prohibition: that on miscegenation. Lévi-Strauss remarks on the seeming paradox that:

incest proper and its metaphorical form as the violation of a minor (by someone 'old enough to be her father', as the expression goes), even combines in some countries with its direct opposite, inter-racial sexual relations, an extreme form of exogamy, as the two most powerful inducements to horror and collective vengeance.[50]

Just such a combination of 'directly opposite' sexual taboos is to be found in Greek and Roman tragedy. Again and again tragedians such as Sophocles and Seneca assume that incest is the most polluting of crimes (*Oedipus* is a particularly striking example of a common theme). Of the two taboos, that on incest is the more inveterate. It is intrinsic to the archaic mythological repertoire which, according to Edith Hall, had to be adjusted by Greek tragedians in the course of the fifth century in order to accommodate the 'invention' of the barbarian, the new Periclean ethos of endogamy and its corollary: a taboo on miscegenation.[51] Euripides's *Medea* – a seemingly archetypal tragic parable of miscegenation between a Greek male and an exotic and barbarous female – illustrates the point nicely. Hall argues that Medea was 'not even foreign' in the original myth and that her 'conversion into a barbarian was almost certainly the invention of tragedy, probably of Euripides himself'.[52] Hence, the official moral of the tragedy – that barbarians don't make good wives – represents a late addition to the source myth. In similar fashion, Sophocles appears to have reshaped a myth of incestuous rape into a parable of miscegenation in a now lost tragedy of Tereus and Philomel. Again, Hall points out, 'Tereus ... had not traditionally been Thracian but a Megarian cult hero ... his ethnic redefinition was probably a Sophoclean innovation' (p. 104). In both these tragedies, therefore, a mythology of miscegenation is fashioned from older mythic material and linked to a more inveterate type of transgression, resulting in a comprehensive dramatic portrait of the transgressive barbarian.

Though Sophocles's tragedy of Tereus has not survived, the legend survives in Ovid's *Metamorphoses* (6.420–676).[53] Ovid's tale is worth extended consideration for several reasons: it represents a mature expression of the Athenian myth of the barbarian; it suggests how completely that myth is assimilated into the Roman discourse of the barbarian; and – as the mythological blueprint of *Titus Andronicus* – it represents a principal means by which the classical myth of the barbarian is transmitted to Shakespeare.

Ovid's narrative might be thought of in terms of three movements or 'Acts'. In the first of these, Tereus – king of the barbarous Thracians – relieves Athens from an infestation by other barbarians. More in gratitude than wisdom, Pandion, the king of Athens, bestows his daughter, Procne, in marriage. The union and the birth of a son, Itys, are attended by evil omens: 'The Furies lighted them with torches stolen from a funeral, the Furies spread the couch, and the uncanny screech-owl brooded and sat on the roof of their chamber' (lines 431–2). After five years in Thrace, Procne begs to be allowed to visit her sister Philomel in Athens, or to have Philomel visit her. Tereus consents to the second proposal and visits Athens in person to fetch Philomel, but while there falls in lust with the girl and – his eloquence fired by lust – prevails on Pandion to allow her to visit her sister. The second movement begins with the voyage to Thrace and the rape of Philomel upon reaching that fatal shore. To prevent disclosure of the double transgression (of incest and rape), Tereus cuts Philomel's tongue out, though not before she accuses him of 'confusing all natural relations' in a phrase (*omnia turbasti*) which epitomises the meaning of the tale (line 537). Deprived of speech, Philomel nevertheless contrives to depict her plight in a tapestry. The third movement begins when Procne sees the tapestry, recognises its meaning, and reacts. In the course of a bacchanalian revel, she releases Philomel and hits upon the idea of revenging herself on Tereus through their son. Itys is subsequently butchered, cooked and fed to his unwitting father. When Tereus attempts to revenge himself on the two women, all three are metamorphosed into birds.

'Confusion' in the comprehensive sense of *omnia turbasti* is the governing idea of all three movements. It is foreshadowed from the very first moment, when an Athenian king commits the ignominy of relying on one group of barbarians to defend the city from another group. From this 'confusion' follows another: the unholy marriage between Athenian princess and Thracian king. In Ovid, the preposterousness of this union of extremes is registered in the inverted character of the marriage blessing, and in Procne's nostalgia for Athens and Philomel. Sophocles possibly made more of this than Ovid does. In a surviving fragment of the tragedy, Procne laments having been 'married into a barbarian household far from home'.[54] Nevertheless, in Ovid, the geographical and human gulf between Athens and Thrace is clear enough in Pandion's reluctance to part with his second daughter. It is also clear in the nature of Tereus's lust for Philomel. True barbarian that he is, Tereus covets Philomel not just for her beautiful body but also for her Athenian 'refinement and apparel' (line 454). Ovid is also careful to mention that 'his own passionate nature pricked him on, and besides, the men of his clime are quick to love: his own fire and his nation's burnt in him' (lines 458–60). Tereus is particularly excited by the sight of Philomel kissing Pandion and throwing 'her arms about her father's neck'; and riots in the contemplation of himself as an incestuous father as well as an incestuous brother-in-law (line 479). All this mental 'confusion' is set in relief by Pandion's solemn injunction that Tereus protect Philomel 'by ... the ties that bind us' and 'guard her with a father's love' (lines 498–9).

The incestuous rape represents the first explosion of the pent-up energy to 'confusion', as well as its only explicit formulation in the phrase *omnia turbasti*. It also marks the first stage of the Athenian sisters' descent into a classical version of Conrad's 'heart of darkness'. The motif of language is an important indicator of this. In an episode which inverts the earlier perversion of eloquence by Tereus, Philomel is depicted as losing the civilising gift of speech along with her 'severed tongue', which Ovid describes as 'palpitating on the dark earth, faintly murmuring' (lines 557–8).[55] It is tempting to suppose that such a detail was originally Sophoclean, and that Sophocles had intended some wordplay on *barbaros*, a word signifying both a 'barbarian' and a 'babbler' (on the assumption that non-Greek speakers were without speech in any proper sense). The first stage of Procne's barbarisation is also conveyed through the motif of language: 'Grief chokes the words that rise to her lips, and her questing tongue can find no words strong enough to express her outraged feelings' (lines 583–5). Procne's plan of revenge is beyond language and the civilisation it represents. The only answer to the 'confusion' of the rape is to 'confound right and wrong' (line 586). In the next stage of their barbarisation, the sisters abandon themselves to the ritual madness of Bacchantes. Finally, in an image which recapitulates earlier bestial images of Tereus as 'a grey wolf' and a bird of prey, Procne slaughters her son 'as a tigress ... on Ganges's banks' (lines 527–8, 636–7). Mere bestiality, however, cannot approach the ultimate 'confusion' represented by inverted sacramentalism of the cannibal banquet. After gorging 'with flesh of his own flesh', Tereus calls for Itys, only to be told: 'You have, within, him whom you want' (lines 651, 655).[56]

The fearful symmetry of this parable suggests how potent is the graft between the archaic mythological theme of incest and the fifth-century tragic themes of miscegenation and the barbarian. The tale also illustrates the full meaning of the idea that barbarians are promiscuous. Rather as in Aristotle, the lustful barbarian is depicted as utterly 'unnatural', as far beyond the moral pale of the *Polis* and the family as he is beyond the geographical pale of *Hellas*. Far from suggesting a mere ethnic foible, the lustfulness of Tereus is a master sign of otherness, of 'confusion', of an 'infamous promiscuity of people and things in the bestial state'. Miscegenation with a barbarian is not only destructive for the individual but for the family: the symbolic economy within which the roles of husband, wife, parent, child, brother and sister have meaning. The antithesis of barbarian and family is perhaps even more fundamental than the link between barbarians and incest. In the Medea myth, for example, the barbarous heroine is not incestuous but she does enact a literal version of 'the death of the family'; or rather, of several families. She dismembers her father's family by eloping with a stranger and by literally dismembering her own brother in order to make good her escape. She destroys the family of Pelias by tricking his daughters into bleeding him to death. She destroys her own family by butchering her children, and that of Creon by poisoning his daughter – Jason's intended bride. In both the Euripidean and the Senecan version of the tragedy, the chorus lays the blame for these disasters on the 'confusion' represented by the miscegenation between Greek and barbarian.

To summarise, the ancient other is constructed in terms of an idiom which recapitulates geographic 'exorbitance' as moral transgressiveness. Literally 'uneconomised' by the geographic structure of the *oikumene*, the other is a force for 'confusion', whether at the biological level (the Herodotean discourse of teratology) or at the most intimate levels of social structure (the discourses of incest and miscegenation).

In view of the Renaissance habit of reading the classics in the light of the Bible, it is useful to observe how much the ancient other has in common with the other of the Old Testament. No less than the barbarian, the Canaanite is generically 'promiscuous' and systematically opposed to the entire bewildering array of observance and prohibition set forth in the Pentateuch. In Chapter 3 of *Purity and Danger* ('The Abominations of Leviticus'), Mary Douglas argues that apparently unrelated taboos – such as those against eating pork, committing incest, sowing one's field 'with two kinds of seed', or wearing a garment 'made of two kinds of stuff' – all testify to a master taboo of 'confusion'; which is the precise meaning of the word *tebhel* (more commonly translated as 'perversion' or 'abomination') (p. 53). Just as the classical barbarian is constructed in terms of the most inveterate of ancient 'confusions' (the incest taboo), so too is the Canaanite constructed in terms of the master theme of 'confusion' in the Pentateuch. Running like a *leitmotif* through Leviticus is the assumption that the Canaanites routinely practise all that is prohibited to the Hebrews: 'Defile not ye yourselves in any of these things: for in all these the nations are defiled which I cast out before you: And the land is defiled: therefore I do visit the iniquity thereof upon it, and the land vomiteth out her inhabitants' (18.24–5).[57] By a Viconian paradox, the aborigines of the land of Canaan are seen to have forfeited their 'natural' right to that land by virtue of their 'unnatural' behaviour, making them 'foreign' in the complex sense that the barbarian is foreign. Indeed, when the genesis of the Canaanites is taken into consideration, the very idea of a 'natural' title to the land is void. As the offspring of Ham, the third son of Noah, the Canaanites were supposed to have inherited the curse of slavery which God had laid upon Ham for looking 'upon the nakedness of his father' (a phrase which may be code for 'homosexual incest').[58] The Canaanites are figured as creatures of 'confusion' in yet another sense which might be thought of as corresponding to Herodotean ethnography. Banished from the tribe of Noah, Ham is supposed to have promiscuously fathered adulterous generations wherever his wanderings took him. These generations were supposed to have propagated themselves with similar promiscuity until all trace of properly human (which is to say Hebrew) heritage was lost. Such a process of racial degeneration explains how the Canaanite can be depicted as the type of 'infamous promiscuity' in the Pentateuch. In the Renaissance, as we shall see, the biblical discourse of the Canaanite was actively concorded with the Aristotelian discourse of the barbarian in order to define the Renaissance other (African and American) as outlandish, transgressive and slavish 'by nature'.

4

If versions of the other personify the marginal 'energies' of the ancient (and biblical) *oikumene*, then so do the mythological ancestors of the Shakespearean voyager. Like otherness, voyaging is dangerous because inherently 'terminal', particularly when imagined in relation to the circumambient river of 'Ocean' or to barbarous lands such as those environing the suggestively named 'Black' Sea.[59] Just to consult the entry on 'Navigation' in the index of *Primitivism and Related Ideas in Antiquity* is to find a formidable array of authorities inveighing against the impiety of voyaging, prime among which is the second chorus of Seneca's *Medea*.[60] But what exactly is 'voyaging' in an ancient context? While Renaissance voyagers (such as Columbus) are conventionally celebrated as reincarnations of ancient prototypes (such as Virgil's Palinurus or Seneca's Tiphys), ancient voyaging simply cannot be imagined in post-Renaissance terms. Its sheer transgressiveness makes it both narrower and broader than its Renaissance equivalent. It is narrower to the extent that the ancient concept lacks the symbolic resonance of the Renaissance concept (voyaging becomes a master sign in the 'age of discovery'). But it is broader to the extent of transcending 'navigation' as such. As a literally 'exorbitant' figure, the ancient voyager tends to be elided with a more strikingly 'exorbitant' figure: the conqueror who, having conquered 'the' world, restlessly scans the ocean for another.

Ideas of oceanic voyaging and exorbitant conquest meet in the legend of Alexander the Great. 'Not content with one world', Alexander is imagined in the *Suasoriae* (a collection of debating exercises on commonplace themes) of Seneca the Elder, as standing at the mouth of the Indus and contemplating a voyage into the ocean to discover other worlds to conquer.[61] The reader – a trainee orator for Seneca's purposes – is required to address himself to the task of dissuading Alexander from so monstrous an enterprise. Alexander might be warned that new worlds are 'fictions easy of invention', or that 'the Ocean cannot be sailed' (1). He might be exhorted to remain 'content to have conquered as far as the world is content to have light', or assured that 'your empire and the world have the same limits' (1.2). He might also be warned that 'the world would rise in revolt if ... Alexander had crossed nature's limits', and reminded that 'it was within the limits of the known world that Hercules won his claim to heaven' (10.1). He must be admonished that 'it is the sign of a great spirit to be moderate in prosperity', that 'even greatness has some end' and that 'you must give greatness its limits, seeing that Fortune does not' (3). The legendary debate is transposed to the discourse of history by Plutarch who has Alexander heeding the counsel of an Indian philosopher: 'that he ought to reside most in the middle of his empire, and not spend too much time on the borders of it' (*Lives*, p. 848). The inexhaustible variety of the rhetorical expressions of the voyager taboo in the *Suasoriae* testifies to the persistence of the 'exorbitance' theme in the Alexander legend. According to Plutarch and Lucan, only death prevented the conqueror from another mad attempt to sail the Ocean: this time a circumnavigation of Africa from the Euphrates to Gibraltar.[62]

A self-consciously similar conjunction of exorbitance and oceanic voyaging is found in the legends of Caesar and Germanicus. Quintilian, for example, suggests that a rhetorical 'invention' of Caesar's invasion of Britain would ideally represent him considering not just military matters but also the ontological 'nature of the Ocean' and the paradoxically 'exorbitant' status of Britain as 'an island' within that alien element.[63] Thus Velleius Paterculus suggests that Caesar 'crossed into Britain, as though seeking to add another world to our empire', while Annaeus Florus relates how: 'Having penetrated everywhere by land and sea, he turned his gaze towards the ocean and, as if this world of ours sufficed not for the Romans, set his thoughts on another'.[64] Even Plutarch is mindful of the topos, to the extent of representing the British campaign as a dress-rehearsal for 1492:

he was the first who brought a navy into the western ocean ... and by invading an island, the reported extent of which had made its existence a matter of controversy among historians, many of whom questioned whether it were not a mere name and fiction, not a real place, he might be said to have carried the Roman empire beyond the limits of the known world. (*Lives*, p. 869)

The legend of Germanicus also shows signs of imitating that of Alexander. Seneca the Elder quotes from a poem celebrating the pioneering voyage of Germanicus in the North Sea:

> Banished from the familiar limits of the world
> They dare to pass through forbidden shades
> To the bounds of things, the remotest shores of the world ...
> Furthest nature shuts off in everlasting shadows
> The world we have left. Are we looking for races
> Beyond, in another clime, a new world untouched by breezes?
> The Gods call us back, forbid us to know the end of creation
> With mortal eyes.
>
> (*Suasoriae*, 1.15)

In spite of the fact that both Caesar and Germanicus seem to have welcomed the idea of outdoing Alexander, a powerful criticism is nevertheless implied. All three conquerors appear to have forgotten that 'it was within the limits of the known world that Hercules won his claim to heaven'. And all three can be thought of as ignoring the warning that Hercules is said to have fixed to his Pillars at the Strait of Gibraltar: *Non Plus Ultra*, or 'No Further'. Their presumptuousness is thus potentially ominous and, indeed, darkens the legends of Caesar and Alexander, though not that of Germanicus. Thus Ben Jonson is able to treat Germanicus as a model of Stoic virtue by comparison with Alexander, who (with Lucan's damning portrayal very much in mind) he describes as 'that voluptuous, rash, / Giddy, and drunken Macedonian'.[65]

Sailing the ocean 'to the bounds of things, the remotest shores of the world' (*ad rerum metas extremaque litora mundi*), presents both a physical and an ontological danger, to, respectively, the voyager and the ordered world which he leaves behind. However, voyaging has other contexts besides the ocean, and other types of danger. Perhaps because the ancient ocean is categorically a 'river', it is possible to commit voyager-transgression merely by crossing a river, especially when the river in question has the significance of a geographical *terminus*. Richard F. Thomas notes the importance of rivers in ancient ethnography: 'Herodotus gave them a special place, and they are clearly important in that so often they define countries. In historical ethnography they assume an even greater importance, in that they serve as natural boundaries which enforce harmony on man, and their being crossed often implies a transgression which leads to disastrous consequences'.[66] By way of illustrating the link between river-crossing and violation, Thomas cites a passage from Virgil in which the Araxes (the border between Persia and Armenia) is described as 'indignant' at being bridged, and argues that Virgil (like Herodotus before him) alludes to 'the defeat of Cyrus the Great, which resulted from his crossing of that river' (p. 43). Thomas also points out that Servius's commentary on this passage confuses Cyrus with Xerxes, because the latter is 'the classic violator of the forces and boundaries of nature, and, as such, naturally came to Servius's mind as the object of the Araxes' *indignatio*' (pp. 43–4).

Like the ocean, then, terminal rivers are exemplary contexts of voyaging and transgression. Alexander's crossing of the Granicus, a stream which Plutarch locates at 'the gates of Asia', portends the oceanic scale of his ambitions in the Orient. Caesar's crossing of the Rubicon – the border between Italy and Cisalpine Gaul – is more ominous. Plutarch relates how Caesar paused to weigh the human consequences of his transgression against the fame, before plunging ahead 'in a sort of passion' (*Lives*, p. 874). But what sort of passion? By a Viconian alchemy, Caesar's geographic transgression assumes strangely Oedipal proportions: 'It is said that the night before he passed the river he had an impious dream, that he was unnaturally familiar with his own mother'.[67] Interestingly, both the meaning and the *mise en scène* of this dream seem to vary with the political sympathies of the narrator. In Suetonius, for example, the dream occurs during Caesar's time as a quaestor in Spain, and is treated as a favourable omen of world conquest (Suetonius conveys the interpretation of Caesar's soothsayers in which Caesar's mother is the Earth or universal parent).[68] In Lucan, however, the dream combines with the river-crossing to present a truly apocalyptic spectacle. Caesar's mother is identified with the Vestal personification of Rome itself, who (in the words of Christopher Marlowe's translation) 'mourning appeared', her 'hoary hairs ... torn, and on her turret-bearing head dispersed' (lines 189–90).[69] Appeals to filial piety prove vain. Like a beast ('a lion of desert Afric'), the son metaphorically violates the mother by renouncing all 'laws ... leagues and covenants' as he plunges into the stream (lines 208, 227–8). The suggestion of 'infamous promiscuity' is quite deliberate. A follower is able to contemplate the most incestuous carnage because it appears already ordained by Caesar's earlier transgressions of the boundaries of the Roman world:

> Is conquest got by civil war so heinous?
> Well, lead us then to Syrtes' desert shore,
> Or Scythia, or hot Libya's thirsty sands.
> This band, that all behind us might be quailed,
> Hath with thee passed the swelling ocean,
> And swept the foaming breast of Arctic's Rhene ...
> ... Should thou bid me
> Entomb my sword within my brother's bowels,
> Or father's throat, or women's groaning womb,
> This hand (albeit unwilling) should perform it.

(lines 367–72, 376–9)

The Viconian mythologisation of this infamous river-crossing – its collective representation in terms of an idiom combining geographic, political and sexual transgression – finds a parallel in the collective fashioning of what the Renaissance saw as the *arche*-myth of voyaging in the ancient world: the story of Jason and Medea. To Euripides, effectively the inventor of this myth in its 'classic' form, the theme of voyaging is of interest chiefly as a symbol of the central tragic theme of miscegenation. Throughout, the transgressiveness of the union between the civilised Jason and the barbarous Medea is metaphorically telescoped into the Argo's passage of the Symplegades, those 'grey-blue jaws of rock' which represent the 'key and barrier to the Pontic Sea' (lines 2, 213).[70] At times, Medea herself seems to embody the danger of all dire straits: she is as pitiless as 'a rock or wave of the sea', and as savage as 'Scylla' – the monstrous female embodiment of the ill-omened strait of Messina (lines 27, 1359). 'Why', the chorus asks her, 'did you come from the blue Symplegades / That hold the gate of the barbarous sea?' (lines 1263–4). The cultural difference between Jason and Medea is expressed in terms of geographic extremity. Medea thinks of herself as 'plunder from a land at the earth's edge', while Jason laments his madness in taking her 'from a land of savages / Into a Greek home' (lines 254–5, 1329–30). In Euripides, then, the transgressiveness of the voyage serves as a metaphoric extension of the miscegenation taboo.

In Seneca, however, this priority is reversed. Miscegenation becomes simply one of several types of 'confusion' resulting from the fundamental transgressiveness of voyaging. The conceptual departure from Euripides is signalled in the second chorus, when the role of arch-transgressor falls not on Jason but on the Argo's helmsman (or navigator). Thus (in the words of John Studley's 1566 translation) '*Typhys* bould' is both celebrated and blamed for being the first who 'on open seas durst show / His hoysted sayles, and for the wyndes decree / New lawes'.[71] As the mother of all merchant ships, the Argo initiates foreign trade ('Traficque far'), and represents the demise of 'the golden worlde ... / Where banysht fraude durst never come in place' (p. 260). Accordingly, it changes the world from one which 'well with seas dissevered lay' to one which is utterly permeable:

> Now seas controulde doe suffer passage free,
> . . .
> Eche whirry boate now scuddes aboute the deepe,
> All stynts and warres are taken cleane away,
> The Cities frame new walles them selves to keepe,
> The open worlde lettes nought rest where it lay.

(pp. 261–2)

The endless violability of this 'open worlde' (*pervius orbis*) is conveyed in terms of a strikingly paradoxical use of river symbolism, which (owing to the clumsiness of Studley's translation) I am obliged to convey in the words of a slightly later translator:

> The Indian, whom at home heate fries,
> Drinkes of Araxis waters cold:
> The Persian, rich in gems and gold,
> Wash in the Rhine and Elbe likewise.[72]

More or less as in the original (*Indus gelidum / potat Araxem, Albin Persae / Rhenum bibunt*), the union of opposites is expressed in the rhetorical figure of a chiasmus ('cross'), in which an extreme south-easterly people (the Indians) pollutively 'drink' the waters of a river which serves as the north-western frontier of their western neighbours (the Persians), who are themselves obtuse enough to 'drink' from yet more distant north-western rivers: the Rhine and the Elbe.[73] In the context of so chiastic a conjunction of peoples and rivers, the imagery of 'drinking' is pollutive. The chorus concludes with a prophecy that the transgression of the Argo is bound to be repeated, not just in the present but in future ages:

> time shall in fine out breake
> When Ocean wave shall open every Realme.
> The wandring World at will shall open lye.
> And TYPHYS will some newe founde Land survay.
> Some travelers shall the Contreys farr escrye,
> Beyonde small Thule, knowen furthest at this day.

(p. 262)

Ironically, as we shall see, no passage of ancient 'geography' was more often cited by Renaissance geographers, nor any so assiduously misconstrued.

5

Assuming for the moment what I shall argue in some detail later – that a dramaturgical version of the ancient poetic geographic economy of difference is to be found in Shakespeare – what *significance* would such a finding have for our understanding of Shakespeare? Evidently, it would allow us to view Shakespeare from a novel perspective composed of what (to the modern eye) will seem a peculiar combination of contexts: geographic, ethnographic, political, domestic, sexual. This is valuable in itself, if merely to remind us of the inevitable degree to which Shakespeare is not 'our' contemporary but a contemporary of Marlowe, Jonson and (in an important sense) of Euripides, Seneca and Plutarch. However, it is much more valuable in providing us with a conceptual purchase on the construction of otherness in Shakespeare that is completely independent of the anachronistic terminology of 'race', 'colour' and 'prejudice'.

Consider, for example, the construction of 'moorish' difference in Shakespeare. As in the ancient poetic geography, all Shakespearean moors combine a generic exoticism or exteriority with an inherent transgressiveness. Their transgressiveness is less a matter of immorality (most Shakespearean moors depart, in any case, from the villainous Elizabethan stage stereotype) than of structure. What this means is that all are imagined in terms of polluting sexual contact with European partners. Aaron in *Titus Andronicus*, Morocco (and the supernumerary female moor impregnated by Gobbo) in *The Merchant of Venice*, Othello, Cleopatra (unhistorically described as 'with Phoebus amorous pinches black'), and finally the regal 'Ethiope' of Tunis whose marriage to Claribel forms so puzzling a passage of *The Tempest* – all are posed in terms of a scenario of miscegenation. The blackness or tawniness of the moor is, I suggest, intimately related to this scenario, much in the way that for one Elizabethan commentator, blackness of skin represented the enduring mark of God's displeasure at the sexual transgression of 'Cham' (or Ham) from whom 'came all these blacke Moores which are in Africa'.[74] Like their colour, the 'exteriority' of moors also has ethical significance. All Shakespeare's moors are associated with a generically 'outlandish' geography; all are 'exotic' in the comprehensive Elizabethan sense of being 'outlandish, barbarous, strange, uncouth'.[75] None has any real existence independent of their transgressiveness of those margins (geographic and marital) whose purpose it is to exclude them.

The strictly Elizabethan (and, of course, ancient) character of this type of otherness is suggested by a comparison between Othello and the black hero of Aphra Behn's Restoration novel, *Oroonoko*.[76] Superficially, Othello seems to resemble Oroonoko far more than the stereotypically villainous moors of the Elizabethan stage. Both heroes are sympathetically portrayed, primitivistically noble, and displaced from their native milieu. Each falls victim to villainous Europeans and each endures extreme suffering before dying with a self-conscious display of magnanimity. Here, however, the resemblances cease. Where Oroonoko is decorously paired with Imoinda (a sexual partner of his own race and aristocratic degree), Othello is transgressively paired with Desdemona. Regardless of his moral worthiness, the social indecorum is extreme. Where Desdemona is young, white and of the highest Venetian rank, Othello is somewhat 'declined / Into the vale of years' (3.3.269–70), utterly black and physiologically Negroid (a 'thicklips' with woolly hair). This in itself makes for a revealing difference from Oroonoko who, though coloured, is lighter in hue than his fellow Africans and decorously European of feature. The combination of Othello's uncompromisingly Negroid appearance and the extreme indecorum of his pairing with Desdemona is purely Shakespearean. In the source (Cinthio's *Heccatomithi*), 'Disdemona' and her nameless moorish partner are both commoners and both of an age. It was therefore Shakespeare's idea to introduce the age discrepancy, to make the girl a senator's daughter and to make the moor a Venetian general. Paradoxically, Othello's military rank does not ameliorate the indecorum. It is instead – rather as in the myth of Tereus – represented (at least in part) as a circumstantial anomaly, enabling a bizarre exception to the rule rather than legitimising miscegenation *per se*.[77] Even Othello (who understandably takes a liberal-minded view of his own suitability as Desdemona's husband) shares Iago's shrewd assessment that the Venetian 'signiory' are more likely to be swayed by his indispensability to Venice's defence than by any urging of what he calls 'my parts, my title, my perfect soul' (1.2.31). It is revealing that Othello should refrain from any attempt at a categorical justification (never, for example, pleading his Christianity). The reason is surely that any attempt to exceed the essentially negative agenda of disarming Brabanzio's rash accusations of magic would have the fatal effect of foregrounding the issue of miscegenation and changing the argument to one which Brabanzio would be sure to win:

> For if such actions may have passage free,
> Bondslaves and pagans shall our statesmen be.
>
> (1.2.99–100)

The meaning of these various differences between Shakespeare's and Behn's heroes is that, whereas Oroonoko's tragedy is accidental, Othello's follows straight from the overwhelming hubris (the transgressiveness) of his otherness. Oroonoko's tragedy is accidental in the sense of being unnecessary: in the sense that slavery has no necessary relationship to his imaginative being (his colour, his primitivism, his Restoration 'exoticism'). Othello's tragedy, by contrast, is structurally necessary. An 'extravagant and wheeling stranger' (1.1.138), he is promiscuously 'everywhere' and intrusively 'here' in the bosom of a Venetian family. As with the tragedy of Euripides's Medea, Othello's tragedy proceeds from a characterological contradiction. In Medea's case, the contradiction is between her married faithfulness to Jason and the barbaric lengths to which she is prepared to go in order to preserve (or revenge) her marriage. In Othello's case, the contradiction is between his romantic pathos and the always potential pollutiveness of his match with Desdemona (a potential which Iago merely serves to interpret and release). In one sense, Othello's tragedy is external to him in requiring the manipulative agency of Iago, but in a deeper sense, Othello's tragedy is endemic. The gross inappositeness of the conjunction between the young 'white ewe' and the old 'black ram' is, after all, the raw material of Iago's deception. To this extent, the play does indeed belong to Othello rather than to Iago. Othello is the protagonist and Iago the agent, the catalyst: the means whereby the 'confusing' and potentially tragic energy (what Mary Douglas would call the 'pollution danger') of miscegenation is converted into the 'pollution danger' of adultery. Somewhat like the tricksters of folktale, Iago punningly elicits a deep structural correspondence (apparently invisible to others) between 'adultery' in the sense of 'violation of the marriage bed' and 'adultery' in the sense of what an Elizabethan homily defines as 'unlawful commixtion' – an idiom which, in 1691, the lawmakers of colonial Virginia would extend to the offspring of interracial sexual liaisons: 'that abominable mixture and spurious issue'.[78]

Beneath the high romance of the first act, therefore, Othello's moral virtue and the 'pollution danger' which he represents to the Venetian republic (and the Elizabethan audience) are in tragic contradiction. Regardless of Desdemona's high-minded justification – 'I saw Othello's visage in his mind' (1.3.252) – the pollutiveness of the other cannot be redeemed by his virtue because virtue and pollutiveness are weighed on different scales. The former belongs to the moral realm, whereas the latter belongs in a realm which Mary Douglas finds to be discontinuous: 'Pollution rules, by contrast with moral rules are unequivocal. They do not depend on intention or a nice balancing of rights and duties. The only material question is whether a polluting contact has taken place or not' (p. 130). The Duke, Desdemona and Othello himself – all those who speak in defence of the marriage – are obliged to defend it in riddles of discontinuity, antithesis and contradiction. When Desdemona sees Othello's 'visage in his mind', she is already conceding the pollutiveness of the visage as such. The Duke makes a similar concession when requiring an improbable leap of faith from Brabanzio: 'If virtue no delighted beauty lack / Your son in law is far more fair than black' (1.3.289–90). Even Othello concedes the pollutiveness of his colour, when bitterly reflecting on the infamy (itself a form of pollution) of cuckoldom: 'my name that was as fresh / As Dian's visage, is now begrim'd, and black / As mine own face' (3.3.391–3).[79] More than the symbolic power of blackness on the Elizabethan stage, such language declares the essential tragic contra-diction of the play, between Othello's moral heroism and the 'pollution danger' which he inevitably symbolises. Again, a comparison with Oroonoko is illuminating. The two Africans are alike in representing inversions of, respectively, an Elizabethan and a Restoration norm of Africanness. For Behn, norm-inversion is a relatively unproblematic exercise simply requiring Oroonoko to be characterised as a noble savage rather than as a plantation slave. For Shakespeare, however, a complete inversion of the norm is impossible because the Elizabethan norm is governed by the full repertoire of the ancient discourse of barbarism. The moral character of the Elizabethan moor can be inverted, but not his generic pollutiveness, nor the generic link with miscegenation.

The difference between Othello and Oroonoko bespeaks a major paradigm-shift in the discursive construction of otherness between the beginning and end of the seventeenth century. Shakespeare's Renaissance imagination of otherness is still heavily indebted to the ancient poetic geography. Behn's Restoration idea of the other, however, is essentially modern and can readily be grasped in terms of post-Renaissance forms of the discourses of race, slavery, the 'noble savage', '*l'exotisme*' and '*Les Indes Galantes*'.[80] The Elizabethan sense of the exotic (the 'barbarous, outlandish and strange') might be characterised as 'hard', in the ancient sense of what Ben Jonson referred to as 'Magick, Witchcraft, or other such exotick arts'.[81] By contrast, Behn's idea of the exotic might be char-acterised as 'soft', suggesting rather the fashionably strange or merely piquant. Like his own romantically off-European appearance (or perhaps like the gorgeously feathered cloak which Behn brought back from Surinam and made available as a costume for Dryden's *The Indian Emperor*), Oroonoko's exoticism is without any 'danger'. It carries no dark suggestion of magic or witchcraft. Othello's exoticism, however, is as dangerous as his colour. Like Medea, he is associated with what Jonson calls 'exotick arts'; both in Brabanzio's mind and in the material form of the charmed handkerchief which he has given to Desdemona:

> ... There's magic in the web of it.
> A sibyl, that had numbered in the world
> The sun to course two hundred compasses,
> In her prophetic fury sewed the work:
> The worms were hallowed that did breed the silk,
> And it was dyed in mummy, which the skilful
> Conserved of maidens' hearts.
>
> (3.4.69–75)

Originally the property of an Egyptian 'charmer', Othello's handkerchief is not only magical, it also combines the rare with the grotesque in the typically ancient manner of Herodotean *thoma*, in which, for example, fragrant spices would be guarded by abominably stinking goats, or Arabian frankincense by winged snakes.[82] The association of magic with Egypt is also Herodotean. As the oldest and wisest of nations, the Egyptians are portrayed by Herodotus as the ultimate magicians, even outstripping such notorious sorcerers as Medea's Colchians (who he believed to have descended from the remnants of an Egyptian expedition in the time of Sesostris).

Magic is but one of several ways in which Othello's difference is 'beholding' to the ancient discourse of exoticism. At various moments, Othello is associated with the marvellous in either of its ancient forms (the grotesque and/or the precious), ambivalently suggesting both his danger and his allure. Desdemona's frankly avowed sexual desire seems rooted in her taste for Othello's tale of monstrous and abominable races:

> ... the cannibals that each other eat,
> the Anthropophagi, and men whose heads
> Do grow beneath their shoulders.
>
> (1.3.142–4)

Ironically, the hunger of Othello's cannibals is echoed in Desdemona's hunger for Othello's Mandevillian narrative: 'These things to hear / Would Desdemona seriously incline ... and with a greedy ear / Devour up my tale' (144–9). Associated with the grotesque, Othello is also often characterised in terms of the precious and rare. Indeed, I would want to suggest that this particular dimension of the ancient category of the marvellous sets the keynote of what has been called 'the Othello music'. For G. Wilson Knight, Othello's imagery was a puzzle:

It holds a rich music all its own, and possesses a unique solidity and precision of picturesque phrase or image, a peculiar chastity and serenity of thought. It is, as a rule, barren of direct metaphysical content. Its thought does not mesh with the reader's: rather it is always outside us, aloof. This aloofness is the resultant of an inward aloofness of image from image, word from word. The dominant quality is separation, not, as is more usual in Shakespeare, cohesion.[83]

One cause of this aloofness-effect (according to Wilson Knight) is Othello's habitual use of 'fine single words, especially proper names' such as 'Propontic', 'Hellespont', 'Anthropophagi, Ottomites, Arabian trees' and so on. It is surely not accidental that these 'fine single words' are all geographic, all connected with phenomenal forms of the exotic and mostly with the marvellous as well. The marvellous is by definition 'aloof' because to insist on 'wonder' is to require 'separation'. Hence, the 'aloof' and lapidary quality of Othello's imagery – the jewel-like glitter of his 'entire and perfect chrysolite', the smoothness of his 'monumental alabaster', the chill perfection of his 'marble heaven' – are (I would want to claim) all of a piece with the poetic geographic quality of his imagination. Whenever Othello wishes to evoke his essential mystery, it is in such terms. Thus, when deciding on revenge, he ritualises Pliny's account of the irresistibility of the current flowing through the Bosphorus:

> Like to the Pontic sea,
> Whose icy current and compulsive course
> Ne'er feels retiring ebb, but keeps due on
> To the Propontic and the Hellespont,
> Even so my bloody thoughts with violent pace
> Shall ne'er look back, ne'er ebb to humble love,
> Till that a capable and wide revenge
> Swallow them up.
>
> (3.3.456–63)

And at the moment of his death, when vainly attempting to reconcile his innermost sense of self with the horror of what he has done, he retreats to a generically Mandevillian heartland where 'Arabian trees' drop 'their med'cinable gum' and where 'the base Indian' (or 'Iudean') throws away 'a pearl richer than all his tribe' (5.2.359, 360, 356–7).

The gulf between Elizabethan and Restoration exoticism is as much a factor of the systematic quality of the Elizabethan concept as of its relative unsentimentality. For Jonson and Shakespeare, the 'outlandish' is 'barbarous' and 'strange' precisely because it is 'outlandish' (and vice versa). For Dryden and Behn, however, the three-way linkage is neither systematic nor even necessary. Just as Behn's African is neither 'barbarous', nor sexually transgressive, nor marvellous (in the sense of being associated with *thoma*); so too the stage Indians of Dryden's *Indian Queen* and *Indian Emperor* observe the same chivalric code as the Spaniards with whom they make war and love.[84]

What is behind the discontinuity between the two representations of the exotic? One factor is likely to have been the prestige of the classics in the earlier period, not just of classical literature but also geography, perhaps in the monumental form of Philemon Holland's 1601 translation of Pliny, or perhaps in the vulgarised form of *Mandeville's Travels*, which was still being taken seriously by technical Elizabethan geographers (to say nothing of the dramatists) as late as 1589 when it was included in the first edition of Hakluyt's *Principal Navigations*.[85] Pliny may well have authorised Jonson's description of magic as an 'exotick art'. Noticing how magic 'is spread over the face of the whole earth', Pliny remarks how exotic nations 'who in all other respects are divided and different ... were conformable enough to the rest of the world in giving entertainment thereto'.[86] Ironically enough, Pliny takes Britain as his example of how 'that art ... hath passed over the wide ocean also, and gone as far as any land is to be seen, even to the utmost bounds of the earth; and beyond which, there is nothing to be discovered but a vast prospect of air and water' (pp. 312–13). Both Pliny and Mandeville testify to the existence of marvels in exotic lands: Pliny asserting that the 'prodigious and incredible' is pre-eminently found among 'those people, especially, who live farthest remote from our seas' (p. 71), and Mandeville claiming that 'earthly beings are more discrepant from one another, because they are in a remote place, and for that reason are more diverse'.[87] The link between difference and distance is virtually axiomatic: 'if therefore in some degree difference can be found near at hand, the greater the distance, the greater must one judge the difference to be, whether in a relatively or in an extremely distant place' (p. 48). Such is the power of this axiom in the period that it is a moot point whether Mandeville be regarded as its cause or its result. One effect of Mandeville's phenomenal popularity among Elizabethans was textual redaction on a grand scale. According to C. W. R. D. Moseley, this had the paradoxical effect of vulgarising a sophisticated medieval travel narrative to satisfy an emerging Elizabethan taste for exotic wonders.[88] Thus, where accounts of monstrous races had filled no more than a page or two of the original, they became the essential Mandeville as far as the Elizabethan reader or audience was concerned.[89] Considered in isolation, therefore, the Mandeville phenomenon hardly accounts for the Elizabethan construction of the exotic. Its true importance is as part of a wider ethnographic discourse to which Holland's Pliny and the Bible also contribute. According to Margaret Hodgen, sixteenth-century ethnography is crucially influenced by the archetypal myth of dispersal in the Old Testament.[90] In three master legends – those of Cain, Babel and Ham – cultural and linguistic difference is seen to derive from divine displeasure and the promiscuous wanderings of accursed outcasts. As Christians, sixteenth-century ethnographers had little choice but to adopt a monogenetic theory of cultural difference, in which 'exotic' cultures were thought to have been 'diffused' from a primitive ur-culture. As in the Old Testament, moreover, 'diffusion' implied 'confusion' or degeneration; a progressive loss of cultural, moral and linguistic integrity.[91] The authority of the classics and the Bible thus combined to produce a set of ethnographic equations between 'wandering', diffusion, confusion, degeneration, difference and remoteness.

Such is the discursive context of Iago's punning description of Othello as an 'erring barbarian' (1.3.354) and Roderigo's description of him as 'an extravagant and wheeling stranger of here and everywhere' (1.1.138–39). Such, too, is the reason for what we might think of as the promiscuous or 'pandemic' quality of Othello's exoticism, the way in which his Africanness is constantly being telescoped into other notorious forms of exoticism: Turkish, Egyptian and Indian. Othello's association with Egyptian charms and the 'base Indian' has already been remarked.[92] His symbolic association with the Turks is a critical commonplace. Throughout, the intimate 'danger' posed by his marriage to Desdemona is paralleled with the military threat posed by the Turks (hence the removal from Venice to the outpost of Cyprus).[93] Also, the name 'Othello' would appear to be derived from 'Othoman', eponymous founder of the 'Ottoman' dynasty. Finally, of course, Othello cathartically identifies with the 'malignant and ... turban'd Turk' who 'beat a Venetian and traduced the state' and whom he 'smote ... thus' (5.2.362–5). Such blurring of racial outline is typical of the representation of exotics in Shakespeare and other Elizabethan dramatists. Thus 'Aaron the moor' in *Titus Andronicus* is as much Scythian or Thracian or Gothic as he is African, whereas the moor of Marlowe's *The Jew of Malta* is said to have been born in Thrace.[94] For Shakespeare and Marlowe there is no geographical incongruity. Turk and African, ancient 'Thracian' and Renaissance 'moor', all share a generic identity as 'erring barbarians', promiscuous wanderers to the round earth's imagined corners. Contemporary travel-writers and geographers appear to have valorised the 'ethnic' and the 'exotic' in similar ways. Thus Thomas Coryat casually mentions 'the barbarous Ethnickes' who resort to the Square of St Mark in Venice.[95] And a frontispiece from the 1636 English translation of Mercator's *Atlas* depicts a group of diverse Europeans confronting a group of diverse non-Europeans, who (regardless of their ethnic variety) are thereby constructed as 'exotic' or 'barbarous' (Plate 14).[96]

It is for this reason that the sharper, more elaborately differentiated and more hierarchical character of post-Elizabethan constructions of racial difference are inappropriate to the problems posed by the Elizabethan other. Not surprisingly, *Othello* has proved particularly intractable to approaches via the post-Elizabethan category of the 'Negro'. In the early nineteenth century, Samuel Taylor Coleridge was completely incapable of countenancing the marriage of a 'beautiful Venetian girl' to 'a veritable Negro', much as he was willing to entertain the sentimental fiction of a 'noble moor'.[97] Similarly Charles Lamb found 'something extremely revolting in the courtship and wedded caresses of Othello and Desdemona', in spite of his willingness to entertain a 'perfect triumph of virtue over accidents, of the imagination over the sense' (unhappily 'the actual sight of the thing' seemed to obliterate 'all that beautiful compromise which we make in reading').[98] For both critics, the tragic contradiction between heroism and pollutiveness is no longer a workable dramatic proposition. The otherness of the 'Negro' has none of the exoticism of the Elizabethan 'moor', none of his theatrically vital mix of danger and allure. It is simply disgusting. The gap between Coleridge's 'veritable Negro' and Shakespeare's moor is partly explained by the institutionalisation of plantation slavery in the New World in the course of the seventeenth century, a phenomenon which (as Winthrop Jordan has argued) required a sharp distinction between 'Negroes' and other types of 'savage' (such as the Amerindian), and a hierarchisation of difference defining the 'Negro' as the lowest of the low.[99]

The demise of the Elizabethan moor came surprisingly early. A mere generation after *Othello* was first played, Thomas Rymer could feel only contempt for the heroine who allows herself to be talked into marrying a 'Black-amoor', and for the playwright who expects his audience to sympathise.[100] Some modern critics concerned to make an issue of 'race' or 'colour' in *Othello* suggest that the Elizabethans were somehow less 'racially prejudiced' than Restoration and nineteenth-century audiences.[101] The truth is otherwise. It was, after all, Elizabethan drama which insisted that 'moors' were sexually polluting. Restoration drama, by contrast, delighted in sentimentalising exotics along the lines of Behn's *Oroonoko* and Dryden's 'Indian' plays. The point is not that Elizabethans were less or more 'prejudiced' but merely that their construction of otherness is significantly different from that of Restoration discourse. In Behn and Dryden, the 'exotic' has parted company with blackness, which is why Oroonoko must be represented as tawny. In Shakespeare, however, the 'exotic' not only embraces the black, the tawny, the monstrous, the savage, the barbarous, the New World and the Old, but touches all with 'wonder' and treats the ancient and Renaissance versions of otherness ('cannibals' and 'anthropophagi') as interchangeable.

The discontinuity between the Elizabethan and Restoration constructions of the 'exotic' is finally suggested by the fate of an epiphenomenon of Renaissance exoticism: the *wunderkammer* or 'wonder-cabinet'. This was a repository for what Steven Mullaney calls 'strange things'; things such as 'an African charm made of teeth, a felt cloak from Arabia . . . an Indian stone axe . . . the twisted horn of a bull seal . . . a flying rhinoceros', or whatever else might have struck the Renaissance collector as suitably bizarre.[102] While one is tempted to identify this as the prototype of the modern museum, Mullaney insists that 'its relation to later forms of collection is a discontinuous one' (p. 61). This is precisely because of its promiscuity; a refusal to categorise its own contents. 'A heteroclite order without hierarchy or degree' (p. 62), the *wunderkammer* was properly a theatrical rather than a scientific phenomenon: 'This is a room of wonder, not of inquiry. It requires and to a certain extent produces an audience that is at once passive and attentive, willing to suspend its critical faculties in order to view "strange things" . . . without "authentic place" . . . in the cultural and ideological topography of the times' (p. 63). This is suggestive. It is under the influence of the similarly ludic discourse of what, in the Folio, is called a 'Travellours historie' that the 'potent, grave and reverend signiors' (and, indeed, Desdemona herself) are charmed into acquiescing in a match which they would be obliged to condemn if only they were able to situate it squarely in terms of 'the cultural and ideological topography of the times'.

6

If Shakespeare's imagination of the exotic is governed by that of Pliny and Mandeville, then what does this suggest of his acqaintance with the atlases of Abraham Ortelius and Gerard Mercator or the voyage compilations of Richard Eden and Richard Hakluyt – in short, with that 'new geography' which was so conscious of having exploded ancient paradigms? One answer is to argue (as Rogers does) that Shakespeare's geographic imagination was somehow blinkered in comparison with that of Greene, Marlowe, Massinger, Beaumont and Fletcher, all of whom avail themselves spectacularly of the global perspectives offered by contemporary voyagers and cartographers.

A more fruitful answer, it seems to me, is that Shakespeare's use of the ancients is a thoroughly Renaissance phenomenon, fully in keeping with the discursive constitution of the new geography in the periods represented by his life (1564–1616) and his career (*c*. 1590–*c*. 1611). In 1570, the first of the great sixteenth-century atlases, Ortelius's *Theatrum Orbis Terrarum*, was published in Latin. The date seems early for it to be considered seriously in relation to Shakespeare, but the influence of this work on European and Elizabethan geography was seminal, and would persist at least until 1606 when an English translation appeared. In 1595,

Mercator's *Atlas* was published, also in Latin. The *Atlas* would usurp the influence of the *Theatrum* and dominate European geography at least until 1636 when it too was Englished. What has been called 'the Shakespearean moment', then, was also the moment of the new geography's most monumental statements. By the same token, it also represented the last flowering of the old 'cosmography', because both Ortelius and Mercator conceived of geography in cosmographic terms. To quote Mercator, 'Cosmographie is the discription of all the world ... as well Elementary, as Celestiall', whereas 'Geographie is properly the description of the situation of the Earth alone'.[103] The prestige of the two great geographers helped ensure that the new geography would continue to be represented in cosmographic terms during the slow decline of 'cosmography' from about 1613, the date of Galileo's *Sidera Nuncia*. This meant that the new geography would continue to be represented also in terms of the ancient poetic geography to the extent that 'cosmography' served as its vehicle.

I want to suggest that the coincidence of the Shakespearean and Ortelian 'moments' was fertile, and in several ways. In the first place, there is no reason to believe that Shakespeare was any less educated in the new geography than he was in the old 'cosmography'. More importantly, Renaissance theatre and 'cosmography' are conceptually interrelated. The theatre was cosmographic and, to an extent, geographic, in its conceptual character (Shakespeare's Globe Theatre is a striking case in point). Cosmography, for its part, was 'theatrical', in the sense that 'theatre' is an important enabling metaphor. (Thanks in part to the popularity of Ortelius's *Theatrum*, atlases were generically 'theatres' before they were 'atlases'.)

The paradox posed by the simultaneously 'new' and ancient character of Shakespeare's geographic imagination should thus be seen in the context of the co-existence of ancient and modern values in the new geography. Eventually the new geography would break from its ancient legacies – both 'cosmographic' and 'poetic geographic' – but not until after the passing of 'the Shakespearean moment'. Perhaps the most compelling reason for the persistence of ancient poetic geographic values within the new geography was the imaginative insecurity of the new discourse. For all its self-consciousness, the new geography had yet to achieve a hermeneutic identity. It required the hermeneutic energy of the ancient geography, as well as the active complicity of Renaissance poets in order to fashion its own *poiesis*. Why? Perhaps because, in the words of Gaston Bachelard, 'inhabited space controls geometric space'.[104] Well over half of the sixteenth-century 'Globe' was composed of geographical entities which were yet to become 'inhabited' (some, of course, being purely fanciful, never could be). For habitation to take place, such spaces needed to be imaginatively possessed, which is to say moralised and mythologised. Poets were needed to make the brave new world feel lived in, and livable in. Ironically, the new geography was inviting to Renaissance poets for the same reason that it remained haunted by the phantoms of the old geography. In the Shakespearean moment, the old geography had the advantage of what Stephen Greenblatt has called 'the power of forms': of historically entrenched mythological and rhetorical forms, over the geometrically more sophisticated forms of the new geography.[105] The Shakespearean moment thus coincided with a moment of unprecedented hermeneutic instability in the *imago mundi*, in which a new geographic poetic was now emerging from, now being swallowed by, the old poetic geography.

To suggest that the new geography was influenced by the 'power' of ancient 'forms' is to claim more than the general prestige of ancient literature, mythology and 'natural history' in the Renaissance. It is to suggest the enduring power of what is perhaps the quintessential form of the ancient geography: Heidel's 'frame of the ancient Greek maps'. The idea that so archaic a feature could have influenced the new geography at all is almost incredible, particularly when the new geography was so conscious of having extended the range of geographic discourse from being (in Ptolemy's words) 'a description of the earth' (in the sense of the 'island of earth') to being a description of the entire terraqueous globe. For all its conspicuous obsolescence in this new context, however, the figure of the frame continued to exercise poetic power. In view of its extraordinary ability to survive technical obsolescence in the ancient geography, and to migrate from one discourse or culture to another, this is not, perhaps, so surprising. Heidel points out that the frame was inherently resistant to advances in Greek geographical thought, such as the massive revision in Greek knowledge of the extent of Asia after the conquests of Alexander, or the novel fifth-century idea that the 'earth' was spherical (p. 13). With inevitable adjustments of orientation and extent, the frame was able to migrate from the Greek *oikumene* to the Roman *orbis terrarum*, where (as J. Oliver Thomson has shown) it continued to demonstrate an ability to survive in the teeth of contradictory geographical evidence, such as the Roman awareness of China (see note 5). The figure of the frame was able to outlive its appeal to the poets of the age of Augustus and survive the highly 'unpoetic' late Roman geography of Ptolemy. It was even able to survive the collapse of the Roman Empire and of late classical geography to become reincarnated as the defining feature of 'Christian Topography'.

As classical civilisation disintegrated in the sixth century, an apparently idiosyncratic and primitive geography was devised by a Christian monk called Cosmas Indicopleustes. Drawing on Ionian and Biblical sources, Cosmas described the world as 'a flat parallelogram twice as long as it was wide'. In the centre of this frame, he placed Jerusalem, apparently on the authority of Ezekiel 5.5 ('I have set her in the midst of the nations and the countries that are round about her'). Such, insofar as it is possible to tell, is the origin of the medieval *oikumene*. For the model of his frame, Cosmas ignored Ptolemy and Eratosthenes (suggesting his complete ignorance of them) and went instead to the most primitive available stereotype in the 'parallelogram of Ephorus', a more or less rectangular border defined by the barbarians which it excluded: Ethiopians, Scythians, Celts and Indians. Even Herodotus had found this geography incredible. Forgotten are virtually all the scientific achievements of the ancient geography: the idea of a spherical earth, the calculation of the earth's circumference by Eratosthenes, the projection of the *oikumene* on to a conical surface by Ptolemy, and his calculation of its position and size relative to that of the globe. Retained, however, is the perennial poetic function of the frame: to define identity in relation to otherness. In a very real sense, medieval geography represents the apotheosis of the ancient frame. The frame appears intact, if reorientated, in generic medieval *mappaemundi*, such as 'the Psalter map' (Plate 6). Amazons, for example, are located in Scythia, exactly where the Greeks had located them, apart from the fact that Scythia now appears in the upper left-hand segment of the map instead of in the upper right-hand segment (as in the ancient Greek map reconstituted by Heidel). This itself is owing to the reorientation of the three ancient continents – Europe, Asia and Africa – by Isidore of Seville. As the direction of Paradise, east is now privileged over north so that Asia is now depicted at the top of the map instead of on the right. Cheek by jowl with the 'anthropophagi' are their biblical counterparts: the hordes of 'Gog and Magog' whose invasion in the latter days had been prophesied by Ezekiel, but who had in the meantime been sealed off by Alexander the Great behind 'a wall of iron and brass'.[106] With its extraordinary resistance to history and epistemic change, the enclosing and excluding frame is a powerful form. Rather as in Vico, its power seems almost prior to the various geographic discourses which serve as its host. Hence the uncanny ability to survive its own technical obsolescence and migrate from one geographic discourse to another; finally into that of the new geography.

   This brings me to the last of my aims. In one sense, this is a book about Shakespeare; it is an attempt to locate a number of Shakespearean plays and themes in the perspective of a new context which, with apologies to Vico, I call 'poetic geography'. In the course of writing, however, it has occurred to me that posing geography – particularly the new geography – in 'poetic' terms is so novel and inherently interesting a task that it should not be treated purely as a 'context' for Shakespeare. In literary history as traditionally understood, a 'context' is supposed to provide a way of 'grounding' the text; a means of anchoring the inherently flighty verbal icon to the bedrock of history and culture. This is to say that the 'context' should function as the *data* or the 'given' against which the text can be *capta* or 'taken'. But the poetics of the new geography can never simply be given. However it may have operated in the world of fact, it can never be posed as hard factual 'ground'. To the extent that it is poetic, then, it warrants treatment as poetry – which is to say, as a 'text' in its own right. Fortunately, this need actually includes an understanding of Shakespearean poetic geography so long as both 'Shakespeare' and 'geography' are thought of in a 'dialogical' rather than a 'textual-contextual' or figure-and-ground relationship. As in Bakhtin's notion of the dialogue in which 'the speaker listens and the listener speaks', the two discourses will be thought of as mutually 'entertaining' and constituting each other.[107] A dialogical spirit is reflected in my chapter outline: Chapter 2 offers a critique of mainstream treatments of geographic themes in Shakespeare and Elizabethan dramatists; Chapter 3 explores the poetic interrelatedness of Elizabethan theatre and sixteenth-century cosmography; Chapter 4 returns to the concerns of the present chapter: the influence of poetic geographic ideas in the construction of otherness and voyaging in Shakespeare; Chapter 5 explores the poetics of the new geography with specific regard to the tension between ancient and Renaissance 'hermeneutic' forms.

To conclude, I express the hope that this book will be of interest to Shakespeareans and geographers alike, as well as to readers whose only interest is in wishing to know more about the geographic construction of the ground they inhabit. Though such readers will probably be unfamiliar with poetic geography, they will certainly be familiar with its results. These persist like the footprints of some prehistoric beast in the sediments of modern geography, especially that of the New World. Every schoolchild has heard of the 'Amazon River'. Few students or even teachers of geography (even of what is now called 'Human Geography') would appreciate the historical and poetic process by which the greatest of the world's rivers acquired its name.

For Herodotus, the Scythians represented the most northerly people of whom a sustained ethnographic account could be given. Beyond them were mythical races, such as the Amazons who dwelt east of the river 'Tanais' (the border between Europe and Asia) and the 'Andropophagi' who dwelt somewhere beyond the point at which the great northern rivers became unnavigable. What did these races – mythical and ethnographic – have in common? Each occupied the darkest end of the earth and represented, as a consequence, a nightmare of Hellenic otherness. In Herodotus and in the ethnographic tradition, all three races tended to become confused: the Scythians mating with the Amazons across the Tanais, and becoming confused with the Andropophagi – rather as in Lear's remark about 'The barbarous Scythian, / Or he that makes his generation messes / To gorge his appetite' (1.1.116–18).[108]

From 1492, just this nexus of poetic geographic associations took root in the new 'end of the earth' across the Atlantic. Well read in Herodotus, Ptolemy, Mandeville and the *Imago Mundi* of Pierre d'Ailly, Columbus himself carried the seeds.[109] The 'Caniba' or 'Cannibals' discovered on his first voyage, quickly took over the generic identity of Herodotus's 'Andropophagi' – to such an extent that the ancient term eventually passed out of usage. Ironically, the invention of the 'Cannibals' was inadvertent. The name had been coined on the assumption that these were people of the Great Khan, but took on its new meaning when evidence of actual anthropophagy emerged. Columbus invested far more energy in an obsessive search for Amazons, whom he reported to be found on islands such as 'Martinina, in whych dwell only women, after the manner of them, called Amazons' or 'Madanio ... inhabited only by women: to whom the cannibals have access at certain times of the year, as in old time the Thracians had'.[110] Unlike 'cannibalism', however, no Caribbean culture seemed to be organised on gynocratic lines. Hence the 'Amazons' tended to remain just out of European reach: originally on some as yet unvisited Caribbean island, ultimately in the remote reaches of the world's largest and most mysterious river, at the very heart of the New World's darkness.

2   Of 'Voyages and Exploration: Geography: Maps'

My exposition of the roots of Shakespeare's geographic imagination in the ancient poetic geography carries us a long way from the terms of the traditional discussion. Traditionally, the argument has been about the extent of Shakespeare's knowledge of 'voyages and exploration, geography, maps'; the degree to which Shakespeare's work was affected by the so-called 'new geography' of the discoveries; and the degree to which *The Tempest* either reflects the sixteenth-century 'invention' of America or 'enacts' the Jacobean colonial experiment in Virginia. In what follows, I shall describe the difference between these approaches and my own, specifically on the question of whether (and how) Shakespeare was influenced by the new geography. To this end, I shall provide a brief overview of the debate so far, before suggesting ways in which the question can be reconsidered in the light of recent (post-Viconian) hermeneutic perspectives on 'geography and maps'.

1

Rogers's essay on 'Voyages and Exploration: Geography: Maps' should be seen in the context of two distinct but interlocking debates about the nature of Shakespeare's geographic imagination. One debate – originating remotely in Ben Jonson's taunt at Shakespeare's ignorance in supplying Bohemia with a sea coast in *The Winter's Tale* – has been over the degree of Shakespeare's literacy in the new geography, and the impact of any such literacy on his dramatic imagination. The other debate has been over the extent to which *The Tempest* is 'about' America. It is largely due to the deftness with which he arbitrates in these debates and then synthesises his findings to form a total and still compelling view of Shakespeare's geographic imagination, that I have taken the liberty of using Rogers as a benchmark in the previous chapter. For the same reasons, Rogers will serve as a convenient introduction to the modern discussion of Shakespeare and the new geography.

Rogers's self-consciously conservative estimation of Shakespeare's geographic literacy or curiosity relative to that of a Marlowe, a Greene or a Massinger, testifies to the existence (as early as 1916) of the alternative view: that Shakespeare was literate in the new geography and significantly influenced by it. To this end, Rogers explicitly addresses R. H. Coote's claim to have identified the original of Maria's striking cartographic allusion in *Twelfth Night*:

> ... He does smile his face into more lines than
> is in the new map with the augmentation of the Indies.
>
> (3.2.74–5)

Maria's comparison of Malvolio's leering countenance to 'the new map' only makes sense if the map in question was unusually 'lined', in addition to showing an 'augmentation of the Indies', and 'new' at the time that *Twelfth Night* was written. The only map to fit all three criteria, argued Coote, is the *Hydrographiae Descriptio* of Edward Wright (Plate 1).[1] Wright's map is heavily scored, featuring not only the standard grid of latitude and longitude, but also clusters of rhumb-lines radiating outwards from arbitrarily placed focal points ('compass-roses'). The date of the map (the late 1590s) roughly matched that of the play (*c.* 1601). Moreover, argued Coote, the 'Indies' were 'augmented' on Wright's map, while the map's cartography was particularly advanced ('new') for its time. Though Coote appears to have overstated the degree to which Wright's map does in fact show an 'augmentation of the Indies'[2], Rogers (like most later commentators) accepted that the *Hydrographiae* was Shakespeare's immediate inspiration, while rejecting the implications which Coote saw in this: namely that Shakespeare's interest in so advanced a map showed that he was not the geographical illiterate of Jonson's taunt, but a true contemporary of Hakluyt:

It appealed ... to Shakespeare because its rhumblines illustrated Malvolio's smiles; and it appeals to commentators on Shakespeare as showing that although Shakespeare knew something of Hakluyt, who dedicated himself to a study of what was outside Europe ... [he] ... did not write of the new-found new world and the new-found old world as momentous additions to the world in which his characters lived and moved. (p. 174)

As far as Rogers was concerned, neither the geographic additions to the *Hydrographiae* nor its cartographic innovativeness materially affected the medievalism of the Shakespearean world view, in which 'nearly all Asia and all America ... were little appendices to his book of life, which book was Europe'.

While reacting to Coote, Rogers was also reacting to a more powerful tendency to see *The Tempest* in specifically 'new geographic' terms. The most persistent and influential of several proponents of this view prior to

1916 was Sir Sidney Lee.[3] In 1898, Lee had argued that Bermuda was the original of Prospero's island and 'Caliban . . . an imaginary portrait . . . of the aboriginal savage of the New World'.[4] In 1907, he asserted that the play was 'a veritable document of early Anglo-American history', while in 1913, he suggested that Shakespeare might have learned about Indians not just from voyage literature but also from real specimens brought back from America to be exhibited as side-show curiosities.[5] Rogers's response to such arguments was both to except *The Tempest* from the rule that the world outside Europe represented 'little appendices' to Shakespeare's 'book of life', and to minimise the significance of the New World echoes in the play. If the New World is there, it is only in an arbitrary and phantasmal way.

If Rogers's position seems familiar, it is partly because of the inconclusiveness and repetitiousness of the subsequent debate. After Rogers, the new geography debate has tended to become subsumed in the *Tempest* debate. This, however, while evolving in ways that Rogers could never have anticipated, seems to have twice come full circle, leaving us uncomfortably near to where Rogers found himself in 1916. In the next decade, three critics made ambitious claims for Shakespeare's interest in the New World. C. M. Gayley tried to establish intellectual links between Shakespeare and 'the founders of liberty in America'.[6] Sir A. W. Ward tried to establish factual links between Shakespeare and 'the makers of Virginia'.[7] R. R. Cawley tried to demonstrate 'Shakespeare's use of the voyagers', both by tracing Shakespearean passages to supposed originals in the voyagers and by drawing suggestive links between themes in the voyagers and in *The Tempest*.[8] In pushing its claims well beyond what Rogers would have thought 'judicious', however, the Americanist case had overreached itself. In 1926, E. E. Stoll effectively discredited Gayley and Ward by pointing out that 'Shakespeare . . . says not a word' linking him to 'the promoters of colonizing in Virginia', nor indicating 'sympathy with their motives and aspirations'. The same tactic served to cast serious doubt on Cawley: 'There is not a word in the *Tempest* about America or Virginia, colonies or colonizing, Indians or tomahawks, maize, mockingbirds, or tobacco. Nothing but the Bermudas, once barely mentioned as a faraway place, like Tokio or Mandalay'.[9] The wheel had come full circle (Stoll's 'faraway place' has a distinct ring of Rogers's 'unknown . . . wonderland of discovery and romance'). For a long time after Stoll, the 'American' debate seems to have stalled. The New World echoes could not be entirely discounted, but nor was anything positively made of them. The uncertainty persists as late as the Arden edition of the play in 1954. On the one hand, the editor, Frank Kermode, is far more prepared than Stoll or Rogers to countenance the contextual relevance of New World material. On the other hand, however, he is reluctant to decide what this relevance might mean because 'there is nothing in *The Tempest* fundamental to its structure of ideas which could not have existed had America remained undiscovered, and the Bermuda voyage never taken place'.[10]

Kermode's caveat notwithstanding, a new and more 'figurative' version of the Americanist argument began to take the conservatives by storm. In the 1960s, and early 1970s, critics like Leo Marx and Leslie Fiedler advanced compelling 'figurative' and/or 'prophetic' readings of the play as a kind of proto-American colonial myth, in which the emerging ideological and political structure of the New World is both anticipated and ironised.[11] Charles Frey's 1979 survey of the critical literature pleads eloquently for the need to regard as 'context' not just 'sources' but also 'congeners': any more or less contemporary New World documents with intertextual links to Shakespeare's play.[12] Stephen Orgel's 1987 Oxford edition of the play pointedly does what Kermode does not: it treats the New World material as a governing context.[13] To explore or even to record the great range and variety of 'figurative', 'New Historicist' and 'Post-Colonial' criticism of *The Tempest* which has emerged since 1980, is neither strictly to the purpose here, nor necessary in view of additional surveys by Alden T. Vaughan (1988) and Meredith Anne Skura (1989).[14] What may be said, however, is that there is again a sign of reaction: of a return to the 'judicious' conservatism of Rogers, Stoll and Kermode. Skura, for example, makes much the same kind of objection to New Historicist readings of Caliban as an Indian, as Stoll had raised against an earlier generation of 'Americanists':

... Caliban is taken to 'be' a Native American despite the fact that a multitude of details differentiate Caliban from the Indian as he appeared in the travelers' reports from the New World. Yet it does seem significant that, despite his closeness to nature, his naiveté, his devil worship, his susceptibility to European liquor, and, above all, his 'treachery' – characteristics associated in the writings of the time with the Indians – he nonetheless lacks almost all of the defining external traits in the many reports from the New World – no superhuman physique, no nakedness or animal skin (indeed, an English 'gaberdine' instead), no decorative feathers, no arrows, no pipe, no tobacco, no body paint, and – as Shakespeare takes pains to emphasize – no love of trinkets and trash. (48–9)

As my present purpose is to provide a critical context for my own study of Shakespeare's geographic imagination, I shall resist the temptation to adjudicate just yet between the rival positions. The present book has grown from the debate as I have (all too briefly) outlined it, but my agenda has not been set by the debate in its present form. Why? In the first place, this is not a book on *The Tempest*, even though it was originally conceived as such. Its agenda is more a throwback to the era of Rogers,

Coote and Lee; an era before (as I have suggested) the issue of Shakespeare's geographic imagination had been completely subsumed in the debate over the New World inheritance of *The Tempest*. Like the earlier writers, I prefer to consider *The Tempest* in the context of a systematic overview of Shakespeare's geographic imagination, rather than vice versa. In part, this more ambitious approach has arisen from a feeling that *The Tempest* could not be adequately treated in isolation anyway. Like Leslie Fiedler, I prefer to see Caliban (for example) in the context of a whole architectonic of otherness deriving from earlier Shakespearean 'strangers': Othello, Shylock, Morocco and Aaron the moor. However, this is not to say that the New World context is somehow superfluous, because 'all can be traced to conventions, literary and philosophical, independent of the new geography'.[15] Thus, like Fiedler, I am not prepared to concede that Caliban's indebtedness to such figures makes him less of an Amerindian; no less than I would concede the same in respect of other prototypes, such as the medieval 'wild man' or the 'satyr'-figure of Italian pastoral tragicomedy. The point is rather that Caliban might be all of these because, as Hayden White has argued, the Renaissance Amerindian owed much to pre-existing 'forms of wildness' anyway.[16] Suggestive as Fiedler has been for me, however, my vision of the Shakespearean other requires an approach which is fundamentally different from his. For Fiedler – I think it is fair to say – Shakespeare's vision of the stranger and his vision of geography are not necessarily related. For me, they *are* necessarily related. Where Fiedler, therefore, includes women as well as ethnic outsiders in his use of the term 'stranger', I would prefer to restrict the term to ethnic outsiders only (which tends to be what is meant by the word 'stranger' in the Old Testament).[17] The vision of otherness that concerns me is an ethnographic vision, the roots of which I have already described as being in the ancient poetic geography. But what of Shakespeare's relationship with the new geography *per se*, particularly its most characteristic artefact, the map? In Chapters 3 and 5, I will suggest that the issue can be considered in much broader terms than traditionally understood if the Globe Theatre itself is thought of as a map, and if Renaissance maps are considered less as individual scientific documents than as a collective and evolving cultural text characterised as much by their pictorial (and often ancient ethnographic) symbolism as by their geographic content. In what immediately follows, I want to lay the groundwork for that discussion by putting three questions: What did Shakespeare actually know about the new cartography (as distinct from the new geography)? Can the question of Shakespeare's relationship with the new geography be submitted to a hermeneutic or poetic analysis? If Shakespeare's 'geographic imagination' is to be thought of in quasicartographical terms (as a 'mental map'), should this entity be thought of in the singular or the plural?

2

Rogers's idea of Shakespeare as an 'instinctive geographer' with a stubbornly parochial window on the wider world of sixteenth-century 'voyages and exploration, geography, maps', owes much to the Jonsonian picture of Shakespeare as a dramatist who was as cavalier with the facts of geography as he was with the neoclassical unities of time and place. One way to cross-examine this stereotype is to ask how typical the geographical absurdity of a Bohemian seacoast is of Shakespeare's geographic practice as a whole (an aim partly addressed in the last section of this chapter), but a more revealing and direct procedure is simply to examine the dramatic use which Shakespeare makes of maps.

In view of the effort invested in identifying Shakespeare's 'New Map', it is surprising to find that a number of cartographically interesting Shakespearean references to maps have gone entirely unremarked.[18] Each of these references says something about Shakespeare's understanding of cartography in the first instance, and his understanding of geography in the second. Characters not only allude to maps, they sometimes actually use them (either on-stage or by report), and they sometimes offer learned comment on matters geographical. Thus a map is actually brought on-stage in *King Lear* for the division of the kingdom into three parts. In *1 Henry IV*, Hotspur, Glendower and Mortimer make use of a map for much the same purpose. In *The Merchant of Venice*, Antonio is imagined as neurotically 'peering in maps for ports and piers and roads' (1.1.19). In *Henry V*, Fluellen offers a view on what is to be found 'if you look in the maps of the world' (4.7.22), while in *The Tempest*, Gonzalo engages Adrian in scholarly debate on whether modern Tunis used to be ancient Carthage. What these references suggest is that the reference to a 'new map' in *Twelfth Night* was not plucked from a discursive vacuum. Each verbal reference presupposes either a distinct cartographic genre (where the reference is to a map as such) or a generic carto-geographic discourse. Collectively, therefore, they tell us something of the generic range of Shakespeare's acquaintance with the rich Elizabethan and Flemish cartographic discourse of the late sixteenth and early seventeenth centuries.

We may begin with *King Lear*. Though there is no explicit direction for a map to be brought on-stage, the implication is clear enough from the phrasing of Lear's formal donation to Goneril:

> Of all these bounds even from this line to this,
> With shadowy forests and with champains riched,

> With plenteous rivers and wide-skirted meads,
> We make thee lady.

$$(1.1.63-6)$$

From the *ecphrasis*[19] (or verbal and gestural indication) of 'these bounds' and 'this line to this', the thought moves to imagined 'forests', 'champains', 'rivers' and 'meads', suggestive of (at best) an impressionistic relationship to the map in question. The imagery does not, therefore, necessarily presume a map upon which such features are notionally depicted. Nevertheless, the imagery is entirely consistent with the rich pictorial ornamentation of Saxton's maps of England and English Counties, in which just such natural features as Lear mentions (forests, fields, rivers, hills, towns) are indicated by a variety of pictorial topographic codes (Plate 4).[20] The very movement of Lear's thought from direct cartographic reference to a rich (almost iconic) imagination of the cartographic content, suggests a national map of monumental or iconic force. Moreover, the use of Lear's map as, effectively, a *Magna Carta* for defining relative spheres of influence is suggestive of what we know of the intensely proprietorial symbolism of Saxton's *Atlas*, each map of which was stamped not just with the Royal arms but also with the arms of the various estates which the map happened to cover.[21] To the Elizabethan aristocracy, at least, the geography of Saxton's English maps was inseparable from the question of their own claims over the property it represented. The *Atlas* was, in effect, a pictorial title-deed; an imprimatur of power. To the historian, Saxton's geography is thus also inseparable from the history of Tudor England, from the dissolution of the monasteries to the rise of a new landholding gentry anxiously seeking the artificial imprimatur of medieval tradition. It is also inseparable – as are cautionary tales of ancient British kings who divide their kingdom – from the still traumatic Elizabethan memory of the fifteenth-century Wars of the Roses.

In *1 Henry IV*, (3.1.67–110), a map of England is again brought on-stage ('Come, here's the map ... ') and used for a similar purpose and with similar (though less evocative) resonance. Here, a 'river' is treated – not, as in *Lear*, as an iconic feature of an almost sacred geography – but as a purely functional boundary between Hotspur's prospective 'third' and Glendower's. The dispute between the two rebels over Hotspur's determination to alter the course of the river in order to take in a rich piece of land which would otherwise be on Glendower's side of the 'border', is richly comic. The comedy is at least partly due to the incongruity between the decorum of the river as a geographic and political icon, and Hotspur's blatantly (and subversively) literal interpretation of cartograpic convention. If the river is a border, and he diverts the river, then he can claim to have solemnly abided by the letter of the cartographically expressed agreement while increasing his own territory at Glendower's expense. Beneath the comedy is an ironic reminder that such logic can be fatal when applied to the complex idiom of national charters.

By contrast with the nationalistic idiom supposed by the maps of these two British history plays, quite another genre of map is presupposed in *The Merchant of Venice*. The image of a maritime trader 'peering in maps for ports and piers and roads' clearly suggests the genre of the maritime map. This type of map was well established in the sixteenth century, and well represented in England, where (from 1588) it appeared within the covers of specialised maritime (or 'hydrographic') atlases.[22] Unlike the monumental, highly decorative maps of Saxton, these maps were primarily functional; as indeed were the maritime atlases, which, in contrast to the great Flemish 'geographic' atlases, were designed with practicality uppermost and appear to have been read in the same spirit.[23]

The generic hint is much more direct in *The Merchant of Venice* than in the case of the two English chronicle plays. Only a maritime map would indicate 'ports and piers and roads' as its principal business. In such a map, 'ports and piers' are exhaustively indicated, and in such a way as to make sense for a mariner approaching by sea. Where the number of 'ports' threatens to obscure the map with text, the names are written at right angles to the shoreline to accommodate as many 'places' as possible without inaccuracy or distortion of the coastline. Sophisticated attempts are also made to indicate the approaches to a 'port' or 'pier', or topographical features of the coastline, 'even as they shew when you passeth before them'.[24] By stark contrast with the careful recording of 'ports', inland places (assumed to be of little interest to the mariner) are either treated cavalierly or ignored. Maritime hazards, such as the 'Goodwins' – a notorious sandbank ('a very dangerous flat, and fatal', 3.1.4–5) in the Thames Estuary – are very clearly and exhaustively marked (Plate 5). Antonio's 'roads' (anchorages) are simply indicated by an anchor symbol. The need to be detailed means that maritime maps tend to show relatively small stretches of coastline in close focus. Accordingly, world maps are rarely of the maritime type because their scale is too compressed for practical navigational use. Its scale aside, Edward Wright's *Hydrographiae Descriptio* represents this type of map: arranging the names of 'ports' at right angles to coastlines, ignoring inland 'places', and displaying rhumb-lines, which contemporary seamen found a more reliable means of calculating distance and position than the Ptolemaic grid of latitude and longitude. The *Hydrographiae* shows the Ptolemaic grid as well, however. The co-existence of both grid and rhumb-lines is perhaps an indication of its double character. It is both practical and monumental.

Where, then, Antonio could not have used such a map to guide his 'argosies' past the Goodwins in the Thames Estuary, he might have used it to send them in the general direction of 'Mexico', that most mysteriously un-Venetian destination which is twice mentioned in connection with Antonio's trading network. It is interesting that the two references to maritime maps in Shakespeare each come from a comedy of the late 1590s; also, that both comedies contain references to the 'Indies'.

Of the 'maps of the world' mentioned by Fluellen in *Henry V*, little can be inferred:

> ... I tell you, captain, if you look in the maps of the
> world I warrant you sall find, in the comparisons
> between Macedon and Monmouth, that the situations,
> look you, is both alike. There is a river in Macedon,
> and there is also moreover a river at Monmouth. It is
> call'd Wye at Monmouth, but it is out of my prains
> what is the name of the other river – but 'tis all one,
> 'tis alike as my fingers is to my fingers, and there is salmons in both.
>
> (4.7.23–30)

What can be inferred, however, is a particular kind of geographic discourse. The idea that Monmouth and Macedon are 'both alike' because each has a river with salmons in it, is a satiric reflection on a common (and highly Viconian) Renaissance idiom which we might think of as 'typo-geographic'. This is essentially a form of geographic moralisation. Places (*loci*) are read in terms of their 'moral' (or historical, or epic, or mytho-logical) significance and then concorded on that basis, opening up the possibility that places bearing similar moral significance might be found to be physically alike also. What Fluellen is doing, then, is paying a clumsily pedantic compliment to his king of the 'learned' type that might be paid by some allegorical personage in the course of a royal entry. The idea is that Hal is another Alexander because his birthplace (Monmouth) recapitulates that of Alexander (Macedon).

The symbolism of 'Milford Haven' in *Cymbeline* is another instance of this discourse. Here, however, the intention is entirely serious. As the port at which Henry of Richmond invaded England in order to topple Richard III, Milford had become a privileged *locus* of Tudor legend; effectively a kind of sacred site.[25] By 1610, the probable date of *Cymbeline*, the Tudor legend of Milford had become merged with the Stuart legend of 'Britain' – the ancient name which James I had revived to describe the geographical entity resulting from the formal union of England, Scotland and Wales. Hence, in *Cymbeline*, as in contemporary Stuart masques, the privileged geography of Milford is concorded with the Roman symbolism of Britain as 'another world', which (as we have seen) was itself the product of

Caesar's desire to portray his invasion of Britain in the light of Alexander's ambition to conquer other worlds (a piece of geographical image-making curiously similar to Fluellen's celebration of Monmouth).

The final instance of Shakespearean 'typo-geography' to be considered, is the odd debate on the relative locations of modern Tunis and ancient Carthage in *The Tempest*:

Adrian.	Tunis was never graced before with such a paragon to their queen.
Gonzalo.	Not since widow Dido's time.
...	
Adrian.	'Widow Dido' said you? You make me study of that. She was of Carthage, not of Tunis.
Gonzalo.	This Tunis, sir, was Carthage.
Adrian.	Carthage?
Gonzalo.	I assure you, Carthage.

(2.1.79–90)

Gonzalo's point is not that modern Tunis occupies the same piece of land as ancient Carthage.[26] The typology of place is more concerned with *loci* than with area as such. The difference is that the *locus* is a moral-geographical entity. Hence the deeper irony of this (again) rather pedantic discussion, is that modern Tunis recapitulates ancient Carthage in moral-geographical terms. This, in turn, provides an exemplary context for reading the curious marriage of Alonso's reluctant daughter, Claribel, to the 'African' King of Tunis. Because modern Tunis recapitulates ancient Carthage, the marriage of Claribel to the African recapitulates the ill-starred relationship of Dido and Aeneas. Indeed, it is potentially more ominous, because – as with the affair of Tamora and Aaron in *Titus Andronicus* – it represents the mischief of a consummated stranger-marriage which Aeneas was piously able to avoid.[27]

What, then, do these passages – of quasi-geographic discourse or direct cartographic reference – tell us of Shakespeare's understanding of cartography, in the first place, and of geography, in the second? They tell us that Shakespeare is demonstrably conversant with quite a variety of geographic discourses and a variety of cartographic genres. An irresistible corollary is that he was also well acquainted with the new geography in the sense of knowledge of new lands and seas as revealed by new discoveries and explorations. This, of course, is the very aspect of the 'new map' to which Shakespeare draws attention in *Twelfth Night*. Here is a map which shows an 'augmentation of the Indies'. Here, too, is a map recording the recent discovery *Novaya Zemlya*, by the Dutch, an event alluded to in Fabian's reproach to Sir Andrew Aguecheek:

> ... you are
> now sailed into the north of my lady's opinion, where
> you will hang like an icicle on a Dutchman's beard
> unless you do redeem it by some laudable attempt
> either of valour or policy.
>
> (3.2.24–8)

I have mentioned how the *Hydrographiae Descriptio* combines the features of a practical maritime map with those of a monumental world map. The doubleness is consistent with the self-conscious novelty of the map. Three large blocks of inserted text inform the onlooker that this map is 'new' in both cartographic and geographic terms. It is cartographically novel in the sense of being set forth on Wright's own revision of Mercator's projection. It is geographically new in the sense of including new areas (*Novaya Zemlya* and parts of the Indies) and it is scientifically rigorous in the sense of omitting cartographic fictions, such as the Strait of Anian, and the southern continent. Here, then, is yet another genre of map which we can say Shakespeare understands: the map whose primary purpose is scrupulously to plot the ever 'newer' outline of the world according to ever-more-recent discoveries.[28]

We can, therefore, conclude with some confidence that the time-honoured stereotype of the 'instinctive geographer', so uneducated or so careless as to depict Bohemia with a seacoast, is grossly exaggerated. Even in the little that he says of maps as such, and the new geography in particular, Shakespeare casually reveals his familiarity with an impressive range of contemporary cartographic genres. Moreover, it is scarcely conceivable that what he chose to reveal so casually represents the full range of his cartographic knowledge. After all, to have understood the novelty of a 'new' map implies, at the least, an acquaintance with older maps (such as Ortelius's *Typus Orbis Terrarum* of 1570, Plate 2) and an understanding of why they were suddenly not 'new'.

One lesson this holds for us is that however parochial Shakespeare's geographic imagination might have been, it could hardly have been primitive in a *cartographic* sense. Rogers makes just this error when comparing Shakespeare's idea of 'the fifteen or more kingdoms of Europe' with the Chinese idea of 'the Middle Kingdom' as described by the Renaissance Jesuit missionary, Matteo Ricci:

They had maps ... pretending a description of the world, but presented (*sic*) only their fifteen provinces with the sea and a few islands, and the names of such kingdoms as they had heard of, all which kingdoms scarcely equalled one province of China. They now wondered to see themselves straitened in an eastern corner of the world. They have a conceit that the Heavens are round, the Earth square, and their empire to be seated in the midst thereof.[29]

'Shakespeare, too', Rogers asserts, 'wrote as if he thought thus' (p. 171). The analogy misleads in much the same way as Coote's suggestions in respect of 'the new map', by confusing cartography with geography. Rogers neglects to point out that Ricci's account of the Chinese geographic 'conceit' is taken from a longer account of how some of Ricci's Chinese friends had been traumatised by seeing an Ortelian world map hanging on the wall of his study.[30] Not only did this map fail to depict 'their empire' in the midst of a square earth, but (like the vast majority of sixteenth-century world maps) it centred its global geography on the Atlantic rather than the Pacific. The result was that China was indeed 'straitened in an eastern corner of the world', where it actually appeared smaller than it should have due to the distorting effect of the ovoid projection in the Ortelian type of world map. The Chinese, it seemed, could cope with the geographic revelations, but not with the cartography. Hence, when redesigning the map for local consumption, Ricci was not only obliged to fashion a more cosmetically appealing version (drawn after Chinese graphic conventions), but also to centre the map on the Pacific instead of the Atlantic, thereby showing China as both bigger and more central than in the Ortelian original.[31] There are two points here. First, Rogers (like Ricci) is hardly being fair to the Chinese. The culture-clash seems to have been as much over cartographic style as over geographic substance. Second, Shakespeare would hardly (like Ricci's Chinese friends) have been fazed by the sight of what was the commonest world map of the later sixteenth century.[32] Not only did Shakespeare know Ortelius's world map, but he was capable of recognising its obsolescence by comparison with the newer *Hydrographiae Descriptio*, with which it appeared in Hakluyt's *Principal Navigations*. However parochial the scope of Shakespeare's geographical imagination, then, it cannot be called 'instinctive'. The Eurocentrism of an educated sixteenth-century European cannot be compared with the Sinocentrism of a sixteenth-century Chinese (prior, at least, to the advent of the Jesuits). One would be the result of preference, the other of necessity. A final point is that any idea of geography (Shakespeare's idea of world geography, or our own idea of that idea) will always seek a cartographic (as distinct from *material*) form, for the reason that geographical ideas require cartographic assumptions. An imagined geography is itself a kind of map in the very real sense that it must presuppose a cartographic idiom of one kind or another, regardless of whether inspired or not by an 'original' such as the *Hydrographiae Descriptio*.

3

Unfortunately, our confidence that Shakespeare was conversant with a significant range of cartographic types is not enough if the essential problem is to assess the impact of the new geography on Shakespeare's geographic imagination. The difficulty here is twofold. On the one hand, Shakespeare rarely appears to have been directly inspired by maps in the way of authors like Marlowe, Milton or Donne. On the other hand, when he is so inspired (as in the allusion to the 'new map' in *Twelfth Night*), the inspiration seems to be localised rather than translated into the symbolic or dramatic structures of the play as a whole.

This makes it impossible to write the kind of study of geography in Shakespeare that has been written of Marlowe and Milton (and remains to be written of Donne).[33] In all three, geographic inspiration can be discussed in relatively straighforward terms. In the case of *Tamburlaine*, for example, the 'new geography' provides a powerful sense of imaginative scale, as in this speech by the Turkish general, Orcanes:

> We have of revolted Grecians, Albanese,
> Sicilians, Jews, Arabians, Turks, and Moors,
> Natolians, Sorians, black Egyptians,
> Illyrians, Thracians, and Bithynians,
> Enough to swallow forceless Sigismond,
> Yet scarce enough t'encounter Tamburlaine:
> He brings a world of people to the field.
> From Scythia to the Oriental plage
> Of India, where raging Lantchidol
> Beats on the regions with his boisterous blows,
> That never seaman yet discoverèd

(II:1.1.61–71)

The epic iteration of nationalities, the heady outward zoom of perspective from the littoral of the Mediterranean and Black Seas to the oceanic 'plage' of the entire Asian continent, is typical of the use of geography in the play. A list of geographical place names from *Tamburlaine* would be a very long list indeed. Moreover, as Ethel Seaton has conclusively shown, Marlowe makes extensive reference to Ortelius's *Theatrum* in a speech in which Techelles, one of Tamburlaine's generals, recounts his conquest of Africa. Beginning with an account of how he followed the Nile deep into the southern reaches of the continent, Techelles tells of marching westward to:

> ... Zanzibar,
> The western part of Afric, where I viewed
> The Ethiopian sea

(II:1.6.194–6)

From there, Techelles relates, he marched north, 'by the coast of Byather' to 'Cubar, where the Negroes dwell', conquered it, and then proceeded to 'Nubia'; whence, after sacking 'Borno, the kingly seat' he brought the king in chains to Damascus. This apparently fanciful itinerary – down the east coast of Africa, across the continent, and up the west coast beside 'The Ethiopian sea' (the South Atlantic) – corresponds in every erroneous detail of locality and orientation with Ortelius's map of Africa. Seaton is thus able to conclude that Marlowe's finger 'walked' through Ortelius's map of Africa even as he composed Techelles's speech. In the case of *Tamburlaine*, then, it can be said both *which* geographic text and which maps were used, *and* that these sources had a powerful impact on the imaginative geography of a play which, like few others in the period, is animated by the symbolism and ideas of the 'new geography'. In the case of Milton, yet more contextual and source evidence is available. Not only are *Paradise Lost* and *Paradise Regained* powerfully influenced by a 'cosmographic' imagination, but the cosmographic sources are readily identifiable.[34] Donne's poetry is also powerfully 'cosmographic', and even if his sources are not as precisely identifiable as Milton's it hardly matters due to his encyclopaedic grasp of 'cosmographic' concepts and 'geographic' imagery.[35]

Where, then, does this leave the study of Shakespeare's geographic imagination? In what follows, I want to put two main propositions. First, that the parameters of Seaton's study of Marlowe's geography are not binding on our study of Shakespeare (no less, indeed, than for Marlowe). Seaton's model is needlessly limited in presuming that only specific documentary 'sources' count in determining the discursive context of an artistic text. And it is flawed, both in presuming a narrow causal relationship between 'source' and artistic text, and in failing to distinguish between geographic content and cartographic convention in both context (the map) and the text (the play/s). Interestingly, an alternative critical procedure is suggested by modern cartography, which redefines 'the map' in ways which make it far easier to think of in intertextual terms (and hence in relation to verbal texts such as Renaissance plays). Cartographic theory has also created a phenomenological model corresponding to what I have been referring to as the playwright's 'geographic imagination': that of the 'mental map'. My second proposition will follow from a discussion of these cartographic notions. This is simply that Shakespeare's geographic imagination is no less map-shaped, no less shaped-by-maps than Marlowe's.

Before discussing what modern cartography understands by the notion of a 'mental map', we should first discuss what it understands by the more fundamental term, 'map'. Both are defined in Harley and Woodward's

History of Cartography, in which nothing less than a complete hermeneutic reorientation of fundamental cartographic concepts is proposed.[36]
In the preface to the first volume, which is entirely concerned with ancient
cartography (and hence with the problem of trans-historical definition),
J. B. Harley observes that:

the apparently simple question, What is a map? raises complex questions of
interpretation. The answer varies from one period or culture to another. The issue
is particularly acute in early societies, but it also occasions difficulty ... with those
maps that can be regarded as a type of picture ... We have not therefore assumed
that the lack of vocabulary is in itself sufficient grounds for dismissing the map as
a latecomer to the cultural scene. On the contrary, this volume provides ample
evidence that maps existed long before they entered the historical record and
before their makers and users called them maps. (p. xvi)

Harley therefore proposes 'an entirely new definition of "map", one that
is neither too restrictive nor yet so general as to be meaningless': 'Maps
are graphic representations that facilitate a spatial understanding of
things, concepts, conditions, processes, or events in the human world'
(p. xvi). Such a definition, Harley continues, reflects his concern 'both
with maps as artifacts and with the way maps store, communicate, and
promote spatial understanding ... The words "human world" (in the
widest sense of man's cosmographic surroundings) signal that the perspective of the *History* is not confined to those maps of the earth whose
description constitutes so much of the existing literature' (p. xvi).

One effect of this definition is to liberate the idea of the map from the
notion of geographic content. In principle, the map's content might be
anything. Another effect is to liberate the idea of the map from the
material forms in which maps are most familiar to modern Europeans.
The map is thus not necessarily of paper or cloth as is suggested by the
etymology of *mappa* (Latin for 'cloth'). Nor does it necessarily suggest
what is implied by the various forms of the word *chart*: 'French *carte*,
Italian *carta*, Russian *karta* ... [which] derive from the Late Latin *carta*,
which meant any sort of formal document' (p. xvi). A map, therefore, can
be in three dimensions (a globe) as well as in two. In short, a map is any
kind of model of any spatial image.

There is perhaps a danger in so abstracting the concept of a map from
its familiar material forms. If virtually any kind of spatial image is a map,
theoretically regardless of its material form, then the field of cartography
is not so much expanded as exploded. Modern cartography addresses this
problem by posing the *reality* of the map in terms of process rather than
product; in terms of a semiological (or signifying) activity rather than an
inert artefact. Any map is thus 'a graphic text', the significance of which
'derives from the fact that people make them to tell other people about the

places or space they have experienced' (pp. 1–2).[37] What finally results is a complex and paradoxical concept. On the one hand 'the map is a relatively simple iconic device', but on the other hand:

> however simple maps may appear on first sight, on analysis they are ... less than straightforward ... maps are two dimensional combinations of 'shapes, sizes, edges, orientation, position, and relations of different masses' that require painstaking interpretation in relation to their original purpose, their modes of production, and the context of their use. Maps created for one purpose may be used for others, and they will articulate subconscious as well as conscious values. Even after exhaustive scrutiny maps may retain many ambiguities, and it would be a mistake to think they constitute an easily readable language. Maps are never completely translatable. (p. 3)[38]

Maps, in short, are like poems. Old maps confront us with the same kinds of interpretative mystery as old poems or old masters. Historical 'contexts' can never be assumed. They have to be painstakingly researched, interpreted and their own textuality declared. The notion of putting a poem in its geographic 'context' should not imply a 'grounding' of the text's figuration. We should instead be thinking of the poetic text as actively encountering a geographic 'context' already charged with poetic possibilities – with ideas, contradictions, traditions, paradoxes, figurations – all of which may take various textual forms within the broad spectrum of 'poetic' discretion available to the Renaissance geographer.

It is for these reasons that a map (a graphic text) should never be confused with its constituent 'geography', where that is supposed to be somehow independent of the act of depiction. To take a simple example, a medieval *mappamundi* of the type commonly associated with Isidore of Seville, will depict the notional continental mass of Europe, Africa and Asia with a radically different combination of 'shapes, sizes, edges, orientation, position, and relations of different masses' from that found in the type of Renaissance world map influenced by Ptolemy's *Geographia*.[39] In the medieval 'Psalter map', for example (Plate 6), east is at the top (because that is the direction of Paradise), west is at the bottom, north is on the left and south is on the right. The earth appears as an 'O'-shaped landmass, encircled by the river of Ocean, punctuated at the top right-hand corner by a sliver of water representing the Caspian Sea, and trisected by another body of water (the Mediterranean and the Black Sea) in the shape of a 'T' (such maps are called 'TO maps' for this reason). In the Ptolemaic map (Plate 7) this apparently counter-intuitive 'orientation' of familiar geographic elements has given way to a more familiar arrangement. North is now at the top, east on the right, west on the left and south at the bottom. The ocean is no longer a river, and no point is privileged as central in the way that Jerusalem is privileged (as an *omphalos* or 'navel')

in the Psalter map. 'Shapes, sizes, edges, orientation, position, and relations', then, are conventionally expressed cartographic dimensions before
they are geographic features.

Failure to appreciate this distinction vitiates much existing discussion
of geography in Elizabethan plays, even when, as in *Tamburlaine*, the
geographic dimension is much more amenable to traditional methods of
literary-historical description than Shakespeare's plays are. The following
passage from Marlowe's play may serve as a case in point:

> I will confute those blind geographers
> That make a triple region in the world,
> Excluding regions that I mean to trace,
> And with this pen reduce them to a map,
> Calling the provinces, cities, and towns
> After my name and thine, Zenocrate.
> Here at Damascus will I make the point
> That shall begin the perpendicular.

(I:4.4.81–8)

Bearing in mind that the action of *Tamburlaine* notionally predates the
discovery of America in 1492, an editor wonders whether the image of
'blind geographers / That make a triple region in the world' presupposes
the geography of an Isidorian map or that of a fifteenth-century Ptolemaic map which would also make 'a triple region of the world'.[40] If the
Isidorian map is intended, then the idea of making 'Damascus' the 'point'
of 'the perpendicular' would suggest that Tamburlaine wants to supplant
Jerusalem as the point marking the junction of the horizontal and vertical
axes of the 'T'. If the later, Ptolemaic map is intended, then Tamburlaine
is merely indicating that 'the initial meridian of longitude' will pass
through Damascus.

The problem with this discussion is not just that it proposes a false
choice between one kind of map and another, but that it reduces a
wonderfully subtle and 'poetic' interplay of cartographic and *geographic*
ideas to a crude question of geographic (as distinct from cartographic)
context. Yet the passage in question actually proposes a distinction
between 'geo-graphy' as a world-creating act of graphic depiction, and
'geography' as a depicted world-object. Tamburlaine's sword is thus the
cartographer's 'pen' which seeks to 'reduce' its geographic object to a
cartographic epitome. Map-making is a conceit for geographical conquest. The interesting point about the word 'perpendicular' is precisely its
hospitality to *both* Isidorian and Ptolemaic interpretation. We should,
therefore, give Marlowe the benefit of the doubt and assume that the
resulting ambiguities are deliberate. The word may easily refer *both* to 'the
initial meridian of longitude' *and* to the perpendicular line of the 'T' shape

which the Mediterranean Sea makes with the horizontal line of the Nile and the Tanais rivers in the TO maps.[41]

Recognising the ambiguity, however, is just the first step in doing critical justice to the passage. The richness of the meaning is lost unless we understand that what Tamburlaine proposes is just as much a contradiction in cartographic terms as it is an abomination in human terms. The dramatic context of the entire conceit is Tamburlaine's refusal to agree to Zenocrate's request that he spare her father's city. I want to suggest that the cartographic conceit be read as a self-subverting justification of the hero's outrageous behaviour. For Tamburlaine, the conquest of the father-city will obliterate Zenocrate's past (just as he had obliterated his own past when changing from his shepherd's clothes to a suit of armour in the first act). A new order will begin in which the hero and heroine – now *autarchs* acknowledging no principle before or apart from themselves – will remake the world in their own self-fashioned image: 'Calling the provinces, cities, and towns / After my name and thine, Zenocrate' (an ambition which effectively recapitulates the precedent of Alexander the Great). The monstrosity of this suggestion – particularly in the light of what can only be a horrified silence from Zenocrate – is further underlined by its cartographic incongruity: which is simply that the idea of privileging one place as the centre of the world is impossible on a new geographic map of the type that Tamburlaine imagines. This is because, on a Ptolemaic map, orientation is a purely mathematical function of the grid rather than (as on the Isidorian map) a function of sacred symbolism. On a Ptolemaic map, no place is sacredly privileged over any other and the question of where to place the 'perpendicular' (or where to begin counting the longitudes) is entirely without moral importance. Tamburlaine's cartographic conceit, then, is as vertiginous as it is exhilarating; a vortex of absurdity as much as a brave new world. We are left wondering which of these two imagined 'geographies' – the new, represented by Tamburlaine, or the old, represented by 'those blind geographers' – is truly blind. The irony of the passage arises from Marlowe's awareness of the profound incongruity, the incommensurability, of the medieval and the Renaissance constructions of space.[42] The point of my reading is to suggest why cartography is not to be taken as a transparent or merely 'given' aspect of geography and why geographic contexts are not to be constructed as the inert 'ground' of the poetic text.

In proportion as his poetic engagement with geographic texts is more problematic than Marlowe's, Shakespeare is even more deserving of the semiological understanding of maps which the *History of Cartography* makes possible. However, the rethinking of the map has greater bearing on the second phase of our project. If the overall aim is to situate

Shakespeare's geographic imagination in the contexts of the 'old' and the 'new' geographies, then the 'new geography' should be submitted to the same order of hermeneutic analysis as that to which the ancient geography has already been submitted. The productions of the new geography – maps, atlases, geographic texts, implements, even architectural spaces designed for the displaying of maps or related types of 'world-image' – all demand a hermeneutic or phenomenological understanding if Shakespeare's geographic imagination is to be fully contextualised. While it is true that Renaissance maps are not so historically or culturally remote as not to satisfy 'normal' expectations of what a map should be (a two-dimensional image of geographic space), it is also true that what we know as the 'new geography' was not known by this name in the period, but by the name of 'Cosmography', which implied quite a different kind of discourse and a symbolism which, as we shall see, was fundamentally at odds with the progressivist and scientist assumptions which modern commentators too easily associate with the new geography. We are not, in other words, to assume that a sixteenth-century world map would have been read by contemporaries in the manner in which twentieth-century geographers are likely to read it. For this reason, Harley and Woodward's perspective on the map is crucial to the project of my fifth chapter: a hermeneutic profile of the 'new geography' in the form of its most characteristic product, the world map. Harley and Woodward's perspective is also vital for understanding another map-related phenomenon of particular relevance to a discussion of Shakespeare's geographic imagination: the Globe Theatre (a discussion of which occupies my third chapter). The idea of a theatre building as a map may seem to stretch the tolerance of the new definition – even though that allows for maps in three dimensions as well as in two. As we shall see, however, the idea of the atlas – a bound collection of two-dimensional maps with text – was actually preceded by the idea of the map room: a self-consciously theatrical display of two-dimensional maps in a three-dimensional space.

Not surprisingly, the new definition of the 'map' has more in common with the notion of a 'mental' map than the traditional definition has. There is less of a gap between an idea of a map as a signifying process and an idea of a map as a purely 'mental' entity, than there is between the latter and the traditional image of the map as artefact. Research into the map as a purely 'mental' or 'cognitive' construction is driven by psychology as much as by cartography. In a review of the literature, Robert Lloyd finds three main ways of posing the 'cognitive map', corresponding to three main positions in 'the so-called "imagery debate" in the cognitive psychology literature'.[43] In essence, the debate is about the degree to which such maps are indebted to purely imaginal processes and the degree to which they are indebted to conceptual/verbal processes. Briefly, 'radical image theory' proposes that 'percepts' are broken into units which are stored and 'can then be assembled into images that are quasi-pictorial, spatial entities' (p. 536). 'Conceptual-propositional theory' proposes that 'knowledge, verbal and visual, is stored as abstract conceptual propositions' and that the 'only difference between the internal representations generated by a verbal description of a map and the ones generated by a visual experience would be in the amount of detail' (p. 540). Finally, 'dual coding theory ... postulates two interconnected memory systems, verbal and imagined, operating in parallel' (p. 540). As yet, the debate is inconclusive. For our purposes, however, it is important to realise that all three positions agree in 'acknowledging that the coding of information may span several layers of cognitive processes, each of which transcribes information in its unique way' (p. 543). Any cognitive map will, therefore, be the outcome of *both* conceptual/verbal *and* imaginal processes: 'It seems that information is imaginally coded at some level of processing, while the same information at another level of processing is conceptually coded' (p. 543).

What possible consequence might such a model have for our discussion of Shakespeare's geographic imagination? The main effect is to suggest that there is little, if any, phenomenological difference between the imagined geography of a play like *Tamburlaine*, which is directly inspired by a 'real' map, and that of a play like *Antony and Cleopatra*, which does not give evidence of having been inspired by a 'real' map. If a mental map represents a fusion of both 'conceptual' and 'visual' processes, then the 'inspiration' may be of less significance than the achievement, which in the case of these particular plays is strikingly similar, according to Eugene Waith who observes that *Antony and Cleopatra* 'ranges like *Tamburlaine* over vast areas and achieves the effect of the sort of magnitude which we normally associate with the epic'.[44] In Shakespeare, as in Marlowe, geographical lore and lists of place names are codes to conjure with:

> ... He hath assembled
> Bocchus, the king of Libya, Archelaus
> Of Cappadocia, Philadelphos, king
> Of Paphlagonia; the Thracian king Adallus;
> King Manchus of Arabia, King of Pont,
> Herod of Jewry; Mithridates, king
> Of Commagene, Polemon and Amyntas,
> The kings of Mede and Lycaonia,
> With a larger list of sceptres.

(3.6.68–76)

If we did not actually know that this particular list originated in North's Plutarch, and that Marlowe's source for the list of African place names referred to earlier was Ortelius, we should be tempted to conclude that both authors had been reading the same books. And would we be so far wrong? How do we know that Shakespeare had *not* drawn inspiration from Ortelius for *Antony and Cleopatra*, just as Marlowe did; or that Marlowe was *not* thinking of classical geography in *Tamburlaine*? Most editions of Ortelius from 1570 included an ever-expanding section entitled the *Parergon* (or 'Supplement') devoted to what we would call historical geography. Among many reconstituted maps of past empires, an Eliza-bethan reader would have seen one of the Roman Empire.[45] While we do not know, it is tempting to think that Shakespeare had seen this map because Plutarch rather assumes familiarity with such a map by present-ing the reader with a mass of undigested geographical detail in his *Life of Antonius*. Such detail is effortlessly spatialised in *Antony and Cleopatra*, in addition to being powerfully energised and moralised. In the case of *Tamburlaine*, we can be rather more certain that the geographical inspir-ation was mixed rather than pure. If Ortelius provided one dimension of Marlowe's Scythian, Lucan's Caesar provided another. The first book of the *Pharsalia* (translated by Marlowe) was, as we have seen, powerfully charged with the moral-geographic symbolism of extravagant journeying and intimate violation (of the mother, the family, the womb). Marlowe draws much the same equation in *Tamburlaine*. The more extravagant the hero's geographic conquests, the more intimate and invasive his violence becomes, to the point where it destroys his family and (arguably) his human being. Shakespeare's Antony (as I hope to show) is a similar kind of figure: a voyager beyond bounds whose extravagance leads directly to the destruction of the Roman family (though this time through his miscegenation with a foreign queen rather than through direct violence). The main point of this comparison is that both playwrights fashion their geographical material (which is probably not as dissimilar as is commonly thought) into generically similar imaginative, dramatic and moral struc-tures. Both combine ancient and Renaissance forms of the moral-geogra-phic myth of the 'voyager' (it is no accident that voyage-imagery plays a prominent role in either play).

This comparison of the expressive uses of world geography in *Tambur-laine* and *Antony and Cleopatra* raises another question upon which recent discussions of maps and 'mental maps' can cast some light: What do *maps* – as distinct from the authors who use them – express? Or rather: what is the expressive link between the Renaissance world map and the imagery of the world map (and the cognate imagery of voyaging) in Elizabethan poetry and drama? In Shakespeare, Marlowe and Donne, the world map (like the voyage) is almost always an image of desire, but precisely because such imagery almost always tends to be linked to an imagery of voyaging and 'Indian' wealth (of either the eastern or western variety), one is tempted to say that the literary or dramatic motive is connected more with voyaging and 'Indian' imagery than with the cartographic image as such. Thus, in *The Comedy of Errors*, we find a mock-Marlovian reference to 'whole armadas of caracks to be ballast' with 'rubies, carbuncles, sapphires' (3.2.140,138), and in *The Merry Wives of Windsor*, Falstaff likens Mistress Ford to 'a region in Guiana, all gold and bounty' (1.3.61–2). Even the image of the 'new map' in *Twelfth Night* is implicitly an image of voyaging (the *Hydrographiae* is, after all, a maritime map), being linked to the image of Malvolio's rival, Sir Andrew, sailing hopelessly 'into the north of my lady's opinion'. To both these voyagers, Olivia represents 'an augmentation of the Indies' or something like what Mistress Ford represents to Falstaff.

The more, however, one looks at late-sixteenth-century world maps, the more it seems that desire is intrinsic to the cartographic image itself, regardless of any iconographic embellishment. This is because the disposition of the major geographic landmasses composes a picture with unconscious expressive force. For Robert Harbison, even modern maps – so pictorially impoverished by comparison with their Renaissance counterparts – pictorialise and dramatise the geography they purport merely to delineate.[46] Geographical orientation, for example, cohabits with pictorial orientation (the conventions governing the expectations of the viewer): 'To look at a familiar coast from the other side shows us that we do not imagine the land out from ourselves flexibly in all directions, but are always standing in the same place when we think of it and facing the same way like a statue' (p. 124). If the world maps of Ortelius and Mercator are read with Harbison's eye, their pictorial bias is immediately grasped. The American landmass is placed on the left and symmetrically juxtaposed with the landmass of the Old World, which appears on the right. It is important to understand that this bias towards symmetry, juxtaposition and conventional 'viewpoint' has nothing to do with cartography as such. Renaissance cartographers had earlier experimented with a 'cordiform' projection, for instance – organised around the figure of a heart rather than a sphere (or oval) – which was focused on the North Pole rather than on the Equator at 0°.[47] And they would have been quite as capable of putting America on the right and the Old World on the left, as Ricci was obliged to do for the Chinese.

Why, then, did the arrangement of Ortelius and Mercator come to be so dominant? The easy answer is that the European viewer needed to visualise America in terms of an Atlantic voyage rather than, say, a voyage via the Indian and Pacific oceans. But a more searching answer is that the European viewer needed to imagine America as a 'New World' in the sense of a teleological or perhaps erotic projection of the Old World.[48] In pictorial terms, Renaissance maps (whether of this or the earlier 'cordiform' type) might be thought of as attempts to cope with the absence of a controlling centre. In the TO map, as we have seen, the entire geography is orientated towards the centre of 'Jerusalem' (just at the juncture of the 'T' and the 'O'). The effect of this privileging of the centre – what Samuel Y. Edgerton calls the '*omphalos* syndrome' – is to settle, to reassure, to emplace.[49] A concentric world is a world which is both harmonious and complete. Outward or centrifugal energy (that of Vernant's *Hermes*) is counterbalanced by inward or centripetal energy (that of Vernant's *Hestia*), resulting in a pleasurable synergy. In this cartographic apotheosis of the *oikumene*, the viewer is truly 'at home'. The effect of a late-sixteenth-century map is utterly different. The strong central focus on the equator at $0°$ carries no suggestion of 'home'. How can it when the centre of the map is somewhere in the Atlantic Ocean? The eye finds no satisfaction in resting here. Instead, this anti-focus forces the eye into a search for compensation, which – in view of the equal gravitational pull exerted by the two landmasses to the viewer's left and right – is literally 'restless'. In place of the comfort of the medieval map we find restlessness, in place of stasis: dynamism, a constant discharge of energy. The difference between the medieval and Ortelian constructions of geographic space is roughly equivalent to the difference which Michel Foucault finds between the ancient and post-Galilean constructions of cosmic space. One is 'a space of emplacement' characterised by 'localisation', the other 'an open space' characterised by amorphic 'extension'.[50] For perhaps the first time in the history of world cartography, world maps post-1492 began to privilege the unknown and unpossessed over the known and possessed. This is the *semiosis* of desire. Its symmetry notwithstanding, the Ortelian map draws the viewer's gaze west rather than east. Why? Because the New World 'beckons', even in this apparently unpoeticised form. Its very emptiness, its nakedness perhaps (the relative absence of graphic density and verbal inscription) invites the eye to 'rove' in the way that Donne imagines his hands roving over the continent of his mistress's body:

> Licence my roving hands, and let them go,
> Before, behind, between, above, below.
> O my America, my new-found-land.[51]

The relationship between Donne's erotic conceit and the geographical image is more intrinsic than it might seem. William G. Niederland finds in sixteenth-century 'cartographic documents' – with 'their rich pictorializations of the sea, the ships, the hidden lands and passages' – 'the haunting lineaments of the feminine form'.[52] Noting how the name 'America' first appears on a world map (in Martin Waldseemueller's *Cosmographiae Introductio* of 1507), Niederland asks himself the secret of the name's immediate and universal appeal, particularly in view of Waldseemueller's deliberate omission of it from his new world map of 1516, by which time he had realised that the honour of discovering the new continent belonged to Columbus and not to Amerigo Vespucci. The answer, Niederland suggests, is that 'America' was immediately identified with 'some of the oldest and most cherished illusions of mankind ... the fantasy of the *Insulae Fortunatae*, the islands of bliss and happiness', the persistence of which testifies to an 'underlying infantile concept ... where ... narcissistic, oral-regressive wishes can be gratified' (pp. 465, 467). The success of the name thus owed less to its association with Amerigo Vespucci than to its association with various European forms and correlates of the word 'mother' which 'are apt to evoke orally- and maternally-tinged images or ideas' (p. 468). Niederland's conclusion is perhaps worth quoting in full:

We can now attempt to formulate the essential characteristics of the historical process under scrutiny in psychoanalytic terms: owing to a combination of special circumstances and under the impact of the excitement aroused by the new discoveries and the momentous changes resulting therefrom (with their accompanying potentialities for expansion, wealth, mastery, freedom), the mental representation of the transatlantic world named America was charged with prevalently narcissistic and pregenital cathexis. The mental representation of these areas thus became overcathected and remained so for centuries. (pp. 468–9)

Lest this psychoanalytic reading of Waldseemueller's cartographic invention seem inappropriately fanciful, it is worth reflecting on Gerard Mercator's own observations on the world map which appeared in his *Atlas* of 1595: 'This universall Globe ... is rather an object of the secret conceptions of humane understanding, than of the sharp-sightednes of our eyes'.[53] The 'Globe' is a visual object, yes, but the visual image is of an object which can never be seen, only imagined. The cartographer, in other words, – like 'the lunatic, the lover, and the poet' of *A Midsummer Night's Dream* (5.1.7) – can be possessed of and by:

> ... such seething brains,
> Such shaping fantasies, that apprehend
> More than cool reason ever comprehends.
>
> (5.1.4–6)

4

The notion of a Shakespearean 'mental map' raises a simple question: should we be talking in terms of one mental map or in terms of as many mental maps as there are plays requiring them? The question arises partly as a consequence of the tendency of conceptual/verbal mental maps towards moralisation, and partly as a consequence of our definition of maps as 'graphic representations of ... events *in the human world*'. Both ideas powerfully imply that all maps (mental and material) are shaped by *human motives*. From this, it follows that different kinds of maps will be formed by different motives, even when their geographic content is identical. When the geographic content differs, as is generally the case when we compare the geography of any two Shakespeare plays, the case for proposing a number of mental maps instead of just one is even stronger. Simply to remember the gallery of Shakespearean characters who either allude to maps, use them, or make learned geographical comment – Lear, Hotspur, Antonio, Fluellen, Gonzalo and Fabian (in *Twelfth Night*) – is to remind ourselves of the range of potential geographic motives we could expect to find in Shakespeare, not to mention the variety of geographic content. If, for the sake of argument, we were to read Shakespeare with Antonio's eye for 'ports and piers and roads', then our notion of Shakespeare's mental map would have a distinctly maritime and mercantile cast. (Something like this has already happened in the 'discovery' of the original of the 'new map'.) If, on the other hand, we were to read Shakespeare from the viewpoint of a Fluellen or a Gonzalo, our idea of Shakespeare's mental geography would be inclined towards the historical and typo-geographical genre. And what if Shakespeare's use of geography were not only figurative (or consciously ungeographical) but shaped by motives which he might not have recognised? Clearly we should be prepared to consider unconscious motives as well as figurative and geographical motives.

Are we, then, to speak of one mental map or many? Let us put the general question in particular terms: Does Shakespeare use an entirely different mental map in a Roman history play (*Antony and Cleopatra*) from that used in a Venetian-Renaissance comedy (*The Merchant of Venice*), *given* that each play shares roughly the same notional geography of a world centred on the Mediterranean?[54]

Whether or not Shakespeare had actually seen Ortelius's map of the Roman Empire, the epic geography of *Antony and Cleopatra* does in fact originate in and suggest the figurative tradition of the *orbis terrarum*. According to Maurice Charney, the geography of the play is not merely a background, but a theme in its own right: 'the imagery of dimension and scope is most powerfully expressed in the world theme, whose cumulative force (forty five examples) is especially significant'.[55] One instance of the 'world theme' is taken from the scene in which the god Hercules leaves Antony; specifically when some soldiers are directed to '*place themselves in every corner of the stage'* (4.3.7–8). Here, argues Charney, the stage itself has become an emblem of 'the four corners of the earth' (p. 81). For the most part, 'the world theme' operates as a figure of hubris. Thus Antony describes Sextus Pompeius as one 'whose quality, going on,/ The sides o' th' world may danger' (1.2.184–5). And, at the moment of his suicide, Antony thinks of himself in the same terms: 'O, cleave my sides! / Heart, once be stronger than thy continent' (4.15.39–40). By this point in the play, the word 'sides' carries an orbic as well as anatomical sense. Such imagery bears an obvious family resemblance to the rhetorical tradition of the *orbis terrarum* – to the *nec sufficet orbis* trope, for example, to the idea of the world as a Roman farm, or to the Ovidian boast that Rome's limits coincided with the limits of the world.[56] For the reason that Roman imperial cartography was itself consciously rhetorical, the geography of Shakespeare's play genuinely mediates officially sanctioned maps of the *orbis terrarum*, such as that compiled by Marcus Agrippa and mounted in the *Porticus Vipsania* near the Forum.[57] In such a map, the world was consciously shrunk to fit the dimensions of the Empire, an idea which must have seemed particularly pointed in the context of a companion map representing the City of Rome.[58]

The Merchant of Venice is a very different kind of play centred on roughly the same Mediterranean geography but not the same Mediterranean 'world'. As a comedy, one would hardly expect its geography to be projected on a 'world' scale in any sense. But it is, because (as I shall argue in Chapter 4) Shakespeare found the Renaissance imperial myth of Venice just as alluring as the classical imperial myth of Rome. The image of the maritime world in *The Merchant of Venice* goes far beyond the kind of map presupposed by Antonio's obsession with 'ports and piers and roads'. Shakespeare insists that Antonio's network of maritime trade is 'world'-wide in the full Renaissance sense. Shylock mentions that Antonio 'hath an argosy bound to Tripolis, another to the Indies ... a third / at Mexico, a fourth for England, and other ventures he / hath squandered abroad' (1.3.17–21). The same catalogue, with the addition of 'India', 'Lisbon' and 'Barbary', is later rehearsed by Bassanio when lamenting the apparently wholesale miscarriage of Antonio's ventures:

> What, not one hit?
> From Tripolis, from Mexico, and England,
> From Lisbon, Barbary, and India,
> And not one vessel scape the dreadful touch
> Of merchant-marring rocks?
>
> (3.2.265–9)

If we match the itinerary of Mediterranean and European destinations *only*, with the model-maps of the Venetian trading empire in Fernand

Braudel's study of Venetian maritime trade from 1482–1534, we will find a very close fit.[59] It is, therefore, quite plausible to imagine Antonio's 'argosies' trading to these locations (if we assume that Shakespeare wants to imagine a Venice at the height of her maritime trade). It is quite implausible, however, that Venetian ships would sail to 'Mexico', 'India' and the 'Indies' (whether 'East' or 'West'). These routes were oceanic. They were never the preserve of Venice, not even of Venice in its maritime heyday; which Braudel supposes to be 'about 1460' (p. 127). The discovery and development of the oceanic routes by the Iberians was, of course, the prime cause of the maritime decline of Venice in the early sixteenth century.[60] What is suggested, therefore, by the intrusion of this geography into a play about 'merchants of Venice', is not the Venetian reality (scarcely even the Venetian myth) but Elizabethan ambitions for London.[61] Shakespeare projects such ambitions in a Venetian fantasy because Venice (no less than Antwerp) represented the *idea* of a world maritime capital which leading Elizabethan merchants had in mind for London.

Should we therefore decide – on the basis of this brief comparison between the geographies of the Roman history play and the Renaissance/Venetian comedy – that the two are indeed different and that it is meaningless to think in terms of a single Shakespearean mental map? Such is the logic of the comparison so far. If we take the comparison a stage further, however, just the opposite is suggested. While the two plays generally presuppose two different geographies, one classical and the other Renaissance/Elizabethan, neither geography is quite exclusive of the other. In 'poetic' terms, indeed, each imagined geography actually *invites* the participation of the other; which is to say that each geography *per se* invites a reading in terms of the 'poetic' energies of the other geography.

Thus, Morocco and Bassanio in *The Merchant of Venice* represent Portia's desirability in terms of the four-cornered classical world. For Morocco, Portia is the focus of a universal pilgrimage:

> ... All the world desires her.
> From the four corners of the earth they come
> To kiss this shrine, this mortal breathing saint.
> The Hyrcanian deserts and the vasty wilds
> Of wide Arabia are as throughfares now
> For princes to come view fair Portia.
> The watery kingdom, whose ambitious head
> Spits in the face of heaven, is no bar
> To stop the foreign spirits, but they come
> As o'er a brook to see fair Portia.

(2.7.38–47)

Morocco himself, of course, epitomises this ethnic migration of 'foreign spirits', which seems half medieval pilgrimage and half barbarian invasion (as if the dynamic outward thrust of the world-city had imploded, drawing the transgressive and pollutive energies of the outside in upon itself). The regions which Morocco imagines as 'throughfares' – 'Hyrcanian deserts' and 'vasty wilds of wide Arabia' – are traditional *termini* or edge-lands of the *orbis terrarum*. They are, of course, two of the four 'corners' of the earth: the north-east corner (Hyrcania) and the south-east corner (Arabia). Morocco himself personifies the African south-west corner. Another version of this orbic trope is voiced by Bassanio, who also imagines Portia as the centre of universal desire:

> Her name is Portia, nothing undervalued
> To Cato's daughter, Brutus' Portia;
> Nor is the wide world ignorant of her worth,
> For the four winds blow in from every coast
> Renownèd suitors, and her sunny locks
> Hang on her temples like a golden fleece,
> Which makes her seat of Belmont Colchis strand,
> And many Jasons come in quest of her.
>
> (1.1.165–72)

Bassanio's 'four winds' are a periphrasis of Morocco's 'four corners of the earth'; much as, in *Cymbeline*, it is said that 'winds of all the corners kissed your sails' (2.4.28). The imagery derives both from the ancient geography and from the decorative symbolism of Renaissance world maps.[62] Understandably, perhaps, the Venetian Bassanio has a different perspective on the four-cornered world from the 'foreign' Morocco. Here, then, the direction of the quest is reversed. Bassanio is a second Jason, voyaging *outwards* from an imagined world-centre to an imagined world-rim: 'Colchis strand', home of Medea and the golden fleece, and (along with Hyrcania) a traditional *locus* of the north-east 'corner' of the Greco-Roman world.[63] Lest, however, the audience be misled into drawing hasty conclusions about the moral character of Portia based on that of Medea (the bloodthirsty witch of Euripides, Seneca and Ovid), she is pointedly compared with 'Cato's daughter, Brutus' Portia', before the potentially ominous image of the golden fleece is raised. The 'poetic geography' of both these rhetorical eulogies of Portia, then, is governed by the classical theme of *termini* or 'limits': limits of geography, of desire, of marriageability and (potentially) of transgression.

The very same classical trope of orbic limits is also found (as we have already partly seen) in *Antony and Cleopatra*. What is truly surprising, however, is that the classical play also seeks a *Renaissance* imagination of limits just as the Renaissance play had sought a classical imagination of limits. As in the Venetian play, this image of limits is also an image of desire. It is the first such image in the play, and perhaps its most potent:

> *Cleopatra.* If it be love indeed, tell me how much.
> *Antony.*   There's beggary in the love that can be reckoned.
> *Cleopatra.* I'll set a bourn how far to be beloved.
> *Antony.*   Then must thou needs find out new heaven, new earth.
>
> (1.1.14–17)

To a degree, the idea of finding out 'new heaven, new earth' can be read in purely Roman terms. It has echoes of Plutarch's disapproving account of the lovers' invention of a 'new' life and their new word for it: '*amimeto-bion*' or (in the words of North's translation) 'no life comparable and matchable with it'.[64] Alternatively, it might recall Cleopatra's 'wonderful attempt' to transport a fleet overland to the Red Sea: 'and so with a great company of men go and dwell in some place about the Ocean sea far from the Mediterranean'.[65] Again, it might suggest the somewhat rhetorical description of Britain as 'another world' in Plutarch's *Life of Caesar*. As we have seen, part of the point of Caesar's conquest of this 'other world' had been to allow him to challenge comparison with Alexander. Here, too, was a man of whom it could be said: *nec sufficit orbis*. Antonius, of course, is not very like the colossal Caesar of Plutarch, but he is more like him than Shakespeare's own (decidedly un-colossal) Caesar is. Antony's resemblance to Plutarch's Caesar is tropological: he too has a tendency to *hubrise* or overflow geographical limits. It is just that his geography is more figurative than literal.

Classical contexts, however, can never account for the marvellous *erhebung* or 'uplift' of Antony's image of 'new heaven, new earth'. This is surely because their commanding context is the Renaissance discovery (and *idea*) of the New World. The immediate context of the phrase is biblical, echoing the language of Isaiah (66.22) and St John (Revelation 21.1). But in concert with the idea of 'finding out' the furthest 'bourn' of love, the words more precisely echo Columbus's famous boast to have actually discovered 'the new heaven and the new earth' spoken of by Isaiah and St John.[66] Even if Shakespeare did not know directly of the Columbus letter, he was certainly acquainted with its underlying symbolism (based on the biblical/classical topos of *Renovatio Mundi*) as his evocation of the Augustan/Christian reign of peace in *Antony and Cleopatra* and *Cymbeline* clearly shows. No less than Columbus, Shakespeare was alive to the apocalyptic symbolism of the New World. Miranda's 'brave new world' is not literally American, but, as an expression of renewal, the words inevitably suggest the geographic construct in which the dream of *renovatio* was so powerfully focused. In all three plays, indeed, Shakespeare suggests something of the nubile iconography of

Revelation 21, in which 'a new heaven and a new earth' is promised for 'the holy city, the new Jerusalem' who 'comes forth as a bride adorned for her husband'. Such a bride and such a figure is Imogen, and Miranda, and (the audacity is breathtaking!) Cleopatra.[67]

If, then, *Antony and Cleopatra*, with its notionally classical geography, invites a reading in terms of a Renaissance 'poetic geography', and *The Merchant of Venice*, with its notionally Renaissance geography, invites a reading in terms of a classical 'poetic geography', we must allow that there is a real sense in which both dramatic 'worlds' are inspired by a unified geographic imagination. Shakespeare simply could not have written either play unless he was somehow able to comprehend a classical geography and a Renaissance geography within a single (if highly flexible) poetic-geographic idiom. It is this 'perspective of the world' (to use Braudel's phrase) that I hope to describe in my fourth chapter.

3   Theatres of the world

If, as Harley and Woodward suggest, maps are 'graphic representations' or 'iconic devices' facilitating 'a spatial understanding of things, concepts, conditions, processes or events in the human world', then our concept of the map is not bound by 'those maps of the earth whose description constitutes so much of the existing literature'. Maps might exist in three dimensions rather than in two. They might even take the form of buildings, as distinct from graphic images on sheets of paper. Here I will consider the Globe Theatre as a kind of map: a quasi-cartographic product of the same type of cosmographic imagination which produced the world maps of Ortelius and Mercator. As such, the Globe Theatre is no less legitimately a context of Shakespeare's geographic imagination than more conventional maps like the *Hydrographiae Descriptio*. 'Shakespeare's Globe' is interesting for another reason. A real theatre, it can tell us much about the conceptual character of the Ortelian *Theatrum*, and vice versa, for the reason that the theatrical metaphor is just as important in Ortelius as the cosmographic or 'global' metaphor is in the discourse of the Elizabethan theatre. Shakespeare's theatre and Ortelian 'cosmography', I suggest, are dialogically related. Each 'reads' the other. Each builds itself in the form of the other. As a corollary, I want to suggest that the Shakespearean other is significantly indebted to the figuration of exotic otherness in the 'theatres' – maps, atlases, ethnographic handbooks – of the new geography.

1

As the theatrical configuration of the later-sixteenth-century atlas will be less familiar than the cosmographic figuration of Shakespeare's Globe, we may begin with the *Theatrum Orbis Terrarum*, which is no less exemplary of Anglo-Flemish cartography in the period 1570–1612, than Burbage's 'Theatre' is of Elizabethan theatre generally.[1] Ortelius not only produced the first Renaissance atlas, but invented the very idea of the atlas. This, in turn, was inseparable from generic labels such as *Theatrum* or *Speculum* ('glass') until a decade or so after the appearance of Mercator's *Atlas* in 1595. Generically speaking, then, an atlas was a 'theatre' or a 'glass' for virtually the entire period of Shakespeare's lifetime.[2]

Nor was '*theatrum*' an idle metaphor. In his address 'to the courteous Reader', Ortelius derives the figurative logic of his 'theatre' from the deep relationship between geography and history:

Seeing, that as I thinke, there is no man, gentle Reader, but knoweth what, and how great profit the knowledge of Histories doth bring to those which are serious students therein; I doe verily beleeve and perswade myselfe, that there is almost no man ... that is ignorant how necessary, for the understanding them aright, the knowledge of Geography is, which, in that respect therefore is of some, and not without iust cause called the eye of History.[3]

Having established that geography is the 'eye of History', Ortelius goes on to explain what kinds of historical event are best suited to geographical illustration: 'especially ... the expeditions and voyages of great Kings, Captaines and Emperours ... the divers and sundry shiftings of Nations from one place to another ... the travels and peregrinations of famous men, made into sundry countreys'. Such events constitute the ideal objects of both history and geography; and hence furnish the ideal rationale of geographical maps:

these Chartes being placed, as it were certaine glasses before our eyes, will the longer be kept in memory, and make the deeper impression in us: by which meanes it commeth to passe, that now we do seeme to perceive some fruit of that which we have read. I omit here, that the reading of Histories doeth both seeme to be much more pleasant, and in deed so it is, when the Mappe being layed before our eyes, we may behold things done, or places where they were done, as if they were at this time present and in doing.

In relation to geography, then, which is imagined as an all-seeing *eye* commanding the spatial and temporal immensities of history, the map is imagined as a *glass* or a means by which the god's-eye view of geography is accommodated to the limited perspective of human sight. But the map (or rather the novel idea of a whole book of maps) is for this very reason *theatrical* in a number of senses, both implicit and explicit. It is implicitly theatrical in two senses. It functions, in the first place, as a memory theatre in which historical events 'will the longer be kept in memory, and make the deeper impression in us'.[4] But it is also implicitly theatrical in the popular sense of making histories 'more pleasant'; enacting them in a virtual sense, 'as if they were at this time present and in doing'.

Turning from the preface to the maps themselves, however, one finds little overt expression or evidence of such theatrical and epic metaphors, but this is less significant than it might seem. The modern regional maps which represent the bulk of the original *Theatrum* were compiled from the work of Europe's leading cartographers *c.* 1570. They are, therefore, neither the original work of Ortelius (his contribution extended only to ornamentation and page-formatting) nor a vehicle of the full Ortelian vision. For this, one must turn to the historical maps of the *Parergon* (or 'supplement'), which came to be included in most editions of the *Theatrum* subsequent to 1570. Here, Ortelius vividly practised his own preaching. Unlike the modern maps of the original *Theatrum*, the maps of the *Parergon* represented Ortelius's own handiwork. In these maps of bygone empires and events, the idea of geography as a historical 'theatre' is made graphically manifest. These are not just maps of regions but of 'expeditions', 'voyages', 'peregrinations'; the very stuff of ancient history, sacred and secular. To their purely cartographic function, Ortelius adds a narrative-theatrical function. As well as describing regions, these maps tell *histories*. Accordingly, the cartography is complemented by a variety of narrative or pictorial devices. Pictures appear either on the body of the map itself (such as the ships of Aeneas or Jason) or framed by cartouches, or set within the ornamental frame. Textual legends appear before or within or beneath maps, in order to convey the historical dimension of the geographic image. One of the more elaborate of these, 'The Peregrination of Abraham the Patriarke', features a comprehensive verbal summary of Genesis, and no less than twenty-two narrative paintings of episodes from Abraham's life (Plate 8). The *Parergon* also illustrates a complementary theatrical development. In as much as these geographic images are the 'eyes' and 'mirrors' of their historical epochs, they are quite as '*chorographical*' as they are *geographical*. They are, that is to say, designed to tell the reader as much about peoples and heroic *characters* as about places.

There is, then, good reason for believing that Ortelius is entirely serious in his preface about the implicit analogies between the function of the atlas and the functions of theatre. Both analogies are underlined by a third and quite explicit analogy when Ortelius explains that wall-maps would be much more saleable:

... were it not by reason of the narrownesse of the roomes and places, broad and large Mappes or Chartes, which are folded or rowl'd up, are not so commodious: nor, when any thing is peradventure read in them, so easie to be look'd upon. And he that will in order hang them all along upon a wall had need have not only a very large & wide house, but even a Princes gallery or spacious Theater.

Here, then, is a third way in which the atlas ('this our Theater') performs a theatrical function. It epitomises the kind of architectural space needed to display a collection of wall-maps. It recapitulates and is functionally equivalent to the 'very large & wide house' of the wealthy merchant, as well as the 'Princes gallery or spacious Theater'. It is, then, doubly an epitome: a *multum in parvo* twice over. Like the Marlovian image of 'infinite riches in a little room', the world has been monumentalised in an architectural space, and this in turn has been bound within the covers of a book.

The idea of theatrical architecture is underlined from the very first page of the atlas by an ornamental frontispiece which resembles nothing so much as a monumental Anverian pageant-stage (Plate 9). Monumental frontispieces are, of course, commonplace features of Renaissance printed 'works' generally. What is remarkable about this one, however, is that it is the first such frontispiece to be employed in a standard work of geography.[5] The editions of the Ptolemaic *Cosmographiae*, which had been appearing in print ever since 1475, were without them.[6] The monumental and theatrical imagery of the Ortelian frontispiece is both original and deliberate, representing (in the words of a Latin *Frontispicii Explicatio* by one Adolph Mekerch) the '*prima foris ... pagina*' or 'the first page of the doorway' of a figurative Renaissance map-room of the type which Vasari describes as impressing the visitor with a spectacle of 'all things relating to heaven and earth in one place, without error, so that one could see and measure them together and by themselves'.[7] Such an 'entrance' makes the atlas itself a textual version of the Renaissance genre of the *studiolo*, the *Kunst-und-Wunderkammer*, the monumental *Guardaroba*, or the *Sala del Mappamondo*. These are but various names for the kind of learnedly decorated room which Paolo Cortesi had recommended in his 1510 treatise on the Cardinalate, as appropriate to the vestibule to the Cardinal's chamber.[8] Again, Ortelius faithfully sustains the monumental suggestions of his preface in his presentation of the geographic material, the decorations of which were taken directly from the very 'Ornament Prints' which were used to decorate the walls and ceilings of Renaissance palaces (and hence of a *Sala del Mappamondo*).[9] In the use of such decorative motifs, indeed, Ortelius mimics the monumental presence of the map-room within the pages of a book: anticipating the conceit of Donne's 'The Canonisation': 'We'll build in sonnets pretty roomes' (where 'roomes' might be understood as a pun on 'stanzas', adapted from the Italian word for 'rooms').[10] This type of decorative motif also became standard in post-Ortelian Renaissance atlases. In their liberal use of the motifs of the 'Ornament Prints' – strap-work, vines, masks, heads, caryatids, monumental and pictorial effects – the maps of the *Theatrum* 'may be taken as models of the Flemish style of cartography which ousted the Italian and was rapidly adopted in every country'.[11] Not only, then, was the new genre of the atlas identified as a metaphor of theatre, but the monumentalising idiom which sustains the metaphor beyond 'the first page of the doorway' also became generic.

The monumental and theatrical imagery of the Ortelian frontispiece is strikingly linked to another Ortelian innovation: the first appearance of personified female continents within a printed cartographic work. Europe is enthroned upon an upper stage forming a canopy beneath which Asia and Africa stand on railings flanking the main stage, upon which America reclines, surrounded by her barbarous attributes. Beside her is a bust of 'Magellanica' (the fictitious southern continent). Such imagery functions to dramatise the 'new' as distinct from the 'old' geography. For all their lowly position within this hierarchy, America and Magellanica are unquestionably the focus of the theatrical composition, thereby signalling a reversal of the tendency of earlier-sixteenth-century *Cosmographiae* to include the geography of the discoveries merely as *addenda* to Ptolemy's geography. The link between the four continents and the theatrical imagery is not casual. A native of Antwerp, Ortelius may have first encountered the 'Continents' in a theatrical milieu – that of the Anverian pageant-stage, where the female personification of 'America', along with various new geographic 'sisters', such as Magellanica, were added to the classical sisterhood of 'Europe', 'Asia' and 'Africa'.[12] Anverian pageantry seems to have given birth not only to 'Miss America' but also the characteristic relationship which Ortelius depicts between the four continents: a great chain of being extending downwards from Europe through the less civilised Asia and Africa to the brutishness of America and her as yet undiscovered sister. Theatre may also be responsible for the paradoxical power of America's position. The bottom of the vertical axis is also the focal point: literally down-stage centre. Exactly what will be enacted here? Like some Polonian prologue, the *Frontispicii Explicatio* rehearses a scenario of 'historical-pastoral-tragical' proportions:

> The one you see on the lower ground is called AMERICA,
> whom bold Vespucci recently voyaging across the sea
> seized by force, holding the nymph in the embrace of gentle love.
> Unmindful of herself, unmindful of her pure chastity,
> she sits with her body all naked, except that a feather headdress
> binds her hair, a jewel adorns the forehead,
> and bells are around her shapely calves.
> She has in her right hand a wooden club, with which she sacrifices
> fattened and glutted men, prisoners taken in war.
> She cuts them up into quivering pieces, and either
> roasts them over a slow fire or boils them in a steaming cauldron,
> or, if ever the rudeness of hunger is more pressing,
> she eats their flesh raw and freshly killed, dripping with darkish gore,
> the steaming joints flutter beneath her teeth, she feeds
> upon the wretches' flesh and darkish blood:

a deed horrible to see, and horrible to tell.
Is there any purpose that barbarous irreligion,
that atheism does not form?
In her left hand, you see a human head
befouled straight from the slaughter. There are her bow and swift
arrows, with which she is wont, as she bends her horn bow
and draws the bowstring, to inflict sure wounds and a sure death on
men. At length, wearied with hunting men and wanting to lie down
to sleep, she climbs into a bed woven in a wide mesh like a net
which she ties at either end to a pair of stakes. In its weave,
she lays herself down, head and body, to rest.[13]

The blend of new geography with ancient poetry and drama is seamless. Vespucci's discovery becomes an Ovidian rape. The language of America's cannibalism and impiety precisely echoes that of Seneca's *Thyestes* and Ovid's story of Tereus.[14]

In view of the density and force of the theatrical metaphor in Ortelius, and in view of the immense prestige of the *Theatrum* for some forty years after its first printing, it is surprising that the generic '*Theatrum*' (like the term '*Speculum*') should have been displaced by the term '*Atlas*'. The common explanation for the success of 'Atlas' is the more considered geography and greater popularity of Mercator's *Atlas*, which – first published in 1595 – gradually supplanted the *Theatrum* as the atlas of choice.[15] As early as 1575, however, the figure of Atlas bearing the terrestrial globe on his shoulders had already appeared as a generic symbol.[16] Yet, whatever the reason for the decline of *Theatrum* as the generic title, two points must be clearly borne in mind. First, the atlas is metaphorically a *theatre* from (roughly) 1570–1610, the crucial years of the Elizabethan theatre. Second, the emblem of the eventual generic title (the figure of Atlas bearing the terrestrial globe on his shoulders) *also* resonates powerfully with the emblem of Shakespeare's Globe Theatre, which is thought to have displayed an image of Hercules carrying the earthly globe upon his back.[17] In both its main generic forms, then, the idea of the atlas resonates powerfully with the idea of Shakespeare's Globe.

2

In what sense (if any) did the idea of Shakespeare's Globe, or the discourse of the Elizabethan theatre, *reciprocate* the attentions of Ortelian geography? Given that the Ortelian atlas proposes itself in the image of theatre, to what extent does Elizabethan theatre respond by proposing itself in geographic or cosmographic terms? Generally, I suggest that there *was* a response and that it was highly inventive. Underlying the dialogue, however, was a common topical heritage which had already substantially determined its direction.

Quite apart from the emblematic figure of 'Hercules and his load', which (at whatever remove) is certainly associated with Shakespeare's Globe, there is the geographic or cosmographic resonance of the name: 'The Globe'. The precise reference and context of this term is unclear. Should 'globe' be understood in a 'cosmographic' context, in which case it may well have the sense of the entire cosmos? Or should it be understood in a strictly geographic sense, in which case it would have the sense of the earthly globe alone? Or should we understand it less exclusively, as roughly equivalent to the Latin *mundus* or 'world'? In any case, the starting point of our enquiry must be the presumptive motto of this theatre: *Totus Mundus Agit Histrionem*, which Shakespeare translates as 'All the world's a stage'.

As with the emblem of 'Hercules and his load', there is some doubt about whether the Globe actually had a motto and whether, if it had, this was it. As with the emblem too, however, it scarcely matters because contemporaries evidently *read* the Globe Theatre in terms of the classical topos of the *theatrum mundi*, from which its presumptive motto derived. When the first Globe was 'casually burnt downe and consumed with fier' on 29 June 1613, for example, the metaphor of the *theatrum mundi* was jestingly invoked.[18] 'See the world's ruins!' apostrophised Ben Jonson. In similar vein, a satirical verse related 'the dolefull tragedie,/ That late was playd at Globe'.[19] Both jokes turn on the metaphoric equivalence of *theatrum* and *mundus*. The analogy appears to have worked both ways. The world was a theatre in the sense of its delusiveness and emptiness. It was, in Macbeth's words, 'full of sound and fury, signifying nothing' (5.5.26–7). For its part, the theatre was a world in the sense of the microcosm's epitomisation of the macrocosm.

For a fuller understanding of the *theatrum mundi*, we must turn to the immediate source of the presumptive motto of the Globe: *Totus Mundus Agit Histrionem*. This, as E. R. Curtius argues, is almost certainly the *Policraticus* (or 'Statesman's Book') of the twelfth-century humanist, John of Salisbury.[20] In the course of several chapters of his third book, John offers what amounts to an extended meditation on the *theatrum mundi* as he understood it from an encyclopaedic range of ancient texts, classical and biblical. The core of the idea is that 'the life of man on earth is a comedy, where each forgetting his own plays another's role'.[21] This implies both that 'almost all the world is playing a part', and that 'the world is the stage on which this endless, marvellous, incomparable tragedy, or if you will comedy can be played; its area is in fact that of the whole world' (pp. 175, 176). The metaphoric equivalence of 'world' and 'stage' has a corollary which is not often remarked. It means that the rest of John's metaphoric theatre – the *auditorium* – is identified with the Christian heaven; which for John meant the celestial spheres which Macrobius had described as encircling the earth in the form of a classical temple.[22]

Strictly speaking, then, it would be truer to equate the *mundus* with the *stage* rather than with the *theatrum* as such, because the latter includes the auditorium which is by definition excluded from the comedy of the world/stage. In John, this distinction between metaphoric stage and auditorium is taken extremely seriously. It explains how it is possible for there to be such an entity as a *valid* identity which virtually the entire human race has alienated by playing false parts. The valid identity is a role assigned by God. It comes, in other words, from the heavenly auditorium rather than from the stage. Virtue is its essence, and this 'has been given to all to enjoy as a kind of solar ray from the fountain of light' (p. 177). At any given period, however, only a handful of sages have realised its celestial effect within themselves, so allowing them to escape the *theatrum mundi* and adopt the position of the heavenly audience which watches the comedy of the earthly stage from its celestial auditorium. Standing apart from the human comedy, these sages – Stoics such as Scipio and Cato, or prophets such as Abraham and John the Baptist – are 'luminaries to dispel the darkness of its night and alleviate the affliction of its blindness' (p. 179). They are the only alternative.

This has a rather startling consequence. If we accept that *Totus Mundus Agit Histrionem* was indeed the motto of the Globe, and if we accept the *Policraticus* as the effective context of that motto, then only the *stage* of the Globe Theatre can be taken as representing the *mundus* (or 'world'). This would mean that the figure of the Globe itself – so clearly identified with the roundness of the auditorium – would strictly suggest the celestial spheres rather than the earthly globe. In fact, as we have seen in the jokes about the burning of the Globe, the metaphor is not quite so strictly applied by the Elizabethans. Jonson's joke about 'the world's ruins' is vague enough to admit ambiguity. Yet within the generally loose Elizabethan idea of the Globe, the economy of John's metaphor seems to remain *potentially* present. In a verse introduction to *An Apology for Actors* (1612), for example, Thomas Heywood manages to suggest John's more precise usage of the topos as well as the looser Elizabethan usage. Asserting that 'The world's a Theater, the earth's a Stage, / Which God, and nature doth with actors fill', Heywood suggests John's distinction between earthly stage and cosmic auditorium, but does not quite sustain it (though he comes very close):

> If then the world a Theater present,
> As by the roundnesse it appeares most fit,
> Built with starre-galleries of hye ascent,
> In which Iehove doth as spectator sit
> And chiefe determiner to applaud the best,
> And their indevours crowne with more then merit
> But by their evill actions doomes the rest,
> To end disgrac'd whilst others praise inherit
> He that denyes then Theaters should be,
> He may as well deny a world to me.[23]

Here, Jehovah occupies the 'starre-galleries' of John's celestial auditorium, judging the human comedy being played out on the stage of the world. But the logic of the metaphor has slackened. Like the stage, the theatre as a whole tends to be identified with the 'world'. Moreover, the metaphoric exchange between 'theater' and 'world' appears to have switched direction. Here, the 'world' is thought 'fit' to 'present' a 'theater' because of its theatrical 'roundness'. The roundness of the theatre, in other words, is remarked *before* that of the world, to yield an interesting conclusion: because the theatre is round, then the round world must also be a theatre.

A final example will serve to illustrate the structure of the analogy between *theatrum* and *mundus* in Shakespeare's (as distinct from John's) period. While almost entirely abstract, J. J. Boissard's *Theatrum Vitae Humanae* (Metz, 1596) contains an emblem (Plate 10) which might have been designed to illustrate Heywood's poetic version of the topos in *An Apology for Actors*.[24] Apart from a few Renaissance touches, the emblem (entitled *Theatrum omnium miseriarum*) might also have been designed to illustrate John's Christian understanding of the ancient topos. The *theatrum* in question here is clearly modelled on the classical amphitheatre or circus.[25] The foreground shows the arena in which chained and trussed figures are tormented by skeletons and a devil. The central figure of the composition is a woman who is chained to a man on one side and the devil on the other. She also appears chained to an angel who kneels at her feet within a sphere. Behind this group is a monumental complex which Frances Yates supposes to be an allusion to the ancient circus.[26] At the centre is an obelisk which, defining the vertical axis of the composition, appears to rise above the crowded galleries to the cloud-fringed heavens, where the divine audience watches from on high. Next to the obelisk stands Hercules with his club and a female figure who might, by allusion to the popular Renaissance scenario of 'The Choice of Hercules', represent Virtue. Significantly, the doomed figures in the foreground appear oblivious of Hercules who appears to point upwards, like his obelisk. Behind the monumental complex are two levels of audience: the earthly audience in the circensian galleries (including a royal box in the centre, directly behind the obelisk); and the heavenly audience, surrounding the ring of light inscribed with mystical Hebrew characters.

Boissard would appear to have solved the difficulty of whether to identify the theatrical auditorium with the celestial spheres or with the earthly globe, by keeping the auditorium within the earthly sphere. At the same time, however, the spherical (but earthly) auditorium is represented as a *type* of the celestial audience above, and hence a type of that celestial identity beyond the *theatrum mundi*. These celestial and earthly realms are linked by two mediating devices. One is the monumental Renaissance iconography of virtue in the centre of the arena. The other device is more directly reminiscent of John of Salisbury. Immediately to the left of the monument, sit two larger-than-life figures swathed in flowing, unclassical, robes. The fact that they are seated at the very end of the audience gallery would seem to align them with the earthly audience. But the fact that both are seated in the arena, and both are depicted roughly according to the scale of the foreground figures rather than that of the audience, would appear to align them with the spectacle of *omnium miseriarum*. Who are they and what are they doing there? The answer is that they represent John's virtuous 'sages', the 'luminaries' who are exempt from the *theatrum mundi* and consequently 'are themselves also spectators at these Circensian Games'.[27] Boissard's figures would appear to be biblical; prophets rather than philosophers or Stoics. This idea of the virtuous sage, who is simultaneously detached from the degrading comedy of life yet available as a counter-example for those with eyes to see and ears to hear, exercised a profound influence on the minds of playwrights like Greene, Jonson and Shakespeare, as well as on philosophers such as Montaigne.[28] For all its apparently purely abstract and moral significance, the *theatrum mundi* provides a conceptual mediation between the discourses of Theatre and Geography in Shakespeare's period.

3

This claim will seem more convincing when it is understood that the *theatrum mundi* also exercised a powerful influence on the geographic image of the globe in Shakespeare's period. Both Ortelius and Mercator, easily the most influential cartographers from the later sixteenth to the mid-seventeenth centuries, employ the figure of the *theatrum mundi* in the global maps of their respective atlases. The theatrical configuration of Ortelius's world map (the *Typus Orbis Terrarum*) is evidently dictated by the theatrical concept of the *Theatrum* itself. As we have seen, this map was the single most famous manifestation of the new geography in the sixteenth century.[29] From 1570 to 1630, it went through three variant states as the copper templates (from which it was printed for the forty-two folio editions of the *Theatrum*) wore out and were replaced. To the degree, then, that any world map could be taken as a *type* or *imago* of the new geographic globe, the *Typus* is that map.

The original *Typus* (Plate 2) figures the *theatrum mundi* both graphically and in terms of textual inscription. An ovoid globe is set laterally across a double page, within a border of dark rolling clouds (some versions of the map are vividly coloured). This suggests that the viewer is looking down on the earthly globe from a vantage point somewhere in the heavens.[30] In conceit, then, the reader who gazes at the map on the page has become like God, gazing down on his earthly creation. He is also in the privileged position of Ortelius himself who, as the *Frontispicii Explicatio* relates, has been translated to the heavens and seen 'the secrets of a distant world' (*mundi arcana remoti*). The impression of a god's-eye view is further underlined by an explicit citation from Cicero in a strap-work cartouche which frames the bottom of the oval:

Quid Ei Potest Videri Magnum In Rebus Humanis, Cui Aeternitas Omnis, Totiusque Mundi Nota Sit Magnitudo.
(For what can seem of moment in human occurrences to a man who keeps all eternity before his eyes and knows the vastness of the universe?)[31]

The force of this exclamation, as we may readily gather from its immediate context in Cicero's *Tusculan Disputations*, is precisely that the 'happy man' is he whose soul is free of earthly entanglement ('human occurrences'); he whose eye is fixed on 'eternity' and 'the vastness of the universe'. The ethic, then, is Stoic and implicitly related to the figure of the *theatrum mundi*. The situation of Cicero's philosopher is analogous to that of John of Salisbury's sage. Each is inspired by the prospect of his cosmic home and rejects the busy emptiness of earthly pursuits. The graphic context which Ortelius provides for this classical text, however, blurs rather than sharpens its meaning. The 'vastness of the universe' is obviously inconsistent with the graphic image of the earthly globe which is presented to the reader. Yet there can be little doubt that Ortelius wishes the reader to meditate on the visual image. Interestingly, Ortelius falls into the same kind of looseness in applying the ancient cosmic figure to his idea of the 'world' that we have already observed in Elizabethan references to the Globe Theatre.

That such is indeed Ortelius's intention is clear from the third and final state of the *Typus* (Plate 3) which was prepared in 1587 and appeared in all subsequent editions of the *Theatrum* from 1592 until 1612 (some fourteen editions).[32] What is interesting about this revision of a map which was already seventeen years old by 1587, is that the primary aim of the revision was *figurative* rather than scientific.[33] This emphasis on figure and ornament tells us something important about the cultural status of this image of the globe in 1587. The first *Typus* had aimed to be as authentic, as accurate and as *new* as possible. To that end, it had been based squarely on Mercator's celebrated wall-map of just a year earlier.[34] By the 1590s, however, when the final state of the *Typus* began to appear in print, it had attained the status of a classic. Accordingly, it ignores mere geographic accuracy and self-consciously asserts its own iconicity with a more monumentalised styling and extra classical citations. The viewer is immediately struck by the absence of the cloudy border of the original map. In its place is a pattern of strap-work and figurative motifs (fruit, birds, masks, heads, vines) such as were readily available in the Ornament Prints. The absence of the clouds, however, does not mean that the fiction of a heavenly viewpoint is abandoned in this state of the map. If anything, it is reinforced by four additional classical citations, each within a circular (but heavily ornamented) cartouche at each corner of the rectangular border. All of these citations (from Cicero and Seneca) powerfully suggest the god's-eye view of earth and the ancient reverence for the macrocosm which underwrites the topos of the *theatrum mundi*.

One citation in particular suggests the *theatrum mundi*. The cartouche at the top left-hand corner contains a citation from 'The Dream of Scipio':

Homines Hac Lege Sunt Generati, Qui Tuerentur Illum Globum, Quem In Hoc Templo Medium Vides Quae Terra Dicitur.
(For man was given life, that he might inhabit that sphere called Earth, which you see in the centre of this temple.)[35]

A key text of the *theatrum mundi*, 'The Dream of Scipio' is echoed by John of Salisbury in his own meditations on the theme. The passage cited by Ortelius epitomises the whole parable nicely. Its context is the very moment when the virtuous Scipio, who has been rapt to the heavens by his legendary ancestor Africanus, gazes back upon the earth from his heavenly vantage. Scipio has just been told of the vanity of life on earth and the bliss which awaits the virtuous man in the heavens, man's true home. To his question, 'why should I remain longer on earth?', Africanus responds as above, in Ortelius's citation.

Curiously (for a seminal work of the new geography), Ortelius's image of the globe is firmly inscribed within the moral space of the ancient cosmos. *Illum Globum . . . Quae Terra Dicitur*, or 'that globe/sphere called Earth', actually conceives of the earthly globe as a *sphere* in the first instance, and indeed, the lowest or least significant of all the cosmic spheres. *In Hoc Templo Medium*, the phrase used to describe the position of the 'sphere called Earth', is interestingly ambiguous. The Loeb editor renders it as 'in the centre of this temple' (p. 267), but *templum* also has the wider sense of 'an open space for observation (in the heavens or on the earth), marked off by the augur', or 'any open space ... quarter of the heavens', or 'a place set apart and consecrated by the augurs for public functions'.[36] Arguably, the reason that *templum* can mean both 'temple' and 'sky' is that ancient temples (like theatres) were understood to have been figured as types of the cosmos.[37] This in turn suggests just how and why the auditorium is privileged over the stage in the *theatrum mundi*. The ancient auditorium bears the same relationship to its stage as Cicero's celestial spheres do to 'that sphere called Earth'. Ortelius is fully alive to the figurative possibilities. His map of the globe (*Illum Globum*) thus corresponds exactly to the position of the stage within the figurative theatre (*theatrum/templum*) represented by the atlas as a whole.

Lest it be thought that Ortelius's penchant for such figurative play is somehow ungeographical or unrepresentative of his discipline, I should stress that geography was not yet a science in the post-Baconian sense of a discourse which rigorously attempts to exclude literary effects from its language.[38] It is significant that the *Somnium Scipionis* survived into the Middle Ages and the Renaissance in the physical form of Macrobius's Neoplatonising *Commentary*, itself a major influence on the geography and astronomy of the Middle Ages and Renaissance.[39] For Macrobius, the passage cited by Ortelius was the key to the whole *Somnium* because it encapsulated the key cosmographic issue of the relationship (physical and moral) between the celestial spheres and the earth (which Macrobius insists on referring to as the 'ninth sphere').[40] The aim of the *Commentary* was to reveal the supposedly hidden meaning of the *Somnium*, conceived as an ancient version of *The Hitchhiker's Guide to the Galaxy*. Macrobius glosses Cicero's elegant parable as an elementary manual of cosmographic (physical and metaphysical) mechanics. No less than John of Salisbury or Chaucer (whose own copy of Macrobius was 'totorn' with continual use), a Renaissance reader of Ortelius would understand his citation of the *Somnium* in its Macrobian context, and would not find it out of place in a work of geography.[41] Ortelius's citation of the *Somnium*, then, is not idiosyncratic or somehow foreign to the discourse of geography, and nor is the figure of the *theatrum mundi*. It is integral to the physical, metaphysical and ethical discourse of the macrocosm which Macrobius helped transmit to Shakespeare. The citation of Cicero/Macrobius in the *Typus* is perhaps another indication of the map's philosophical self-consciousness. This is the new geography's version of the monumental *mappaemundi* of previous centuries.

Ortelius's other classical citations are all in keeping with the celestial contempt for the earth which is so characteristic of both Cicero and Macrobius. The lower left-hand cartouche contains a citation from Seneca:

Hoc Est Punctum, Quod Inter Tot Gentes Ferro Et Igni Dividitur,
O Quam Ridiculi Sunt Mortalium Termini.
(Is this that pinpoint which is divided by sword and fire among so many nations?
O how ridiculous are the boundaries of mortals!)[42]

The 'ridiculous' image of the earth as a mere 'pinpoint' represents a late Stoic moralisation of Aristotle's discussion of the earth's sphericity. Aristotle's essentially geometrical argument had stressed both the smallness of the earthly globe in relation to the stars and the smallness of the *oikumene* in relation to the earthly globe (which he had thought to be as large as 400,000 stades in diameter).[43] Seneca's *Hoc Punctum* has the sense of the 'inhabited earth' rather than of the earthly globe as such, because *Mortalium Termini* has the sense of the geographic boundaries which divided the *orbis terrarum* from the regions beyond. Seneca offers a list of such *termini* immediately after the passage which Ortelius cites:

Let our empire confine the Dacians beyond the Ister; let it shut out the Thracians by means of the Haemus; let the Euphrates block out the Parthians; the Danube separate Sarmatian and Roman interests; the Rhine establish a limit for Germany; the Pyrenees lift their ridge between the Gallic and Spanish provinces; between Egypt and Ethiopia let an uncultivated wasteland of sand lie. (pp. 7–8)

The point is that while it makes practical sense for the Romans to parcel up the inhabited earth by means of such natural *termini*, they are meaninglessly petty in the cosmic scheme of things (the only valid perspective). Much the same thought is found in the *Somnium*, when Africanus warns Scipio against the vanity of world conquest: 'Do you suppose that your fame or that of any of us could ever go beyond those settled and explored regions by climbing the Caucasus, which you see there, or swimming the Ganges? What inhabitants of those distant lands of the rising or setting sun, or the extreme north and south, will ever hear your name?' (pp. 275–6). In each text the ethic is the same: earthly concerns are ultimately as insignificant as earthly *termini*. Cicero's emphasis departs, however, from Seneca's rather defensive imagery of the *termini*, in taking the form of an exorbitant, Alexander-like conquest or exploration beyond the limits of the *orbis terrarum*. The virtuous man's business on earth is not to aggrandise himself but to do his duty by the Republic.

In Chapter 5, I shall discuss what may already be apparent: that the physics, metaphysics and ethics of these ancient texts with their lofty disdain of the earth and specifically their contempt for the exorbitant business of exploration, discovery and conquest, are profoundly at odds with the very *idea* of a new geography priding itself on the discovery of 'distant lands of the rising or setting sun' unknown to the ancients. At this point, it is enough to note that all Ortelius's citations inscribe the new geography within the ancient cosmography, for which the earth was merely the last and least of all the spheres.[44] In view of the investment of Ortelian geography in the old cosmography, it also seems likely that the decline of '*Theatrum*' as a generic for the atlas is linked to the rapid disintegration of the Macrobian or 'Ptolemaic' universe in the early- to mid-seventeenth century. Unlike '*Theatrum*', the term '*Atlas*' makes few assumptions about the place of the earth within the cosmos at large. It would, therefore, have allowed more freedom for the new geography to develop independently of the old cosmography which, especially from 1613, began to disintegrate apace. In that year, the 'new philosophy' which Donne had lamented in his *Anniversaries* two years previously, arrived unmistakably in the form of Galileo's *Sidera Nuncia*, a pamphlet describing what the author had seen when looking at the moon through the new invention of the telescope. Instead of a perfectly spherical heavenly body, Galileo described a body which bore all the marks of corruption and mutability. No longer would it be possible to claim, as Macrobius had, that the sphere of the moon (the eighth sphere) marked the division between a corruptible sublunary nature and an incorruptible 'meta-physical' supernature. Without the macrocosm, the ancient contempt for the 'ninth sphere' and the ancient figure of the *theatrum mundi* would lose much of their 'cosmographic' point.[45]

4

Shakespeare's theatre of the world resonates with Mercator as well as Ortelius. While the cosmography of the *Atlas* is more original than that of the *Theatrum*, the ornamentation owes much to the earlier work. The monumental and quasi-'theatrical' frontispiece of the first edition in 1595 (Plate 11) registers the Ortelian influence, as does Mercator's scholarly edition of Ptolemy in 1578 (Plate 12). The influence of Ortelius's theatrical architecture is perhaps clearest in the latter work, which reproduces essentially the monumental stage of the *Theatrum*. Here, however, there are no personified continents. Instead, the cosmographers Ptolemy and Marinus stand on the railings which had supported Asia and Africa, looking down on a terrestrial globe which rests amid other cosmographic instruments (including books) on the centre of the stage (about where America had reclined in the *Theatrum*). The upper stage throne which had been occupied by Europe in the *Theatrum* is here occupied by a celestial globe. As in Ortelius, the economy of the *theatrum mundi* is plainly figured. The terrestrial globe occupies the stage. Ptolemy and Marinus occupy liminal positions in the wings of the stage (and slightly above it), thus corresponding to John's enlightened sages or Boissard's prophets, or perhaps to the figure of the metatheatrical commentator in a Jonsonian comedy of humours. The celestial globe occupies the upper stage, which may also be taken for a seat in the celestial auditorium.

A version of this architecture (without the figures) appears in the frontispiece of the 1595 edition of the *Atlas*. Here, however, the theatrical suggestion is less insistent. The upper stage has been reduced to a kind of recessed gallery, where an armillary sphere is upheld by two classically draped figures. The stage, as such, is entirely occupied (and hence obscured) by two large pediments upon the upper of which Atlas (in a reversal of the terms of the mythological image) is shown sitting on the earth (as distinct from upholding it) while considering terrestrial and celestial globes.[46] The new image effectively recapitulates the cosmographic theme of the edition of Ptolemy, while omitting its specifically theatrical suggestiveness. The theatrical theme, however, was not about to fade away. In volume two of the self-styled *Editio Ultima* of the *Atlas* edited by Henry Hondius in 1636 and translated into English by Henry Hexam, the 1595 frontispiece has been enlarged to accommodate the Ortelian iconography of the continents (Plate 13). Six continents are shown either standing within niches or seated upon architraves in and about the ornamental frame, the centre of which remains occupied by the figure of Atlas as before. Admittedly, the theatrical possibilities of this explosion of figurative life are poorly accommodated by the architecture of frontispiece, its extensions notwithstanding.

The theatrical theme returns, however, in the cosmographic symbolism of the famous world map which – a feature of all editions of the *Atlas* from 1595–1636 – rivalled and eventually usurped the currency of the Ortelian *Typus*. Versions of the map found in early editions are generally sparing of ornament, but later versions, such as those in editions produced by the Hondius family and their collaborators, abound in ornament and figurative life: mainly personified continents, elements and seasons. There are also famous cosmographers (Julius Caesar, Ptolemy and Mercator), among which company Hondius saw fit to depict himself with (in some versions) his personal emblem, a hound. Generally, it may be said that the figures of the four elements predominate over other figures, which (as we shall see) implicitly privileges cosmography over geography.[47] In the 1636 edition (Plate 15), for example, elaborate depictions of the elements occupy most of the rectangular border, along with Caesar, Mercator, Ptolemy and Hondius.[48] The seasons are absent and the four continents appear within a single cartouche, at the bottom of the vertical axis formed by the two joined hemispheres.

This vertical axis is interesting for the way that it figures the *theatrum mundi* within an expression of 'the great chain of being'. At the top is a celestial sphere, figuring the heavens. Between that and the junction of the two hemispheres is the sun. Both images are reinforced by the iconography of fire and air on either side. Below the junction of the hemispheres is the moon, below which is a pageant-like tableau of Europe – sheltered by an elaborate canopy and enthroned upon a pedestal – receiving offerings from Asia, America and Africa, who, along with various forms of vegetable life and inanimate matter, occupy the lowest place in the entire vertical sequence. The lower group is flanked by the elements of water and earth. Again, however, as with Ortelius and the Elizabethans, the figure of the *theatrum mundi* is scrupulously included only to be blurred. While 'earth' and 'stage' clearly figure the sublunary creation, as distinct from the untheatrical celestial globe which figures the heavens at the top of the axis, the earthly *theatrum* is not *farcical* in the sense of Cicero or John of Salisbury. It is, in fact, a form of sacred, even *cosmographic* theatre: a necessary expression of the great chain of being, in which lower forms of life (Asia, America and Africa) serve the needs of higher forms of life (Europe).

As this configuration, like most of the map's iconographic adornment, is the work of later engravers, it cannot be counted as directly integral to Mercator's own cosmographic imagination of the earthly globe. It is, however, indirectly integral to the discourse of the *Atlas* in the sense that this is how it was figured in the *readings* of later engravers. It has, then, as much right to our consideration as does the work of the great cartographer's own hand because our interest is as much in the *generic* idea, as in the original idea. In any case, it is clear that Mercator's own perspective was cosmographic, and that this as much as anything could have inspired the cosmographic symbolism of later editions. Mindful of Ptolemy, Mercator thought of geography as a part of the larger whole comprised by cosmography.[49] Accordingly, the *Atlas* is divided into two parts: cosmographic and geographic. The first part, entitled 'The Booke of the Creation and Fabrick of the World', is concerned with 'the scope of all Cosmographie'. This involves a Christian account (reminiscent of du Bartas) of the creation, and a highly sophisticated yet recognisably Macrobian account of the structure of matter and the universe. Surprisingly, it concludes with a section entitled 'Portraiture of the Universall

Earth', which is in fact a prologue to the map of the earthly globe. The surprise is that the map of the earth features in the cosmographic section and not in the geographic section, along with the maps of continents and countries. Mercator's 'earth', then, is a 'universall' as distinct from a 'geographicke' conception. The very idea of a 'Universall' earth suggests a gentler, less agonised, idea of the relationship between earth and the cosmos than is to be found in Ortelius.

The gentler tone, and to a significant extent, the phraseology of Mercator's description of this relationship are, I suggest, echoed in Shakespeare's *Hamlet*. Mercator begins by insisting on an idea of the world as a cosmic manifestation: 'This universall Globe, which is rather the object of the secret conceptions of humane understanding, than of the sharp-sightedness of our eyes ... is called by ... the Latines *Mundus*. Plinie ... saith, it is that, *in the compasse whereof all things are enfoulded*' (vol. 1, p. 39). To the authority of Pliny is added that of Apuleius and Aristotle, both of whom also imagine the 'world' as a 'compasse', but more specifically as a 'coniunction' or a 'congregation' of the earth (in the elemental rather than the geographic sense) with the heavens:

Apuleius describing this excellent frame, worthy of all admiration, saith, It is that, *which consisteth of the coniunction of heaven, and of earth, and of the nature of the one, & the other*. Aristotle, in his booke of the world, describeth it by the causes, to wit, *that it is in the order and disposition of things universall preserved by God*, and by its part, *a congregation of the Heaven and of the Earth, and of the natures of them*. (p. 39)

The architecture of 'this excellent frame' (Mercator's own phrase for the union described by his classical authorities) is further described in the words of Apuleius:

The world (saith hee) *is an ordinance well adorned by the gift of God, a proper guarde of the Gods. The supporter whereof, for so I call the Center, is the earth, strong and immovable, which is the Genetrix and Nurce of all living Creatures; all high things being environed and covered after the manner of a roofe, by the clearnesse of the aire. Moreover it is the house of the Gods, which wee call* Heaven, *which wee behold, laden with Celestiall bodies, with most beautifull & lucent torches of the Sunne, the Moone, and the rest of the Planets* ... (p. 39)

Mercator goes on to explain how the world is 'a perfect Globe', and why the figure of the globe is perfect, before explaining that: 'The parts of the world are two, the *Aethereall*, or *Celestiall*, & *Elementarie* or *Sublunarie*' (p. 39). The perfect figure of the sphere is then used to pose the relationship between these two 'parts of the world'; a relationship which is exemplified in the roundness of the ancient temple: '*Numa Pompilius* for the same consideratiò dedicated to the Goddesse *Vesta*, a Temple of a round forme' (p. 40). Mercator next touches on the topos of the smallness of the earth in relation to the heavens; and manages by a judicious quotation from Pliny to state what Ortelius's citation of Seneca's *Hoc Punctum* passage had only implied: the vanity of earthly conquest. This finally brings Mercator to the 'Earth' as such, which he discusses in the figure of a '*venerable mother*' who:

> ... is sweete, gentle, and indulgent, accommodating herselfe, as a handmayde, for the use of man. What is it she engendreth not? what is it she doth not produce of her owne accord? what sweet odours? what sap, and juice? what diversitie of colours? how faithfully doth she render the use of that, which is concredited to her? how many things doth she nourish for our sakes? (p. 40)

Such a passage strikingly exemplifies the tonal difference between Mercator's view of the earth and the Ortelian view, indebted as it is to the 'world'-contempt of Cicero and Seneca. While the elements of Mercator's cosmography are indistinguishable from that of Ortelius, their rhetorical formation is quite new. Where Ortelius sees hierarchy and disjunction (the earth as a kind of universal sink-hole), Mercator sees harmony and conjunction, with the earth imagined as a providential mother-figure.

Albeit that the English translation from which I have quoted did not appear until 1636, Mercator's tone, his cosmographic vision and his very words seem echoed in Hamlet's description of his melancholy to Rosencrantz and Guildenstern:

> ... I have of late – but
> wherefore I know not, lost all my mirth, forgone all
> custom of exercise; and indeed it goes so heavily with
> my disposition that this goodly frame, the earth, seems
> to me a sterile promontory. This most excellent canopy
> the air, look you, this brave o'erhanging, this majestical
> roof fretted with golden fire – why, it appears no other
> thing to me but a foul and pestilent congregation of
> vapours. What a piece of work is a man! How noble
> in reason, how infinite in faculty, in form and moving
> how express and admirable, in action how like an
> angel, in apprehension how like a god – the beauty of
> the world, the paragon of animals! And yet to me what
> is this quintessence of dust?
>
> (2.2.296–309)

Particular words, phrases and images strongly suggest the 'Englished' Mercator: 'this goodly frame' echoes 'this excellent frame'; 'congregation' echoes the Aristotelian word 'congregation' and the Apuleian image of 'coniunction'; the imagery of 'this most excellent canopy the air' and 'this majestical roof fretted with golden fire' echoes the Apuleian account of 'all high things being environed and covered after the manner of a roofe, by the clearnesse of the aire ... laden with Celestiall bodies, with most beautifull & lucent torches of the Sunne, the Moone, and the rest of the Planets'.[50]

To establish whether Mercator was actually the *source* of Hamlet's speech, one would have to establish direct verbal links with the Latin text of 1595. This I will not attempt to do because my aim is merely to demonstrate a general *intertextual* link, rather than to decide how that link arose. Shakespeare may have read Mercator in Latin or perhaps second-hand in a redaction. He may even have gone directly to the classical authors cited by Mercator. Alternatively, the words, phrases and images may have been so commonplace that a direct textual encounter need not be assumed. The point, however, is that not only particular words, but also Mercator's cosmographic vision and, even more important, its tone, are all assumed in Hamlet's speech. In this connection, it is instructive to ask ourselves what kind of speech Shakespeare might have written for Hamlet had his reading been limited to the more saturnine cosmography of Ortelius and Macrobius, neither of whom imagine the earth as a fertile and nourishing mother. Hamlet speaks of 'this goodly frame the earth' as 'a sterile promontory'. Not only does this invoke the warm optimism of Mercator's vision of the earth as a fertile mother, even in denying it, but the highly unusual conjunction of the earth image with the word 'promontory' also occurs in Mercator who abruptly breaks off his eulogy to the earth-mother to list various geographic features (such as the gulf, the isthmus, the island), the first of which is the promontory: 'But it will not be amisse to adde that which is called a *Promontorie*, an extent of earth which reacheth upward, and appeareth a farre off' (p. 40). Mercator's description of the earth-mother even suggests the deeper level of Hamlet's meaning. In order to do full justice to the fertility of his earth-mother, Mercator unconsciously slips into a demure eroticism. Thus, she is 'sweete, gentle, and indulgent, accommodating herselfe, as a handmayde, for the use of man'. The image of the mother is unobtrusively elided with that of the concubine. A similarly Freudian doubleness characterises Hamlet's image of the 'sterile promontory' encased by 'a foul and pestilent congregation of vapours'. The earth has lost its savour for Hamlet because it wears the face and sex of the over-accommodating mother whose fertility has gone sterile through very rankness. The incestuous and teeming energy of 'a foul and pestilent congregation of vapours' bespeaks the latent fertility denied by the image of the 'sterile promontory' and echoes the earlier image – also prompted by thoughts of 'sullied' quasi-maternal flesh – of that 'unweeded garden that grows to seed' possessed by 'things rank and gross in nature'. Hamlet detests his own flesh because it is ultimately the incestuous mother's. It follows that 'the beauty of the world, the paragon of animals' is likewise a 'quintessence' of earthly 'dust'.

If we accept Mercator as a discursive context, then Hamlet's speech becomes rather more interesting than a recent editor supposes. For Philip Edwards:

> What we should discount as an index of Hamlet's feelings is the famous speech 'What a piece of work is a man' ... So often pointed to as a brilliant perception of the anguish of Renaissance man in general and of Hamlet in particular, it is a glorious blind, a flight of rhetoric by which a divided and distressed soul conceals the true nature of his distress and substitutes a formal and conventional state of *Weltschmerz*. At the end of it he punctuates the rhetoric himself.[51]

Can we not, however, imagine the speech functioning *both* as an evasion of Rosencrantz and Guildenstern *and* as a pitiless mirror of Hamlet's private obsession with the soiled and earthy mother? Mercator takes us deeper into the text, not away from it. Nor does Shakespeare rely exclusively on Mercator as such. As Neville Coghill suggests, Hamlet's utterance actively gestures towards the cosmically figured architecture of the Globe Theatre itself.[52] Again, cosmographic imagery resonates deeply with dramatic and personal meanings. The 'theatre of the world' is simultaneously microcosmic and macrocosmic, subjective and objective, a measure of personal obsession and also of contagious *miasma*.

The three-way dialogue between Mercator's 'Portraiture of the Universall Earth', Hamlet's speech and the Globe Theatre forces us to confront the fact that all Elizabethan plays were 'uttered' within the physical context of what was effectively a world map in its own right.[53] No less than the monumental medieval *mappaemundi* which were characteristically displayed over altars or in other monumental settings, the purpose of Shakespeare's Globe Theatre must have been 'to exhibit in one synoptic image the firmly rooted and universally held idea that the events, features and phenomena of the created world are infinitely many and yet all one, for they are all emanations of one divine principle, links in one great chain of being'.[54] This quotation represents the second part of a modern definition of the semiotic function and character of *mappaemundi* as distinct from more functional types of medieval map such as the 'Portolan Chart' (or nautical map) or the Pilgrim's itinerary. In contrast to such maps, Juergen Schulz argues, the apparently impractical *mappaemundi* had the very real function of providing an 'ideal' image of the world:

> By far the greatest number of Medieval ideal maps ... are philosophical ... in meaning. This is the content of innumerable *mappaemundi*, world maps large and small, meant to illustrate the unity and diversity of creation, not the exact shapes

of, and relationships between, ground features. They show in greater or lesser detail depending on the availability of space, the continents, seas and rivers of the *oikumene*, the flora, fauna, and human races of its different regions, the events of biblical and ancient history that took place in them, the missionary travels and martyrdoms of saints, and still more. (p. 112)

I want to take the liberty of applying the concluding sentence of *this* definition to Shakespeare's Globe for the same reason that Schulz finds it appropriate to the *mappaemundi*. The semiotic character of both 'theatres of the world' is the same. Both represent an ideal image of the world in an idealised cartographic form. By this definition, then, the Globe Theatre was a three-dimensional *mappemonde*. But it was also a sixteenth-century *Typus Orbis* to the degree that the world maps of Ortelius and Mercator – though several *quanta* removed from the primitive geography of the *mappaemundi* – deliberately inscribe and figure themselves within a cosmography which predates even the *mappaemundi*.

Shakespeare's Globe Theatre also qualifies as a map in terms of Harley and Woodward's definition: 'Maps are graphic representations that facilitate a spatial understanding of things, concepts, conditions, processes or events in the human world'. More specifically, the Globe is a cartographic structure in the sense of those monumental and theatrical map-rooms which Ortelius so cleverly duplicated (and rendered obsolete) within the pages of his printed *Theatrum*. No less than the first Renaissance atlas, then, it represents a prototypically Renaissance idea of a 'theatre of the world'. This phrase, of course, echoes the book in which Frances Yates suggestively places the architecture of the Globe Theatre in the context of the ancient theatrical architecture of Vitruvius, whose *De Architectura* was translated early enough to have influenced the building of the 'Theater' – the prototypical building from which the Globe and its generic offspring descended.[55] For Yates:

The Globe Theatre was a magical theatre, a cosmic theatre, a religious theatre, an actors' theatre, designed to give fullest support to the voices and gestures of the players as they enacted the drama of the life of man within the Theatre of the World ... His theatre would have been for Shakespeare the pattern of the universe, the idea of the Macrocosm, the world stage on which the Microcosm acted his parts. All the world's a stage. The words are in a real sense the clue to the Globe Theatre. (p. 189)

I agree entirely. The allusion to Yates's title in this chapter is intended as a compliment. I differ only in suggesting that the idea of a cosmic theatre was available to Shakespeare (as to the men who built the original 'Theater' in 1576) in two contexts that were independent of Vitruvius and his Renaissance disciples.[56] It was present in the form of the ancient/

medieval discourse of the *theatrum mundi*, as well as in the form of a contemporary dialogue with the new geography which, like the Elizabethan theatre, was attempting to constitute itself as a 'theatre of the world' in the ancient cosmic sense. As with the Elizabethan theatre again, the failure of the attempted imitation produced something entirely new.

5

There is every suggestion that the Elizabethan theatre was a 'theatre of the world' in specifically geographic and ethnographic senses as well as in the cosmic sense. Plays such as *Tamburlaine* and *Henry V* powerfully suggest the exhilaration of dramatist and audience alike with the imagined conquest of geographic space. The same exhilaration is to be found in Cunningham's *Cosmographicall Glasse* (1559), when 'Spoudaeus', an apprentice cosmographer, draws his first map:

Nowe I perceive by the makinge and describying of this onely Mappe ... I may in like sorte at my pleasure, drawe a Carde for Spaine, Fraunce, Germany, Italye, Graece, or any perticuler regio: yea, in a warme & pleasant house, without any perill of the raging Seas: danger of enemies: losse of time: spending of substaunce: werines of body, or anguishe of minde. O how precious a Iewell is this, it may rightly be called a Cosmographicall Glasse, in which we may beholde the diversitie of countries: natures of people, & innumerable formes of Beastes, Foules, Fishes, Trees, Frutes, Stremes, & Meatalles. (fol. 120)

Like some armchair Tamburlaine, Spoudaeus reduces the world to a map in order to control it. Like Tamburlaine, too, he sees no end to map-making and the possession of geographical abundance. Here, as in all 'Cosmographicall' contexts, the glass metaphor is not to be confused with the common mirror. Its function is not so much to present a full-sized image of the original object but to shrink that object, to reduce it to manageable scale; in Macrobius's words, 'just as the image of a large object in a small mirror reproduces its exact features and lineaments on a reduced scale in their correct proportions' (p. 208). Spoudaeus's 'glass', therefore, is a curved mirror like a 'Claude Glass' (the later-seventeenth-century aid to landscape painting), presumably the oval, mirror-shaped object represented on Cunningham's ornamental title-page.

It seems likely (though beyond my present scope to establish) that the commonplace use of 'glass' metaphors in Elizabethan theatre has at least some 'cosmographical' significance in addition to the more obvious moral significance of (in Hamlet's words) holding 'as 'twere the mirror up to nature, to show virtue her own feature, scorn her own image, and the very age and body of the time his form and pressure' (3.2.12–24). When Marlowe's prologue asks the audience to 'hear the Scythian Tamburlaine

/ Threatening the world with high astounding terms, /And scourging kingdoms with his conquering sword', and then asks them to 'view but his picture in this tragic glass', the glass metaphor may be predicated on a curved mirror suggesting therefore a metaphorical instrument for reducing immensity in addition to the conventional moral suggestion predicated on a plane mirror. Whether this is so or not, Marlowe's prologue speaks the language of Cunningham's Spoudaeus: 'We'll lead you to the stately tent of war'. The images are all of vicarious movement, geographic energy. It is the same language spoken by the chorus in *Henry V*:

> The King is set from London, and the scene
> Is now transported, gentles, to Southampton.
> There is the playhouse now, there must you sit,
> And thence to France shall we convey you safe,
> And bring you back, charming the narrow seas
> To give you gentle pass – for if we may
> We'll not offend one stomach with our play.
>
> (2.34–40)

Just as the 'Cosmographicall Glasse' allows Spoudaeus to voyage 'without any perill of the raging Seas', the Elizabethan playwright guarantees his audience against sea-sickness. Theatre, and indeed the *theatrum mundi*, seem to have been thought of in specifically geographical terms as early as Richard Edwardes's *The Excellent Comedie of the two most faithfullest Freendes, Damon and Pithias* (1565):

> Pithagoras said, that this world was like a Stage
> Whereupon many play their partes: the lookers on the sage
> Phylosophers are saith he, whose parte is to learne
> The manners of all Nations, and the good from the bad to discerne.[57]

Here, the metatheatrical sages, whom John of Salisbury imagined gazing on the theatre of existence for moral purposes, use the theatre as a source of ethnographic information. The moral emblem is partly a metaphorical instrument, equivalent perhaps to a chorographical map or a common ethnographical handbook, such as Johannes Boemus's *The Fardle of Façions* (London, 1555). The idea of its instrumentality arises for the same reason as the 'glass' metaphor in works of geography. While geography may be the 'eye' of history, it is not (as Mercator reminds his readers) itself the object of human sight ('the sharp sightedness of our eyes'). Mere mortals can 'see' the geographic object only in their minds' eye, and then only with the aid of Spoudaeus's 'Glasse'.

How different this 'theatre of the world' is from the ancient theatre which Frances Yates sees as its inspiration. It is true (as Yates insists) that both are built around what the Renaissance architect, Leon Battista

Alberti, called 'the orb of the voice'. But voice in the Elizabethan theatres mediates a special quality of geographic vision – a fascination with imagined scenes and places for their own sakes – which has no real equivalent in the ancient drama. While it is true, therefore, that physical scenery is either rudimentary or non-existent in both Elizabethan and classical theatres, the *meaning* of this absence is very different in either case. According to Vitruvius, scenery on the Roman stage was represented by a pair of three-sided devices (*periaktoi*) placed on either side of the doorways in the rear stage wall. Each device was capable of representing any one of three types of scene – tragic, comic and satyric – on each of its three surfaces:

> Now the subjects of these differ severally one from another. The tragic are designed with columns, pediments and statues and other royal surroundings; the comic have the appearance of private buildings and balconies and projections with windows made to imitate reality, after the fashion of ordinary buildings; the satyric settings are painted with trees, caves, mountains and other country features, designed to imitate landscape.[58]

For all the realism of the three 'scenes', their function is less to do with geography than decorum. They exist in order to indicate the genre of the action played between them, rather than to create the illusion of geographic place or (crucially) of travel. Thus, in a play of any one given genre, the *periaktoi* would remain locked into the single appropriate setting. In the Greek theatre, whence *periaktoi* originated, the same logic applied, only more so. Vitruvius notes several key architectural differences from Roman theatre:

> the Greeks have a wider orchestra ... The scenery is more recessed. The stage is narrower: this they call *logeion* (speaking-place), for the reason that the tragic and comic actors deliver their speeches on the stage. The other artists carry on their action in the orchestra. Hence the Greek gives them separate names: stage players and chorus (*scaenici* et *thymelici*). (p. 291)

Bearing in mind that Vitruvius's word for 'scenery' (*scaenam*) primarily refers to the rear stage wall rather than to a 'scene' painted on or before it, the visual element seems even more rudimentary than in the Roman theatres. Here, indeed, the stage is actually a 'speaking place' as distinct from the orchestra which is a dancing and singing place. And the actors, or speakers, are designated by the Vitruvian term *scaenici*, sufficiently indicating the complete subservience of the visual to the vocal principle.

Lacking scenery of even these rudimentary kinds, the Elizabethan stage has been represented as even more visually impoverished than the ancient. This, however, is misleading. We have merely to look closely at the text which is most commonly cited as evidence of the totally unvisual nature of the Elizabethan stage, to realise the error. On the face of it, the opening speech of the chorus in *Henry V* is an apology for the visual inadequacy of the Elizabethan stage. But this actually assumes a potent expectation of presentness, of physical immediacy and visual pleasure: an expectation of 'seeing' the geographical sweep of an epic action in the mind's eye. Shakespeare's apology for the pathetic inadequacy of the Globe as a *theatron* (a place for *seeing*) is, of course, splendidly disingenuous:

> But pardon, gentles all,
> The flat unraisèd spirits that hath dared
> On this unworthy scaffold to bring forth
> So great an object. Can this cock-pit hold
> The vasty fields of France? Or may we cram
> Within this wooden O the very casques
> That did affright the air at Agincourt?
> O pardon
>
> (lines 8–15)

The rhetorical disclaimers bespeak, rather, Shakespeare's absolute confidence in the power of the spoken word to conjure the 'great object', the 'vasty fields' and the 'very casques' within the 'wooden O'. The difference between this use of the spoken word and that by the ancient nuntius-figure or the ancient chorus, is that Shakespeare's chorus harnesses speech to the geographical muse. This, as Ortelius understood, was a muse of the eye ('geography is the eye of history'), a commonplace observation more vibrantly expressed by Leonardo: 'The eye ... is the master of astronomy. It makes cosmography ... The eye carries men to different parts of the world. It has created architecture, and perspective and divine painting ... It has discovered navigation'.[59] The eye, as Mercator cautioned, was in the mind of course. And this is exactly Shakespeare's point in the prologue to *Henry V*. In the very act of apologising for the visual inadequacy of his theatre, Shakespeare appeals directly to the geographic muse, conjuring a kaleidoscopic sequence of imagined scenes beyond the capacity of any known scenographic illusion to represent. The scenes that the chorus invites the audience to 'piece out' with their 'thoughts' are on both the chorographic and geographic scales. The mind's eye is never still, but 'zooms' from one place and scale to another. Paradoxically, the audience's visual pleasure at a performance of *Henry V* would be no less than what Marlowe found in the maps of Ortelius. The theatrical means whereby so 'great an object' was crammed within the 'wooden O' were, in any case, similar to the techniques of cartographic epitomisation. Both kinds of 'theatre' used codes of contraction, varieties of Shakespeare's 'crookèd figure' which 'may / Attest in little place a million' (lines 15–16).

In one obvious way, Shakespeare's theatre was able to break free from the strait-jacket of the code, and to do so in a way that was actually beyond the ability of the Ortelian theatre to emulate. This was in the *living* representation of exotic peoples by actors 'properly habited' (to use a stage direction from *The Tempest*), made-up, and speaking in appropriately 'exotic' registers. Though it cannot be conclusively shown, it is probable that the costuming and make-up of exotics in Shakespeare and Marlowe were ethnographically inspired: based, that is to say, on the same ethnographic tradition from which the exotic inhabitants adorning the Renaissance *carte à figures* are taken.[60] A portrait of Edward Alleyn as Tamburlaine from the 1590 edition of *Tamburlaine I* is actually thought to have inspired a Turkish portrait in Richard Knolles's *The General Historie of the Turkes* (London, 1603).[61] Shakespeare's exotics must also have seemed authentic by the standards of the time. Like all Elizabethan moors, Shakespeare's come in two versions: 'black' (or Negroid) and 'tawny' (or Arabic). Each type has its own costuming and make-up. Morocco, a tawny moor, is dressed 'all in white' (2.1.) – suggesting a flowing Arabic garment – and carries a scimitar. Aaron and Othello are completely blacked-up and wear wigs of tightly curled hair. Shylock's 'Jewish gaberdine' (1.3.109) complements his impressively Rabbinical register (so unlike Marlowe's Barabas whose speech owes more to the tradition of the stage 'Machevil' than the Old Testament, and whose false nose owes more to *commedia dell'arte* and popular anti-semitism than the ethnographic tradition).[62] The word 'gaberdine' is interesting because, while indicating a domestic English garment, it is also used in relation to Caliban (2.2.37). While it is generally thought that this indicates a certain carelessness with ethnographic detail, it is more likely that the word 'gaberdine' is being used in the catch-all sense that characterises the language of Renaissance travel-writing generally. Faced with garments and phenomena for which there was no English equivalent, the travel-writer was forced to improvise with whatever English words were to hand. The way in which Caliban can strike one observer as 'a plain fish' (with 'fins like arms' or arms like fins, notwithstanding his 'long nails'), another as an 'islander', another as a 'mooncalf' or 'monster' suggests that Shakespeare was sufficiently aware of the problem to mock it. As we shall see in the next chapter, a more complex irony at the expense of ethnographic reportage informs *Antony and Cleopatra*, particularly in Antony's description of the crocodile. In view of the patent unreliability of such descriptions, it is perhaps impossible to be certain of the actual appearance and provenance of Caliban's 'gaberdine'. A hint, however, is supplied by the 'blanket' worn by Edgar as 'poor Tom' in *King Lear*. This, it seems clear from the language of Lear's meditation on Tom, is a stage code for nakedness.

Thou wert better in a grave than to answer with thy
uncovered body this extremity of the skies. Is man no
more than this? Consider him well. Thou owest the
worm no silk, the beast no hide, the sheep no wool, the
cat no perfume. Ha, here's three on 's are sophisticated;
thou art the thing itself. Unaccommodated man is no
more but such a poor, bare, forked animal as thou art.

(3.4.95–101)

There is no reason that a 'gaberdine' ('a cloak of coarse cloth') might not
perform the same theatrical function, particularly if – as seems certain in
Caliban's case – it is not worn with anything else, or is not a sleeved and
full-length garment (as Shylock's presumably was).[63] That Caliban's
garment is neither sleeved nor full-length is suggested by the visual
humour of Trinculo's encounter with Caliban. For the joke to work,
Caliban must appear plausibly shapeless, but with protruding arms and
legs. The 'gaberdine' must also be loose-fitting enough for Trinculo to be
able to 'creep under' it and present an even more shapeless spectacle to
Stephano. Without sleeves, there would be little to distinguish Caliban's
gaberdine from Edgar's blanket. And this would make perfect sense
because, as a savage, Caliban is also 'unaccommodated man'.

A good idea of the exotic image in the theatres of Ortelius and
Mercator is given by the frontispiece of the first volume of the 1636
edition of the *Atlas* (Plate 14). Intriguingly, the architecture is that of a
fully functional stage, which – aside from a curious semi-circular recess in
its centre for the purpose of accommodating the title description – is far
more reminiscent of the large, open stage of a public theatre than it is of
the smaller stage of a monumental pageant-device.[64] This is a stage
designed for acting, not just for posing. Accordingly, it is crowded with
naturalistic 'characters' who move about and interact; rather than simply
being occupied by static allegorical personifications. These 'characters',
moreover, fully realise the *chorographic* (as distinct from geographic)
emphasis of the original *Theatrum* of sixty-six years earlier.

The costumes of these figures are in fact derived from the Renaissance
ethnographic tradition (by then almost a century old).[65] To the left of the
stage is a group of some eight figures, all of whom are attired in recognisably European clothing. To the right is a group of some nine figures, all of
whom are attired in a variety of barbarous or savage garments. Some are
almost naked, and some seem distinctly Negroid. Three wear feather
head-dresses; two of whom are almost certainly American, while the other
is perhaps 'East Indian'. The turbaned figure is Turkish, while the goateed
spear-holder would appear to be Mongolian (or 'Scythian'). All are
distinctly reminiscent of the repertoire of exotics in the pages of

seventeenth-century voyage publications, such as the *Great Voyages*, effectively a serialised encyclopaedia of discovery published by the de Bry family between 1590 and 1634.[66] They are also distinctly reminiscent of the generally seventeenth-century genre of *cartes à figures*: maps which showed not just the geography of the relevant country or region, but also the inhabitants in their native garb.[67] These two probable contexts of Hondius's figures are in fact one, because the inhabitants of the *cartes à figures* are almost certainly based on the voyage illustrations. A single example must suffice. Though an allegorical abstraction rather than an 'inhabitant', Hondius's 'Magalanica' from the frontispiece to the second volume (Plate 13) is in fact based on a figure (by then generic on *cartes à figures*) representing the typical 'Fuegian'. This was a female figure holding a dead sea-bird by the neck. She is naked except for a primitive skin-cloak – counterpart perhaps of Edgar's 'blanket' and Caliban's 'gaberdine' – which, falling over her back, leaves her genitals exposed. Exactly this image (described as a 'Magellanican') can be found in John Speed's entirely derivative (and thus exemplary) world atlas of 1626, in which (along with other Indian types) she flanks a map of America.[68] But, though she is also found in numerous other maps of the period, she originates as an illustration to de Bry's edition of the voyage of Van der Noort in the *Great Voyages*.[69]

The frontispiece to the first volume of the 1636 *Atlas* is suggestive of the Elizabethan stage in one final respect. The figures are grouped in a way that suggests an *encounter* (perhaps a confrontation) between the 'civilised' Europeans on the left and the barbarians (Turkish and 'Scythian') and savages (African, 'East Indian' and American) on the right. The logic is just that of the ancient poetic geography, the geography of difference that distinguishes 'civilised' from 'barbarous' above all else. The scene might almost be emblematic of the drama of the exotic in Shakespeare.

Plates

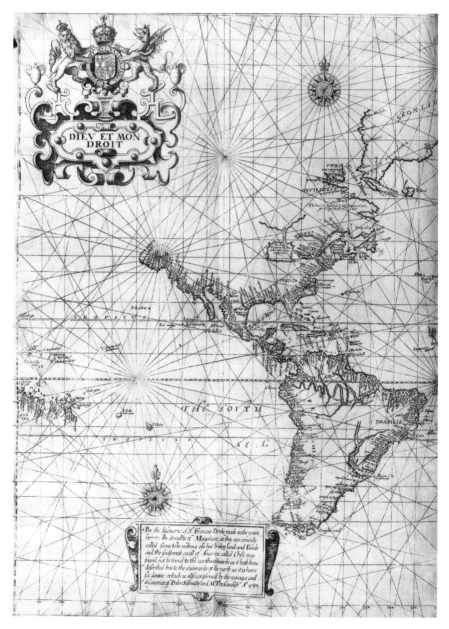

1. World map: Edward Wright's *Hydrographiae Descriptio*, London, 1599.

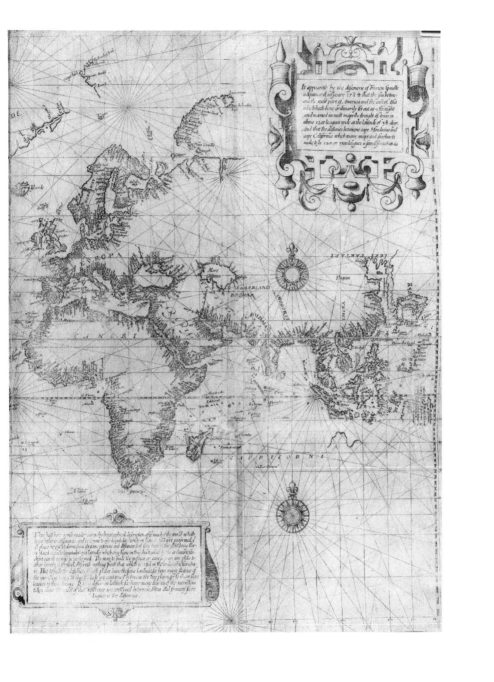

It appeareth by the discoverie of Francis Gualle
a Spaniard in ye yeare 1584 that the sea betweene the west part of America and the east of ʃa-
pan, which here ordinarily set out as a streight
and named in most maps the streight of Anian, is
above 1200 leagues wide at the latitude of 38 degr.
And that the distance between cape Mendocino and
cape California which many maps and ʃeacharts
make to be 1400 or 1500 leagues is ʃcant ʃomuch as the

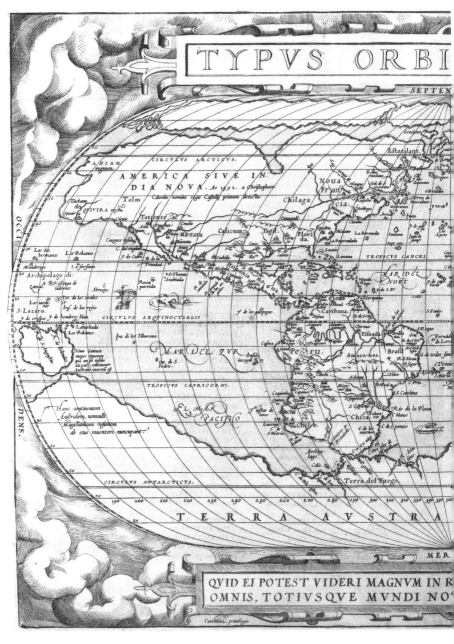

2. World map: Abraham Ortelius's *Typus Orbis Terrarum* (first state), from the *Theatrum Orbis Terrarum*, Antwerp, 1570.

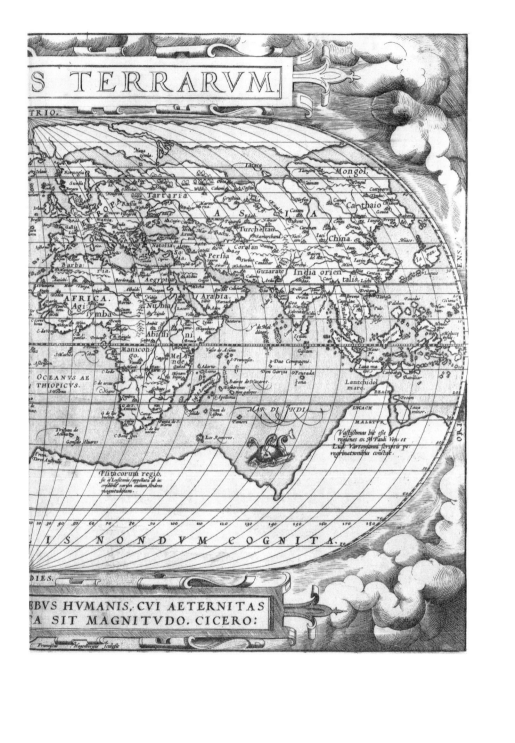

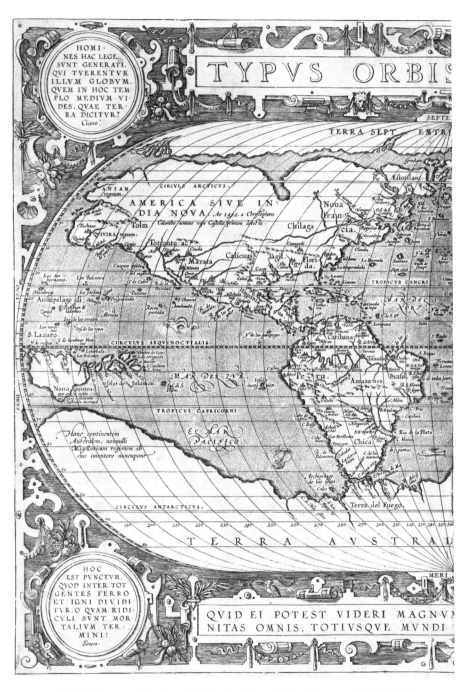

3. World map: Abraham Ortelius's *Typus Orbis Terrarum* (third state), from *The Theatre of the Whole World*, London, 1606.

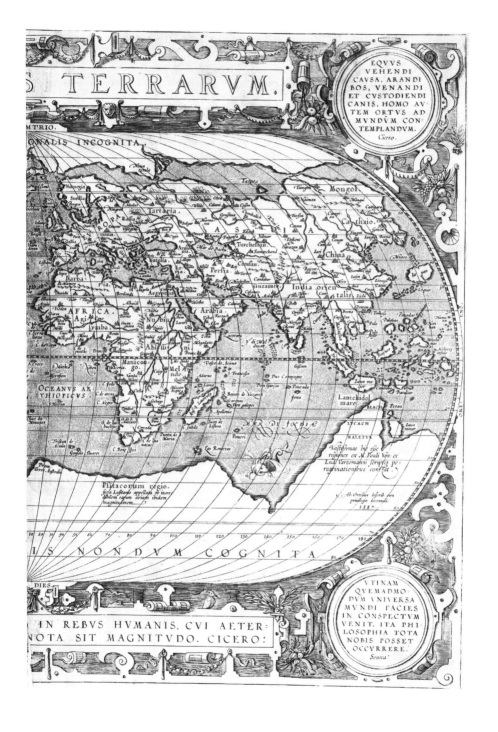

4. Christopher Saxton's map of Cornwall, from *An Atlas of the Counties of England and Wales*, London, 1576.

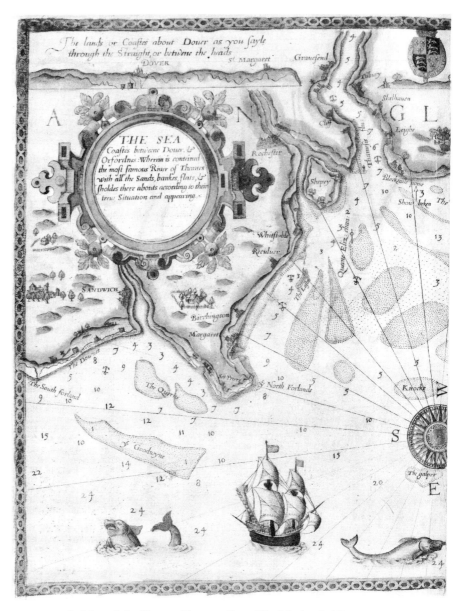

The lands or Coastes about Douer as you sayle through the Streight, or betwene the heads

DOVER   St Margaret   Grauesend

THE SEA
Coastes betweene Douer, &
Orfordnes Wherein is contained
the most famous Riuer of Thames
with all the Sands, bankes, flats, &
sholdes there abouts according to their
true Situation and appearing.

Rochester

Whitstable
Reculuer

Shepey

Cliff

Tilbury

Skelhauen

Leighe

Blacktaile Rome

Show broken

The

Queene Eliz. shai

The Lide

SANDWICH

Birchington

Margaret

The Downs

The Quernes

St North Forlands

The South forland

Y Goodwyne

Knocke

The galper

5. Map of the Thames Estuary, from *The Mariner's Mirrour*,
London, 1588.

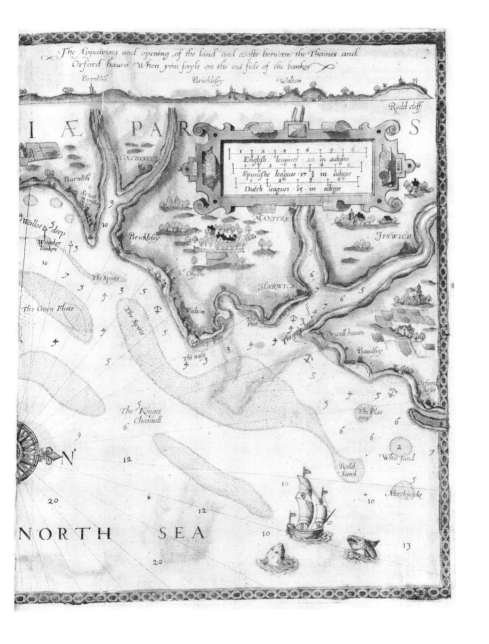

The Appearing and opening, of the land and coaste betwene the Thames and
Orford hauen When you sayle on the out side of the bankes

Burnffes   Brickelsey   Walton

Redd cliff

I Æ   P A R   S

COLCHESTER

| | | | | | |
English leagues · 20 · in adegre
| | | | | | |
Spanishe leagues 17½ in adegre
| | | | |
Dutch leagues · 15 · in adegre

Burnhill

South reason

9

Wallot   deep   5
10
Winker   5
beaken   5

Brickelsey

10

7

5

The Spits

4   5   5· Olythe

3

5

5   MANTRE   5

Walton   6

6

HARWICH   6

The Pret   6   5
The Corn Flete
The Spits   5   The wet
5
Orwell hauen
IPSWICH

The nate
4   3   5   4   Thegal

5   Baudsey

Orford nesse

The Kinges
Channell   5
6   5   5   5
The Plat   5
texte   6

6
9   6

12   5   6
2   7
Whit sand

Redd
Sand   5
10   10   Abertnocke

N   20   12   10   13

NORTH   SEA   20

6. 'The Psalter Map'.

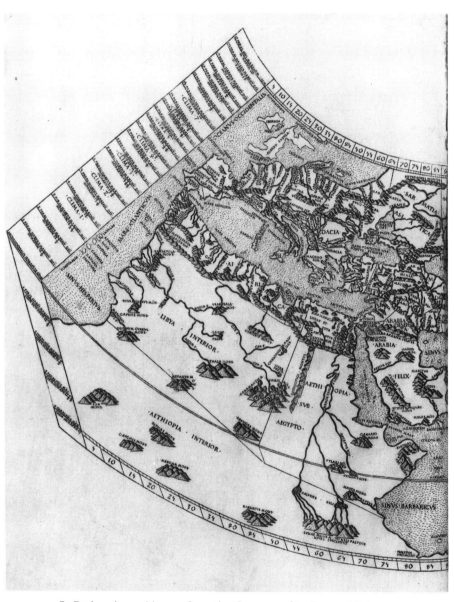

7. Ptolemaic world map, from the *Cosmographia*, Rome, 1478.

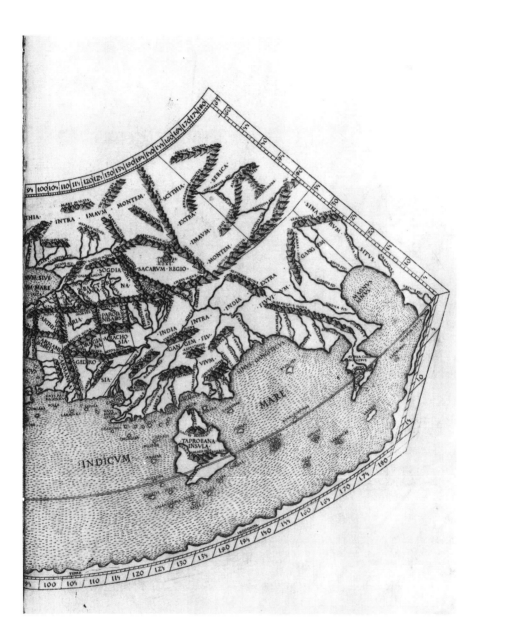

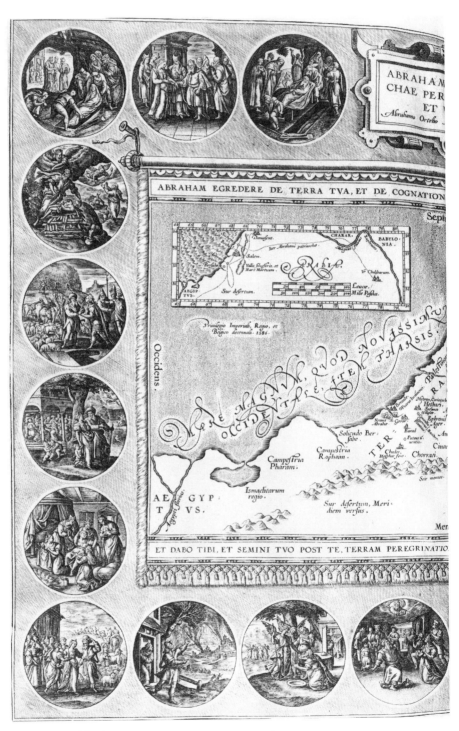

8. Abraham Ortelius's *Abrahami Patriarchae Peregrinatio Et Vita*, from *The Theatre of the Whole World*, London, 1610.

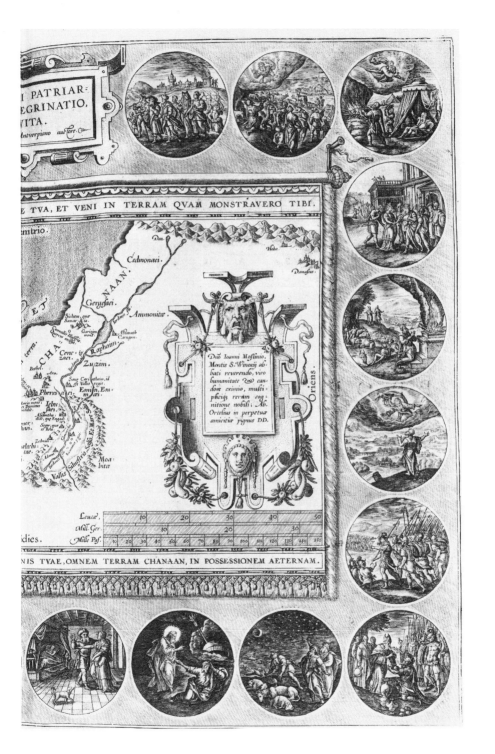

PATRIAR·
EGRINATIO,
VITA.

Antverpiano au
Fore Cu...

E TVA, ET VENI IN TERRAM QVAM MONSTRAVERO TIBI.

emtrio.

Dan.

Cedmonaei.

Hoba.

Gergesaei.

Damascus.

Ammonitæ.

Sichem, quæ
Samar. Aia.

Garizim
mons.

Silo enih
Carna...

Cene-
zaei.

Raphaim.

Zuzim.

Bethel.

Emim, Em-
mæi.

Pheres.

Iebus,
sei.

Zeboim.

Moa-
bitæ.

Vallis.

Dño Ioanni Moflinio,
Montis S. Winoci abbati reverendo, viro
humanitate & candore eximio, multiplici rerum cognitione nobili; Ab.
Ortelius in perpetuæ
amicitiæ pignus DD.

Oriens.

Leucæ.   10   20   30   40   50
Mill. Ger.   10   20   30
Mille Paf. 10 20 30 40 50 60 70 80 90 100 110 120 130 140 150

dies.

NIS TVAE, OMNEM TERRAM CHANAAN, IN POSSESSIONEM AETERNAM.

9. Frontispiece: Abraham Ortelius's *Theatrum Orbis Terrarum*, Antwerp, 1570.

THEATRVM VI-
TÆ HVMANÆ.

CAPVT I.

VITA HVMANA EST TANQVAM
Theatrum omnium miseriarum.

Vita hominis tanquam circus, vel grande theatrum est:
Quod tragici ostentat cuncta referta metus.
Hoc lasciva caro, peccatum, morsque, Satanque
Tristi hominem vexant, exagitantque modo.

A

10. Frontispiece: J. J. Boissard's *Theatrum Vitae Humanae*,
Metz, 1596.

11. Frontispiece: Gerard Mercator's *Atlas*, vol. 1, Düsseldorf, 1595.

12. Frontispiece: Gerard Mercator's *Tabulae Geographicae Cl: Ptolemei*, Cologne, 1578.

13. Frontispiece: Gerard Mercator's *Atlas*, vol. 2, Amsterdam, 1636.

GERARDI   I.HONDII.

MERCATORIS

ATLAS
OR
A Geographicke
description of the Regions,
Countries and Kingdomes of
the world, through EUROPE,
ASIA, AFRICA, and
AMERICA, represen-
ted by new & ex-
act Maps.

Translated by HENRY HEXHAM,
Quarter-maister to the Regiment of
Colonell GORING.

Printed at
AMSTERDAM,
By HENRY HONDIUS,
And
IOHN IOHNSON,
Anno 1636.

14. Frontispiece: Gerard Mercator's *Atlas*, vol. 1, Amsterdam, 1636.

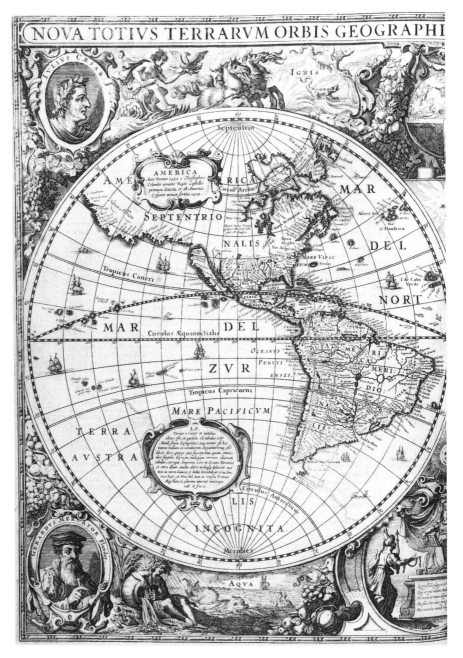

15. World map: Gerard Mercator's *Atlas*, vol. 1, Amsterdam, 1636.

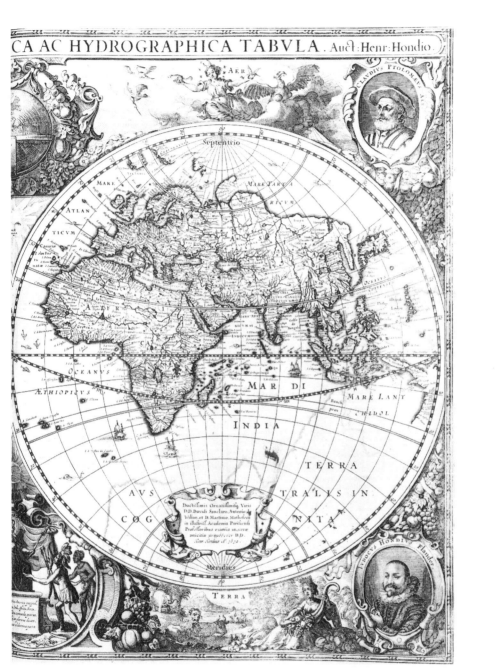

CA AC HYDROGRAPHICA TABVLA . Auct : Henr : Hondio .

CLAVDIVS PTOLOMEVS Alex.

Septentrio

AER

MARE   MARE TARTA

ATLAN   RICVM

TICVM

Canaria

OCEANVS
ORIENTALIS

A   F   E   R

CICVM

INDICVS

MAR DI

OCEANVS   MARE LANT

ÆTHIOPIVS   CHIDOL

INDIA

TERRA

AVS   TRALIS IN

COG   NITA

Ductissimis Ornatissimiq, Viris
D.D.Davidi Sanclaro, Antonio de
Willim, et D.Martino Mathelou
in illustriss. Academia Parisiensi
Professoribus examiis in, veræ
amicitiæ argumentum D.D.
Henr Hondius Aº 1632.

Meridies

TERRA   HENRICVS HONDIVS Flander

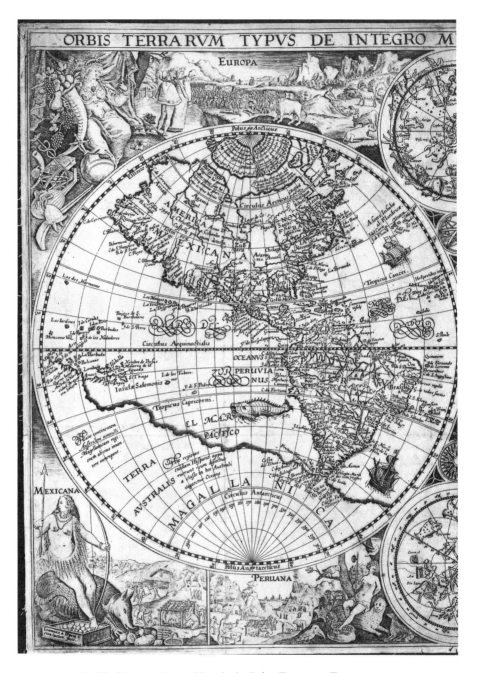

16. World map: Petrus Plancius's *Orbis Terrarum Typus*,
Amsterdam, 1594.

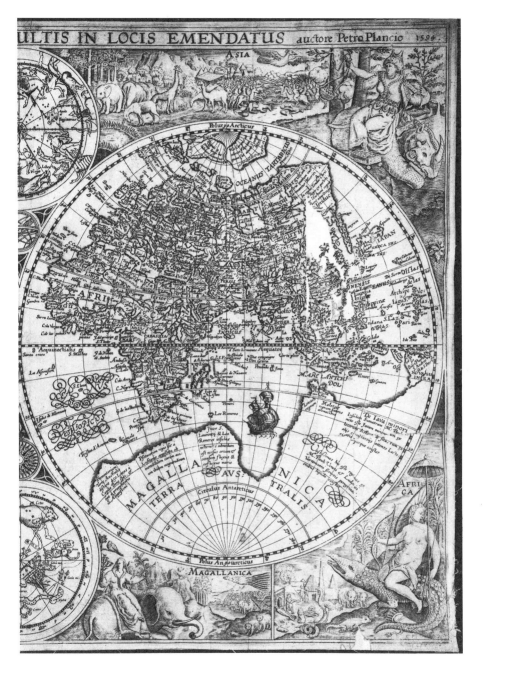

17. World map by Claes Janszoon Visscher, Amsterdam, *c.* 1617.

18. World map: Sebastian Münster's *Typus Cosmographicus Universalis*, from the *Novus Orbis Regionum*, Basle, 1532, by Johann Huttich and Simon Grynaeus.

CVS VNIVERSALIS

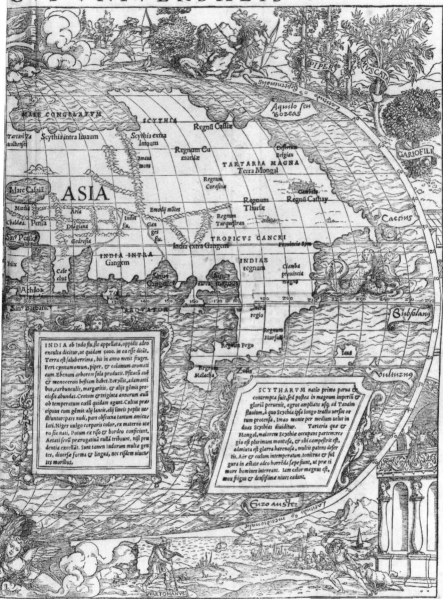

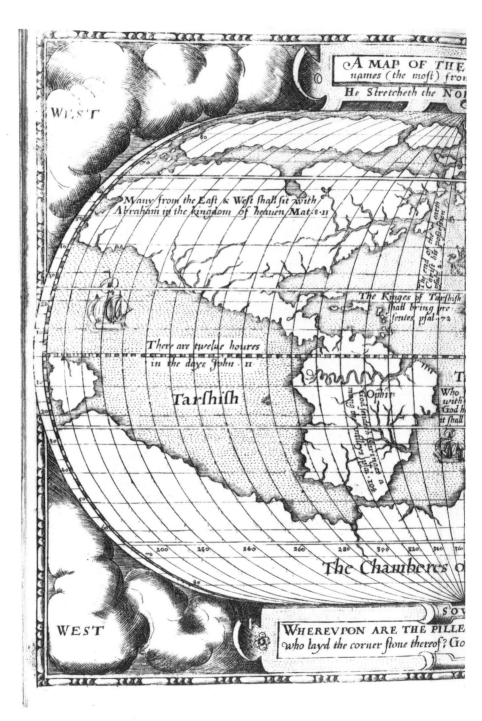

WEST

A MAP OF THE
names (the most) fro[m]
He Stretcheth the NO[R]

Many from the East & West shall sit with
Abraham in the kingdom of heauen Mat. 8.11

The Kinges of Tarshish
shall bring pre-
sentes psal. 72

There are twelue houres
in the daye John. 11

Tarshish

Ophir

The end of the N. earth
Chrift: of the possession
shall a

Who
with
God h[e]
it shall

The Chamberes o[f]

SO[V]

WEST

WHEREVPON ARE THE PILLE[RS]
who layd the corner stone thereof? Go[d]

19. World map: Hugh Broughton's *Map of the Earth with names (the most) from Scriptures*, from the *Concent of Scripture*, London, *c.* 1590.

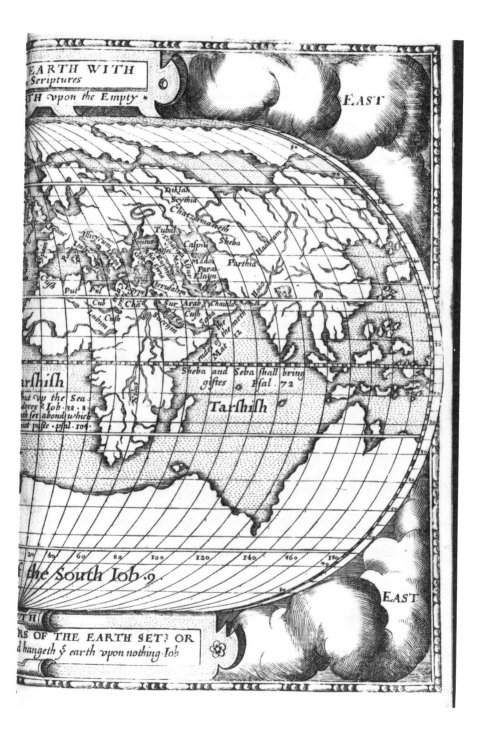

EARTH WITH
Scriptures
TH vpon the Empty *

EAST

Diklah
Scythia
Chatzarmaueth
Tubal
Ponus
Caspii
Sheba
Illyrium
Hadslau
Caspii Sea
Madai
Para
Parthia
Pul
Klaiŋ
Jerusalem
Houd
Cub
Chā
Sur Arab
Chauila
Cuſh
Cuth
Soerim
Cush
Seba
Lubim
[ende] of the earth
Mai 12

Sheba and Seba shall bring
giftes Psal 72

arshish
Tarſhiſh
hut up the Sea
dores Iob 38.8
th set abond which
not paſſe psal 104

20   40   60   80   100   120   140   160   180
                                              70

of the South Iob 9.

EAST

TH
RS OF THE EARTH SET? OR
d hangeth y earth vpon nothing Iob

20. World map: *The Christian Knight Map of the World*, Amsterdam, *c.* 1597, by Jodocus Hondius.

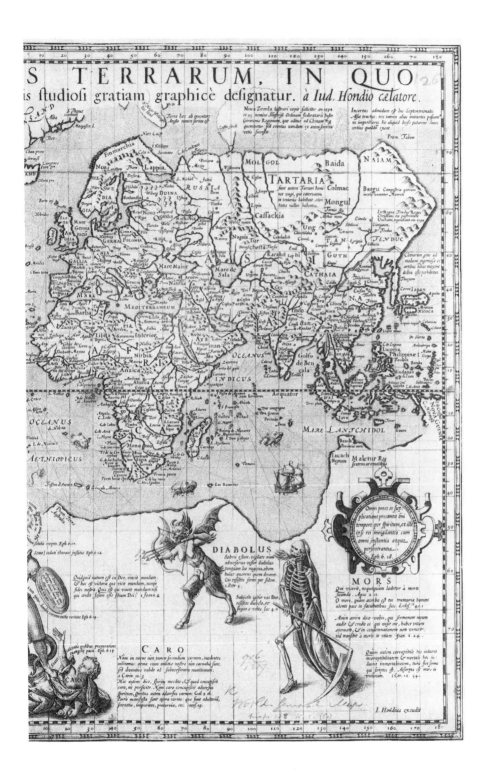

4 'The open worlde': the exotic in Shakespeare

The Cytes frame new walles them selves to keepe,
The open worlde lettes nought rest where it laye.
(Medea, 2nd Chorus, *The Tenne Tragedies of Seneca*
Translated into English, London, 1581)

Having suggested the need for a poetics of Renaissance geography, and having (in the previous chapter) outlined one direction along which such a poetics might proceed, I now propose to return to the question with which we began: how to define Shakespeare's idea of the 'exotic'? An obvious procedure is simply to catalogue and analyse whatever seems to correspond to the Elizabethan usage. Thus, the exotic in Shakespeare would include all phenomena – persons, imagery, settings, objects, props, costumes, speaking-registers – suggesting the 'barbarous', 'outlandish' or 'strange'. In practice, such a discussion would inevitably focus on Shakespeare's ethnic others: figures in whom (as I have suggested in the introductory discussion of *Othello*) the exotic is personified, both directly (through make-up, costume, props, vocal-register) and indirectly (in imagery suggestive of the 'outlandish' and 'strange'). Focusing on such figures should not be reductive because (again as we have partly seen in Shakespeare's Elizabethan tendency to telescope different exotic types) there is a compelling sense in which 'exoticism' in general controls 'ethnicity' in particular. Thus, the etymology of Othello's name suggests the 'Ottomans' rather than the moors. Thus, too, Shylock is at one point compared to 'stubborn Turks and Tartars never trained / To offices of tender courtesy' (4.1.31–2). And Cleopatra – who in Plutarch is represented as ethnically Greek – is represented with the 'tawny front' of a moor consistent with Egypt's proximity to Libya, and consistent perhaps also with her sultry temperament.

Ultimately, however, Shakespeare's idea of the exotic amounts to more than the sum of exotic phenomena or exotic characters in the plays; it is an action rather than a phenomenon, a kind of relation rather than a kind of character. Like the 'barbarians' of Athenian tragedy, Shakespeare's exotics are innately transgressive. And, like the sexually intrusive moors of the Elizabethan stage, their transgressiveness is less a matter of individual immorality than of dramatic structure. Regardless of how they may differ in character, Shakespeare's exotics all resemble Ovid's Tereus in a tendency to 'confuse all natural relations'. This is because they are never isonomic. Exclusion, liminality, and a fatal attraction towards some version of the excluding Aristotelian 'commonwealth', is their essence. This is true even of Cleopatra and Caliban, the only Shakespearean exotics who are located in 'native' settings, beyond the geographic pale of a generic 'commonwealth'. Each seeks to prey sexually upon a 'European', with potentially disastrous consequences, whether to Rome or to Prospero's 'brave new world'. Shakespeare's other 'strangers' are potentially even more threatening for being geographically displaced. Not only do they seek some form of pollutive 'incorporation' with a host-city, but their very existence in the city (on any terms) is dangerous. Shakespeare's cities have nowhere to 'put' their aliens, no institution capable of containing or articulating their liminality. Far from suggesting an embryonic cosmopolitanism, however, the lack of such an institution (effectively a ghetto-mechanism of the Renaissance Venetian type) means that Shakespeare's aliens are perpetually dangerous and in danger. The city's toleration of the alien is less a sign of nascent broadmindedness than of a shameful compromise of political integrity; a compromise which must be expiated by the end of the play. Thus all Shakespeare's aliens end by losing their tenuous place within the commonwealth. Death, slavery, conversion, confiscation or some equivalent annulment of difference is their generic fate. Only one intermarriage remains intact: that between Jessica and Lorenzo in *The Merchant of Venice*.[1] But this, while notionally acceptable within the contexts of conversion and confiscation, remains hubristic, divisive, morally ambiguous and decidedly ill-omened.

When the transgressiveness of the exotic is seen in the light of an action rather than as a character-attribute, its wider social dimension emerges. For exotics to pose a danger to the commonwealth, they must first be tolerated. This itself is transgressive. In the context of Shakespeare's commonwealths, toleration appears less a proto-democratic virtue than a weak-minded inability to draw the line, to exclude or place or contain. Interestingly, the *OED* identifies two Elizabethan senses of the word 'toleration'. It seems to have suggested either 'the action of allowing; permission granted by authority, licence' (1517–18), or 'the action or practice of . . . allowing what is not actually approved' (1582). The second of these two meanings is the more suggestive of Shakespeare's commonwealths. In these cities, 'toleration' (in deed rather than in word) is precisely a tolerance of the ambiguous or liminal. It may be expressed as an occasional error of policy or diplomacy. Thus, in *Titus Andronicus*, the new emperor adopts a family of barbarians, whose proper place is that of 'base bondmen to the yoke of Rome' (4.1.108). And, in *Othello*, the defence of Venice is entrusted to a moor whose name punningly invokes that of Venice's arch-enemies:

> Valiant Othello, we must straight employ you
> Against the general enemy Ottoman
>
> (1.3.48–9)

'Toleration' may also express itself in a deeper institutional malaise. In *The Merchant of Venice*, Antonio sees his plight as due in part to a shameful failure to distinguish between the judicial privileges of Venetian and 'stranger', Christian and 'Infidel':

> The Duke cannot deny the course of law,
> For the commodity that strangers have
> With us in Venice, if it be denied,
> Will much impeach the justice of the state,
> Since that the trade and profit of the city
> Consisteth of all nations.
>
> (3.3.26–31)

Even though Portia eventually discovers a provision 'in the laws of Venice' (4.1.345) that protects the citizen from the utmost malice of the 'stranger', the dominant impression is of an impotent duke and a fatal flaw in 'the justice of the state'. The generic link between this type of toleration and that in *Othello* is suggested by an echo of the expression 'the justice of the state' in the later play (1.1.141). Again this occurs in the context of a 'mangled matter' (1.3.172) between a citizen and an alien, and again it leads to a trial scene presided over by a compromised duke. 'Toleration', then, may take a number of forms: the compromise of a city's judicial institutions, the 'dotage' of a particular ruler, or a military/political compromise. Whatever form it takes, it opens the door to the more intimate 'confusion' of miscegenation. The other presents a danger only when the gate of the city is left ajar.

It is for this reason that, in addition to exploring the exotic both as phenomenon and action, I shall also discuss it in relation to the voyager. Like the rulers by whose 'dotage' the exotic enters the city, Shakespeare's voyagers are dangerous representatives of the commonwealth. Unlike the ruler, who characteristically controls the centre, the voyager controls the boundaries. It is the voyager's function to manage the exotic: which may mean either bringing it safely within the pale or excluding it entirely. In practice, again as I have suggested earlier, Shakespeare's voyagers tend to form deeply compromising relationships with the exotic, to the point where the two types sometimes merge in the same character. This, I want to suggest, is partly due to the way in which Shakespeare's voyagers tend to combine Renaissance heroism with classical hubris. Explorers like Columbus, Shakespeare's voyagers are also like Lucan's Caesar or Seneca's Tiphys: boundary-violators by whose means the outside chaotically intrudes. If the voyager approaches the exotic via a paradoxical liminality, the exotic approaches the voyager via another kind of paradox. From the very first, Shakespeare's interest in exotic characters far outweighs their notional ideological justification. Shakespeare either goes out of his way to include exotics in plots which don't strictly require them, or he elaborates exotic roles well beyond what they are in the sources. The roles of 'Aaron the moor' and Othello are elaborated far beyond those of their nameless moorish prototypes in, respectively, the prose *History of Titus Andronicus* and Cinthio's *Heccatomithi*.[2] Nor is there much precedent for the roles of Shylock and Morocco in the sources of *The Merchant of Venice*.[3] The intensity of Shakespeare's interest in the exotic, however, emerges less in the numbers of exotics he invents or in the size of their parts, than in their ability to monopolise attention. Characteristically, the exotic character courts our sympathy even as the voyager forfeits it. The separate ambiguity of each figure, then, leads to a blurring of the lines between them.

In what follows, I intend to test these interlinked theses on the constitution of the exotic, by examining all five plays in turn. In the case of the two classical plays (*Titus Andronicus* and *Antony and Cleopatra*), I intend to focus on the complementary aim of illuminating the ancient roots of Shakespeare's idea of the exotic. In the case of the two 'Venetian' plays (*The Merchant of Venice* and *Othello*) and the one 'island' play (*The Tempest*), the focus will be more on how the ancient construction reacts to Renaissance pressures.

1

If it is true that Shakespeare's 'plots, themes, and scenes are almost exclusively European', then it is odd that the idea of the exotic should emerge as early as his first tragedy. The exotic presence in *Titus Andronicus* is systemic rather than casual. Behind it, I will suggest, lies the ancient tragic drama of the 'barbarian'. Not only are Shakespeare's barbarians constructed along ancient lines, but the action of the play articulates the ancient tragic myth of barbarian intrusion in which an exemplary city is entered, polluted and violated at the level of an exemplary family. Shakespeare is not, however, content merely to imitate. He improvises on his ancient models, departing only so far as to disturb them with the hint of a more ambivalent idea of the exotic.

The clearest gauge of Shakespeare's debt to the ancient *mythos* of barbarism is his imitation of the Tereus legend. Far from concealing his debt to Ovid's grisly tale, Shakespeare advertises it right where it would most be noticed: at the rape of Lavinia and the cannibal banquet. Thus, when Lavinia enters with 'her hands cut off and her tongue cut out, and ravished' (2.4), we hear how:

> Fair Philomel, why she but lost her tongue
> . . .
> A craftier Tereus, cousin, hast thou met,
> And he hath cut those pretty fingers off
> That could have better sewed than Philomel.
>
> (2.4.38–43)

Every allusion to Ovid becomes a competition. It is not enough for Lavinia to lose her tongue, but also her hands. Deprived of Philomel's remedy of weaving her fate in tapestry, Lavinia opens a copy of the *Metamorphoses* with her stumps (or mouth), earmarking 'the tragic tale of Philomel' (4.1.47) in her own blood. Nor is Ovid forgotten at the moment of revenge. As good as his boast ('worse than Philomel you used my daughter, / And worse than Progne will I be revenged', 5.2.193–4), Titus serves up two sons to Progne's one. But the important debt to Ovid has little to do with *grand-guignole* and name-dropping. Shakespeare meticulously preserves and intensifies the deep structural logic which makes the Tereus myth so compelling an instance of the ancient narrative of barbaric intrusion.

As we have already seen, Ovid's narrative unfolds in three basic movements: the anomalous or contradictory incorporation of the barbarian, the 'confusion of all natural relations', and the death of the family. In the first movement, the barbarian is accepted into the Athenian royal family as a direct result of a military-political contradiction (Athens relies on barbarians to repel a barbarian attack). In the second movement, the family is annulled by the crime of incestuous rape. In the third movement, the family literally devours itself as the Athenian mother brutally murders her son and tricks her husband into eating him. Particularly in view of his complete departure from Ovid's setting and personnel, Shakespeare's preservation of the deep structural logic of Ovid's narrative is remarkable.

Ovid's first movement is recapitulated in the first act of *Titus Andronicus*, wherein we see a family of barbarians incorporated into Rome as a direct result of contradiction or anomaly. Interestingly, Shakespeare multiplies Ovid's single contradiction by four. To begin with, Rome's relationship with the barbarians is uncompromised and uncompromising: the Goths enter the city in the course of a triumph, the ritual purpose of which is to assert the state's power over its others. Almost immediately, however, the clear superiority of Roman over barbarian is compromised.

By sacrificing a son over the protests of his mother, Titus shows a gross disregard of 'natural' piety, that explicitly recalls one of the most infamous 'barbarisms' of ancient tragic legend: the murder of Hecuba's infant son by the 'Thracian tyrant' (1.1.138), Polymestor.[4] So polluted, Titus commits several more impieties. He chooses the vicious Saturnine over the virtuous Bassianus as emperor of Rome. He promiscuously insists on Saturnine's right to marry Lavinia, when he has already betrothed her to Bassianus. And he kills his own son, Mutius, when attempting to reclaim Lavinia for Saturnine. The common denominator of all four acts is a 'confusion of natural relations', at the levels of family and state. Accordingly, Titus's killing of Mutius is accompanied by the exit of Saturnine and the barbarians, and their almost immediate re-entry 'aloft' from which position Saturnine declares his contempt for the Andronici and his intention to wed the queen of the Goths. The inversion of hierarchy is expressed as a vertical movement of barbarians from a position of inferiority in the triumph to a superior position 'aloft' (1.1.294ff.). By compounding the element of contradiction and stressing its linkage with the theme of barbarous infiltration, Shakespeare emphasises deep structures in Ovid's tale which are easily overlooked in a casual reading. As an 'imitation' of Ovid, then, *Titus Andronicus* is somewhat paradoxical. Shakespeare actually uses his radical departures from Ovid's setting and personnel to achieve a more archetypal (possibly Sophoclean) statement of the Tereus legend than is found in Ovid.

Shakespeare's second act corresponds to the second movement of the Tereus legend. Here, however, the 'imitation' of Ovidian themes is deeper and more powerfully inventive. The rape and mutilation of Lavinia, of course, begs comparison with the rape and mutilation of Philomel, but the deeper interest lies in what Shakespeare does with the Ovidian theme of 'confusion'. At least three layers of symbolic meaning are added. In the first place, Shakespeare invests the rape and mutilation with a directly political symbolism which is only implicit in Ovid.[5] The name 'Lavinia' deliberately recalls the Italian princess in the *Aeneid*, who, by marrying Aeneas, becomes the mother of the Roman people. The spectacle of a raped and dismembered Lavinia, then, deliberately inverts the symbolism of the founding marriage in Virgil. In place of Virgil's foundation myth, we are presented with a 'con-founding' myth: an emblem of the pollution and dismemberment of the Roman body-politic. Significantly, the last words that Lavinia utters are: 'Confusion fall' (2.3.184).

The second layer of meaning with which Shakespeare invests his rape comes from the symbolism of the forest setting. Physically, the forest amounts to a property tree beside an open trap, which (fringed by property nettles) represents a 'pit'.[6] Symbolically, it is rather more complex. Echoes of at least three classical forests are present. In the first place, Shakespeare echoes the *silvis vetustis* ('ancient wood') of Ovid's Thrace. Thus Titus imagines Lavinia being raped 'as Philomela was ... in the ruthless, vast, and gloomy woods' (4.1.52–3), and by extension imagines Rome as 'a wilderness of tigers' (3.1.53).[7] To the Ovidian suggestions of his forest, Shakespeare adds echoes of Virgil and Seneca. At the beginning of the rape scene, Tamora's amorous inclinations, her hunting dress, and her very words remind the audience of the lyrical hunting scene which is the prelude to the love-making of Dido and Aeneas in their 'counsel-keeping cave' (2.3.24).[8] Shortly after, when confronted by Lavinia and Bassianus, Tamora sees the forest as a very different kind of place:

> A barren detested vale you see it is;
> The trees, though summer, yet forlorn and lean,
> Overcome with moss and baleful mistletoe.
> Here never shines the sun, here nothing breeds
> Unless the nightly owl or fatal raven,
> And when they showed me this abhorrèd pit
> They told me here at dead time of the night
> A thousand fiends, a thousand hissing snakes,
> Ten thousand swelling toads, as many urchins
> Would make such fearful and confusèd cries
> As any mortal body hearing it
> Should straight fall mad or else die suddenly.

> (2.3.93–104)

The *locus classicus* here is the haunted grove from Seneca's *Thyestes*:[9]

> Down in a hollow, is an ancient grove,
> The sanctuary of the royal house.
> Here grow no trees of pleasant aspect, none
> That any pruner's knife has cultivated ...
> Sometimes the grove is filled with sounds of barking ...
> Sometimes gigantic phantoms haunt the palace.
> Daylight brings no relief from these alarms;
> The grove's own darkness is the dark of night,
> And even at high noon the ghostly powers
> Retain their sway.

> (lines 650–3, 678–82)

All three classical forests are related, but Shakespeare appears to have been drawn to the Virgilian and Senecan forests for their quality of primal depth. Ovid's 'ancient wood' has a hint of this in the 'low hut' which serves as Philomel's prison. In Virgil's forest, the suggestion is stronger in the image of the cave within the 'primal earth'. In Seneca's malign grove, the sense of depth is greater still. The 'hollow' *(regio secessu)* is a door through which the underworld pollutes the daylight. What Shakespeare seems to be drawn to, then, is the sense of the forest enfolding a womb-like 'heart of darkness'.

Shakespeare creates his own 'heart of darkness' with a startlingly original use of the stage 'pit'. This becomes the focus of dramatic attention from the moment that Lavinia begs to be thrown 'into some loathsome pit' (2.3.176), rather than be raped by Chiron and Demetrius. Our attention is momentarily distracted from the pit as Lavinia is dragged off, but it is immediately refocused as the body of Bassianus is thrown in. Hereafter, the pit is remorselessly anthropomorphised. When Aaron enters with Titus's sons, he too describes the pit as 'loathsome' (line 193). When the first son (Martius) falls in, the second (Quintus) describes it almost as a kind of womb:

> ... What subtle hole is this,
> Whose mouth is covered with rude-growing briers
> Upon whose leaves are drops of new-shed blood
> As fresh as morning dew distilled on flowers?
> A very fatal place it seems to me.

(2.3.198–202)

Subsequent references are more explicit. To Martius, it is 'this unhallowed and bloodstainèd hole' (line 210), and to Quintus it is 'the swallowing womb / Of this deep pit, poor Bassianus' grave' (lines 239–40). But the womb is also a gut, with 'ragged entrails' (line 230), and a mouth 'detested, dark' and 'blood-drinking' (line 224), a 'fell devouring receptacle, / As hateful as Cocytus' misty mouth' (lines 235–6). What, then, are we to make of it? More than just a landscape, the pit is an inverted gynaecological emblem. It is an unnatural womb which 'swallows' rather than gives birth.[10]

The 'swallowing womb' is an audacious blend of tradition and improvisation. To some extent it recalls traditional medieval and Renaissance depictions of womb-enchantment, such as the familiar Renaissance epic scenario in which a knight is lulled asleep by an enchantress in a womb-like 'bower of bliss'. There is no enchantress here, but there is a clear association between the pit, and images of lust and sleep. The pit is where Aaron claims to have 'espied the panther fast asleep' (line 194). Failing to comprehend that the panther (like Aaron himself) is a symbol of lust, Quintus complains, 'My sight is very dull, whate'er it bodes' (line 195). Similarly overcome, Martius proposes to 'leave our sport to sleep awhile' (line 197). The sequence in which both brothers fall into the pit will seem absurd unless played hypnotically and understood in the context of the web of associations between wombs, darkness, lust, sleep and holes. If Spenser is one context of such symbolism, then the tale of Dido and

Aeneas is another. Virgil's 'council keeping cave' was commonly allegorised as a womb, and the love-making itself as a figure of adultery.[11] Shakespeare himself thinks along these lines in *King Lear*. Thus Gloucester's blindness is related to his fondness for adultery and the cavernous womb which produced Edmund: 'The dark and vicious place where he thee got / Cost him his eyes' (5.3.164–5). And for Lear, the womb is not only a cavern, but an infernal pit, a place where – as in Seneca's malign grove – the underworld irrupts into the daylight:

> But to the girdle do the gods inherit;
> Beneath is all the fiends'. There's hell, there's darkness, There's the
>   sulphury pit.
>
> (20.121–3)

It is not, of course, Shakespeare's intention to suggest that the Andronici are adulterous because they fall blindly into the pit. The symbolism is far more flexible than the allegorical tradition from which it remotely derives. The 'pit' sequence creates its own context in the simultaneous off-stage rape of Lavinia and her immediate entry as a spectacle of 'ravishment'. As in a diptych, the audience is forced to juxtapose and relate. They are expected to recognise that the monstrous activity of the 'swallowing womb' is the symbolic counterpart of the rape of Lavinia. As Lavinia's archetypically Roman womb is polluted and forever disabled as a source of true Roman issue, the 'loathsome' womb/pit devours Rome's remaining sons while spreading a miasma of adulterous contagion. To summarise: the second layer of meaning which Shakespeare adds to the Ovidian theme of 'confusion' transforms Ovid's generically 'wild' landscape into a 'heart of darkness' which is at once a kind of landscape and a kind of body. More precisely, it is an antitype of the state conceived in Aristotelian terms as a 'natural' body.

The hint of adultery makes sense in terms of the third layer of meaning which Shakespeare adds to Ovid's idea of 'confusion'. The rape scene actually begins with the love-making of Tamora and Aaron. Evoking, as she does, the 'conflict such as was supposed / The wand'ring prince and Dido once enjoyed' (2.3.21–2), Tamora courts a Virgilian comparison with Lavinia. In the *Aeneid*, Dido is opposed to Lavinia at the levels of family and empire. She represents adulterous love as opposed to married love, and Africa as opposed to Italy/Europe. For all his sympathy with Dido, Virgil is careful to portray her dalliance with Aeneas as adulterous and as a potential miscegenation (thus Venus wonders 'whether Jupiter ... approves the blending of peoples', *si Iuppiter ... miscerive probet populos*).[12] Had the union of Dido and Aeneas been consummated, Lavinia could never have been the genetrix of the Roman empire. But it is just this possibility that Shakespeare wants to suggest by the union of Tamora and Aaron. The adulterous miscegenation of Roman empress and African 'confounds' the empire no less than the rape and dismemberment of Lavinia.

It is of particular interest for our exploration of the exotic, that Shakespeare should make such a major issue of miscegenation. In Ovid, the theme of miscegenation is secondary to that of incest. Miscegenation is wrong because it facilitates the greater and more immediate 'confusion of all natural relations': incestuous rape. In Shakespeare, however, miscegenation takes the place of incest as the structural expression of 'confusion' within the body-politic. There are, indeed, two 'confounding' miscegenations here rather than one. In the first, Tamora marries the Roman emperor, thus becoming of one flesh with the Roman body-politic: 'I am incorporate in Rome' (1.1.459). In the second, Tamora and Aaron infect the body-politic with the taint of a 'blackamoor child' (4.2.51ff.). While this figure develops, as we shall see, in a quite unclassical direction, it is deeply rooted in the classical symbolism of defilement that we have been examining. The 'blackamoor child' might be thought of as representing the defiled womb in its fertile aspect, as distinct from the 'ravished' Lavinia who represents the defiled womb in its infertile aspect. The womb in question is not just Tamora's but, by virtue of her 'incorporate' bond with the emperor, Rome's also. Thus is the child described as 'stately Rome's disgrace'.

In Shakespeare, then, the theme of 'confusion' is not only much more elaborately stated than in Ovid, but it takes on a quite different character owing to the substitution of miscegenation for incest. The emphasis on miscegenation creates an entirely un-Ovidian plot-line (based on Aaron, his child and Lucius) which requires an un-Ovidian conclusion in addition to the patently Ovidian conclusion (based on Titus, Lavinia and Tamora) of the cannibal banquet. It is, I want to suggest, in this second and unclassical conclusion that *Titus Andronicus* not only parts company with the Tereus myth but also (to a degree) with the classical drama of the barbarian. But before enquiring into the new direction in which this takes the play, we may ask how Shakespeare handles his Ovidian conclusion. In Ovid, the cannibal banquet is precisely calculated to counterpoint the 'confusion' wrought by incestuous rape. As one Elizabethan editor of the *Metamorphoses* put it, Procne 'strikes at her husband ... through her owne bowells'.[13] By murdering her own child and feeding him to her husband, Procne revenges herself in a peculiarly incestuous way: the mother becomes the means by which the family swallows itself, or more precisely completes the process of self-annihilation which the crime of incest had set in train. From a structural point of view, what is important about this revenge is less its savagery than its capacity to devastate the incestuous husband with a homology of his own crime. This is just what Procne achieves. If incest is viewed in René Girard's terms, as a slaying of 'distinctions' within the family, then the cannibal banquet may be viewed in the same light, as 'the violent abolition of all family differences'.[14] Such indeed seems the thrust of Procne's reply to Tereus's request to have Itys join him at the table: 'You have, within, him whom you want'. Given, then, so intimate a relationship between the cannibal banquet and the crime of incest in the Tereus myth, it is hardly surprising that Titus's revenge (for all its competitive excess) lacks the precision of Procne's. Titus is able to make Tamora devour her own children, but he can't, like Procne, revenge himself 'through his owne bowells'. It is the *incestuousness* of the rape that justifies Procne's revenge, and the intimacy of the kinship bond which makes it so terrible. While therefore Shakespeare assiduously imitates Ovid's conclusion, he fails to do so with the penetrating intelligence which marks his imitation of the first two movements of Ovid's tale. For all its excessiveness, there is a perfunctory and random quality about Titus's revenge. The murder of Lavinia may be intended to match Procne's murder of Itys but it has no logical connection with the cannibal banquet itself.

Interestingly, the intelligence which we might have expected from Shakespeare's imitation of Ovid's conclusion, is found instead in the alternative conclusion centred on Aaron, the 'blackamoor child' and Lucius. Aaron's child, as I have suggested, begins his stage existence as a living sign of the pollution of the Roman body-politic. So, at least, the Roman characters insist. 'Here is the babe', cries the nurse with a theatrical flourish, 'a joyless, dismal, black, and sorrowful issue ... as loathsome as a toad ... stately Rome's disgrace' (4.2.66–7, 60). 'Behold the child', cries Marcus (as if in an anti-nativity play), 'the issue of an irreligious moor' (5.3.118, 120), and embodiment of the 'dire events' of which its parent has been the 'breeder' (5.3.177). Ominously, Lucius describes the child to Aaron as 'this growing image of thy fiendlike face' (5.1.45). Apart from Aaron, then, everyone refers to the child as a kind of theatrical equivalent of the imagery of blood-defilement in *The Rape of Lucrece*. The context of this imagery is Lucrece's agonised debate on the question of whether the victim of rape incurs a form of adultery-pollution. In a classic illustration of Mary Douglas's distinction between pollution rules and moral rules, Lucrece decides that she is indeed polluted regardless of her moral innocence.[15] Her own blood makes the point emblematically:

> ... bubbling from her breast, it doth divide
> In two slow rivers ...

Some of her blood still pure and red remain'd,
And some look'd black, and that false Tarquin stain'd.

(lines 1736–7, 1742–3)

Just as Lucrece's body is 'adulterated' by rape, so is the Roman body-politic adulterated by the 'blackamoor child'. It is for this reason that Aaron's baby is publicly held up for comparison with Lucius, Titus's last remaining son, who represents himself as the unadulterated issue of Rome, 'That have preserved her welfare in my blood' (5.3.109).

Given the starkness of this juxtaposition between the pure and the adulterate Roman issue, it is surprising that Aaron's baby is not made to share the fate of his polluting parents or his barbarian half-brothers who are served up to their mother in the cannibal banquet. Death is the generic fate of the hybrid or the monstrous in classical tragedy for the reason that such drama vehiculates a particularly intense form of pollution-awareness characteristic of a classical 'shame culture', as distinct from the moral awareness characteristic of a Christian 'guilt culture'. In Seneca's *Hippolytus* (a source of several details in *Titus Andronicus*), therefore, the innocent mixed-race hero is torn apart by a beast from the sea which recapitulates the monstrous form of the minotaur: 'the crossed offspring' of Pasiphaë's bestial amours.[16] In *Oedipus*, the hero is doomed to suffer for the 'crime' of incest regardless of having been completely ignorant of Jocasta's identity. And in classical versions of the Lucretia legend, the innocent heroine expunges the taint of rape-pollution only at the cost of her own death.[17]

Why, then, given the force of the classical theme of womb-pollution in *Titus Andronicus*, is the mixed-race baby spared? The easy answer is that Shakespeare manipulates the audience into a sentimental view of the child. We are at least as likely to identify with the father's humorously indulgent response to his son, as with the outrage of the humourless Romans. We are also more inclined to sympathise with the father's courageous, and finally self-sacrificing defence of his child, than with the homicidal self-righteousness of those who seek to destroy it. But more than audience-manipulation is involved here. The child actually becomes a force for redemption. The first to be affected is Aaron himself who discovers a capacity for parenthood that should surprise us as much as it does Tamora's sons. As the most demonic of all the barbarians, Aaron should be incapable of any such 'natural' feelings. However, his protection of his child 'maugre all the world' (4.2.109) not only compares favourably with Tamora's command to 'christen it with thy dagger's point' (4.2.70), but also with Titus's treatment of his own children, two of whom he murders. In redeeming his own father, moreover, the child also exercises a redemptive power over Lucius. Already blooded by his enthusiastic participation in the sacrifice of Tamora's child, Alarbus ('Alarbus' limbs are lopped / And entrails feed the sacrificing fire', 1.1.143–4), Lucius's first thought upon being confronted with the two moors is to hang the child in the sight of its father. Aaron's feat in extracting a promise of clemency for his child thus spares Lucius from incurring the very blood-debt in which the tragedy had originated. This, in turn, creates the conditions for a redemptive ending instead of a Senecan or Ovidian holocaust. By promising to see Aaron's child 'nourished' (5.1.60), Lucius converts a typically tragic economy of 'violent reciprocity' into a typically comic order in which 'reciprocity' works for the good of the 'commonwealth'.[18] Violence, of course, remains. Aaron is executed by being set 'breast-deep in earth' (5.3.178) and famished. But this is a discriminating and cleansing violence, clearly recapitulating the emblematic spectacle in which Rome's true issue are 'swallowed' by the earth. Compared with the lawless and 'confounding' revenge of the cannibal banquet, then, Aaron's death has the 'founding' character of law. The difference between revenge and justice is signalled by a subtle shift in Lucius's symbolic role. Though he enters Rome at the head of a foreign army, like Coriolanus, he succeeds to power as an Aeneas. Instead, therefore, of re-enacting the sad history of an impious and potentially 'confounding' invader, he re-enacts the foundation of Rome by the pious Aeneas.[19] Curiously, it is the existence of the black baby which allows Lucius to assume the latter role, because – as living proof of adultery and miscegenation – the child allows the Romans to recognise Tamora as a promiscuous barbarian rather than as Rome 'incorporate'. The sheer visibility of the child's pollutiveness makes possible a redrawing of the confused boundaries between Roman and barbarian, pure and impure. The boundaries are not, however, the same as the old boundaries. 'Rome' now seems to include an army of mysteriously reclaimed Goths who anticipate the ancient Britons of *Cymbeline*.

It is clear that the generous inclusiveness of this ending directly contradicts the ancient narrative of barbarous intrusion which Shakespeare is at such pains to reconstruct. But where does the contradiction come from? It is tempting to suppose that a more 'enlightened' or 'cosmopolitan' view of the exotic is struggling to find expression, but the contradiction can in fact be traced to an alternative ancient view of the barbarian. To the extent that the ancients thought of barbarians as 'primitive', they also credited them with primitivistic virtues: physical hardihood, courage, and an uncorrupted taste for the simple life.[20] This tradition certainly contributes towards Shakespeare's revaluation of Aaron and the Goths. Thus Aaron plans to raise his child like a primitive Goth rather than like a Roman:

I'll make you feed on berries and on roots,
And fat on curds and whey, and suck the goat,
And cabin in a cave, and bring you up
To be a warrior and command a camp.

(4.2.176–9)

Aaron's heroic defence of his child, and his indifference to suffering, would also seem to be in line with the tradition.[21] But if the context of the contradiction is ancient, what is its logic here? Why would Shakespeare want to offer this radically alternative view of the barbarian? Whatever his sources, his *motives* cannot have been ancient. Here it is worth pointing out that Goth and moor are not included to the same degree at the end of the play. Assimilated into the new order which they have helped bring about, the Goths seem less like barbarians than honorary Romans, cousins perhaps of the primitive but proto-Christian 'Britons' of *Cymbeline*.[22] The place of the moor, on the other hand, is deeply paradoxical. Aaron dies a barbarian: excluded in the physical sense, abominated by the Romans, yet recognisably 'human' to the audience. The 'blackamoor child' is included to the extent that Lucius promises to see it 'nourished', but excluded in the sense that his position within the new order is left unclear.

To conclude: the paradox of the moor in *Titus Andronicus* is a measure both of Shakespeare's indebtedness to the classical idea of the barbarian, and of his invention of a more problematic tropics of barbarism. Aaron begins by representing all the viciousness and pollutiveness of the classical barbarian writ large (he is precisely 'a craftier Tereus'). Yet the very excess of his outrageousness – his begetting of a 'blackamoor child' upon the Roman empress – leads to a rebirth of just those familial and civic bonds which he has so spectacularly violated. Humanly appealing yet inevitably 'confusing', all Shakespearean moors inherit Aaron's paradox.

2

Creative worlds removed from the primal drama of barbarism in *Titus Andronicus*, *Antony and Cleopatra* nevertheless represents the exotic as insidiously threatening. Exoticism is hardly the reigning theme in the later play, but it remains an important dimension in the complex polarity defined by Rome and Egypt. The exotic of the later play differs again in its mythic or narrative character. Instead of invading or intruding on a geographical and moral centre, the exotic is now encountered in the course of an outward or literally 'exorbitant' adventure beyond the geographical and moral confines of the Roman world. 'Exorbitance', as we have seen, is a type of geographical and moral adventurism associated with ancient ideas of conquest and navigation, and with the ancient figure of the 'voyager' as I have defined him. Here I want to suggest that Shakespeare's Antony is such a figure. Yet how might the voyager myth have found its way into Shakespeare's play? The question arises because (as we shall see) the myth does not figure significantly in Shakespeare's main source: Plutarch's *Life of Antonius*. It has not, I think, been sufficiently recognised how much Shakespeare's Antony owes to the non-Plutarchan legend of Antonius, nor how closely this legend approximates that of the ancient voyager.

Master of an insidiously 'Asiatic' rhetorical style, admirer of Alexander, proponent of a subversively 'cosmopolitan' model of empire as against the hallowed Romanocentric model, spurner of his Roman wife and Roman mores, lover of a foreign queen, and finally leader of invading hordes from the East – the 'historical' Antonius is a case-study in 'exorbitance'; the classic example of a conqueror who 'went too far'. If the tendentious moralism of Antonius's legend reflects the influence of Augustan propaganda, its basic features were of his own making.[23] Antonius had consciously sought to fashion his career on 'exorbitant' role models such as Alexander.[24] Thus, seeing his eastern empire as a recapitulation of Alexander's, Antonius invaded Parthia in an arbortive attempt to assimilate the Macedonian's former territory. Of greater political consequence, Antonius championed a 'cosmopolitan' or 'ecumenical' philosophy of empire in which the Roman Empire was conceived in Alexandrian terms as a brotherhood of nations instead of in Aristotelian terms as a ring of vassal nations dominated by a single city-state.[25] Antonius had also sought to represent his miscegenation with Cleopatra in Alexandrian terms. Not only was Cleopatra herself a descendant of Alexander, but Alexander was supposed to have authorised mixed-race marriages by his own union with the Persian princess, Roxana. Antonius drew attention to the parallels both by nominating his mixed-race children as Alexander's successors and investing them in the garb of the various eastern nations they were to rule.[26] Yet Alexander was not Antonius's only 'exorbitant' inspiration. Insofar as he wished to be seen as a champion of the East over the West, Antonius played the part of the eastern god, Dionysus. Insofar as he was notoriously promiscuous where Alexander was not, Antonius claimed to be following in the steps of Hercules. In a subversive twist to the Hercules myth, Antonius pointed to the hero's habit of propagating descendants outside the bounds of family and nation.[27] Thus, where a Roman might have understood Hercules as a figure of restraint (in keeping with the legendary motto of the Pillars of Hercules: *Non Plus Ultra*), Antonius was able to represent him as a pattern of heroic promiscuity.

All these potentially 'exorbitant' elements were, then, already available to the Augustan counter-legend of Antonius which (aside from Plutarch's *Life of Antonius*) formed the basis of Antonius's myth in the Renaissance.[28] In the most illustrious of these Augustan counter-myths, Virgil's *Aeneid*, the idea of Antonius is constantly present as a negative measure of Virgil's hero. Unlike the impious Antonius, therefore, the 'pious' Aeneas preserves his family and household gods in the direst of circumstances. Unlike the promiscuous Antonius, Aeneas heeds the advice of the gods and forsakes the embraces of an African queen. Unlike the 'cosmopolitan' Antonius, Aeneas single-mindedly focuses his energies on founding a dynasty which, it is prophetically revealed to him, will one day produce the Julian rulers of a new Trojan empire. In the prophetically inspired decorations on the shield of Aeneas, Antonius is depicted as a degenerate Alexander: 'Here Antonius with barbaric might and varied arms, victor from the nations of the dawn and from the ruddy sea, brings with him Egypt and the strength of the East and utmost Bactra; and there follows him (O shame!) his Egyptian wife'.[29] The idea that Antonius's defeat represented the triumph of Rome over eastern barbarism (*Aurorae populis*) rather than a purely Roman affair, is fully in keeping with the tenor of Augustan propaganda.[30] The same idea is found in Horace who expresses outrage that 'a Roman consul ... has turned his back on the ways of his City to wallow in Pharaonic luxury ... enslaved himself to a woman, and humiliated himself to the point of obeying her eunuchs'.[31] Not surprisingly, the Augustan legend of Antonius also served as a foil for Augustus's own legend. Augustus made a point of invoking Apollo against Dionysus, and of privileging Roman mores over foreign.[32] He also established the Augustan idea of the empire as a completed 'natural' artefact in place of the Alexandrian idea of an empire constantly expanding.[33]

In terms, then, both of his Augustan counter-legend and of his own political myth, Antonius should have seemed 'exorbitant' to any educated Renaissance poet, including Shakespeare. Here, however, we encounter a paradox. Plutarch's *Life of Antonius*, by far the dominant classical influence on Shakespeare's play, propagates an essentially different legend. The Antonius legends I have been describing have an archetypal, even cartoon-like, quality befitting their immediate public and political contexts. As a biographer, however, Plutarch was less interested in such material than in material of a more personal, intimate and 'documentary' nature. The result is that Plutarch's narrative is too rich, too complex and too 'real' to fit the simple lines of the Augustan counter-legend (even though most of the Augustan elements are preserved). Plutarch, of course, disapproves of Antonius, but in a moral rather than a political and ideological sense. Two factors help explain the change of emphasis. In the first place, Plutarch was writing roughly a hundred years after Antonius's death, when the immediate need for political myth-making had passed. In the second place, Plutarch was himself Greek and an enthusiastic proponent of the 'cosmopolitan' view of empire attributed to Alexander and championed by Antonius.[34] In Plutarch, therefore, we get little sense of the archetypally Roman drama of 'exorbitance' in which the renegade commander 'goes native', joins forces with the 'exotic' queen, and leads the eastern hordes against the mother-city.[35] Nor is Cleopatra primarily the 'exotic' queen in Plutarch. While strongly disapproving of her, Plutarch does so on moral rather than racial grounds. Thus Cleopatra is ethnically Greek in Plutarch rather than the dangerously exotic 'Egyptian wife' (*Aegypta coniunx*) as in Virgil. Antonius's affair with Cleopatra is an adultery rather than a miscegenation. In conclusion, we can say that while the outline of the Augustan legend of Antonius is visible in Plutarch, it is obscured by other political interests and another narrative tendency.

Plutarch's importance to Shakespeare should sharpen rather than diminish our appreciation of how Shakespeare systematically returns to the mythic, pre-Plutarchan themes of 'exorbitance' and 'exoticism' in *Antony and Cleopatra*. Shakespeare transforms these themes in several ways.

'Exorbitance' permeates *Antony and Cleopatra* in the form of 'the world theme'. Such imagery bears a family resemblance to a type of image which Shakespeare elsewhere uses in relation to Julius Caesar: in *Cymbeline*, where Caesar's ambition is imagined as having 'swelled so much that it did almost stretch / The sides o' th' world' (3.1.49–50), and in *Julius Caesar*, where Caesar is explicitly imagined as a Colossus:

> Why, man, he doth bestride the narrow world
> Like a Colossus, and we petty men
> Walk under his huge legs, and peep about
> To find ourselves dishonourable graves.

> (1.2.136–9)

The reappearance of this type of image – most obviously in Cleopatra's vision of Antony as a Colossus 'whose legs bestrid the ocean', whose 'rear'd arm crested the world' – is interesting for several reasons. In the first place, it suggests that Shakespeare envisaged Antony partly through the patently 'exorbitant' legend of Julius Caesar, whom Plutarch describes in *The Life of Antonius* as driven by 'an insatiable desire to reign, with a senseless covetousness to be the best man in the world'.[36] More interesting still, however, is that Shakespeare actually seems to prefer Antony to Caesar as the 'exorbitant' type *par excellence*. Shakespeare's Caesar is not the superman of Plutarch or Lucan. Cassius's ironic image of him as a 'Colossus' merely underlines the difference. Unlike Marlowe, Shakespeare never seems to have been inspired by the obvious exemplars of empire and overreaching ambition.

This brings us to the second level of 'exorbitance' in *Antony and Cleopatra*. Antony's brand of exorbitance is erotic or existential rather than imperialistic. If 'exorbitance' is a quasi-divine dissatisfaction with the limitedness of one's world, then Antony is 'exorbitant' in love. The first words of the play inform us how 'this dotage of our General's / O'erflows the measure' (1.1.1–2). Philo is amazed that Antony should turn his eyes 'upon a tawny front' (1.1.6); suggesting perhaps the proverbial madness of the lover who, in *A Midsummer Night's Dream*, 'Sees Helen's beauty in a brow of Egypt' (5.1.11). Antony, of course, makes a point of refusing to set a 'bourn' or limit on love unless in some 'new heaven, new earth'. And characteristic of the voyager, his new world necessarily requires the dissolution of the world he once possessed:

> Let Rome in Tiber melt, and the wide arch
> Of the ranged empire fall. Here is my space.
> Kingdoms are clay. Our dungy earth alike
> Feeds beast as man. The nobleness of life
> Is to do thus.
>
> (1.1.35–9)

Plutarch's account of the 'order ... called amimetobion' by which Antonius and Cleopatra live – '(as much to say, "no life comparable and matchable with it") ... exceeding all measure and reason' – is here translated into geographic terms.[37] Thus Plutarch's 'measure' becomes 'the wide arch of the rang'd empire', or again the Tiber into which Rome is envisaged as 'melting'. Throughout, Shakespeare shows a grasp of the Roman idea of rivers as defining geographic *termini*. Hence, Antony – with the exorbitant man's contempt for *fines* and mores alike – translates the Tiber from a symbol of definition into one of dissolution. He surrenders himself to Cleopatra on the Cydnus (the terminus of Asia), and takes the grotesque Nile as his measure.

If rivers represent one metaphoric site of Antony's 'exorbitance', the sea represents another. The sea is Antony's symbolic element. Thus 'his delights' are 'dolphin-like', showing 'his back above / The element they lived in' (5.2.88–9). But if the sea is a liberating and festive element (Pompey's feast is held afloat), it is also fatal. Thus Antony twice makes war by sea with disastrous consequences. An interesting polarity exists between sea and land, as between an element of instability and 'exorbitance', and one of solidity and limits. Antony's first decision to make war by sea is opposed by a soldier who reminds him that 'we / Have used to conquer standing on the earth' (3.7.64–5), and swears 'by Hercules' (line

67) to reinforce the point. Shortly after the defeat of Actium, Shakespeare inserts an emblematic scene in which soldiers keeping watch hear solemn music 'i' th' air' and 'under the earth', and interpret it as a sign that 'the god Hercules, whom Antony loved / Now leaves him' (4.3.13–14). The scene is loosely based on Plutarch's account of how Bacchus deserted Antonius in the form of 'a marvellous sweet harmony of sundry sorts of instruments ... with the cry of a multitude of people, as they had been dancing and had sung as they use in Bacchus' feasts' (p. 275). Shakespeare seems to have substituted Hercules for Bacchus partly in order to confirm the sea/land polarity. As the soldiers hear solemn music beneath the stage, they stand in its four corners in order to suggest the four-cornered earth.[38] Ironically, Antony wins his next battle, which is on land, but loses the last confrontation by trusting again to water: 'Their preparation is today by sea; / We please them not by land' (4.11.1–2). Throughout, the sea represents more or less what the ocean represents in Seneca's *Suasoriae* : it is chimeric, formless, endless, uncertain, phantasmal. Accordingly, perhaps, the image of the sea in *Antony and Cleopatra* is linked to other types of water imagery which more directly suggest evanescence and illusion. Such is Caesar's image of the 'vagabond flag upon the stream' which 'Goes to, and back, lackeying the varying tide, / To rot itself with motion' (1.4.45–7). Such again is Antony's final vision of existential despair, when reviewing his life as a cloud-like succession of phantasmal shapes, ultimately 'indistinct / As water is in water' (4.15.10–11). While such sentiments are foreign to Plutarch's Antonius, they are in keeping with the mythology of voyaging. In Seneca's *Suasoriae*, Alexander is warned that he will be swept into nonentity at the boundaries of creation.

The idea of Antony as a voyager is further underlined by another departure from Plutarch. Rather than conceiving Antony's career as a kind of rake's progress – a graded escalation of excesses – Shakespeare represents Antony as abandoning himself all at once to Cleopatra. Before meeting Cleopatra, Antony is assumed to have been a pattern of *Romanitas*. Philo's opening remarks convey shock at the suddenness and completeness of Antony's collapse into 'dotage'. The contrast is more forcefully stated by Caesar:

> ... Antony,
> Leave thy lascivious wassails. When thou once
> Was beaten from Modena, where thou slew'st
> Hirtius and Pansa, consuls, at thy heel
> Did famine follow, whom thou fought'st against –
> Though daintily brought up – with patience more
> Than savages could suffer. Thou didst drink
> The stale of horses, and the gilded puddle

> Which beasts would cough at. Thy palate then did deign
> The roughest berry on the rudest hedge.
> Yea, like the stag, when snow the pasture sheets,
> The barks of trees thou browsed. On the Alps
> It is reported thou didst eat strange flesh,
> Which some did die to look on.
>
> (1.4.55–67)

Virtually all the details of this passage originate in Plutarch – except for the point. For Plutarch, Antonius's capacity to survive on the Alps illustrates his native strength of body and mind. In Shakespeare, however, Antony's endurance becomes proof of an almost Stoic virtue. The new point is signalled by a slight change of detail. In Plutarch, Antonius eats 'the barks of trees and such beasts as never man tasted of their flesh before' (p. 192). In Shakespeare, Antony eats 'The barks of trees' and 'strange flesh, / Which some did die to look on'. The alteration, I suggest, is prompted less by a taste for hyperbole than by a desire to imagine the earlier Antony as a kind of Cato. Shakespeare may actually be thinking of Lucan's lurid account of Cato's journey through the desert of the Syrtes, in which the hero's self-sufficient virtue insulates him from exotic perils which some indeed 'die to look on'. But if the touch of hyperbole suggests Lucan, the passage as a whole suggests any number of literary journeys in which Stoic virtue is measured against exotic perils (Horace's *Integer Vitae* is a case in point). Before meeting Cleopatra, then, Antony is a pattern of Stoic 'patience' (precisely a patience '*more* / Than savages could suffer').[39] After meeting Cleopatra his ability to endure fatally 'strange flesh' becomes an active lusting after 'much more monstrous matter of feast' (2.2.189).

Cleopatra's exoticism is the counterpart of Antony's exorbitance. Shakespeare not only exoticises Cleopatra – actually representing her as 'tawny' and 'a right gipsy' (4.13.28) rather than Greek – but systematically augments the portrait that he found in Plutarch with at least two varieties of ancient exoticism: the Roman discourse of the 'Orient' and the Herodotean discourse of Egypt.

The 'orientalism' of Cleopatra's court – with its luxury, decadence, splendour, sensuality, appetite, effeminacy and eunuchs – seems a systematic inversion of the legendary Roman values of temperance, manliness, courage and *pietas*. In one sense the opposition seems ironic. It is only from the vantage point of Egypt that Rome actually seems 'Roman'. In another sense, the opposition is apocalyptic. Antony's Egypt-inspired vision of Rome 'melting' into the Tiber rivals Juvenal's mock-apocalyptic vision of the Tiber being swamped by the alien waters of 'Syrian Orontes' with 'its language and its morals ... its national tambourines'.[40] At the simplest level, Egypt attacks Antony through his senses: particularly in a blended imagery of feeding and sex ('he will to his Egyptian dish again', 2.6.126). At another level, Antony's judgement is bewitched by the 'enchanting queen' (1.2.123) who is 'cunning past man's thought' (line 138). Nowhere is the idea of the oriental enchantress stronger than in Enobarbus's description of the meeting of Antony and Cleopatra on the Cydnus. Once again, virtually everything in this speech is Plutarchan – except the point. In North's translation, all is fuss and detail:

Therefore when she was sent unto by divers letters ... she made so light of it that she mocked Antonius so much that she disdained to set forward otherwise but to take her barge in the river of Cydnus, the poop whereof was of gold, the sails of purple, and the oars of silver, which kept stroke in rowing after the sound of the music of flutes, howboys, citherns, viols, and such other instruments as they played upon in the barge. And now for the person of herself: she was laid under a pavilion of cloth of gold of tissue, apparelled and attired like the goddess Venus commonly drawn in picture. (p. 201)

In Shakespeare's version of the scene (2.2.197–212) – too well known to need quoting – much the same parade of detail has the force of vision. The differences are extraordinarily subtle. Vocalisation is an important factor, as is the fact that Enobarbus exchanges his customarily sceptical and prosaic register for a register of lyricism and wonder, virtually as he speaks. It is the quality of the wonder here that is important, however. Just as Rome is never more 'Roman' than when viewed from Egypt, so Cleopatra is never more 'exotic' than when viewed from Rome. Enobarbus has suddenly become a classical Mandeville, filled with the wonder of the Orient, fettered (no less than his stage audience) by the strong enchantment that he describes. At its most powerful, the exotic beggars description. Thus, where Plutarch is content with the figure of analogy ('she was ... apparelled and attired *like* the goddess Venus commonly drawn in picture'), Shakespeare prefers the figure of incomparability: 'For her own person, / It beggared all description ... *O'er-picturing* that Venus where we see / The fancy outwork Nature' (lines 204–6, my italics). The deeper lesson of this 'enchantment' is that the exotic is less a fact than a trick of perspective. There can only be an Orient if there is an Occident.

For all Cleopatra's orientalism, however, there is a sense in which she is irreducibly 'Egyptian'. The Herodotean character of Shakespeare's Egypt has never (so far as I am aware) been recognised. To understand it, we must first consider how Egypt is constructed in Herodotus. The Egyptian *logos* in Book Two of the *Histories* is narratively and conceptually prior to all other Herodotean ethnographies, such as the Scythian *logos* which immediately follows. It is not merely a particular ethnography, therefore, but the first ethnography: a blueprint of the entire tradition of ancient ethnography (and of much in the Renaissance). Herodotus is first struck by the 'marvels' of Egypt: 'But concerning Egypt I will now speak at length, because nowhere are there so many marvelous things, nor in the whole world beside are there to be found so many works of unspeakable greatness. Therefore I shall say the more concerning Egypt' (2.35).[41] The 'marvels' actually justify the ethnographic project in the first place. The combination of 'marvels' and geographic extremity (Herodotus takes Egypt to be the most southerly of lands) institutes the first axiom of ancient ethnography: that 'the fairest blessings (*thoma*) have been granted to the most distant nations' (3.106). The combination of 'marvels' and geographic extremity is in turn recapitulated at a human level: 'As the Egyptians have a climate peculiar to themselves, and their river is different in its nature from all other rivers, so have they made all their customs and laws of a kind contrary for the most part to those of all other men' (2.35). To Herodotus, the Nile was 'different' in several senses. Its source was unknown, it spawned monsters, its size was out of keeping with the arid regions through which it flowed, and it brought fertility only when in flood. The inhabitants of this Nile-defined country are just as different. They reverse sexual hierarchy ('women buy and sell, the men abide at home ... women make their water standing, men sitting', 2.35), and the proper relationship between inside and outside ('they relieve nature indoors, and eat out of doors in the street ... they knead dough with their feet and gather mud with their hands', 2.35). The antipodean geography is recapitulated in a carnivalesque society.

In Shakespeare, too, the character of Egypt and the Egyptians is epitomised by the Nile. The feast on Pompey's barge begins with a geography lesson on the flooding of the Nile:

> ... The higher Nilus swells,
> The more it promises; as it ebbs, the seedsman
> Upon the slime and ooze scatters his grain,
> And shortly comes to harvest.

(2.7.20–24)

But it is not long before the lesson takes a carnivalesque turn. Lepidus interrupts with a drunken question: 'You've strange serpents there?' (line 24); and a drunken observation: 'Your serpent of Egypt is bred now out of your mud / by the operation of your sun; so is your crocodile' (lines 26–7). As in Herodotus, Egypt means the Nile and its natural wonders. As in Herodotus, too, monstrosity in the natural sphere goes with carnival in the human sphere. It is, therefore, no accident that the most sustained display of Egyptian ethnography in the play should be found in the play's most carnivalesque scene. Egypt, the Nile, and carnival all burgeon in the atmosphere of intoxication. The drunker he gets, the deeper Lepidus penetrates into some Egypt of the mind ('these quicksands, Lepidus, / Keep off them, for you sink', lines 58–9) like some mockery Cato being swallowed by an imaginary Syrtes.

At their most interesting, Shakespeare's echoes of the Herodotean discourse of the Nile are not just festive but oneiric, mysterious, even absurd. When Lepidus asks 'What manner o' thing is your crocodile?' (line 40), Antony answers:

> It is shap'd, sir, like itself, and it is as broad as
> it hath breadth. It is just so high as it is, and moves
> with it own organs. It lives by that which nourisheth
> it, and the elements once out of it, it transmigrates.

> (2.7.41–4)

The joke works on two levels. In the first place, Antony is spoofing what Hartog has described as the Herodotean rhetoric of comparison and analogy, the generic ethnographic strategy by which the different is translated into the code of the same.[42] The technique is strikingly evident in Herodotus's description of the hippopotamus ('they are four-footed, with cloven hoofs like oxen; their noses are blunt; they are maned like horses, with tusks showing, and have a horse's tail and a horse's neigh; their bigness is that of the biggest oxen', 2.71) and again in his description of the crocodile:

I will now show what kind of creature is the crocodile ... It has four feet, and lives both on land and in the water ... its eggs are not much bigger than goose eggs, and the young crocodile is of a bigness answering thereto ... It has eyes like pigs' eyes, and great teeth and tusks answering to the bigness of its body. (2.68)

At its simplest, Antony's joke works by setting up just this sort of comparison and then withholding it. But the joke also has a philosophical edge. By withholding analogy, Antony is denying the possibility of 'translation', linguistic appropriation, even knowledge itself. He is insisting that the different is essentially untranslatable into the Roman code and hence unknowable. One appropriates the exotic only by moving outside of one's code. Nor can the exotic ever be displaced or decoded without ceasing to be truly exotic. The deeper point of the joke may pass unnoticed until we realise that the crocodile is Cleopatra's heraldic beast:

> He's speaking now,
> Or murmuring, 'Where's my serpent of old Nile?' –
> For so he calls me. Now I feed myself
> With most delicious poison. Think on me,
> That am with Phoebus' amorous pinches black,
> And wrinkled deep in time.

> (1.5.24–9)

Not unlike Antony's crocodile, Cleopatra is here unsearchable in her difference. She is ancient, black, sun-burned, reptilian, intoxicated with her own poison: a Herodotean blend of the monstrous and the marvellous that resists language and category. The image is deliberately inconstruable in visual terms, thus actualising the paradoxicalness which Enobarbus spells out in more conventionally rhetorical terms in his more conventional vignettes of Cleopatra:

> Age cannot wither her, nor custom stale
> Her infinite variety: other women cloy
> The appetites they feed, but she makes hungry
> Where most she satisfies. For vilest things
> Become themselves in her, that the holy priests
> Bless her when she is riggish.

(2.2.241–6)

The untranslatable mystery – the autonomy – of Cleopatra's difference is what is at issue in the last act of the play. Shakespeare's interpretation of Cleopatra's suicide differs markedly from Plutarch's. In Plutarch, Cleopatra kills herself out of a sense of despair and bereavement. In Shakespeare, however, Cleopatra commits suicide essentially to escape appearing in Caesar's triumph.[43] Ritual 'translation', as distinct from a simple desire to avoid disgrace, is what is at issue here. Both Cleopatra and Caesar show a general grasp of the politics of ceremony: Caesar when complaining of Octavia's unceremonious return to Rome (3.6.42–55), and Cleopatra when imagining herself burlesqued in the Roman streets. Both also show a precise grasp of the politics of the triumph. Cleopatra understands it as a ritual means of translating the exotic into so many 'scutcheons and . . . signs of conquest' (5.2.131). Caesar understands it as a theatre of abjection and self-glorification. In a revealing slip, Proculeius explains to Cleopatra how her suicide would rob Caesar of the chance to 'let the world see / His nobleness well acted' (5.2.43–4). What he wants Cleopatra to hear is that Caesar would like the opportunity to seem generous and magnanimous. But what Cleopatra actually does hear ('he words me, girls, he words me' 5.2.187) is the thought behind the words: 'her life in Rome / Would be eternal in our triumph' (5.1.65–6). Cleopatra's suicide, then, robs Caesar of his 'eternal' triumph. But there is more to it than this. By ritualising her death, Cleopatra counters one form of theatre with another, and preserves her mystery from translation.

3

Patterns of 'intrusion' and 'exorbitance' blend disconcertingly in Shakespeare's 'Venetian' plays. To the degree that these plays are about exotics who seek to 'incorporate' themselves with a neo-imperial (if republican) city which persists in regarding them as alien, they may be said to recapitulate the 'intrusive' pattern of *Titus Andronicus*.[44] To the degree, however, that Shakespeare's Venice is somehow complicit with the 'exotic', the 'Venetian' plays may be said to anticipate the 'exorbitant' pattern of *Antony and Cleopatra*. The connections are not direct. *Titus Andronicus* is not a source for either 'Venetian' play, nor they for *Antony and Cleopatra*. How, then, do we explain the presence of the 'Roman' themes of 'intrusion' and 'exorbitance' in the 'Venetian' plays? Part of the answer can be found in the Elizabethan idea of Venice.

To the Elizabethans, Venice was a glorious – yet unsettling – contradiction. The idea originates as a celebratory topos in Venetian authors such as Gasparo Contarini who (in the Elizabethan translation of his *Commonwealth and Government of Venice*) describes the city as a *coincidentia oppositorum* : 'so unspeakeablie strange' as to make 'the straungest impossibilities not seeme altogether incredible'.[45] Thus, Venice is a 'Citie', but 'seated in the middle of the sea' (A3). 'Founded upon quagmires', it yet has 'pallaces ... reaching up to the clouds' (A3). Governed by 'unweaponed men in gownes', it yet controls an empire (A3). Lacking defensive walls, it has remained 'like a pure and untouched virgine, free from the taste or violence of any forraine enforcement' (A3). For Contarini, Venice excites contradictions in order to reconcile them. For his Elizabethan readers, however, Venice's contradictions were more than simply rhetorical. In particular, they seem to have been exercised by a contradiction unremarked by Contarini: between the idea of Venice as the constitutional heir of the ancient city-state ('Athens, Lacedaemon and Rome' (p. 6), and the idea of Venice as an open or cosmopolitan city whose citizens mingled promiscuously with the peoples of the world. Thus Lewkenor's translation of Contarini is prefaced by a sonnet of Edmund Spenser castigating Venice as the 'third Babel' (after Rome and 'The antique Babel, the empire of the East'). The allusion is to the legend of Babel in Genesis 11.1–11, and in particular to the ideas of confusion and dispersal therein exemplified: 'Therefore was the name of it called Babel: because the Lord did there confound the language of all the earth: and from thence did the Lord scatter them abroad upon the face of all the earth' (Genesis 11.9).[46] Interestingly, Spenser may well have derived this highly unflattering analogy from Contarini himself, who praises the city as 'a common and general market of the whole world', and enthusiastically describes 'the wonderful concourse of strange and forraine people, yea of the farthest and the remotest nations' (p. 1). Both writers want to suggest the cosmopolitanism of the city, but a value-free term for the fact does not yet exist.[47] Venice might have recalled Babel in yet another respect. The much remarked splendour of its buildings ('pallaces ... reaching up to the clouds') should have called to mind the Babelesque presumption of building a tower 'whose top may reach unto heaven' (Genesis 11.4). The ambiguity of the Elizabethan response to Venice is nicely caught in Thomas Coryat's description of St Mark's Square:

> Truely such is the stupendious (to use a strange Epitheton for so strange and rare a place as this) glory of it, that at my first entrance thereof it did even amaze or rather ravish my senses. For here is the greatest magnificence of architecture to be seene, that any place under the sunne doth yeelde. Here you may both see all manner of fashions of attire, and heare all the languages of Christendome, besides those that are spoken by the barbarous Ethnickes; the frequencie of people being so great ... that (as an elegant writer saith of it) a man may very properly calle it rather *Orbis* then *Urbis forum*, that is, a market place of the world, not of the citie.[48]

For all the obviousness of his debt to Venetian celebratory topoi, Coryat's admiration is uneasy. The Elizabethan tourist is 'ravished' by a Babel-esque tumult of impressions: 'magnificence of architecture', 'frequencie of people' and confusion of tongues. What is here a hint of unease – perhaps of disorientation – becomes stronger in Coryat's account of visiting the Jewish ghetto (where an intemperate theological dispute with a Rabbi almost starts a riot) and the synagogue, where the Law of Moses is recited: 'not by a sober, distinct, and orderly reading, but by an exceeding loud yaling, undecent roaring, and as it were a beastly bellowing of it forth. And that after so confused and hudling manner that I thinke the hearers can very hardly understand' (p. 231). The 'ethnicke' theme is addressed again in Coryat's description of a curious frieze on the wall of the doge's palace, depicting four barbarous Albanian brothers (Turks), 'and each couple consulting privately together by themselves' (p. 188).[49] These, having arrived at Venice in 'a ship laden with great store of riches' (p. 188), conspire against and kill each other in order to monopolise the treasure: 'Whereupon the Signiory of Venice seised upon all their goods as their owne, which was the first treasure that ever Venice possessed, and the first occasion of inriching the estate' (p. 190). Coming shortly after the slightly hysterical account of the teeming activity in St Mark's Square, this verbal still-life bespeaks a need to affirm ultimate control over the exotics and barbarians upon whose wealth Venice relies. Perhaps like an earlier generation of Venetians for whom this origin-myth had been invented, Coryat wants to be assured that Venice is *not* a Babel; that the city (*urb*) will govern the world (*orb*) rather than being dissolved in it, that Venice will be able to profit from 'barbarous ethnickes' without compromising its integrity as a civilised and Christian state.

At once an empire and an outpost, Shakespeare's Venice has just this doubleness. It is thus that the themes of 'exorbitance' and 'intrusion' enter the Venetian plays. The antithesis between these Shakespearean themes corresponds closely to the contradiction within the Elizabethan idea of Venice. Self-consciously imperial and a 'market place of the world', Shakespeare's Venice invites barbarous intrusion through the sheer 'exorbitance' of its maritime trading empire.

In *The Merchant of Venice*, the contradiction is expressed in the opposition between Antonio and Shylock. Rather in the spirit of Spenser and Coryat, Shakespeare rejects Contarini's magical reconciliation for an implacable antagonism which can only be settled by the elimination of one of the contending parties. Antonio represents Venice in its ancient or 'Augustan' aspect: that of the Aristotelian city-state which – regardless of its imperial extent – remains a community bounded by the interlocking circles of kin, 'commonwealth', religion and 'kind'. Shylock embodies Venice in its 'cosmopolitan' or Babelesque aspect. His very existence in the city – on what are effectively his own commercial and legal terms ('the commodity that strangers have / With us in Venice', 3.3.27–8) – represents (to Antonio at least) a fatal compromise of 'the justice of the state'.

Shakespeare seems at pains to represent Antonio as an embodiment of the Venetian civic ideal. More than a mere merchant, he is a 'royal merchant' (4.1.28), a kind of merchant-prince whose trading empire embraces the whole of the Renaissance maritime world. Power and magnificence, however, are but the façade to an ethical integrity corresponding to that which Contarini finds in the Venetian citizen; a virtue which (he insists) protects the city better than city walls. Hence, perhaps, is Antonio described as 'one in whom / The ancient Roman honour more appears / Than any that draws breath in Italy' (3.2.292–4). And so is he imagined as an ancient Stoic for whom (as for Cicero's Scipio) the world is 'a stage' (1.1.78) for the tragi-comedy of human existence.

Antonio's *Romanitas* has two active forms of civic expression. In the first place, Antonio regards wealth as a means towards living virtuously, rather than an end in itself. Thus, he refuses to 'lend nor borrow / Upon advantage' (1.3.68–9), is conspicuously generous, and redeems 'worthy' debtors from the clutches of usury. In this respect he may be said to exemplify the free-handed, public-spirited, Ciceronian view of riches formulated in Bacon's *Of Riches*; or the generosity of Cato who converted an estate 'all into ready money, which he kept by him for any of his friends that should happen to want, to whom he would lend it without interest'.[50] Again he may exemplify the idealised merchant of certain Renaissance Venetian writers, who '... was required to be entirely disinterested, bound to his work not by a desire for profit but for the "convenience and advantage" of others, and ... not permitted to speculate ... nor ... make an illicit profit by asking more than a "just price"'.[51] If Antonio's idea of riches is Ciceronian, it is also Aristotelian in the sense of distinguishing firmly between 'natural' and 'unnatural' means of acquisition, or *oikonomia* and *chremastike* (by which term Aristotle meant not just usury, but also trade itself when pursued solely for individual profit, or for ends unrelated to the good of the community).[52] By the same token, Antonio's idea of wealth is Christian. Hence is he like the merchant of Matthew's parable who, seeing a pearl of great price, goes and sells all he has in order to buy it (thereby, in the terms of the parable, 'redeeming' spiritual value in exchange for material possessions). Whatever the allusive context, Antonio's brand of merchandising is an instrument of the wider good, serving the needs of 'friendship' and 'kindness'. Exchange, in his hands, approximates the economy of the 'gift' as described by Marcel Mauss.[53] It is 'a total social fact', an 'event which has a significance that is at once social and religious, magic and economic, utilitarian and sentimental, jural and moral'.[54] Above all, it stands in a reciprocal (redemptive) relation to the 'commonwealth', from the perspective of which it appears as a form of 'housekeeping', or (to use Aristotle's approving term) *oikonomia*.

The second 'active' expression of Antonio's civic virtue is closely related to the first. Antonio's detestation of usury expresses itself in an active persecution of Shylock. It is important to realise that more than mere race-hatred is involved here. Antonio's exclusion of Shylock, both as usurer and as Jew, is as much a 'total social fact' as his own idea of riches. It is strongly implied that unless Shylock is excluded from the circle of reciprocal and 'kindly' exchange that comprises Antonio's idealistic conception of the 'commonwealth', then the 'commonwealth' must lose all meaning as a 'natural' political entity, and degenerate into a kind of Babel. Antonio's position on usury and Jews is supported by the symbolism of the 'bond of flesh'. This benighted contract is both a parody and a negation of the reciprocal bondedness presupposed by the ideal Venetian body-politic. It is a parody to the extent that it echoes the 'flesh and blood' symbolism of other forms of kinship bonding in the play: bonds between parents and children, and bonds between husbands and wives. It is a negation to the extent that Venetian law (in the person of the impotent Duke) is shown as allowing the most barbaric of all forms of human 'incorporation' (that of cannibalism) over the civilised ideal notionally represented by the 'commonwealth' itself. The idea that extending 'commodity' to 'strangers' must somehow lead to the abomination of the bond of flesh, involves a revealing conflation. The use by Antonio and Shylock of terms such as 'commodity', 'charter' and 'your city's freedom', suggests the contemporary practice by which foreign nationals were granted limited trading privileges within the emporia of Europe (privileges such as the English themselves enjoyed in Antwerp under a deed with the suggestive name of 'The Intercourse').[55] The bond of flesh story has quite a different context in traditional folklore, and ultimately in an ancient Roman law on debt, which (according to the first-century legal historian, Aulus Gellius) stipulated that debtors were to be 'confined for sixty days', during which time they were to be produced before the Praetor on 'three successive market-days', and, 'on the third day ... capitally condemned or sent across the Tiber to be sold abroad'.[56] The lawmakers, moreover:

made this capital punishment horrible by a show of cruelty and fearful by unusual terrors ... For if there were several, to whom the debtor had been adjudged, the laws allowed them to cut the man ... in pieces, if they wished, and share his body. And indeed I will quote the very words of the law, less haply you should think that I shrink from their odium: '... Let them cut him up; if they have cut more or less, let them not be held accountable'. (p. 425)

The conflation of this barbaric and quasi-legendary statute on debt with a sophisticated contemporary device for facilitating foreign trade, powerfully suggests the Aristotelian bias of Shakespeare's own conception of the Renaissance trading city. That bias is underlined in the deeper symbolism of the two legal caveats by which Portia denies Shylock's claim on Antonio. The first caveat ('Shed thou no blood, nor cut thou less nor more / But a just pound of flesh', 4.1.322–3) symbolically denies the quasi-sacramental character of the flesh-bond as a rite of 'incorporation' or kinship. Without blood, Shylock's pound of flesh cannot partake of the symbolism of the 'blood-covenant', which, according to W. R. Smith, is a sacramental assertion of kinship for the reason that 'there can be no kinship except by blood and no bond except by kinship'.[57] Nor can it operate as 'flesh and blood' imagery operates elsewhere in the play, within a symbolic lexicon of kinship and marital incorporation.[58] The second of Portia's caveats is also powerfully Aristotelian:

It is enacted in the laws of Venice,
If it be proved against an alien
That by direct or indirect attempts
He seek the life of any citizen,
The party 'gainst which he doth contrive
Shall seize one half his goods; the other half
Comes to the privy coffer of the state,
And the offender's life lies in the mercy
Of the Duke only, 'gainst all other voice.

(4.1.345–53)

The effect of this is to assert the absolute distinction between 'alien' and 'citizen' which is blurred by the practice of granting 'commodity' to 'strangers'. Interestingly, the caveat reproduces the logic of the ancient Roman law on debt which is the source of Shylock's bond. Instead, however, of the *debtor* suffering death, dismemberment or 'alienation' (literally through being sold 'beyond the Tiber'), it is here the *creditor* (an intruding 'alien') who suffers a version of 'dismemberment' or death. Shylock's ducats – as intrinsic to his 'flesh and blood' as his daughter is – are here parcelled out to Antonio and the Venetian state. The way in which Portia belatedly redeems Venice from the apparently fatal contradiction between its Aristotelian and Babelesque tendencies can be seen to correspond to the subtextual juxtaposition in Coryat between the wholesale 'intercourse' of Christians and 'barbarous ethnickes' in St Mark's Square, and the uncompromising distinction between barbarians and Venetians implied in the frieze of the Albanian brothers on the walls of the doge's palace. Both Shakespeare and Coryat entertain the spectre of a promiscuously 'open' city, only to exorcise it by appealing to archaic mythologies of civic origin.

Where Shakespeare systematically represents Antonio as the ideal Venetian, he is no less systematic in representing Shylock as other. More than just a 'Jew', Shylock is a 'stranger', an 'alien' and an 'infidel'. His Jewish otherness has the pandemic quality that we have already noticed in *Othello*. In this connection, it is interesting to notice Shylock's mischievous facility with 'voices': his tendency to make debating points by slipping into registers which, while not quite his own, might easily be:

> What should I say to you? Should I not say,
> 'Hath a dog money? Is it possible
> A cur can lend three thousand ducats?' Or
> Shall I bend low, and in a bondman's key,
> With bated breath and whisp'ring humbleness,
> Say this: 'Fair sir, you spat on me on Wednesday last;
> You spurned me such a day; another time
> You called me dog; and for these courtesies
> I'll lend you thus much moneys'?

> (1.3.119–27)

In the trial scene, this tactic is not merely embarrassing but downright subversive:

> You have among you many a purchased slave
> Which, like your asses and your dogs and mules,
> You use in abject and in slavish parts
> Because you bought them. Shall I say to you,
> 'Let them be free, marry them to your heirs.

Why sweat they under burdens? Let their beds
Be made as soft as yours, and let their palates
Be seasoned with such viands.' You will answer,
'The slaves are ours.' So do I answer you.

                                                              (4.1.89–96)

Shylock's facility with 'voices' allows him to conjure up an entire under-class of 'slaves', 'bondmen' and metics who – in 'Roman' plays such as *Julius Caesar* and *Coriolanus* – are characteristically represented in the form of a hydra-headed rabble, the ultimate symbol of political 'con-fusion'. In this connection, it is also worth pointing out how often Shylock talks at cross-purposes to his Venetian interlocutors, and how uncouth he sounds to the Venetian ear. Thus Bassanio is outraged to hear that the sentence, 'Antonio is a good man', means only that Antonio 'is sufficient' (1.3.12, 17). And thus Solanio regales Salerio by rehearsing the 'passion so confused, / So strange, outrageous, and so variable / As the dog Jew did utter in the streets' (2.8.12–14).

Shylock's usury coincides with his barbarism. The bond of flesh inverts both the transcendental moral of Matthew's parable, and the 'natural' or 'kindly' function of riches advocated by Cicero and Aristotle. Shylock's claim that his bond is 'dearly bought' (4.1.99) inverts Portia's protestation to Bassanio ('Since you are dear bought, I will love you dear', 3.2.311) and – behind that – Elizabethan 'transcendentalisations' of the marriage bond (such as in the homily on adultery), themselves founded on the redemptive idiom of Matthew, and Paul's echo of it in the Epistle to the Corinthians.[59] In Aristotle's terms, the usurer shares the 'unnaturalness' of the barbarian. Just as the barbarian is excluded from the 'natural' body of the *Polis* and of the family, so is the usurer excluded from the 'economy' of the city – that *oikonomia* (literally 'household management') by which the city is imagined as replicating the structure of household and family on a larger scale.

In all these senses, the confrontation between Antonio and Shylock amounts to a struggle over the political and economic heart of Venice. Thus the forum of Antonio's many assaults on Shylock is always the market-place – 'Even there where merchants most do congregate' (1.3.47), Shakespeare's version of Coryat's *urbis forum* – where Venice is both most and least itself. Like Christ chasing the money-changers from the temple or Cato denying Roman citizenship to 'strangers', Antonio seeks to recover the sacred core of the city from the twin abominations of 'interest' and intrusion.[60] Significantly, there is no suggestion of Shylock's person or activities being *contained* in the ways that they must have been in Venice or any of the major emporia of Europe. Shylock does not, for example, live in a ghetto; nor is there any suggestion of his 'commodity' being strictly controlled – of his actually being required to practise usury and usury alone. The absence of either form of containing boundary (geographic or commercial) has the effect of making Shylock seem much more liminal, and thus more dangerous, transgressive and polluting, than he might otherwise have seemed. Again – as with the telescoping of the idea of 'commodity' into the archaic legend of the 'pound of flesh' – what is suggested here is less Shakespeare's ignorance of the existence of the Venetian ghetto or of the true nature of foreign trading privileges, than a need to totalise Shylock's otherness. What is also suggested is a specifically Elizabethan perspective on these comparatively enlightened continental civic institutions. While the English enjoyed certain trading rights within the city of Antwerp (under the terms of 'The Intercourse'), they refused to grant similar trading rights to foreign merchants in London. Technically, foreign merchants were simply forbidden to conduct business, in the way that Englishmen themselves were forbidden to charge 'interest' beyond a nominal rate of some 8–10 per cent. London was to be protected from the Babel-like 'openness' of Venice and Antwerp. Hence there were no ghettos and no 'commodity' with 'strangers' as such. At fairs, however, all such Aristotelian restraints on 'strangers', their 'commodity' and 'interest' were abandoned. Babel was given free rein. The difference between the English mechanism for granting 'commodity' to 'strangers' (the fair) and the Venetian mechanism (the ghetto) may account for the unsettling degree of liberty enjoyed by Shylock in Shakespeare's Venice.[61] With the equivocal xenophobia of the Elizabethan Londoner, Shakespeare imagines Venice as a glorified fair in which – apart from Antonio's high-minded harassment – the 'stranger' conducts business as he pleases ('for were he out of Venice I can make what merchandise I will', 3.1.118–19).

To see *The Merchant of Venice* in these terms is to see it as an attempt to recuperate the Elizabethan idea of Venice from its chief contradiction. The emphatic repudiation of the bond of flesh (a perverted rite of incorporation) and the conversion of Shylock (in the legal sense of 'converting ... to one's own use', as well as in the religious sense) signify the victory of Venice in its Aristotelian aspect over Venice in its Babelesque aspect. This, however, is to overlook Shakespeare's energetic subversion of his own ideological agenda. The entire stage history of *The Merchant of Venice* testifies to its ambiguity. As early as 1598, the play is described as 'a book of the Merchant of Venice, or otherwise called the Jew of Venice'.[62] Shylock not only upstages Antonio but blurs issues and distinctions to such a degree that Portia's questions: 'Which is the merchant here, and which the Jew?' (4.1.171) – remarkable questions indeed, considering Shylock's 'Jewish gaberdine' – mock their apparent innocence. Shylock's notional 'unkindness' (in both senses of that punning word) is, for example, seriously complicated by Shakespeare's decision to represent him as a householder, a family man and a man of impressive (if idiosyncratic) piety. Much is said by Jessica and Gobbo of Shylock's unkindness as a father and as a master, but 'kindness' in both capacities emerges in small but telling details. Thus, in the midst of what seems a stock-comic lament for the loss of his ducats and his daughter, Shylock surprises us by the dignity of his outrage at Jessica's exchange ('for a monkey') of the betrothal ring that he 'had ... of Leah when ... a bachelor' (3.1.111–13). In a play where rings function as master symbols of human bonding, the implication is clear. There is also a compelling suggestion of Shylock having compassion for the wretched Gobbo. Shylock refers to Gobbo as 'that fool of Hagar's offspring' (2.5.43), meaning Ishmael (the mixed-race son of Abraham who was banished in favour of his pure-blooded brother, Isaac) yet he also allows that 'the patch is kind enough' (45). The very idea of an Ishmael being 'kind enough' for the 'tribe'-conscious Shylock, says much for his deeper humanity. The significance of Shylock's being shown in the contexts of family and household is heightened by the fact that both these dimensions are missing in the portrait of Antonio. In the sources, the Antonio character has a clear kinship relationship to the Bassanio character. In Shakespeare, however, Antonio is effectively a 'friend' rather than a kinsman, in which capacity he actually poses a danger to kinship in the form of the fundamental 'bond' between Bassanio and Portia. From Portia's perspective, indeed, 'the merchant' and 'the Jew' do have something in common. In their different ways each poses a threat to her marriage with Bassanio and thus to the 'commonwealth' which it redeems and renews – hence, perhaps, the point of her questions: 'Which is the merchant here, and which the Jew?'

The blurring of the lines between Antonio and Shylock is related to Portia's emphatic usurpation of Antonio's role as defender of the 'commonwealth'. *Romanitas*, and all that it signifies here, is betokened by the very name of 'Portia', the first mention of whom is accompanied by a reference to 'Cato's daughter' (1.1.166). Portia not only usurps Antonio's role as defender of the 'commonwealth' but exposes the hollowness of his pretensions to disinterested giving. Antonio's loan may seem disinterested in the mercantile context of Shylock's usury, but not in the domestic context of Portia's donation of herself and her property to Bassanio:

> Myself and what is mine to you and yours
> Is now converted. But now I was the lord
> Of this fair mansion, master of my servants,
> Queen o'er myself; and even now, but now,

> This house, these servants, and this same myself
> Are yours, my lord's. I give them with this ring.

$$(3.2.166-71)$$

The splendid clarity of this formal 'donation' contrasts with the ambiguity of the moment in which Antonio agrees to finance Bassanio's voyage to Belmont:

> Thou know'st that all my fortunes are at sea,
> Neither have I money nor commodity
> To raise a present sum. Therefore go forth –
> Try what my credit can in Venice do.

$$(1.1.177-80)$$

What sounds like a qualified refusal turns into an agreement – with unwonted complications. The ambiguity deepens when we learn that Antonio is first prepared to borrow at interest and then to offer a pound of his own flesh as security. The obscurity of his motives in accepting so ominous a condition is suggestively illuminated by the symmetry of the exchange as a whole. As the apparent generosity of Antonio's loan to Bassanio is echoed by the apparent 'kindness' of Shylock's interest-free loan to Antonio, so too the real claim by Shylock on Antonio implies a correspondingly real (if undeclared) claim by Antonio on Bassanio. Where the ostensible purpose of the loan is to liberate Bassanio from 'the great debts . . . in money and in love' (1.1.128–31) which he owes Antonio, its effect is to bind him further to Antonio 'in love' if not exactly 'in money'. Thus Bassanio must continue to 'owe the most' (line 131) to Antonio in spite of being 'dearly bought' by Portia.

Compared with Portia's donation to Bassanio, Antonio's loan seems anything but disinterested, appearing to owe more to 'the protean character of trade' than to the strict economy of the 'gift' in Mauss's sense. According to Jean-Christophe Agnew, gift-exchange has the effect of clarifying 'the grounds and bounds of all exchange', whereas in money-exchange, such 'grounds and bounds' ('the boundaries of self and social grouping') are obscured. This is precisely the difference between Portia's donation and Antonio's loan. The former is a gift in the sense of clarifying identity and confirming mutuality. The latter is a form of trade in the sense of obscuring identity and confusing alliances ('the grounds and bounds of . . . exchange'). The gap between the two forms of alliance and exchange is unbridgeable, as may be seen in Bassanio's equivocal attempts to mediate between them. Bassanio begins by representing his voyage to Portia as a kind of trading venture, a way of repaying the debt 'in money and in love' which he owes Antonio. Accordingly, he imagines Belmont as 'Colchis' strand' (1.1.171), himself as Jason, and Portia as a kind of female *El Dorado* ('her sunny locks/ Hang on her temples like a golden fleece', 1.1.169). In the course of the casket ordeal, however, he abandons the mercantile perspective, recognising 'those crispèd, snaky, golden locks' as 'the dowry of a second head, / The skull that bred them in the sepulchre' (3.2.92, 95–6), and valuing his bond with Portia as a sacrament rather than as a commodity. After the trial, however, Bassanio yields to Antonio's advice to give his betrothal ring to the 'doctor' in exchange for favours granted. The marriage bond has again become commodified and relativised ('Let his deservings, and my love withal, / Be valued 'gainst your wife's commandèment', 4.1.447–8). While it is true, then, that Antonio uses his money for 'kindly' ends, it is also true that he uses it to commodify, dislocate and corrupt them.

On closer inspection, indeed, Antonio's Venice begins to look more and more like Shylock's. The polemical opposition between Christian *oikonomia* and Jewish *chremastike* is undercut by the fact that all the Venetian characters have recourse to a common commercial vocabulary. Ideologically 'loaded' and yet equivocal terms such as 'commodity', 'use', 'merchandise' and 'thrift' are used in relation to Christian and Jew alike, with the effect of further blurring the lines between them. Superficially, such terms are consistent with 'pure' as distinct from 'tainted' forms of commercial activity. In practice, however, it is rarely possible to be sure which form of activity is being referred to. Thus Antonio's use of 'commodity' ('neither have I money nor commodity / To raise a present sum') probably has the innocent meaning of 'goods'. But how can we be sure that it doesn't involve the more sinister forms of 'commodity' enjoyed by 'strangers' in Venice? Jean-Christophe Agnew remarks that, 'for the late-sixteenth-century reader, the word "commodity" still signified, above all, a profit or advantage' (p. 78). This is surely because the term was actively equivocal rather than merely ambiguous; as, for example, when used as code for a covert form of interest in which part of a loan would consist of worthless commodities, the *notional* money-value of which (effectively the interest) would be restored in cash on settlement of the loan. How can we be sure, then, that Antonio's use of the word 'commodity' is entirely untainted by the usage of 'young Master Rash' in *Measure for Measure*, who is jailed 'for a commodity of brown paper and old ginger ... of which he made five marks ready money' (4.3.4–7)?[63] The terms 'use' (shorthand for 'usury') and 'merchandise' are also employed to equivocal effect. Though the main thrust of *The Merchant of Venice* is to portray these practices as sharply antithetical (in line with mainstream contemporary opinion), there are hints of a deeper alliance.[64] Thus we find Shylock speaking of making 'what merchandise I will', and Antonio of holding Shylock's fortune 'in use' (4.1.380). 'Thrift' (or 'thrive') is also used equivocally. According to the *OED*, the noun was capable of comprehending anything from 'prosperity, success, good luck' (1679), to 'Savings, earnings, gains, profit', to 'frugality ... parsimony, niggardliness' (1553). Shakespeare appears to use it in either of two ways depending on the speaker. Thus, in Bassanio's mouth ('I have a mind presages me such thrift / That I should questionless be fortunate', 1.2.175–6), the word appears to have the sense of 'good luck'. In Shylock's mouth ('This was a way to thrive ... And thrift is blessing if men steal it not', 1.3.88–9), the word appears to have the sense of 'profit' (the context being a polemical justification of 'interest'). But is it this simple? 'Profit' is hardly irrelevant to Bassanio ('In Belmont is a lady richly left, / And she is fair', 1.1.161–2). Moreover, there is perhaps more than a hint of irony in that both usages of 'thrift' occur in the context of 'fleece' myths – the Jason myth and the Old Testament story of Laban's sheep – each of which signifies a legendary origin of 'profit' and 'advantage'. The latent homology between these two 'fleece' myths threatens to deconstruct the whole idea of Venice as a Christian *Polis*. The Jason myth is exemplary not just for Bassanio but for Graziano and Lorenzo (who also 'venture' for women and wealth). Antonio, too, is a Jason, his argosies laden with the 'fleece' of eastern 'spices' and Mexican gold.

The near-subversion of the laboriously constructed antitheses of *The Merchant of Venice* bespeaks a nagging suspicion that the contradictions which were supposed to be reconciled in the Renaissance idea of Venice (where 'the straungest impossibilities' were not 'altogether incredible') were indeed irreconcilable. The market-place of the world does not, apparently, fit into the ideological clothing of the Aristotelian *Polis*. The strict 'natural' proportions of the Aristotelian civic ideal are distorted by the 'unnatural' (ethnic and economic) openness of the Renaissance maritime city. At this level, *The Merchant of Venice* is not really about Venice as such. Venice is merely a stage-set for a cluster of more abstract, more universal and more culturally endemic contradictions. The contradictions of Shakespeare's Venice, for example, were potentially those of other Renaissance maritime capitals – such as Antwerp and London – which, in order to become world emporia, were obliged to open themselves dangerously to the world.[65] Again, the equivocal opposition of merchant and usurer reflects not so much Venice in particular as a fundamental contradiction in the Renaissance idea of economic exchange: between a contemporary version of Aristotle's *oikonomia* (eloquently set forth in Bacon's *Of Riches*) and a nascent capitalism which (like Bacon's *Of Usury*) haltingly acknowledged the fundamental importance of 'interest' to trade.

A third cultural contradiction reflected in the play relates to the Renaissance mythology of voyaging. This, as we have seen, ostentatiously departed from the ancient idea of voyaging by glorifying the voyager as a discoverer (Columbus, Drake) instead of abominating him as a transgressor (Jason, Tiphys). Yet, to the extent that voyaging was linked to trade, it was implicitly linked to the problematic ideological status of trade and to the subversive 'openness' of the maritime trading city. 'Implicitly' but hardly, it seems, explicitly or officially. The sheer power of the Renaissance myth of the voyager (and the prospect of wealth beyond the dreams of avarice) appears to have ensured the triumph of faith over doubt. This is exactly what makes the 'unofficial' and ambiguous celebration of voyaging in *The Merchant of Venice* so intriguing. The merchant adventurers of Shakespeare's Venice are at once triumphant and problematic. Shakespeare clearly has reservations about Antonio and the young Venetian 'Jasons' but is unable to express them fully. It is almost as if a Renaissance performance of the Jason myth is being haunted by the ghosts of the classical past (Seneca in particular) – as if by a repressed unconscious.

Repression and displacement certainly mark Shakespeare's handling of the Jason myth in *The Merchant of Venice*. Bassanio's initial identification with Jason and his vision of Portia as a female embodiment of the 'golden fleece' (1.1.170) suggests that she is to be identified with Medea. The suggestion is abandoned, of course, along with the 'golden mind' (2.7.20) that brought Bassanio to Belmont ('Colchis' strand', 1.1.171) in the first place. The Jason-function survives, however, in Graziano (the most crassly materialistic of the 'Christian husbands') as well as in Lorenzo (the most troubled). Thus, at Bassanio's moment of triumph in Belmont, Graziano boasts: 'We are the Jasons; we have won the fleece' (3.2.239). Lorenzo's identification with Jason is less explicit, but more profound and haunting. Intriguingly, the intimation of Medea which is repressed in the case of Portia, returns in the figure of Jessica. Unlike Portia, Jessica combines wealth and femaleness with the essential Medean attribute of otherness. Like Medea assisting Jason to the 'golden fleece', Jessica assists Lorenzo to her father's 'gold and jewels' (2.4.31). Like the chorus in both classical tragedies of Medea (and to some extent like Jason himself), Lorenzo betrays deep unease at the thought of marrying a 'stranger'. For all its material success, the marriage seems ominous. In profaning her father's betrothal ring, Jessica shows a barbarous disregard for marriage itself, and increasingly betrays an obscure sense of disillusion which culminates in the curious exchange of allusions to tragic love stories (including that of Medea) at the opening of the fifth act. Meanwhile, Gobbo (supposedly Jessica's friend) continually harps on the impropriety of miscegenation, and the damage which Lorenzo thereby does to 'the commonwealth' (3.5.32). While ostensibly, then, the function of the Medea myth here is to celebrate the merchant-adventuring ethic of Shakespeare's Venetians, its deeper purpose is to intimate anxieties which are all too clear in ancient versions of the myth: anxieties about trade, intermixture and miscegenation. Such intimations are at once a means of expression and yet of repression. Medean anxieties are expressed but displaced and unagonised. They are denied narrative and dramatic focus.

Yet Shakespeare is sufficiently aware of the unconscious – the disregarded ancient dimension – of the Jason myth to be haunted by it. In this, as in other aspects, the play intrigues us by actually producing the content which it represses. This contrasts with the bland revisionism of 'official' Renaissance performances of the Jason myth in the civic pageantry of London and Antwerp. In London, 'Jason and his Golden Fleece, a favourite everywhere, naturally becomes a particular emblem of the Drapers' (effectively a guild which served as a front for the Merchant Adventurers).[66] In the Drapers' pageants, the golden fleece appears to have been little more than a logo for the themes of money and trade. In Antwerp, the myth is used with similar unconcern in celebrations sponsored by the mint. The most famous of these will serve to illustrate what I mean by the 'official' or public construction of the myth. In 1635, Rubens designed a pageant arch on commission from the mint for the entry of the Cardinal-Infante Ferdinand into Antwerp. *The Pageant of the Mint* consisted of a mountain, 'intended as a half-naturalistic, half-emblematic image of the proverbial Mount Potosí, richest and most famous of the Spanish silver mines in the New World'.[67] Upon this were various South American images culled from illustrations in Theodore de Bry's *America*: a chinchilla, Indian miners and parrots. The parrots, however, were perched on a most un-American tree, 'that legendary dragon-guarded oak, native to the kingdom of Colchis, from which the hero Jason snatched the Golden Fleece with the aid of Medea's enchantments' (196). At the summit of the mount and to one side of the tree, stood Jason reaching for the fleece which hung from the branches. To the other side stood a female 'personification of *Felicitas*, or *Prospera Navigatio*', evidently a very different consort from Medea:

Like flying Fortune, Lady Felicity raises her cloak into a billowing sail, and she carries a model of a Spanish merchant carrack, for without her help in securing its ships a safe and happy passage, the priceless treasure of the Golden Fleece would never bring its benefits home. For the Golden Fleece is the golden Indian wealth that has been won for Spain. It had been a commonplace among humanist writers of the sixteenth century to liken the venturesome *conquistadores*, on the trail of Spanish gold, to the intrepid band of ancient Argonauts. Compared to Jason, those heroes Cortés and Pizarro can even be seen to advantage ... they have brought to Spain not one, but an annually repeated Golden Fleece of treasure. (196)

It is as if Seneca's *Medea* had never existed. Jason is simply uprooted from the Euripidean and Senecan narrative of geographic and marital transgression and replanted into a brand new narrative in which voyaging is nothing but happy and prosperous. Where the unofficial Shakespearean revision of the myth represses the Medea-function by displacing it from Portia to Jessica, this 'official' revision represses simply by editing Medea (and all the bad karma she represents) entirely out of the story. Without Medea, there can be no marital transgression. And without that, voyaging itself is untransgressive. *Prospera Navigatio* is the kind of girl one might introduce to one's parents. Not unlike Venice in the legend of the Albanian brothers, Antwerp collectively attempts to erase any anxiety attaching to its status as a maritime city, one that has perhaps been over-beholden to 'strangers' for the golden fleece of its prosperity. Shakespeare indulges the Venetian wish-dream of the golden fleece only to disturb it with intimations of the ancient nightmare.

4

The disturbing porosity of Antonio's Venice is also felt in *Othello*, revealingly in the first act, where Shakespeare is entirely unbeholden to the Italian *novella* which provided him with the narrative structure of the remaining acts. There is nothing in Cinthio corresponding to the elopement of Othello and Desdemona; to Brabanzio's complaint; to the 'trial' before the Duke and the 'signiors' of Venice; to the essentially comic structure; nor to Shakespeare's 'high romantic' tone. Where, then, does the inspiration come from? Why does the first act have the structure that it does? Leslie Fiedler reads it suggestively as a topsy-turvy continuation of *The Merchant of Venice* in which Portia elopes with Morocco, the thwarted fathers of Portia and Jessica merge into Brabanzio, and Graziano matures into Iago.[68] I want to argue that the later 'Venetian' play recapitulates the earlier because it also recapitulates the *ur*-narrative of 'intrusion' and 'exorbitance'.

It is instructive to read the first act of *Othello* in the light of the Tereus myth. In both narratives, a 'barbarian' marries into a ruling family as a direct result of becoming militarily indispensable to the state. There are two main differences. First, Othello is actually a Venetian general and not (like Tereus) the leader of a barbarian horde who happen to be allies. Second, Othello takes the girl against her father's wishes instead of accepting the girl at her father's hands. Neither difference obscures the deeper similarity. In the first place, while Othello's rank within the city may differentiate him from Tereus, he is essentially like Tereus in defending the city from invading barbarians ('the general enemy Ottoman') with whom he is symbolically allied. Here it is worth recalling the hints that Othello's rank might owe as much to contingency as to virtue. Had the Turkish threat not been so pressing and had 'Marcus Luccicos' not been mysteriously absent, Othello might never have been chosen as commander in chief.[69] In the second place, while Brabanzio's opposition is indeed a complicating factor, it is clearly suggested that the Duke (like Pandion) actively complies with a forbidden marriage out of an overriding sense of obligation to (and reliance on) the barbarous defender; thereby confirming the predictions of Iago ('the state ... Cannot with safety cast him, for ... Another of his fathom they have none / To lead their business', 1.1.149–55) and Othello ('My services which I have done the signory / Shall out-tongue his complaints', 1.2.18–19). The equivocation of the ducal ruling and the shiftiness of this particular duke have yet to be fully appreciated. The very setting of the 'trial scene' (in the context of an emergency war-council) powerfully suggests that 'the justice of the state' might be subordinated to military necessity. That suggestion is fully borne out in the extraordinary behaviour of the Duke, whose first reaction is to allow Brabanzio to act as judge and jury in his own complaint:

> Whoe'er he be that in this foul proceeding
> Hath thus beguiled your daughter of herself
> And you of her, the bloody book of law
> You shall yourself read in the bitter letter
> After your own sense, yea, though our proper son
> Stood in your action.

> (1.3.65–70)

How different is his reaction when the identity of the accused is revealed. Fulsome support turns to frosty reservation. Brabanzio is denied the luxury of reading 'the bloody book of law' in his 'own sense', charged with making wild accusations and required to furnish 'more overt test'. The Duke's next somersault is in relation to the 'overt test'. While both parties agree to accept Desdemona's testimony as the deciding factor, the Duke effectively decides the case before she enters in the strikingly implausible (and legally irrelevant) remark: 'I think this tale would win my daughter, too' (1.3.170). However 'liberal' this may sound to the modern ear, the suggestion is clearly that the case has been rigged in Othello's favour. The issue of allowing miscegenation at such a high political level – 'if such actions may have passage free, / Bondslaves and pagans shall our statesmen be' (1.2.99–100) – is simply ignored. The dubious credibility of the Duke in *Othello* matches the impotence of the

Duke in *The Merchant of Venice*. In each play 'the justice of the state' (in this very phrase) is compromised by the city's reliance on the alien. Both dukes are effectively obliged to countenance especially intimate forms of alien intrusion or incorporation (*mariages d'état*), for having already allowed versions of accommodation (*mariages de convenance*).

It is hardly necessary to suppose that either *The Merchant of Venice* or the Tereus myth is a 'source' of *Othello*, merely that all three articulate the essential dialectic of 'intrusion' and 'exorbitance'. Another (perhaps more plausible) context for the pattern is provided by Contarini. *Othello* might just as easily be read as deconstructing Contarini's claim that Venice was able miraculously to combine geographical openness (as the unwalled market-place of the world) with political chastity (as 'a pure and untouched virgine, free from the taste or violence of any forraine enforcement'). Shakespeare explodes the symbolic economy of Contarini's political metaphor by vividly suggesting the nested vulnerability of the geographical, political, domestic and bodily spheres. The moor's political and military penetration of the city is thus recapitulated at the level of Brabanzio's house, and thence at the level of Desdemona's body.

There are also hints of a yet more intimate, oneiric, penetration. Brabanzio invites Othello into his house in order to indulge a taste for the exotic and the 'extravagant'. He and his daughter court their own seduction through an 'errant' and voyeuristic wish-dreaming, a desire for the exotic as an embodiment of the repressed contents of mental domains (*terrae incognitae*) which they have previously refrained from 'discovering'. Thus Brabanzio actually dreams a version of his daughter's seduction ('This accident is not unlike my dream', 1.1.144) where the less suggestible Iago does not ('If ever I did dream of such a matter, abhor me', 1.1.6).[70] And thus Desdemona – she who was 'never bold, / Of spirit so still and quiet that her motion / Blushed at herself' (1.3.194–6) – is ravished by the dynamic spaciousness of Othello's 'traveller's history' (1.3.138), and by the imagery of monstrous orality which – 'with a greedy ear' (148) – she devours up. This might not be 'enchantment' in the literal sense, but it certainly is in a literary sense. Desdemona's and Brabanzio's taste for exotic narrative approximates what Hayden White has described as the construction of America as a fetishised object in sixteenth-century voyage accounts. According to White, the early European fascination with the Amerindian is inseparable from the fact that the standard description contained 'no less than five references to violations of taboos regarded as inviolable by Europeans of that age: nakedness, community of property, lawlessness, sexual promiscuity, and cannibalism'.[71] The 'fetishization' of such beings would thus suggest 'a projection of repressed desires onto the lives of the natives (as the references to the health and longevity of the natives suggest), but if it is such, it is a desire tainted by horror and viewed with disgust' (pp. 186, 187).[72] As Karen Newman suggests, Othello seems to excite a similar *frisson* of desire, horror and disgust in Desdemona.[73] But the mysterious root of the attraction is repressed and rationalised as a conventionally austere regard for virtue: 'I saw Othello's visage in his mind' (1.3.253). In Brabanzio, the dialectic of desire and disgust evolves in a different direction. Desire is converted into disgust, much as (according to White) the fetishised image of the Amerindian was doomed 'to fall apart into contending ideals in the years to follow: Wild Man and Noble Savage, respectively' (p. 187). The vehemence of Brabanzio's abhorrence for 'the sooty bosom / Of such a thing' (1.2.71–2) provokes the speculation that his original idea of Othello was that of the Noble Savage. Ironically, Othello also comes to regard himself with disgust rather than idealism. Hence Desdemona is condemned for no more and no less than the audacity of having desired him. The virginal image of Desdemona is exploded by another image of Desdemona as 'that cunning whore of Venice / That married with Othello' (4.2.93–4). The description is self-confirming. Desdemona is a whore *because* she married Othello. In much this way, Contarini's idealised image of Venice was self-subverting. The image of the 'pure and untouched virgine' was haunted by its opposite, the image of Venice as the whore of Babylon, the universal courtesan whose legs were perpetually open.[74]

5

To the extent of actually being set in 'a wonderland of discovery and romance, where monsters dwelt and miracles were common', *The Tempest* creates a more conventionally geographic impression of 'the exotic' than any of the foregoing plays. However, since the setting of *The Tempest* is – like its characters, plot and themes – notoriously elusive, the task of defining 'the exotic' in this play is less than straightforward. For all this, Prospero's island seems the obvious place to start.

Rather as in the 'Bermuda Pamphlets', the story of the island is set within a voyage narrative: framed by an initial moment of shipwreck and a final moment of deliverance. The importance Shakespeare attaches to this framing device – and to the idea of voyaging which it mediates – is suggested by the unique construction of the opening scene. The shipwreck is at once plausibly 'real' and an emblem of the contingency, boundedness and fragility of human order.[75] The writing, moreover, conveys dramatic immediacy and nautical understanding at levels unprecedented in Shakespeare, and – one suspects – in voyage literature too (the various accounts of the storm in the Bermuda pamphlets are woodenly rhetorical by comparison).[76] Both as immediate fact and as governing idea, voyaging establishes a commanding perspective on the island. Soon after the opening scene, we hear that the wrecked 'ship' represents the last of three ill-starred voyages to the island: each occasioned by varieties of hubris through which first Sycorax, then Prospero and now Alonso, are cast out from the world of men. The exorbitance of these and other castaways is mirrored in the 'terminal' geography of the island. A desert 'where man doth not inhabit', the island befits those ''mongst men ... most unfit to live' (3.3.57–8). Storm-infested (like 'the still-vexed Bermudas' 1.2.230), the island mirrors the disordered passions of the castaways in its own weather. To have ventured so far is not merely to have spanned a gulf of sea, distance and time, but in some way to have overstepped the limits of the properly human. The traditional debate about the island's exact geographic whereabouts is beside the point. Like More's 'Utopia' – or *Meta Incognita* ('Unknown bound', Martin Frobisher's name for Greenland) – the island is a seamless compound of geography and poetry. It is a Renaissance version of what Seneca the Elder called 'the bounds of things, the remotest shores of the world' (*rerum metas extremaque litora mundi*).

In the second scene, Prospero rehearses what a Renaissance geographer might have recognised as the island's 'natural and moral history'.[77] This unfolds in three poetic geographic 'moments' corresponding respectively to the 'voyages' of Sycorax, Prospero and Alonso; each moment (effectively, a generation) having its own identity and tropology. The original moment of the island's 'natural and moral history' is a species of dispersal myth, governed by the trope of 'confusion'. The second moment is a species of 'plantation' myth, governed by the trope of separation. The third is a species of 'renewal' or 'regeneration' myth, governed by the figure of *discordia concors* (and the emotion of 'wonder'). While I use the word 'myth' loosely to describe the narrative character of all three moments, each does in fact have a subtly distinct discursive character. The original moment (performed as a ritualised narrative of remote or first things) has a properly 'mythological' character. The 'colonial' moment has a more 'historical' (or dialogical or 'controversialised') character. The moment of 'renewal' has a prophetic or visionary character.

The ritual or mythic character of Sycorax's story emerges in the manner of its telling. The narrative is rehearsed by Prospero to Ariel in an urgent, quasi-liturgical monologue. Responses are invited, but as in a liturgy, their purpose seems only to confirm. No room is allowed for disagreement or even minor variations in detail. There is also a suggestion of ritual repetition. Prospero assures Ariel that he 'must / Once in a month recount what thou hast been, / Which thou forget'st' (1.2.263–65). Like origin myths generally, the purpose of this monthly performance is to create identity and confirm subjection. In what we might think of as a per-formance-within-a-performance (*The Reign of Sycorax*, perhaps), the island is remembered as entering narrative or 'history', and thereby becoming a geographical entity: a land (*geos*) capable of description (*graphos*). What it 'becomes' is a new version of Scythia, the eternal *eschatia*. The name 'Sycorax' is glossed by Stephen Orgel as 'an epithet for Medea, the Scythian raven', largely on the basis of the roots *Sy* ('Scythia') and *korax* ('raven').[78] *Corax*, however, resonates with Scythia in a more direct way. In John Speed's 1626 map of Europe, the Caucasus Mountains are labelled 'Ye Montaine Corax'.[79] Not only are these at the Colchian end of the Black Sea, but they are inscribed within the Medea myth by George Sandys in his edition of the *Metamorphoses*, when he explains the golden fleece as a poeticism for gold originating from mines in the Caucasus.[80]

Sycorax does not so much *find* 'a howling wilderness', as *make* one (literally). Thus she imprisons Ariel ('a spirit too delicate / To act her earthy and abhorred commands') within 'a cloven pine', where Ariel's groans 'Did make wolves howl' (1.2.274–5, 279, 290). The very existence of Ariel (a combination of 'airy' spirit and *genius loci*) on the island suggests an inherent capacity for nurture. While Ariel could hardly be said to possess a moral nature, he/she is clearly associated with a motif of 'temperance', which figures the island as 'temperate' in both a climatic sense and a moral sense.[81] In the first instance (as I have argued else-where), this motif derives from a topos of Virginian propaganda.[82] Ulti-mately, however, the motif of 'temperance' derives from the ancient moral-geographic discourse of *temperies* which explained the moral quali-ties of particular races by reference to the temperateness of their native climates.[83] The suggestion of the motif of 'temperance' in *The Tempest* is that, for all its remoteness and apparent inhospitability, the island is potentially 'temperate' and 'fruitful'. Under Sycorax, however, such potential (*meliora natura*) is stifled and perverted or 'confused'. Thus Sycorax tries to force an 'airy' spirit to perform 'earthy' commands. Thus, too, she adopts a New World 'devil' (another kind of *genius loci*) as a god.[84] The name 'Setebos' is more than just a random echo of the voyage narratives. By worshipping the god which Antonio Pigafetta describes as being worshipped by the Patagonian Indians of the storm-beaten wilder-ness of Tierra del Fuego, Sycorax is identified with the most remote, God-forsaken and degenerate of sixteenth-century Amerindian types.[85] The 'infamous promiscuity' of such worship is recapitulated at a sexual level. If Prospero is to be believed, Sycorax has had intercourse with 'the devil himself', resulting in Caliban, 'the son that she did litter here' (1.2.284). The word 'litter' suggests her complete abandonment of the maternal role. Caliban is born and reared 'in the bestial state', without nurture, culture or 'language'. While an entirely original piece of myth-making, *The Coming of Sycorax* is recognisably a species of dispersal myth. Like Ham, progenitor of the Canaanite, the Negro and other supposedly bestial and slavish races, Sycorax is an outcast from the world of men, a wanderer beyond bounds and an active promoter of the degeneracy of her 'vile race'. Renaissance geographers would have recognised a telling consonance between the ideas of dispersal, isolation, sorcery, matriarchy and degeneration.

While Sycorax reduces nature on the island to the state of wilderness and abomination, Prospero and Miranda attempt to reclaim it (both in the sense of improving it, and in the sense of taking possession of it). The second moment in the island's history is patently colonial: the island is nurtured, worked, territorialised, troped, 'translated', idealised and commodified. All these themes are present in Caliban's memory of his 'first encounter' with Prospero. Caliban's name (an anagram of 'cannibal') and his education permanently implicate him within the full colonial discourse of reclamation, demarcation and territory-formation. Prospero and Miranda are inveterate line-drawers, dichotomising between: good and bad, pure and impure, useful and useless, fertile and barren, cultivated and uncultivated, bestial and human, languaged and languageless. Having learned their 'language', Caliban has no choice but to dichotomise too. Even in the act of cursing the time he showed Prospero 'all the qualities o' th' isle', Caliban automatically distinguishes between 'fresh springs' and 'brine-pits', 'barren place and fertile' (1.2.340–41); which is to say between the useful or commodifiable and the useless or uncommodifiable. There is also a distinction here between different types of commodities. 'Brine-pits' might seem useless by comparison with 'fresh springs' but they were mined for salt in the New World and seem privileged by comparison with the unreclaimable nature associated with Sycorax: an 'unwholesome' fenland possessed by the creeping or hybrid abominations of Leviticus ('toads, beetles, bats', 1.2.340). The fact that the first-encounter phase of the colonial experience is bitterly remembered from a post-encounter perspective, discourages any temptation to idealise it. It is significant, too, that there are two narratives to contend with here and not just one. Unlike *The Coming of Sycorax*, the early relationship of Prospero and Caliban is a matter of dispute. Caliban sees his education as a pretext for dispossession. Prospero and Miranda regret the over-optimism of their early attempt to educate Caliban, as well as the incaution of lodging him in their 'own cell' (1.2.340). Neither party is entirely right or entirely wrong. Colonialism, it seems, is inherently controversial. But Caliban is right to see his education as a strategy of subjection and a step in the direction of his present 'abjection': his excommunication from the clean, the human and the natural. Like the Hebrews in Canaan, or like Conrad's Kurtz (with his 'society for the suppression of savage customs'), Prospero and Miranda identify the impure (in the form of what Julia Kristeva calls 'the abject' or outcast) as a way of defining the pure. As colonisers, they correspond to what Kristeva calls the 'deject' (one who defines himself by excluding another), a 'deviser of territories, languages, works'.[86]

The third moment in the 'natural and moral history' of the island is intimated rather than lived. Though renewal is experienced by various characters after the second scene – most notably by Ferdinand, in the fourth-act masque of Ceres – the idea is already present in Ariel's song and Ferdinand's 'wonder'. As in the masque of Ceres, discord becomes concord, opposites are harmonised and bereavement is translated into 'something rich and strange' (1.2.405).

Each of the three moments of the island outlined in the second scene – origin myth, colonial history and prophecy of renewal – recur throughout the play. Echoes of the dispersal/degeneration myth represented by *The Reign of Sycorax* can be detected in the curious reference to Alonso's daughter, Claribel, and in the apparition of 'several strange shapes' with a banquet. The function of the Claribel 'story' is obscure unless we understand it as a dispersal myth. Alonso has recently sailed from the African city of Tunis, having married his daughter – very much against her own inclination and the advice of his court – to 'an Ethiope'. The combination of geographical and moral 'extravagance' figures him as a voyager in the ancient mould: a confuser of categories like Seneca's Jason, or an impious overreacher like Paterculus's Crassus – recognising 'no limits' (*modum*) and accepting 'no bounds' (*terminum*). Appropriately, Alonso's exorbitance results in utter 'confusion'. Insofar as both his children are abandoned or castaway (in both a geographical and a moral sense), Alonso also recapitulates the example of Ham. Such contexts may help to explain the severity of Prospero's view of Ferdinand, and the brutality of his corrective regime:

> I'll manacle thy neck and feet together.
> Sea-water shalt thou drink; thy food shall be
> The fresh-brook mussels, withered roots, and husks
> Wherein the acorn cradled.

(1.2.465–8)

Though Ferdinand's re-education turns out to be rather more genteel in practice, the harsh primitivism of this symbolic diet identifies him as a version of unreclaimed 'natural' man; hence a symbolic relative of Caliban.[87] The connection is underlined by the symbolic identity of their corrective ordeals: Caliban entering '*with a burden of wood*' at the opening of Act 2 Scene 2, and Ferdinand entering '*bearing a log*' at the opening of the very next scene, Act 3 Scene 1. Both are treated as slaves, the generic occupation of the outcast and naturally degenerate.

The mythology of dispersal and degeneration is echoed again in the masque of 'shapes'. While the stage direction (*Enter several spirits, in strange shapes bringing in a table and a banquet, and dance about it with gentle actions of salutations, and inviting the King and his companions to eat, they depart*, 3.3.19–20) implies a scene of pure fantasy, it is significant that the shapes should 'depart' rather than vanish, and that the stage audience should take them as real rather than imaginary. Thus Sebastian thinks he sees 'a *living* drollery' (3.3.21, my italics), and Antonio and Gonzalo believe they have just been presented with living proof of travellers' tales. Realism is again underlined when Prospero – having just complimented Ariel on his performance as the harpy – compliments his 'meaner ministers' for having performed 'their several kinds' with 'good *life* and observation strange' (3.3.86–7, my italics). If, then, the performance seems real to the stage audience and realistic to the stage-manager, what is it supposed to be imitating? Gonzalo takes the 'shapes' for 'islanders':

> For certes these are people of the island,
> Who though they are of monstrous shape, yet note
> Their manners are more gentle-kind than of
> Our human generation you shall find
> Many, nay almost any.
>
> (3.3.30–34)

Beneath the compliment lurks a commonplace anthropological distinction based on the dispersal theory. The 'islanders' are 'people' but not 'of / Our human generation'; they are 'gentle-kind' but not humankind (hence, 'of monstrous shape'). They are 'people' in the sense of having descended from Adam, but they are not 'of our human generation' in the sense that their cultural and biological evolution has become side-tracked through geographic dispersal and isolation. If the logic seems biblical or Mandevillian ('earthly beings are more discrepant from one another, because they are in a remote place, and for that reason are more diverse'), it is also scientific by the most advanced sixteenth-century criteria. Thus, in a typical rationalisation of dispersal mythology, Francis Bacon explained the cultural backwardness of the Amerindians as a product of the 'oblivion' wrought in that part of the world by vast inundations. All Amerindians would, supposed Bacon, be descended from mountain-dwelling peoples, 'the remnants of generation ... [who] ... were, in such particular deluge, saved'.[88] The descendants would be correspondingly degenerate because 'the remnant of people which hap to be reserved are commonly ignorant and mountainous people, that can give no account of the time past, so that the oblivion is all one as if none had been left' (p. 228). In moral-geographic terms, mountains are like islands: both are isolated and correspondingly likely to produce oblivious 'generations' of *semi-hommes*. This may be why Gonzalo detects 'mountaineers' among his 'islanders':

> When we were boys,
> Who would believe that there were mountaineers
> Dewlapped like bulls, whose throats had hanging at 'em
> Wallets of flesh? Or that there were such men
> Whose heads stood in their breasts? Which now we find
> Each putter-out of five for one will bring us
> Good warrant of.
>
>   (3.3.43–9)

An educated man, Gonzalo sees what Renaissance 'anthropology' would have led him to see on a remote island: a selection from the traditional gallery of monstrous types – 'people' who are not just culturally or racially different from 'our human generation', but absolutely different: the products of what Bacon (following Pliny) called a 'pretergeneration', an errant or unnatural birth of a type commonly recorded in popular 'Mirabilaries'.[89] The simultaneously 'mythological' and yet 'scientific' character of Gonzalo's construction of the 'islanders' suggests much about Prospero's mythological construction of the island's prehistory. Specifically, it reinforces the point that Prospero's prehistorical myth (*The Reign of Sycorax*) is indeed a species of dispersal myth, and as such closely related to the speculations of Renaissance anthropologists and geographers concerning 'the natural and moral history' of remote and newly discovered regions of the world. By the same token, it provides us with a 'scientific' context for Caliban.

The second moment in the island's 'natural and moral history', that of 'discovery' and colonisation, is re-enacted at greater length. The 'discovery' phase of this moment, represented by the original encounter of Prospero and Caliban, is echoed in the encounter of Caliban with Trinculo and Stephano. Just as before, Caliban falls at the feet of a seemingly god-like European (Stephano) who confers the gift of 'language' upon him – though this time in a bottle of sack. The allusiveness of this discovery-episode makes it more explicitly colonial than the first. Thus, confronted by Caliban's prostrate body, Trinculo is not reminded of Mandevillian monsters so much as of 'a dead Indian' (2.2.33). While Trinculo is at a loss how to identify Caliban – who, like Antony's crocodile, conspicuously frustrates the categorising rhetoric of 'comparison and analogy' – he is full of ideas for making money out of him. Virtually all the jokes of his first speech ('What have we here, a man or a fish?', 2.2.24ff.) are about turning Caliban into a sideshow exhibit. Cashing in on Caliban is also Stephano's first reaction: 'If I can recover him and keep him tame and get to Naples with him, he's a present for any emperor that ever trod on neat's leather' (2.2.68–70). Most other jokes at Caliban's expense also turn on the idea of commodification. In the last of his 'first encounters' with Europeans, Caliban is identified by Antonio as 'a plain fish, and no doubt marketable' (5.1.269). Another phase of the colonial moment is echoed in the progress of Trinculo, Stephano and Caliban. The comic insurrection plot is a replay of Caliban's original insurrection. Just as before, the goals are sovereignty of the island, sexual possession of Miranda and the begetting of a dynasty.

The third moment, that of renewal, is also developed at some length. Though renewal is experienced by most characters – even Caliban in the course of his encounter with Stephano (''Ban, 'Ban, Cacaliban / Has a new master – Get a new man!' 2.2.183–4) – it is epitomised by Ferdinand and some members of the courtier group. This is because, in order to be renewed, a character must be capable of recognising past errors and enduring whatever penitential ordeal Prospero thinks fit to impose. For Ferdinand, this means undergoing a ritual of humility and restraining his sexual feelings for Miranda. His reward is the betrothal masque of the fourth act, a prophetic vision of harmony in which spring is reconciled with summer, earth with air, air with water, and temperance ('temperate nymphs', 4.1.132) with sexual appetite ('sunburned sicklemen', 4.1.134).[90]

The tripartite structure of the 'natural and moral history' of Prospero's island has an obvious resonance with the discourse of the New World in general and that of Virginia in particular. Within a year or so of the play's first performance, a pamphlet entitled *The New Life of Virginea* was published. In the dedication, the author, Robert Johnson, explains his intention of dividing the story of Virginia into three parts: 'The first is nothing else but a briefe relating of things alreadie done and past: The second, of the present estate of the businesse: And the third doth tend as a premonition to the planters and adventurers for the time to come'.[91] Though primarily a short history of the colony's progress up to the time of writing (1612), the first part includes an account of the pre-colonial settlement of the country, which Johnson sees as originating in the dispersal of Babel. The presumption of 'the race and progenie of *Noah*' in building the infamous tower:

> ... so highly provoked the Maiestie of God, that ... he subverted their devices and proud attempt, infatuating their understanding by confounding their tongues, and leaving each one to his severall waies, to follow the pronesse and follie of his owne heart, so that from this scattering and casting them out like unprofitable seed upon the dust of the earth, did spring up (as weeds in solitarie places) such a barbarous and unfruitfull race of mankinde, that even to this day (as is very probable) many huge and spatious Countries and corners of the world unknowne, doe still swarme and abound with the innumerable languages of this dispersed crue, with their inhumane behaviour and brutish conditions. (pp. B-B1)

'The sundrie nations of *America*: which as they consist of infinite confused tongues and people' represent a conspicuous case in point; as does the aboriginal region corresponding to Virginia, where God 'did never vouchsafe the hand of the weeder, to clense and give redresse to so desolate and outgrowne wildernesse of humaine nature' (pp. B1–B2). Having thus accounted for the physical existence and the moral condition of the natives, Johnson procedes to describe the discovery and naming of Virginia and the ultimate goal of the colonial enterprise: 'to replant this unnatural vine to make it fruitfull' (p. B3). The initial attempt at settlement, however, does not effectively alter Virginia's moral status:

> the common sort (of colonists) ... grew factious and disordered out of measure ... in which distemper that envious man stept in, sowing plentifull tares in the hearts of all, which grew to such speedie confusion, that in a few moneths Ambition, sloth and idlenes had devoured the fruits of former labours, planting and sowing were cleane given over ... and so that Virgine voyage ... which went out smiling on her lovers with pleasant lookes, after her wearie travailes, did thus returne with a rent and disfigured face. (pp. C-C1)

The early 'plantation' is thus represented as having reverted to the wilderness which it is supposed to be reclaiming. Mutiny is described in the language of the aboriginal dispersal myth. Suggestively, in view of the rebelliousness of the younger male generation (Ferdinand and Caliban) in *The Tempest*, a clear sense of a generation gap emerges between the mutineers and the colonial government. Thus Johnson blames 'those wicked Impes ... or those ungratious sons that dailie vexed their fathers hearts at home, and were therefore thrust upon the voyage', for fomenting rebellion and then returning 'with false reports of their miserable and perilous life in *Virginea*' (p. C2). The first phase of Johnson's narrative ends with the arrival of Sir Thomas Dale and Sir Thomas Gates at the colony, and with the restoration of order and the establishment of a 'temperance' among the colonists, befitting the 'temperateness' of the climate. As 'their first and chiefest care was shewed in setling Lawes divine and morall', Dale and Gates finally succeed in bringing 'the hand of the weeder' to Virginia (pp. D, B2).

The second part of Johnson's narrative – a brief account of the present state of the colony and the commodities of the country – effectively serves as a prologue to 'the third and last division' of his discourse: that concerning 'The New Life of Virginea' (p. D4). The project of renewal is divided into a three-fold labour: 'upon yourselves, upon your English, and upon the poore Indians' (p. E2). In the spirit (and to some extent in the hierarchising idiom) of Prospero, Johnson insists that government is impossible without austere self-discipline. Thus: 'you shall lay the foundation in your owne steps ... When thus your light shall guide their feete, sweete will that harmonie be betweene the head and members of the bodie, then may sleepe the rigour of your lawes' (pp. E2, E3). With self-discipline established, colonial government (the second labour) becomes not only possible but easy. Martial law (Dale's 'Lawes divine and moral') may be dispensed with, and the colonists can be allowed to 'live as free English men, under the government of iust and equall lawes, and not as slaves' (p. E3). The third labour of renewal concerns 'the poore Indians' (p. E4). These 'however they may seeme unto you so intollerable wicked and rooted in mischiefe' are to be considered as 'no worse then the nature of Gentiles' and thus redeemable in principle (p. E4). The strategy which Johnson suggests bears an extraordinary resemblance to Prospero's initial treatment of Caliban:

Take their children and traine them up with gentlenesse, teach them our English tongue, and the principles of religion ... make them equal with your English in case of protection wealth and habitation ... Instead of Iron and steele you must have patience and humanitie to manage their crooked nature to your forme of civilitie: for as our proverb is, Looke how you winne them, so you must weare them. (p. F)

While not corresponding in all respects, the symbolic structure of *The New Life of Virginea* has an obvious homology with the discourse of Prospero's island. This in turn would suggest that Shakespeare's play is vitally rather than casually implicated in the discourses of America and the Virginia colony. Though appearing some year or so after the play was written, Johnson's pamphlet is fully representative of the pamphlet literature sponsored by the Virginia Company of London in previous years, notably the 'Bermuda Pamphlets' which are universally accepted as Shakespearean sources. The notion that the Amerindians had evolved from the biblical dispersals is vigorously asserted by William Strachey (author of the most important of the 'Bermuda Pamphlets') on the authority of earlier geographical classics, such as Boemus's *Fardle of Façions* and Acosta's *Natural & Moral History of the Indies* (translated in

1604 by Edward Grimstone).[92] A pictorial version of the master metaphor of 'planting' adorns the frontispiece of *A True Declaration of the Estate of the Colonie in Virginia* (London, 1610), where two bearded patriarchs in flowing biblical robes plant saplings on stony ground.[93] Johnson's providentialist account of the difficult early years of the colony is also entirely typical, reflecting the tone of the 'Bermuda Pamphlets' and of earlier material such as an influential group of sermons published by the Virginia Company in 1609.[94] Typical, again, of Company policy in these years is Johnson's relatively benign attitude towards the Indians, who are to be tolerated, converted, educated and assimilated rather than conquered and enslaved.

On this point, however, there is a striking difference between the policy of the Virginia Company and the colonial politics of the play. Shakespeare represents the civilising task as having comprehensively failed well before the moment of the play. Prospero and Miranda have already given up on Caliban, and – regardless of any doubts as to the justice of their native policy – their denigration of Caliban is generally endorsed in the text as a whole (the 1623 description of Caliban as a 'salvage and deformed slave' strongly suggests that this is how he was played on the Jacobean stage). In a recent review of the debate over the importance of New World and colonial contexts to the play, Meredith Anne Skura uses the discrepancy between the relatively kind view of the Indian in contemporary Virginia Company documents and the harsher view of the native which is often (as here) attributed to Shakespeare, to argue that the relevance of the New World material has been overstated.[95] I cannot agree. Instead, it seems to me that the discrepancy makes *The Tempest* even more intriguing as an early American and colonial document. We need merely to assume that Shakespeare wished to confront or take issue with the contemporary Virginian ideology rather than reflect it. Assuming this to be the case – and the assumption is modest in view of the characteristic freedom with which Shakespeare treats his sources – what are we to make of Shakespeare's position in relation to the other in *The Tempest*?

In the sense that Shakespeare's construction of Caliban as an 'abject' anticipates the sudden reversal of the Company's Indian policy from 1622 (when a massacre of colonists triggered a systematic denigration, exclusion and finally annihilation of the natives), the harsh anti-primitivism of Shakespeare's view may be judged 'prophetic', or what an earlier generation of critics has thought of as shrewdly 'realistic'. In the sense that his construction of Caliban as naturally inferior and therefore slavish echoes Aristotle's doctrine of natural servitude, Shakespeare's view might seem reactionary by comparison with his own previous dramatisations of otherness – with the single possible exception of *Titus Andronicus*. The word 'reactionary', of course, is anachronistic in this context. Yet it remains true that (however sympathetic) the 'salvage and deformed' Caliban represents a reversal of what is virtually a career-long tendency in Shakespeare's construction of the other: one in which profound ethnic difference is always offset by a corresponding dignity of character. In Shylock and Othello especially, Shakespeare's ability to see through cultural stereotypes is – like Desdemona's ability to see Othello's visage 'in his mind' – truly radical. In Caliban, however, Shakespeare is actually *less* willing than his contemporaries were to dispense with the more egregious Amerindian stereotypes. As this cannot have been due to conceptual or imaginative limitations, the explanation can only be political. Shakespeare *chose* to represent the Amerindian as monstrous and to ignore more favourable character models, such as that promoted by the Virginia Company in which the Indians were likened to the 'gentiles' converted by St Paul.

Is 'reactionary' the right word for the colonial politics of *The Tempest*? It may help if both Shakespeare and the Virginia Company are seen in a longer perspective. In 1550, some half a century after what has been called the 'first widespread meeting of the races in modern times', the human status of the American Indian was formally debated at the Spanish imperial capital of Valladolid.[96] The principals were Juan Ginés de Sepúlveda, who had recently completed a monumental translation of Aristotle's *Politics*, and Bartolomé de Las Casas, who had returned to Spain after spending fifty years as a missionary in the New World.[97] Sepúlveda argued that the standard Spanish practice of enslaving Indians was justified by the doctrine of 'natural servitude'. In reply, Las Casas argued that slavery was unjustified because, in his own extensive experience, the Indians were no less human than Europeans. On the surface, the argument appears to be a classic contest between what Bacon called 'the library' (or the accumulated lore of traditional learning) and 'the road' (the experiential and experimental method which he saw exemplified in Columbus).[98] In fact, however, it was not so straightforward. Las Casas never disputed the *terms* of the Aristotelian doctrine, nor its relevance to this most un-Athenian form of slavery. Thus he conceded the fundamental validity of barbarism as a natural and political category, and confined himself to arguing that the Indians were not barbarous in Aristotle's sense because they had a demonstrated capacity for culture, language, reason and piety. Two more features of Las Casas's strategy are of interest. In conceding Aristotle's authority, Las Casas overlooked a glaring logical contradiction. Though stating that 'it is nature's purpose to make the bodies of free men differ from those of slaves, the latter strong enough to be used for necessary tasks, the former erect and useless for that kind of work, but well suited for the life of a citizen of the state' (*Politics*, 1254b16), Aristotle also admits that the difference is effectively theoretical. Thus, some people 'have the right kind of bodily physique for free men, not the soul', while others 'have the right soul but not the body'. Moreover, 'it is much more difficult to see beauty of soul than it is to see beauty of body' (*Politics*, 1254b32). The inescapable logic of these admissions is that it is impossible to tell who is naturally fitted for slavery and who for mastery. Failing to attack the doctrine of natural servitude at its core, Las Casas was obliged to represent the Indians as an exception to the rule.[99] A second noteworthy aspect of this strategy is that, having conceded Aristotle's authority in respect of the Indians, Las Casas not only recognised the legitimacy of slavery, but vastly increased the likelihood that a more eligibly barbarous race would be found to supply the place of the Indians in the slave economy. The paradoxical result of Las Casas's humanitarian efforts on behalf of the Indian is that the modern 'West Indian' is black.[100]

The debate at Valladolid is essential to a historical understanding of the 'native question' in both Shakespeare and the Virginia Company. The Indian policy of the Virginia Company was itself an indirect result of Las Casas's agitation. In the early 1540s, Las Casas had exposed the cruelty of Spanish treatment of the Indians in a treatise which was probably intended for official use only. In 1522, following the debate at Valladolid, this was printed as the *Brevissima relación de la destrución de las Indias*, and thence disseminated throughout protestant Europe in a variety of translations, including French (1579) and English (1583). In this way, a 'black legend' of Spanish atrocities in the New World spread throughout protestant Europe.[101] One outcome was that any prospective colonising effort by a protestant power in the New World was obliged to distinguish its own treatment of the Indians from that of the Spaniards. Thus it was that the English emphasised the peacefulness of their relations with the Indians and the legitimacy of claiming land in exchange for the higher gifts of language, civilisation and religion. The Spanish claims, by contrast, were represented as illegitimate and deriving from conquest alone. A fanciful way of putting it was to portray the English as foster-parents and the Spanish as lustful rapists.[102] Under English rule, 'Virginia' would retain her maidenhood intact, until embraced by godly settlers in lawful marriage. For all this, however, an undercurrent of impatience with the Indians can be detected in even the rosiest statements of the Company's evangelising mission. William Crashaw, for example, explains that the English policy is motivated more by generosity than moral duty. Strictly speaking, the English would be justified in simply expelling the Indians as the Hebrews had expelled the Canaanites from the promised land. So persistent was the Canaan theme that the complete reversal of the Indian policy after the massacre of 1622 could be represented as a simple change of emphasis. In his *Virginia's Verger* of 1623, Samuel Purchas had merely to bring Leviticus from the margins of Virginian discourse to the centre, and press the parallel between Indian and Canaanite:

Temperance and Justice had before kissed each other, and seemed to blesse the cohabitations of English and Indians in Virginia. But when Virginia was violently ravished by her owne ruder Natives, yea her virgin cheekes dyed with the bloud of three Colonies ... by so manifold losses adding to the price of Virginias purchase: Temperance could not temper her selfe, yea the stupid Earth seemes distempered with such bloudy potions and cries that she is ready to spue out her Inhabitants.[103]

The last line of this passage echoes Leviticus 18.25, 'And the land is defiled: therefore I do visit the iniquity thereof upon it, and the land vomiteth out her inhabitants'. The point I want to make is that the Company's debt to Las Casas had always been more apparent than real: owing more to protestant polemic than to the ethical imagination.

This being so, it scarcely makes sense to judge Shakespeare's colonial politics as 'reactionary' by contrast with those of the Virginia Company. It is true that Shakespeare is of Sepúlveda's party in representing Caliban as a 'salvage and deformed slave'. By insisting on deformity, moreover, he actually goes beyond Aristotle in making the difference between the naturally slavish and the naturally masterful appear self-evident. But if this is 'reactionary', it is also interestingly subversive. By implying the impossibility of any type of exchange between Prospero and Caliban, Shakespeare subtly undermines Prospero's title to the island. One reason Caliban so infuriates Prospero is that he is constantly able to expose the embarrassing truth that there is no social basis for their relationship; that Prospero's rule has no authority beyond force. Slavery is no relationship at all when the slave refuses to acknowledge the master's authority. Without 'rough magic' and his 'books', Prospero is (as Caliban puts it) 'but a sot as I am' (3.2.94).

Shakespeare's version of the renewal topos reveals a similarly interesting blend of reaction and subversion. In associating renewal primarily with Europeans – particularly Ferdinand and Miranda – Shakespeare effectively distances it from the 'native' theme in a way which (again) anticipates the hardening of English attitudes towards the Indians after the massacre of 1622. In *Virginias Verger*, Samuel Purchas would envision Virginia as a kind of walled garden from which the Indians – like so many weeds – were to be eradicated. Likewise, there is no place for Caliban in the symbolic vision of the earthly paradise represented in the masque of Ceres (which is perhaps why, when Caliban gatecrashes, the dream of

renewal fades along with 'the baseless fabric of this vision', 4.1.151).[104]
Nor is there a place for Caliban in what is perhaps the most luminous
statement of the 'renewal' theme in the play, when Miranda beholds
Europeans as if for the first time:

> O wonder!
> How many goodly creatures are there here!
> How beauteous mankind is! O brave new world
> That has such people in't!

(5.1.184–7)

One of several intriguing ironies about this moment is how it echoes the
first encounter topos (the wondering encounter of European and the
other in the New World) without actually *being* one (for the reason that
the other is absent). Erased from the scene, however, the other remains in
spirit or perhaps in voice. In *Decades of the Newe Worlde or West India*
(London, 1555), Peter Martyr relates how a 'reverende owlde governour'
of the Indians was so wonderstruck by his encounter with Columbus that
he volunteered to accompany him to Europe. His family, however, dis-
suade him, whereupon: 'not ceasing to woonder, and of heavy countenance bycause he myght not departe, he demaunded oftentymes if that
lande were not heaven, which browght foorth suche a kynde of men'.[105]
The haunting consonance between Miranda's words ('O brave new world,
/ That has such people in't') and the old Indian's ('he demaunded
oftentymes if that lande were not heaven, which browght foorth suche a
kynde of men') underlines the strategic dislocation involved. By giving the
other's lines to his European princess, Shakespeare is able to invest them
with a sublimity and pathos entirely lacking in some of his own (generally
farcical) versions of the first encounter topos; such as when Caliban meets
the same group of Europeans a few minutes later: 'O Setebos, these be
brave spirits indeed' (5.1.261). But irony is present nonetheless. Quite
aside from Prospero's comment (' 'Tis new to thee', 5.1.187), the very
presence of the word 'brave' in the moment of Miranda's wonder impli-
cates it in the earthier ironies of the moment in which the 'brave monster'
encounters his 'brave god', Stephano. In detaching the renewal topos
from the native theme, then, Shakespeare privileges it, but hardly in the
uncritical way of colonial apologists such as Samuel Purchas. In celebrating (to an extent, inventing) its beauty, he also exposes the dream-
structure of the American colonial myth: its origins in the psychology of
narcissism and utopian wish-dreaming.[106] It is almost as if Shakespeare
catches himself in the act of inventing the American myth in its modern
form. On the one hand, Miranda's wonder is both homogenised (purified
of its Indian underpinnings) and 'sublimed' into a romantic discovery
myth, a Keatsian mantra:

Then felt I like some watcher of the skies
When a new planet swims into his ken;
Or like stout Cortez when with eagle eyes
He stared at the Pacific – and all his men
Look'd at each other with a wild surmise –
Silent, upon a peak in Darien.[107]

On the other hand, the structure of the repression is disclosed in the latent homology between Miranda (sublime wonder) and Caliban (absurd wonder). Miranda's name, of course, means 'wonder'. But wonder is also Caliban's element: an ignorant savage, he is a congenital wonderer (in Vico's terms, 'the child of ignorance') and a marvellous monster (*thoma*). Oddly, the difference between the sublime and the absurd is one of emphasis. Miranda and Caliban are brother and sister, children of ignorance.

5   The frame of the new geography

Yet have they seen the maps, and bought 'em too,
And understand 'em, as most chapmen do.

(Ben Jonson, The New Cry)

Thus far, Shakespeare's geographic imagination has been rotated through a broad spectrum of poetic geographic traditions and performances: his own 'exotic' dramas; the Renaissance ethnographic tradition; the ancient poetic geographic tradition; the geographic imaginations of fellow poets and dramatists; the geographic symbolism of Elizabethan theatres; and the theatrical symbolism of the Renaissance atlas. One large question, however, remains: is Shakespeare's geographic imagination fully of a piece with the new geography or not? By now, I hope, it should be clear that this is less a question about Shakespeare than about the so-called 'new geography'. Typically, this term denotes not just the geography of the Renaissance but an essentially *scientific* geography as opposed to a primitive 'topography of myth and dogma'.[1] Here I want to suggest that the whole idea of a 'new geography' (as a species of Baconian 'instauration') is inadequate to describe the geographic culture of the sixteenth and early seventeenth centuries, to the extent that it back-projects the scientific bias of the modern geographic historians who invented it. In what follows, I propose to describe that phenomenon in cultural rather than 'scientific' terms, through a 'thick description' of its most characteristic cultural product: the world map. This will involve a profile of the whole semiotic activity of these maps: their geography, cartography, textual legends, and the iconography of their ornamental frames. My purpose, then, is to dispel the pseudo-Baconian aura surrounding these maps, by disclosing their conscious mythological agenda which (as I have already suggested in Chapter 3) was at least as open to the ancient poetic geographic values as to the 'new', regardless of the deep paradoxes which this inevitably entailed.

1

Just beneath the highest scientific and scholarly expression of the new geography in the work of geographers such as Mercator and Hakluyt, one finds a popular discourse which – while vitally affected by such work – was all too liable to subordinate achievement to prestige. Ironically, it is for the very reason that the groundwork of the new geography was laid by 'real' geographers such as Mercator and Hakluyt, that it should not be pictured as evolving steadily upwards towards ever higher scientific and scholarly levels. Hakluyt's reputation ensured that his voluminous collection of voyage manuscripts would be reissued under the title *Hakluytus Posthumus*, but it could not ensure an editor with the meticulous scholarship of Hakluyt himself. In the hands of Samuel Purchas, the rigorously established canon of English voyages became *Purchas His Pilgrimes*, the sprawling Gothic romance which would eventually inspire Coleridge's *Kubla Khan*. The difference in editorial rigour is illustrated by Purchas's reinstatement of Mandeville to the *corpus*. (Hakluyt had excluded Mandeville from the second edition of the *Principal Navigations* in 1598.) Purchas seems to have conceived of the history of voyaging not so much as a 'battle of the books' between fact and fantasy, but as a seamless compound of the two; a palimpsest to be endlessly elaborated and scribbled over. His conception of the editor's task extended to the insertion of vapid remarks in the margins of voyage accounts which were already refreshingly to the point. Coleridge would find Purchas's running commentaries 'poetic' and immortalise them in the margins of his own *Rime of the Ancient Mariner*.

In the Netherlands, the cartographic example of Mercator was succeeded by the less scrupulous (and, in general, less scientifically educated) industry of map-makers like Jodocus Hondius, the Visscher family and Willem Blaeu. It is a commonplace that the geographic and cartographic sophistication of Mercator's great sixteenth-century maps was never systematically built upon during the entire seventeenth-century ascendancy of the Dutch cartographic industry. Even Willem Blaeu – a map-maker who was 'keenly interested in science and did not forget his earlier training under Tycho Brahe'; and who in 1633 was appointed head of the department of hydrography in the Dutch East India Company – made little effort to improve the general level of the Dutch geographic and cartographic culture which he did so much to mould. A cartographic historian remarks that 'many of his maps ... are far from scientific achievements ... none of his charts is laid down on a Mercator projection, though other chart makers had been using it for years. The majority of his maps are drawn without parallels or meridians; a few have parallels, but usually there are no meridians'.[2] The answer, according to the same historian, is that:

he probably made two kinds of maps and charts: one for the carriage trade, pretty things with bright colors and gold leaf to please the eye and decorate the home; and one for seamen and officialdom who knew and demanded the best in scientific documents. Blaeu was not stupid or uninformed; he was a shrewd business man who gave his customers what they wanted. His working maps and charts were worn out or were destroyed as a safety measure, while his beautiful maps and atlases, because they were usually locked up in a gentleman's library ... have survived. (pp. 171–2)

Brown's thesis about Blaeu is in keeping with a generic distinction commonly remarked in the cartography of earlier periods: between maps emphasising accuracy and functionalism, and maps emphasising ornament and style. The former tend to be for private, the latter for public consumption. Thus, the map which the doge actually used to plot a Venetian trade route or plan a defence against the Turk, would not be the monumental map which adorned the outer wall of the Venetian council chamber.[3] The very latest cartographic information was often too valuable to be published. The same generic distinction is made between the monumental character of Agrippa's map of the *orbis terrarum* and the functional character of Roman road maps, sailors' charts (*periplii*), and the maps of the *agrimensores* (or surveyors). The distinction also applies for medieval cartography: between the monumental *mappemonde* (the chief surviving examples of which appear to have been used as altarpieces) and the functional 'Portolan chart' or maritime map.

What such a distinction suggests of the general culture of map production and consumption over much of the seventeenth century, is that it was far from the scientific ferment it is supposed to have been. Indeed, from the latter half of the sixteenth century until the eclipse of the Dutch industry by the French towards the close of the seventeenth century, it would scarcely be an exaggeration to claim that the new geography was 'new' in name only. Mercator's maps were copied, and the copies copied, for the best part of a hundred years. A genuinely 'new map' was actually a curiosity. When, in 1599, Edward Wright's *Hydrographiae Descriptio* pointedly omitted the entire fictitious southern continent of 'Magellanica' – a popular staple since Mercator's great world map of thirty years earlier – the 'advance' simply failed to register with the general cartographic culture.[4] 'Magellanica' continued to be depicted on world maps until (and even beyond) the middle of the next century.

If the cartographic industry of Antwerp and Amsterdam was fuelled by a taste for maps which Brown describes as 'pretty things with bright colors and gold leaf to please the eye and decorate the home', then it is perhaps in terms of such maps (and not the 'advanced' ones) that we should assess the cultural or 'poetic' dimension of the new geography. To suppose that the 'poetry' of such maps is a matter of 'bright colors', however, is seriously to underestimate them. The colour is but an aspect of a highly complex interplay of geography with ornamental and symbolic design. If one takes the time to pore through the 640 or so entries of Rodney Shirley's exhaustive 'cartobibliographic' survey of 'Early Printed World Maps 1472–1700', one is struck by the *generic* character of their design and symbolism. This is not to say that the design and symbolism never vary or evolve. They do. But the variety and evolution generally remain within clear generic parameters. These too were subject to change. After 1570, for example, the cordiform projection gives way quite suddenly to the ovoid and double-hemispherical projections. Again (to take a specifically iconographic example) it is rare, after this date, to find a world map adorned with 'wind-heads' in the fashion of those in late-fifteenth-century editions of Ptolemy. Instead, one is likely to find a host of other classical devices. Various combinations of personified continents, elements and seasons occupy the decorative margins (and occasionally the cartographic body) of the maps. Roughly from the appearance of Ortelius's *Theatrum* of 1570 and Mercator's *Atlas*, such imagery tends to assume a programmatic form.[5]

2

The idiom of this programme is overwhelmingly classical. Thus, where the geography of the maps themselves afforded scant opportunity for the ancient 'poetic' values to congregate and regenerate, the symbolism of the ornamental frame compensated abundantly. The ancient 'frame', as such, could hardly be adapted to a *global* geography whose *omphalos* was the Atlantic Ocean. Nevertheless, the mere portrayal of the round globe on a rectangular page seemed to afford the ancient poetic values a window of opportunity. The decorative borders of these maps suggest the 'poetic' values of the ancient geography almost as if the new geography had never happened. The four elements, the four seasons, the four winds and the five zones, are all classical. The 'four' continents are also classically based: in the usage they imply of the word 'continent', in the iconography of the three ancient continents, and in the tendency for various personified New World 'Continents' ('Mexicana', 'Peruvana', etc.) to be subordinated to a single continent ('America'), thereby giving a total of four. As a foursome, the continents are then imagined and arranged in ways that recapitulate the four ends of the earth. In addition to these mostly ancient personifications, it is not uncommon to find troops of stage Romans disputing rights of cartographic possession with the true heirs of the new geography, the great Renaissance voyagers: Columbus, Vespucci, Magellan, Drake, Cavendish, and others. In the case of each of the classical motifs, a deep contradiction between ancient poetry and new geography is observed. But the very tolerance of such a level of contradiction will demonstrate yet more forcibly the power of ancient formations within the new geographic *poiesis*. This will emerge from a brief survey of the function of the classical motifs within the maps.

The use of classical wind-heads at the corners of Renaissance world maps is perhaps the most obviously paradoxical transposition of the ancient 'poetic geography' to the 'new' geographic context. In strictly geographic terms, the iconography of the winds – recapitulating, as it does, a Mediterranean climate and geography – directly contradicts the global dimensions of the new geography. (We have already seen how, in *The Merchant of Venice*, Bassanio's 'four winds' define 'the four corners of the earth', while Antonio's Mexican trade route suggests the terraqueous globe.) Wind-heads are most popular in the early Renaissance, where they are often to be found (in groups of either four or twelve) in Ptolemaic maps. They were still current in world maps of the mid-sixteenth century, such as the 1564 world map of Abraham Ortelius.[6] In his next world map, however, the *Typus Orbis Terrarum* of 1570, Ortelius abandoned them, setting a powerful precedent for the entire Flemish and Dutch industry. In *chorographic*-scale maps, however, wind-heads were still in use by 1675, when William Salmon instructed artists in how to draw them.[7] For 'Eurus', the east wind, the artist should 'draw a youth with puffed and blown cheeks (as all winds must be), wings upon his shoulders, his body like a Tauny Moor, upon his head a Red Sun'.[8] Clearly, Eurus can be an *east* wind only if Africa is imagined to the east or south-east of Italy. An exclusively Mediterranean orientation is also presupposed in two other winds. Zephyrus, the west wind, should be a youth with a merry look, holding in his hand a swan with wings outspread as though he were about to sing. On the youth's head should be a garland of all sorts of flowers, 'because it cherisheth and quickeneth, bringing life'. Again, this hardly makes sense when transposed to global dimensions. Salmon's young Bacchus is a long way from home on Gerard de Jode's world map of 1555, where, as 'Occidens', he blows his quickening gales from the equatorial eastern shores of the Pacific.[9] A similar incongruity is felt with 'Auster', the south wind, who is to be drawn 'with head and wings wet, a pot or urn pouring forth water, with which descend frogs, grasshoppers, and the like creatures which are bred by moisture'. Only Boreas, the north wind, continues to make sense on the global scene. Salmon describes him as an old man 'with a horrid, terrible look; his hair and beard covered with snow, or the hoar-frost; with the feet and tail of a Serpent'.

Because the 'four' winds had (since antiquity) been mixed up with the 'twelve' winds, the precise identity of the 'four' sometimes differs according to which of the 'twelve' are taken as the most representative foursome. As Africa stretches right across the southern littoral of the Mediterranean, the 'African' wind might be coming from anywhere between west-south-west and east-south-east. In the 1555 map of Gerard de Jode, 'Africus' blows from west-south-west. Salmon's 'Eurus' appears as 'Surocus' (the Sirocco), blowing from east-south-east. In the 1564 map of Ortelius, 'Occidens' is not Bacchic (as in de Jode) but clearly African. 'Africus', as such, blows from west-south-west; and 'Euro-notus, Scirocco' blows from east-south-east. The traditional confusion over character and naming must have contributed, scarcely less than the geographical incongruities, to the abandonment of the entire system. Before we too abandon the winds, however, we should notice an interesting implication of this 'African' family of sub-equatorial wind-heads. In addition to the ethnic-African look suggested by Salmon for 'Eurus', it is common to find African winds represented by death's-heads.[10] It is suggestive that Africans seem to be interchangeable with skulls. It is also suggestive that Shakespeare's Morocco, one of the 'renowned suitors' whom 'the four winds blow in from every coast' is not only ethnically *African* but also rewarded with a *death's-head* for failing to win Portia. Morocco is almost literally an ill 'African' wind who, like the dry 'Sirocco', blows nobody any good.

The iconographic motif of the four continents is also something of a geographical paradox. Strictly speaking, a 'continent' suggests the 'continuous land' of its Latin root *terra continens*; a fact which was well understood by the Elizabethan geographer Richard Eden, who defines a continent as 'the firme lande not inclosed with water, or no Ilande'.[11] Hardly surprisingly, only the ancient continents, Europe, Africa and Asia, properly qualify in terms of this classically based definition. America, for all its vast size, is an island, and therefore anomalous. Recognising the paradox, Gerard Mercator redefined the word 'continent' to mean a huge island rather than continuous land. This meant that the three ancient 'continents' – Europe, Africa and Asia – became one. It also meant that there were now three 'continents' where, according to the old definition, there should have been five (assuming that 'Magellanica' was taken seriously). Mercator's usage and his results are acknowledged by Ortelius in the course of his own inconsistent retention of the classical definition:

Gerardus Mercator the Prince of moderne Geographers in his never-sufficiently-commended universall Table or Map of the whole world, divides this Circumference of the earth into three continents: the first he calles that, which the Ancients divided into three parts, and from whence the holy Writ beares record, that mankinde had their first originall, & first was seated: the second, is that which at this present is named *America* or the *West Indies*: for the third, he appoints the South maine, which some call *Magellanica*.[12]

Where Mercator departs from the root meaning of the word 'continent', his usage at least has the advantage of consistency. By contrast, the usage implied by the four continents of Ortelius is quite inconsistent. Europe, Africa and Asia are 'continents' in the ancient sense of being adjoining land. America, however, is a continent in the insular sense of Mercator. The status of 'Magellanica' is left vague.[13]

Why was the quite inconsistent and geographically meaningless idea of *four* continents so successful? Part of the answer may be found in the prestige of ancient precedent. Another part may lie in Europe's need of identity as defined by contrast with the 'other' nations of Africa and Asia. Europe's perceived racial and cultural superiority to Africa and Asia would thus find expression in the idea of a separate 'continental' identity (thus answering a 'poetic' or 'moral' need which Mercator's superior geography ignored). Finally, the idea of four continents may have re-capitulated the ancient 'poetic' symmetry of the four corners of the earth. They may have been a very long shadow cast by the ancient frame. We will never know just how far that shadow may have reached into the geography of sixteenth- and seventeenth-century atlases, but it does appear that the ancient frame took a number of symbolic forms in the new ornamental frames.

It is not uncommon, for example, for the four continents – either as allegorical personifications, or as miniaturised maps within circular cartouches – to be set within the gaps between the ovoid frame of the map itself and the four corners of its decorative rectangular frame. In either case, the disposition is the same. Europe will be at the top left-hand corner, America at the bottom left, Asia at the top right and Africa at the bottom right. Both variations of this formula – allegorical and cartographic – derive indirectly from Ortelius. The geographic images of the four continents are set within cartouches at the four corners of the frame in an interesting map from the *Parergon*, in which Ortelius projects the Ptolemaic *oikumene* upon an otherwise empty Renaissance globe.[14] The miniaturisation of the four continents within four corner cartouches then becomes a convention in a number of Ortelian world maps of the seventeenth century.[15]

The allegorical version of the formula begins with the 1594 *Orbis*

Terrarum Typus of Petrus Plancius (Plate 16) which depicts six personified
continents (and copious repertoires of their attributes) in the interstices of
a stereographic or double hemispherical map. *Europa*, *Mexicana*, *Asia*
and *Africa* occupy the four corners of the ornamental frame; while
Peruana and *Magallanica* occupy the central interstices between the two
hemispheres at the bottom of the frame. 'The elaborate pictorial borders'
were, Rodney Shirley claims, 'inspired by drawings in the works of
Theodore de Bry ... and established a pattern of cartographical decor-
ation that lasted for over a century'.[16] In a few years, the rectangular logic
of the frame seems to have asserted itself, and the six continents of
Plancius are reduced to the four of Adam Elsheimer in a world map
drawn in 1598 to illustrate the voyage of Cornelis Houtman.[17] *Magallanica* disappeared perhaps because of her inability to evolve from fantasy
into history. The reason for the disappearance of *Peruana* and *Mexicana*
from the repertoire is less easily accounted for, but it may be due to the
fact that, as 'continents' in the ancient sense of 'adjoining land', they were
at odds with the idea of an island 'continent' (in the sense of Mercator)
which was also a 'New World'.

The resonance of the continents with the four corners of the classical
frame is nowhere more marked than in a world map of *c.* 1617 by Claes
Janszoon Visscher (Plate 17). Perhaps the most elaborately decorated
map of the post-Ortelian tradition, it is described by Rodney Shirley as 'a
masterly combination of all the emblems of the age'.[18] Visscher not only
has six continents, four elements and four seasons, but also the twelve
months and the seven *opera charitatis* ('charitable works') of St Matthew.
The relatively modest area devoted to geography is stereographically
divided into two spheres along a horizontal axis. The vertical axis is
occupied by two celestial spheres. The ornamental frame not only
embraces this geography, but invades its every interstice. At the outermost corners of the entire overloaded design are four 'stage' ancients on
horseback, each bestriding a fallen foe and each confronting a body of
water from which a monstrous beast rears threateningly.[19] At the top of
the page are '*Ninus*' on the left and '*Cyrus Maior*' on the right. At the
bottom are '*Alexander Magnus*' and '*C. Iulius Caesar*'. What are they
doing there? I have yet to find an explanation, but I suggest that they
represent four ancient conquerors legendarily credited with extending the
boundaries of the ancient world. The bodies of water would thus represent the encircling ocean-river. The monstrous beasts would symbolise the
chaos of the margin and the taboo on venturing *ad rerum metas extremque
litora mundi* ('to the bounds of things, and remotest shores of the world').

The contradiction between the symbolism of the ancient frame and that
of the 'new geography' which we have posed as *generic* of Renaissance

world maps is starkly manifest in Visscher's map. With typical incongruity, the great voyagers pose as if for their portraits over the vacant expanse of *Magellanica*. Visscher must have wanted his viewers to appreciate the symmetry between his ancient world-conquerors and his Renaissance explorers. However, the very ingenuity of the juxtaposition serves to underline its oddity.

Of the four elements, little can be added to what has already been said of them in Chapter 3. Their function is essentially *cosmographic* in the sense of suggesting that however strange the new geography may appear, however alien to the classical tradition of the *orbis terrarum*, its substance was always identical with the substance of the world as traditionally understood. The earth was always 'sublunar'. Everything on it – no matter how monstrous or novel – was an imperfect compound of four elements. As long as the new geography could be so inscribed within the familiar cosmography, it was controllable; or would be until the 'new philosophy' of Copernicus, Galileo, Brahe and Kepler had penetrated deep enough into general cartographic culture for the ancient cosmographic scheme to be abandoned. This, however, would not begin to happen until the mid- to late-seventeenth century, when world maps began to depict the Ptolemaic cosmos alongside the new formulations of Copernicus, Galileo, Brahe and Kepler. Until then, however, the four elements, like the four seasons, would remain as a constant motif – usually at the interstices of stereographic globes rather than in the frame itself. Unlike the winds and continents, however, they would remain relatively static. They never evolve.

The final classical motif worthy of notice is that of the five zones. Unlike all the previous motifs, this was never an iconographic feature as such, but a purely cartographic feature, part of the map's native graphic idiom. Ostensibly, at least, the incongruity between the classical zones and the 'tropics' of the new geography is far less than the incongruities already observed. This is perhaps because the zones had been adapted to the global model of the earth by the Greeks of the fifth century. Vico, however, would wish us to search out the primitive origins of zone theory, before the sphericity of the earth had been dreamed of or mathematically projected. Just such an account of 'poetic' origins is provided by Heidel, who finds the most primitive imagery of zones inseparable from the idea of the *uninhabitability* of regions immediately north or south of the primitive *oikumene*.[20] To the south, the torrid zone set an impassable limit to inhabitation (even by those monstrous races best equipped for torrid conditions). To the north, inhabitation is impossible because of the extreme cold. The *oikumene* itself is found to occupy the most temperate mean between these unendurable extremes. In essence, the idea of the zones was flexible enough to survive any number of outward revisions of the limits of the classical *oikumene*. Even the realisation that the earth was a sphere and not a flat circle or rectangle could be accommodated. It merely meant that the zonal experience of the northern *oikumene* would be duplicated in the theoretical southern hemisphere: the Antipodes. The three zones would therefore become five: northern frozen, northern temperate, torrid, southern temperate, southern frozen.

Ortelius graphically illustrates both the fit and the discrepancy between the ancient zones and the new geography in the theoretical 'theme' map, the *Aevi Veteris, Typus Geographicus*. Here, the Ptolemaic *oikumene* is shown not just in relation to the globe but also in relation to the delineation of the ancient zones on a global scale. The delineation itself, therefore, is entirely 'new'. The frozen zones are marked by the Arctic and Antarctic Circles respectively. The torrid zone is encompassed within the two tropics. And the two temperate zones are respectively to the north and south of the northern and southern tropics. Such a scale hardly corresponds to the ancient poetic tradition of the zones, in which the frozen wastes of the north are imagined a good deal further south than the Arctic Circle. Similarly, the torrid wastes of Africa are imagined a good deal north of the 'new' Equator. The 'Garamantes', for example, a famous extreme southern race in Augustan literature, are here no further south than the Tropic of Cancer. These discrepancies are unremarked by Ortelius, perhaps because he is so concerned to point up another discrepancy: between the ancient myth of the 'uninhabitability' of the torrid zone and the Renaissance realisation that the Equator was inhabited. Bordering his Equator, therefore, is the following legend: *Zona torrida, et ob Solis nimium fervorem a veteribus inhabitabilis credita* ('the torrid zone, believed uninhabitable by the ancients due to the extreme heat of the sun'). Typically of his entire approach to the new geography, Ortelius tries to reconcile the new with the ancient, before rejecting what he perceives to be the irreconcilable elements of an ancient theory. The desire to reconcile and newly define leads to a confusion. Appropriately enough for a poetic geographic idea, the ancient zones had been highly flexible. They migrated outwards along with the boundaries of the *oikumene*. They only became fixed in mathematically sophisticated geographic systems such as that of Ptolemy, which are unrepresentative of the poetic dimensions of the idea. By insisting on the fixture of the zones *and* insisting on the classical myth of the uninhabitability of the torrid zone, therefore, Ortelius pretends to be preserving the *scientific* essence of the ancient zones while disputing their 'poetry'. In fact, he has confused ancient 'poetry' with modern 'science'.

3

This brief survey of classical motifs within and around the ornamental frame of sixteenth- and seventeenth-century Flemish and Dutch maps, has also been a record of the incongruities between each individual classical motif and the new geography it is supposed to suggest. But the full incongruity can only be grasped when the geographic *imago* as such is seen in relation to the iconographic programme as a whole. Quite apart from their verbal legends and iconographic programme, the geography of these maps is powerfully (if mutely) poetic.

It is sometimes suggested that the Ptolemaic grid was inherently resistant to the poetry of the ancient '*omphalos* syndrome'.[21] It would be truer to say that the grid was resistant to poetic tendencies *in the context of Ptolemy's geography*, for the reason that the relationship between the *oikumene* and the grid is entirely unsymmetrical (see Plate 7). At its left, the *oikumene* begins at about 5° longitude and terminates at about 180°, with the effect that its vertical mid-point (approximately longitude 87.5°) is entirely without wider symbolic reference. The horizontal mid-point is equally unpoetic, passing well north of the Equator. The Tropic of Cancer comes close to dividing the *oikumene* horizontally, but any resulting impression of symmetry is dissipated by the effect of the conic projection whereby the lower portion of the map exceeds the upper portion. Essentially because its reference is global rather than 'ecumenical', the grid fails to impose symmetry on the *oikumene*.

For just this reason, however, the grid exerts a powerful symmetry on the global geography of the Ortelian world map. The horizontal axis is now 'the Equator', and the central axis the meridian. Furthermore, respect for symmetry led Renaissance and ancient geographers alike to suppose that the combined landmass of the southern hemisphere would equal that of the northern hemisphere. Just this respect dictates the rough parity between northern and southern landmasses in the seminal maps of Mercator and Ortelius (Plates 2, 3 and 15). Both show sub-equatorial Africa, America and the gigantic Australian continent in the south, counterbalancing a huge North America, the old world and a large Arctic strip in the north.[22]

In both, too, the addition of an entire 'New World' in the west creates an equally powerful vertical symmetry between eastern and western hemispheres. Thus, instead of the concentricity of an ancient *oikumene* upon the *omphalos* of an Athens or a Rome or a Jerusalem, we find a clear bifurcation into two 'worlds'. In the ovoid projection of Ortelius, the division occurs precisely along the line of the central meridian. In Mercator, the bifurcation is expressed stereographically, with the hemispheres shown as matching spheres rather than as halves of a single oval. In part, no doubt, the vertical division is due to the accident of America's sheer size. But it is also true that the size of America (particularly North America) is grossly overstated by the new geography, with a consequent understatement of 'Scythian' Asia and the Pacific. A reason sometimes alleged for the exaggerated width of North America is the inadequacy of sixteenth-century technology for measuring longitude at sea. This may be so, but inaccuracy of measurement alone cannot account for the *systematic* nature of the overestimation of America and the underestimation of North Asia and the Pacific. Mere inaccuracy produces mere randomness, but 'poetry' produces system. The marked tendency of the grid to divide the new geography into matching 'worlds' along a vertical axis is immediately seen when comparing the maps of Ortelius and Mercator with any world map showing the proper dimensions of the Pacific relative to the Atlantic and Indian Oceans. On a global scale, therefore, the grid tends to exert an axiological force on the landmasses of the new geography. The new 'continents' and 'worlds' in the western and southern hemispheres are responsive to (and partly the products of) new 'poetic' tendencies unencountered by Ptolemy.

Apart from the number and size of the 'continents' in such maps, and the vertical and horizontal symmetry of their grouping, we may be struck by a related carto-poetic feature: the 'straits' of 'Magellan' and 'Anyan' and a nameless north-east strait across the top of Europe and Asia. These 'straits' are related to the continents to the degree that the size and number of the continents drastically reduces the extent of ocean on this 'terraqueous' globe. It is perhaps because there is so much *less* ocean, that the sea-routes between the vast continental expanses tend to take the form of 'straits' rather than of open sea. The great 'straits' of the new geography are all fictitious and for much the same reason. The 'Strait of Magellan' was in fact the route by which Magellan crossed from the Atlantic into the Pacific in 1522. But a Magellan-like strait is depicted on world maps 'years before Magellan's expedition'.[23] And, as we have seen, it continued to be depicted as the only southerly link between the two oceans well after 1599, when Edward Wright pointedly omitted the southern continent in his *Hydrographiae Descriptio* (Plate 1), and announced that Drake had rounded the Horn in open sea. Accordingly, as late as 1636, Mercator's reissued *Atlas* continued to insist that Magellan was among the noblest 'streights of the Ocean' (p. 40). On some maps the significance of the great straits is further advertised in chorographic depictions of each strait, individually set within cartouches along the decorative border.[24]

The northern 'Strait of Anian' is also fictitious, not because it did not exist, but because of what it portended: a north-west passage across the top of America. On Ortelius's *Typus*, the passage is almost half the circumference of the globe at that latitude. Its delineation is suspiciously smooth, without the fiddly bits which bespeak an authentically mapped coastline. Unlike the 'strait' of Magellan, the north-west passage was as yet undiscovered and would remain so for centuries (Cook would lose his life on a fruitless voyage to 'discover' it from the Pacific end). The north-east passage across the top of Asia can almost be considered an extension of the north-west passage over the top of America. Such it appears on the map of Ortelius where it forms the other half of the circumference constituting the Strait of Anian. Both straits, therefore, form a virtually continuous line separating the northern landmasses of the New and Old Worlds from the landmass of the Arctic. Such also it seems to have appeared to Mercator when, responding to Ortelius's news that Drake had rounded the Horn, he opined that the English fleet meeting Drake in the Pacific 'had returned on a course west and north of Asia by way of the strait which surrounds the northern coasts of America, a route already explored by Frobisher'.[25] This is to say that the fleet travelled from east to west over the top of the Old World but via the *same* strait 'which surrounds the northern coasts of America'.

Ultimately, the poetry of these great cartographic fictions is more than a mere corollary of understated oceans and overstated continents. One of its springs is perhaps the primal collision between the unstoppable force of Columbus's dream of a westerly sea-route to Asia, and the immovable objection of the American continent. All Columbus's subsequent voyages to the Caribbean were motivated by the idea of eventually finding a 'passage' to China through the massive irrelevancy of that land 'vaguely realising westward'. One ironical *poiesis* resulting from this collision is indeed the word 'cannibal', which is thought to have been formed from the telescoping of the native word 'carib' and the Columban word 'Khan'.[26] When Columbus asked the Indians the way to the land of the great 'Khan', and also the way to the land of their man-eating enemies, the Indians seemed to gabble of 'Caniba' who lived to the west. When no strait was found through the middle of the continental wall, but another was found between its bottom tip and the presumed mass of the Australian continent, the profound hermeneutic investment in the first was perhaps transferred to the second, and then the third (at the top of the continental wall). Fictions they may have been, but like the 'missing link' of nineteenth-century evolutionary theory, the great 'streights of the ocean' were geographically 'necessary'. My echo of Wallace Stevens's *Notes Towards a Supreme Fiction* is not entirely undesigned. Ultimately, as with all 'supreme fictions', the inspiration of these straits was perhaps unconscious. They authorised, even as they promised to disclose, what Ortelius thought of as 'the secrets of a distant world' (*mundi arcana remoti*). The context of this phrase is the moment when the geographer is imagined – in the course of his 'explication' to the frontispiece of the *Theatrum* – as gazing back on the earth after being rapt to the heavens like some Renaissance Scipio. Instead of viewing the earth with Scipio's lofty disdain, Ortelius takes advantage of his heavenly viewpoint to spy out 'the secrets of a distant world'. The situation and the pleasure here suggest what Mark Kanzer describes as 'the phallic-voyeuristic impulses' of Robert Louis Stevenson's childhood reminiscence, *Foreign Lands*:

> I held the trunk with both my hands
> And looked abroad on foreign lands.
> I saw the next door garden lie,
> Adorned with flowers, before my eye,
> And many pleasant places more
> That I had never been before.[27]

Noting the absence of overt romantic interest in the work of the mature Stevenson, Kanzer suggests that it is displaced into 'the sea, the ships, the hidden treasures of Stevenson's tales', all of which 'mark the haunting lineaments of the feminine form' (p. 433). Exploring the geographised body of his mistress ('Before, behind, between, above, below') with his hands, Donne seems rather more conscious of the erotic source of his geographic pleasure.[28] It is also perhaps relevant to mention that ancient straits such as Messina and the *Symplegades* were overtly female (the first guarded by the monstrous forms of Scylla and Charybdis, and the second elided with the figure of Medea).

The final 'poetic' expression in the cartographic face of the 'new geography' can be read as an energetic correspondence between the sheer extent of undiscovered *terrae incognitae* and the explicit depiction of voyagers thereupon. After (but not in or before) Ortelius, it is common to find portraits of Columbus and later explorers usually over the accommodating emptinesses of America, Magellanica or the ocean (see Plate 17). As well, it is not uncommon to find navigational instruments, maps, globes, astrolabes, or even a cosmographer adorned with the personal emblem of the map-maker himself. Ships, of course, are always to be found (sometimes juxtaposed with sea-monsters) in various parts of the cartographic oceans. Exotic beasts (parrots, elephants, crocodiles, armadillos) and savages may also be shown, suggesting the character of the *terrae incognitae*, and a collective bio-geographic object of the voyaging impulse. As we have seen, this explicitly iconographic expression of the new geography is challenged by the entire repertoire of classical iconography which surrounds it. Thus 'framed', however, the voyager is not overpowered. He has strategic advantages over the encircling forces. He inhabits the body of the map, rather than its margins. He has the authenticity of recent and documented history as against the purely abstract representativeness of the classical figures. And in the generic sense if not personally, he authorises at least half the land surface of the map. It is, indeed, primarily in the person of the voyager that the new geography achieves its full poetic identity, its difference from the powerful archaism of the decorative frame.

To appreciate the significance of the voyager, we have simply to look again at Ortelius's *Typus Orbis Terrarum* (Plates 2 and 3). None of the many states and varieties of this ubiquitous map shows a voyager. The map is as free of voyagers as it is of figures of any kind, including those of classical mythology. Lacking figures, however, the map is not without *figuration*. The classical poetry is powerfully present in its classical citations, a single one in the original 1570 version and another four in the 1587 version, which remained the standard version of the map until 1612.[29] There is no need to rehearse these texts again, but we may simply note that their combined effect is to inscribe the new geography within the ancient ethic of respecting the limits set by earthly *termini*, while piously contemplating the insignificance of the earthly globe in relation to the heavenly spheres.[30]

Nothing could be further from the Renaissance romance of discovery. When, therefore, the figure of the voyager finds his way on to post-Ortelian world maps, a whole new geographic ethos arrives with him. The secular canonisation of the voyager dates from the early sixteenth century, certainly from 1516 when Charles V implicitly adopted the voyager as his imperial mascot.[31] The imperial emblem was two pillars with a scroll inscribed with the motto: *Plus Ultre* ('Ever further'); an inversion of what was perhaps the most famous symbol of the ancient piety of the *terminus*: the two pillars which Hercules was supposed to have set up at the strait of Gibraltar, adorned with the command: *Non Plus Ultra* ('No further'). But, as Earl Rosenthal has exhaustively shown, the imperial *ultre* was not directly derived from the Latin *ultra*.[32] The immediate source was Dante's *oltre*, from the verse describing Ulysses' impious passage of:

> ... *quella foce stretta*
> *dov'Ercule segnò li suoi riguardi,*
> *acciò che l'uom non si metta*
> (that narrow outlet where Hercules set up his landmarks so that men
>   should not pass beyond.)[33]

The damnation of Ulysses for having transgressed the *terminus* of Hercules is one of the last ringing declarations of the ancient ethic in Western literature. Rosenthal even supposes that in Ulysses – who, with

Jason's helmsman Tiphys, is an exemplar of the ancient idea of the voyager as transgressor – Dante had intended an allusion to the Vivaldi brothers, who had disappeared after voyaging into the Atlantic. In Luigi Pulci's *Morgante* (1461–83), however, and certainly after 1492, the Renaissance figure of the voyager is born.[34] Exorbitance and audacity are celebrated rather than damned. Tiphys, whom Seneca had abominated for opening a maritime freeway between Europe and Asia, becomes the patron saint of the sixteenth-century mariner, and is regularly honoured in maritime atlases (as in the dedication to *The Mariner's Mirrour* of 1588). Venice, Antwerp and London would adopt the Burgundian imagery of the golden fleece, and the Herculean pillars along with the motto *Plus Ultre*, as signals of their own pretensions to maritime empire.[35] Collectively, such imagery suggests the nature of the European perception of the New World and also their relationship with it.[36] In the poetry of Donne and many others, the New World voyage explicitly operates as a sign of desire. In Bacon, it becomes the master metaphor of a new science.[37] In common parlance, the imperial motto produces the neologism 'nonplus', 'a state in which no more can be said or done; inability to proceed'.[38] When, therefore, the figure of the voyager makes his appearance on early seventeenth-century maps, all these 'poetic' resonances appear with him. The 'new geography', now a kind of Nietzschean *gai savoir*, is hermeneutically complete.

However, at no stage of the entire ascendancy of Flemish and Dutch cartography, is the new geography ever quite free of the old poetry. The victory of the new poetry over the old is always qualified, always relative. Classical iconography would remain idiomatic well into eighteenth-century cartography, and even beyond. Over Shakespeare's career, from the 1580s to 1611, the struggle between the new geography and its classical frame was just beginning to be resolved. This means that our aim of providing a sharp hermeneutic profile of the new geography as Shakespeare would have known it, is impossible. Just as Montaigne found his own inner profile to be *divers et ondoyant*, so the hermeneutic of Shakespeare's new geography is necessarily unfixable, unquantifiable and unmappable. It is, at least, not to be understood as a fixed quantity but only as a process of becoming. In no contemporary map, not even those of Mercator or Ortelius, does it achieve final and definitive statement. It is, perhaps, partly due to the immense prestige of both great Flemish cartographers over exactly this period, that the geographic hermeneutic is so unstable. Were the *Theatrum* and the *Atlas* not so exemplary, it is possible that the classicising perspective would not have taken such a deep root, and the new geography might have sooner divested itself of the old poetry.

4

One more question must be asked before our hermeneutic profile of the new geography is complete: Why was the iconography of the decorative frames of these maps almost exclusively classical rather than biblical or an amalgam of the two? As we have seen, the biblical poetic was dominant in medieval geography, even though the TO map had been built on the back of the archaic Greek frame. Why, therefore, is it now excluded? Part of the explanation must consist in the prestige of Ptolemy's *Geographia* from its discovery in 1400. The conceptual sophistication of this late classical geography, with its geometric grid (allowing a *scientific* sense of orientation, distance and proportion) and its modern refusal to privilege a sacred *omphalos*, defined the very possibility of a new geography. Without Toscanelli's calculation (on Ptolemaic principles) of the width of the Atlantic, Columbus's voyage would not have been possible. But Ptolemy was more than a mere precursor. His true significance is to have broken the imaginative hold of the 'Christian topography' of Cosmas and Isidore in the fifteenth century; much as, in the sixth century, he had shattered the poetic mould of the *orbis terrarum*. In the sixteenth century, however, Ptolemy would prove less a barrier to the return of the latter than of the former.[39]

It is not, however, until the flowering of the new geography after the *Theatrum* in 1570, that the classical programme (as I have described it) comes truly into its own. Insofar as Ptolemaic *Cosmographiae* of the fifteenth and early sixteenth centuries have a generic poetry, this tends to be a mixture of biblical and classical elements in which the latter slowly gains the ascendency. The biblical element, however, would never entirely disappear from the repertoire. It is marginalised rather than excluded, always potential rather than systemically manifest.

Because of a general lack of pictorial iconography in the fifteenth-century editions of Ptolemy, we may begin with a Ptolemaic world map – luminously entitled *Das ander alter der Welt* ('The other age of the world') – from the 1493 *Nuremberg Chronicle* of Hartmann Schedel.[40] Though Columbus had reached the New World in the previous year, his achievement was insufficiently publicised or understood for any of it to have registered on the map. As the title implies, the 'theme' of this map would appear to be the population of the world in archaic times. The entire left-hand border of the map is devoted to illustrations of various monstrous races suggested by the ancient teratological tradition of Herodotus, Pomponius Mela, Solinus and Pliny. A portion of the textual legend informs us: 'This is how the sons of Noah divided it up after the Flood. And Sem and his children owned Asia, Japhet Europe and Cham Africa, as the writings of Crisostomus, Isidore and Pliny say'.[41] Accordingly, the Noachides are shown at three of the map's four corners. A dignified and patriarchal Japhet occupies the top left-hand corner (notionally over Europe). A sneaky-looking Shem occupies the top right-hand corner, notionally over Asia. A leering Ham is shown at the bottom right-hand corner, suggesting not just Africa but also, perhaps, India. A border of classical wind-heads separates the Noachides from the map as such.

The influence of Christian poetic geography extends beyond the pictorial border and into the terminology of orientation. While the map itself is generally Ptolemaic, a textual legend describes the relative distribution of the continents as follows:

... Now the world is divided into three parts, namely Asia, Africa and Europe, but not in equal proportions. For Asia extends from midday through (sun)rise to midnight, but Europe from midnight to sunset and Africa to sunset from midday ... Between these parts a great sea flows from the common sea and differentiates them. So the world is now divided into two parts, sunrise and sunset. In the one part there is Asia, and in the other Africa and Europe.

East and west, in other words, are resolved into the more archaic or poetic antithesis of 'sunrise' (Orient) and 'sunset' (Occident). Nor is the archaism purely a matter of etymology. Schedel seems entirely ignorant of the Ptolemaic grid, and incapable of describing distance geometrically. Instead he prefers to describe the absolute and relative widths of the continents in terms of a solar itinerary. While, then, east is not absolutely privileged as in the TO map, it is privileged in that the direction of the 'sunrise' remains the *alpha* point not only of the west as such but of any place along the line of the sun's path across the earth.

This rapprochement between biblical and classical iconographies would neither develop nor systematically endure. The *Typus Cosmographicus Universalis* of Sebastian Münster (Basle, 1532) illustrates a growing preponderance of classical over biblical motifs (Plate 18).[42] The map shows an ovoid globe set horizontally within a rectangular frame populated by an interesting mix of Christian, classical and contemporary imagery. Two angels (at top and bottom) turn the globe with crank handles, so providing a vertical axis and four areas of composition. The top right-hand corner is inhabited by Scythian archers and spice plants. Below them, Jason is depicted removing the golden fleece while Medea encourages him from a palace balcony. Text within a cartouche immediately above this scene describes the barbarous Scythians and their inhospitably cold climate. Another text over the Indian Ocean describes an India which reaches from the Indus river to the Pacific Ocean, as the home of spices, gold and barbarous natives. Here, then, is the link between the anachronistic grouping of Scythian archers, spice plants and the myth of the golden fleece in the right-hand border of the map. All suggest the riches and perils of the East Indies: the golden fleece represents a classical imagination of the gold of the modern East Indies (as well as the geography of ancient Scythia, which is more directly suggested by the Scythian archers above Siberia). The spices, which incongruously appear beside the Scythian archers, are an image of the contemporary spice trade.[43] The left-hand half of the border is inhabited by abominations. Naked *Canibali* are shown butchering and roasting corpses in the bottom section, while naked and monstrous savages appear with monstrous and predatory beasts in the top section. This composition encloses a relatively primitive geographic depiction of America, the northern part of which is still ambiguously close to Japan.

The sheer range of cartographic and iconographic experiment between this eclectic repertoire of 1532 and the severely classical Ortelian repertoire of 1570, makes generalisation difficult. It is, however, clear that the iconographic repertoire is almost exclusively classical from the appearance of the *Theatrum* of 1570. Yet for all its failure to achieve a generic iconographic expression, the biblical frame of reference remained available for individual moralising application. In 1590, for example, Ortelius's world map appeared in Hugh Broughton's *A Concent of Scripture* (Plate 19).[44] In straight geographic terms, Broughton's version of the map is identical to that of the original version in 1570 (even down to the cloudy border). All the legends, however, are changed along lines suggested by its new title: 'A Map of the Earth with names (the most) from Scriptures'. The general tendency of such 'inscription' is to present the ultra-biblical expanses of the new geography in terms of biblical references to 'ends of the earth'. The following citation from the second Psalm is set neatly between two meridians, over the North Atlantic: 'The end of the earth Christ his possession'. A quotation from Psalm 72 is set at right angles to form an inverted 'T': 'The kinges of Tarshish shall bring presentes'. The phrase 'the endes of the earth' (this time, from Matthew 12) also appears in the Indian Ocean at the outlet of the Red Sea. And yet again, we find a text which imagines the bringing of 'presentes'. On the east coast of Africa, at about the Equator, is the phrase: 'Sheba and Seba shall bring giftes' (Psalm 72). Apart from general references to the 'ends of the earth' and to exotic kings who bring gifts, two specific biblical place names are indicated. 'Ophir' appears in South America, between the upper reaches of the Amazon and the 'Plate' river. Most striking of all, however, the name 'Tarshish' appears in large fonts over all three oceans: Pacific, Atlantic and Indian.

Here, then, is an individual reading of the new geography in purely biblical terms: which is to say, in terms of the Old Testament experience of a tiny slice of the Middle East beyond which anywhere would have qualified as the 'ends of the earth'. To a modern reader, the projection of such restricted terms of geographic reference on a global scale will seem idiosyncratic. The question we must ask, however, is: *Was* it idiosyncratic at all? In general terms, no. Broughton's main idiosyncracy is to have been so thorough in applying a commonplace moralisation of the new geography. An old woodcut world map of 1527 included in Hakluyt's *Divers Voyages* of 1582, labels the spice islands of the East Indies as *Insule Tharsis et Offir*.[45] The modern 'Solomon Islands' will also stand as mute testimony to the sixteenth-century habit of locating Solomon's Ophir at a notional three years' sail east of the Holy Land: through the Red Sea and into the Indian Ocean (or beyond). It was not at all unusual to site this mythical source of biblical gold as far 'east' as America. Jonson echoes this tradition in *The Alchemist*:[46]

> Come on, sir. Now you set your foot on shore
> In *Novo Orbe*; here's the rich Peru,
> And there within, sir, are the golden mines,
> Great Solomon's Ophir! He was sailing to 't
> Three years, but we have reached it in ten months.
>
> (2.1.1–5)

He may, however, have got the notion directly from Broughton whose *Concent* is savagely satirised elsewhere in the play.[47] But the tradition was known to Ortelius who took it upon himself to summarise the debate about *Ophir* in a miniature world map set within a large map of the biblical *Geographia Sacra*.[48] Here, *Ophir* is variously located in Peru, South Africa, the East Indies and the Caribbean.

The logic of Broughton's 'Tarshish' is perhaps more obscure than that of the legendary 'Ophir'. While inscribing 'Tarshish' over all three oceans, Broughton nevertheless appears to favour the Atlantic as its site *par excellence*. This is where we find the text: 'The kinges of Tarshish shall bring presentes'. The Old Testament portrays Tarshish as a site of 'jewels and precious stones'.[49] Like Heidel, Broughton appears to equate 'Tarshish' with what Aristotle knew as 'Tartessus' in Spain.[50] Tarshish not only corresponds to Ophir in respect of its fabled wealth, but also complements it in that Tarshish was west of the Holy Land whereas Ophir was to the east. 'East' and 'West' are so important to Broughton that each word is *repeated* at the top and bottom of each side of the map. Where, in other words, we might have expected that *four* cardinal directions (NE, SE, NW, SW) would be advertised at the four corners of the map, we find only two. The reason for this would seem to be that the biblical 'ends of the earth' which Broughton was interested in (Tarshish and Ophir) were at the eastern and western 'ends' of the biblical *oikumene*. These were the mysterious sources of gold and precious stones.

But what does Broughton mean by 'the kinges of Tarshish' and 'Sheba and Seba' bringing gifts? Psalm 72 provides a context:

> He shall have dominion also from sea to sea,
> And from the river unto the ends of the earth.
> They that dwell in the wilderness shall bow before him;
> And his enemies shall lick the dust.
> The kings of Tarshish and of the isles shall bring presents:
> The kings of Sheba and Seba shall offer gifts:
> Yea, all kings shall fall down before him:
> All nations shall serve him.
>
> (verses 8–11)

The 'sea to sea' and 'river' of the first verse rather suggest that these 'ends of the earth' might be from the Mediterranean to the Caspian, or perhaps from the Atlantic (Tharsis) to the Indian Ocean (Sheba and Seba) via the Nile and the Red Sea. The 'kings' of Sheba here recall the visit of the Queen of Sheba to Solomon, suggesting that they are as African as she was. For Broughton, however, the legendary wealth of 'Sheba' seems to equate it with yet another 'end' of the earth. Only this would explain why 'Sheba' appears as a place name over the Caspian Sea, close enough to the site of Medea's Colchis to suggest that the two golden women from opposite 'ends' of the earth have been fused in Broughton's imagination.

The tributary and enforced character of all these 'presentes' is further underlined by the Messianic and imperialistic idiom of the second Psalm which is the context of the citation accompanying the reference to the kings of Tarshish:

> Thou art my son;
> This day have I begotten thee.
> Ask of me, and I will give thee the nations for thine inheritance,
> And the uttermost parts for thy possession.
> Thou shalt break them with a rod of iron;
> Thou shalt dash them in pieces like a potter's vessel.
>
> (verses 7–9)

The contexts of other citations, however, suggest a gentler, less imperialistic motive for the gifts. In Matthew 12, Jesus proposes an analogy between himself and Jonah, whose mission to 'Nineveh' (actually Tarshish) is imagined as a mission to an end of the earth:

> An evil and adulterous generation seeketh after a sign; and there shall
>   no sign be given unto it but the sign of Jonah the prophet:
> For as Jonah was three days and three nights in the belly of the whale;

so shall the Son of man be three days and three nights in the heart of
the earth.

The men of Nineveh shall stand up in the judgement with this
generation, and shall condemn it: for they repented at the preaching
of Jonah; and behold, a greater than Jonah is here.

The queen of the south shall rise up in the judgement with this
generation, and shall condemn it: for she came from the ends of the
earth to hear the wisdom of Solomon; and behold, a greater than
Solomon is here.

(verses 39–42)

This rather gentler image of 'terminal' peoples hungering for conversion
is echoed by a verse from Matthew which appears over North America:
'Many from the East & West shall sit with Abraham in the kingdom of
heaven' (Matthew 8.11). Its context is the episode of the faithful centurion
of whom Jesus said: 'I have not found so great faith, no, not in Israel'
(Matthew 8.10).

Broughton's reinscription of the *Typus* – the most prominent icon of
the new geography *c.* 1590 – in the biblical idiom of the 'ends of the earth',
is beyond mere idiosyncracy. It is systematic in a way that points beyond
the poetic geography of the Bible to a powerful proto-colonial discourse
in which the peoples of the 'ends of the earth' are written as objects of
missionary and imperialistic attention. They may be 'good' strangers, like
Solomon's Sheba, or 'proud' and wealthy strangers like the 'kings of
Tarshish' who might legitimately be humbled, despoiled and broken by
the people of God. Does the appearance of the name 'Tarshish' over all
three of the world's oceans imply that all 'terminal' peoples are fair game?
So it would appear. But the biblical association between 'Tarshish',
'treasure', 'fleets' and 'Spain', may also conceal an allusion to the oceanic
empire of Philip II whose yearly treasure fleet, the *carrera de las Indias*,
made the hazardous journey from the Caribbean to Cadiz: which the
Romans knew as *Gades* and the Greeks may have known as *Tartessus*.

It is curious that Broughton should omit all reference to the *Noachides*
(the sons of Noah) from his biblicised *Typus*, when his familiarity with
the tradition is beyond question. Part of the *Concent* is devoted to an
impenetrably dense explication of the Messianic mission of 'the blessed
Sem'. It occurred to Broughton, as it later would occur to Donne, that all
the continents of the new geography were once 'where Japhet dwelt, or
Cham, or Shem'. Broughton and Donne remind us of the resilience of the
biblical poetic geography. Though never allowed to establish itself as a
system within the generic repertoire of Ortelian maps, it was always at the
service of discourses that might be 'poetic' in the formal sense of Donne,
'typo-geographical' in the scriptural sense of Broughton, or perhaps
'typo-chorographic' in the sense of 'moral histories' of the New World.

Nor, indeed, would the biblical 'poetry' remain entirely excluded from the classical repertoire of seventeenth-century maps. The tendency of the genre towards greater decorative elaboration finally enabled some elements of biblical symbolism to be accommodated within the frame, though always on an idiosyncratic basis.

The frequent use of Christian symbolism in the maps of Jodocus Hondius will serve to illustrate. Like many Flemish map-makers, Hondius moved to London after the fall of Antwerp, where he spent a busy decade from the late 1580s to the late 1590s. In this time he worked with fellow expatriates engraving a number of important maps and making the acquaintance of important English geographers and colonial promoters. Like the geographic productions of Hakluyt, de Bry and later Purchas, his cartographic engraving has a deeply protestant character. His famous 'Christian Knight Map of the World' (*c*. 1597) is a good example (Plate 20). Dedicated to a group of nameless English 'friends', whose interests Hondius claims to have represented, the map is one of the first to be based on Mercator's projection 'as expounded by Edward Wright whose name appears among three English mathematicians to whom the map is dedicated'.[51] While the geography as a whole is taken from Plancius's world map of 1594, Hondius is careful to note 'places relating to the discoveries of the English in Virginia (1585), Davis's attempts to find the north-west passage (1585–87) and later explorations around Novaya Zemlya (1594–95)'.[52]

What is particularly striking, however, is that a map which, in Shirley's words, was 'as up-to-date as geographical knowledge of the time allowed' (p. 219), would devote a third of its area (that of the southern continent) to a kind of Christian morality play featuring *Mundus* (The World), *Peccatum* (Sin), the Christian Knight, *Caro* (Flesh), *Diabolus* (Devil) and *Mors* (Death). We have seen how this programme derives from the specifically moral tradition of the *theatrum mundi*. The idea of the 'world', then, like the figure of *Mundus* herself, has a predominantly moral meaning. Yet the very transposition of the emblem into a cartographic context gives her a geographic resonance, suggesting that the drama of redemption might take a colonial form, as in Virginia, or in whatever colonies might one day be planted on the southern continent.[53]

There are other maps in which Hondius expressed his protestant sympathies. In 1607, he engraved a curious thematic map: the *Designatio Orbis Christiani*, which showed the relative influence of Christianity, Islam and miscellaneous idolatry with appropriate symbols.[54] In 1611, he engraved a sumptuously decorated stereographic world map, in which the *Noachides* were reintroduced at the corners of the frame.[55] The numerical discrepancy between the three sons of Noah and the four corners is got around by presenting Noah's donation of the 'three' parts of the world in the fourth corner. The upper and lower niches between the twin hemispheres are occupied by scenes from Genesis and the Apocalypse. The geography, no less than the frame, is richly decorated. Over North America is an elaborate *Memento Mori* composition: a cartouche filled with skeletons, a death's-head, and other figures, framing a legend which announces that the wages of sin is death. The outer border is occupied by no less than sixty vignettes of animal life. Christian iconography was, therefore, no stranger to the maps of Hondius. For all its elaborate profusion, however, and for all its occasional supplantation of the classical programme, it never evolved into a fixed form. Each of Hondius's 'Christian' maps is different.

Because Hondius never achieved a systematic use of Christian iconography on his own maps, he can hardly be seen as representative of cartographic uses of Christian or biblical iconography in the period. Nor, indeed, shall we attempt to discuss a representative selection of such maps here. What we can do, however, is suggest an approximate range of *possibilities* for incorporating Christian iconography within the frames of world maps. One possibility which Hondius was never able to achieve was the complete harmonisation of Christian, classical and specifically new geographic symbolism all in a single map. Such a feat is achieved in the very elaborate Visscher world map of 1617 (Plate 17), already discussed in relation to Renaissance cartographic transformations of the four corners of the earth. Along with an encyclopaedic gallery of classical and new geographic icons, the map includes a border of panels successively illustrating the seven works of charity from Matthew's gospel. The coherence of this eclectic scheme is remarkable. Without the apparently superfluous Christian elements, indeed, the iconographic profusion of this map is without purpose or direction.

The significance of the illustrations of the *opera charitatis* along the lower border of the frame is manifest only when we grasp their specific relationship with the large panel along the top, the twelve panels at the sides and the four panels in the corners of the map. The large panel at the top depicts Queen Europa seated between Asia and Africa on our left and Magallanica, Mexicana and Peruviana on our right. Further to our left, just beyond Asia (who is seated on a treasure chest full of gold coins) is a representative Asian landscape with pyramids, devil-worship and an elephant. Just to the right of this scene, two men are in the process of robbing a grave of a naked body. A third bears another naked body away from a tree upon which other naked bodies are hung, towards the scene of devil-worship to the left. European ships loom on the horizon. To the extreme right, immediately behind Peruviana (who is seated on an armadillo) are more exotic creatures (a parrot and a long-eared sheep) and scenes of cannibalism. An Indian armed with bow and arrow is mounted on an elephant. All these features are part of the standard iconography of the New World.

Two organising motifs are worthy of further comment. A forest of trees occupies most of the background of the composition, providing a link between the Asian scene on the left, the court of Queen Europa in the centre, and the American scene on the right. A more precise link is that abominations are practised under the shade of both Asian and American trees. Thus the naked bodies of the Asian section are recapitulated by the cannibalised bodies of the American section, bits of which hang from branches. The second motif is the rustic fence in the middle ground which separates the clearing in which Queen Europa holds court from the encircling trees in the background. If the trees represent something like the *silvis vetustis* ('ancient wood') of Ovid's Thrace, or the 'malign grove' of Seneca's Atreus – in effect, a 'heart of darkness' – the fence represents something like a provisional city wall, dividing the domain of the human from that of the savage and monstrous. The terminality of the fence is suggested in several ways: it serves as a perch for a parrot, a liminal blend of exoticism and harmless curiosity; but it also protects Queen Europa's court from monstrous creatures such as the long-eared sheep, the serpent and the elephant outside. Paradoxically, the monstrous armadillo remains within the pale, serving in the office of a mount for Peruviana. This, however, gazes fixedly towards the scenes of monstrosity and barbarism beyond. Interestingly, the less civilised members of Queen Europa's court also gaze wistfully outside, suggesting a Caliban-like intractability. The more civilised-looking and perhaps more docile Peruviana turns her gaze inward upon the queen.[56]

By contrast with the scenes of wild abandon in the upper panel, the twelve panels at either side of the map, depicting the twelve months of the year, invoke the harmony of nature and art. No less than nine of these panels (from March to November) portray the seasonal rhythm of agriculture. Two, the panels for January and February, portray domestic scenes, a fire in a parlour and a family sitting down to dinner, reminding us that there are no interiors in the upper panel. The panel for October portrays labourers being paid for the harvest; while December portrays men apparently amusing themselves by floating a ship on a frozen lake. Agriculture, in other words, occupies the entire yearly cycle apart from the very coldest months. We are reminded that the civilised domesticity of January and February and the financial transaction of October are supported by agriculture – the oldest of the civilised arts, and the key to civilisation itself.[57] We are also reminded of the figurative conjunction between the idea of civilisation and the idea of the seasons in the classical myth of Proserpine and Ceres. In the golden age of Proserpine (in whom is figured perpetual spring), men had no need of agriculture because the earth supplied all their wants. With the rape of Proserpine, however, spring departed from the earth, only to return for six of the twelve months on the intercession of Jupiter. Only after this classical 'Fall' does man experience what, in *As You Like It*, Shakespeare calls 'the penalty of Adam, / The season's difference' (2.1.5–6). Only now do the gifts of agriculture and civilisation become necessary and only now does Ceres grant them. The traditional conjunction of the seasons with the idea of civilisation determines not just the seasonal imagery on the sides of Visscher's map, but also the absence of any seasonal imagery from the top panel. In accordance with the prevailing commonplace, Visscher perceives the savages of the New World as lacking in agriculture *and therefore* in civilisation as well. They are in a state of innocence and of degeneracy at one and the same time.[58] Hence the harmonious imagery of the seasons does not apply to the chaotic scenery of the upper panel; at least not until Queen Europa's civilising mission has got well under way.

The patently colonialist composition of the upper panel is echoed by the seven panels at the bottom. The key to these panels is provided by a superscript over the first: *Haec sunt opera charitatis. Matth: 25.* In Matthew, the works of charity are sixfold:

> For I was an hungred, and ye gave me meat:
> I was thirsty, and ye gave me drink:
> I was a stranger, and ye took me in;
> Naked, and ye clothed me:
> I was sick, and ye visited me:
> I was in prison, and ye came unto me.

(Matthew 25.35–6)

Visscher illustrates all six works of charity on the next six panels, each of which bears a Latin inscription to the purpose. Interestingly, he reverses Matthew's order: beginning with the last work (*In carcere eram et venistis ad me*) and ending with the first work (*Essurivi et dedistis mihi quod ederem*). Only the two central panels relating to the housing of strangers and the clothing of the naked retain the order they have in Matthew. Visscher also departs from Matthew in his first panel, which depicts men burying a coffin in a churchyard (a bier is visible in the middle ground). Why, then, does Visscher depart from Matthew to the extent both of rearranging, and adding a seventh work of charity? The answer, I suggest, lies in the need to have the lower panels correspond to the upper panel. If the upper panel is 'read' from the viewer's left to right, it forms a sequence corresponding to that in the lower panels. The scene of Asiatic grave-robbery thus corresponds to the Christian burial of the dead. The scene in which Queen Europa holds court to the exotic nations corresponds to the three panels concerned with visiting the imprisoned, ministering to the sick, and clothing the naked. Finally, the scenes of cannibalism at the right of the upper panel correspond to the panels concerned with giving drink to the thirsty and feeding the hungry. What is the meaning of this iconographic dialogue? In essence, the works of charity have become an apology for European colonialism in the Far East and the New World.[59] Visscher's seven *opera charitatis* not only suggest the form that Europe's civilising mission will take, but suggest an antipathy between European and savage customs and the probable need of armed might.

The iconography of the four conquerors of the ends of the earth is now fully declared. They (and the armada in the upper panel which would seem to translate the ancient imperial symbolism into Renaissance terms) provide the earthly means for converting Asian gold into godly capital. They imply that the Christian ethic of the lower panels will be imposed by the sword on the nations of the upper panels. In this connection, it may be worth pointing out that the monstrous chimeras and the bear in the four corner panels – symbolising, as we have suggested, the monstrosity of the orbic margins – find their counterparts in the exotic beasts in the upper panel: the elephants, the over-sized armadillo and the long-eared sheep. The ancient imagery of the edge, in other words, has become flesh in the monstrous fauna of the New World. The new conquistadores – like their ancient counterparts who, bestriding their human foes, now challenge bestial nature itself – must similarly reduce the savage nature of the New World to the harmonious order of the four seasons and the twelve months.

5

The high level of improvisation required in order to balance so many competing 'poetics' illustrates the inventiveness of the map-maker and the receptiveness of the new geography to figurative play. The role of the engraver of this map is far more than that of a mere transcriber or copyist of established formulae. It is closer to the role of the Renaissance artist who creates surprise out of stereotype and new architectures from available repertoires. Ultimately, the difference between the poetic map-maker and the cartographic poet is less important than their similarity. To test this proposition, I want to conclude this semiotic profile of the post-Ortelian world map with an analysis of cartographic imagery in a metaphysical poem: Donne's *Hymn To God My God In My Sicknesse*. No less than Visscher, Donne creates within a repertoire of poetically charged geographic ideas which is all the more open to improvisation for its hermeneutic instability. Donne, of course, used words where Visscher used a stencil, but the essential difference lies in his greater insight into the poetic possibilities of the new geography.

Burdened by a needlessly 'Baconian' idea of the new geography, even the best critics have tended to underestimate the force and richness of the geographical conceit in the *Hymn*. For this reason, my reading begins as a counter-reading; specifically of the first four stanzas:[60]

> Since I am coming to that holy room,
> Where with thy choir of saints for evermore,
> I shall be made thy music; as I come
> I tune the instrument here at the door,
> And what I must do then, think here before.
>
> Whilst my physicians by their love are grown
> Cosmographers, and I their map, who lie
> Flat on this bed, that by them may be shown
> That this is my south-west discovery
> *Per fretum febris*, by these straits to die,
>
> I joy, that in these straits, I see my west;
> For, though their currents yield return to none,
> What shall my west hurt me? As west and east
> In all flat maps (and I am one) are one,
> So death doth touch the resurrection.
>
> Is the Pacific Sea my home? Or are
> The eastern riches? Is Jerusalem?
> Anyan, and Magellan, and Gibraltar,
> All straits, and none but straits, are ways to them,
> Whether Japhet dwelt, or Cham, or Shem.
>
> (stanzas 1–4, lines 1–20)

I think it is fair to say that discussion of the geographic imagery of these stanzas has been guided by three related assumptions. The first is that Donne introduces the image of the map in stanza two primarily because 'he regularly thinks of a map as a scanty and inadequate picture of the world which it represents'.[61] The second is that 'even though Donne was keenly interested ... in new geographical discoveries, his imagination worked most characteristically in terms of the old geography' (the 'geography of myth and legend' rather than the geography of Baconian science).[62] The third assumption is that the poem is a closed text with a 'unilateral' meaning which, while obscure to the twentieth-century reader, was transparent to Donne himself and to any reader familiar with the medieval geographical code.[63] In each case, I want to suggest, the geographical conceit and the poem are better understood if just the opposite assumptions are made.

To begin with, it seems perverse to suppose that the primary conno-
tation of the map conceit is negative. Donne may well have been in the
habit of remarking on the inaccuracy of contemporary maps elsewhere,
but inaccuracy is hardly the issue here. All new geographic world maps
imply the identity of east and west, rather as Toscanelli admonished
Columbus: 'do not marvel at my calling "west" the regions where the
spices grow, although they are commonly called "east"; because whoever
sails westward will always find those lands in the west, while one who goes
overland to the east will always find the same lands in the east'.[64] The
relevant distinction, then, is less between cartographic convention and
reality than between two different forms of cartographic projection: the
two-dimensional 'flat map' and the three-dimensional globe. Further, it is
via the cartographic conceit that the authoritative imagery of the three
'straits', the 'south-west discovery', the 'Pacific Sea' and the 'Eastern
riches' is introduced. Donne may be more insightful than his cosmo-
grapher-physicians in realising that west becomes east and 'death doth
touch the resurrection', but all are thinking along the same cosmographic
lines. And what kind of cosmography is this? Strikingly for a poem
written no earlier than 1623 (and possibly as late as 1631), the kind of map
Donne imagines is Ortelian; the kind on which the 'straits' of Anian and
Magellan represent the only means of access from the Atlantic to the
Pacific; a kind which had been fully evolved two years before Donne's
birth in 1572. If cartographic accuracy is at all an issue, why authorise a
type of map which must have seemed conspicuously outdated to a man of
Donne's geographic literacy? The answer is that the idea of the great
straits is the key to the poem. A more strictly accurate map, like the
Hydrographiae Descriptio, in which the Strait of Magellan is exploded,
was therefore useless ('none but straits are ways to them'). For Donne,
then, the allure of the map has less to do with accuracy than with poetry,
the myth, the 'necessary fiction'. Apart from the great straits, Donne
appears to have been inspired by the semiotic activity of the Ortelian
world map, as I have described it in Chapter 2: by its pictorial energy, its
tendency to disperse focus and draw the eye from east to west in the track
of an imaginary voyage. It is in this way that Donne is able 'in the midst of
comparing himself to a map', to change 'without warning into a navigator'.[65] Were George MacDonald able to see the Ortelian map with
Donne's eye, he might have been less affronted by the 'grotesque' image
of Donne as 'alternately a map and a man sailing on the map of himself'
(p. 460).

If we reject the notion that Donne's experience with the 'notoriously
inaccurate and incomplete' maps of the Renaissance was mostly irritating
and unsatisfying, we may dispense with the next assumption: that the true

poetry of the conceit arises exclusively from the medieval geography, and not the new.[66] Clay Hunt, Helen Gardner and Louis Martz all read the crucial fourth stanza as a mimesis of the search for the earthly paradise, which medieval typology had equated with Jerusalem. New geographic names appear, but are denatured: remorselessly typologised and sacralised, incongruously translated into the patristic geography in which all places point towards the ultimate place (the centric *omphalos* of Jerusalem) and in the sacred direction (east). Thus, the questions 'Is the Pacific Sea my home? Or are / The eastern riches? Is Jerusalem?' are read as transparently rhetorical and as versions of the same question, because all these apparently incongruous places are (typologically speaking) identical: 'the Pacific Sea' equals 'Jerusalem' ('Vision of Peace'), and 'the eastern riches' equals 'the New Jerusalem, the Heavenly City shining with gold and precious stones'.[67] On this reading, then, the new geography is poetically inert and completely swallowed by the old. Hunt finds it 'strange that Donne could be aware of the discovery of America in stanzas 2 and 3 ... and oblivious to it in stanza 4'; and explains such intellectual amnesia or regression as 'one of the symptoms of a crisis period in intellectual history when the elaborate logical structure of the Medieval synthesis was crumbling', but persisted 'as ingrown habits of imaginative association' (p. 243). All three critics agree in regarding the fourth stanza as the emotional climax of the poem and as a blissfully untroubled illustration of the proposition advanced in the third stanza: that 'death doth touch the resurrection' because the Occident (*occidere*: 'to fall down') becomes the Orient (*orire*: 'to rise').

My quarrel is not with the scholarship of these readings but with their apparent need to simplify what is actually highly elliptical, and to explain away a deliberate *aporia*. Unlike Louis Martz, I do not think that 'the very questions [of stanza four] imply the goal' or answer themselves.[68] And, unlike Hunt, I am not obliged to explain the sublime equanimity of this stanza as intellectually regressive. Instead, I prefer to think of Donne as no less intellectually engaged in this meditational poem than in an intellectual *tour de force* such as *The First Anniversary*, which (according to Martz) is so conspicuously sceptical as to fail of its meditative purpose.[69] In the *Hymn* no less than in the *Anniversaries*, I suggest, the integrity of the new and unsacralised form of learning is respected in spite of the fact that the meditative purpose prefers the patristic geography to work its alchemy. Essentially, I am suggesting that the sceptical mind is engaged as well as the believing soul, the new geography as well as the old.

The poem begins in the expectation of arriving at a specific place. 'That holy room' may not be describable as a place. In *The Progress of the Soul*, indeed, the word 'room' is code for a revelation that can only be known by the risen soul, for which:

> Heaven is as near, and present to her face,
> As colours are, and objects in a room
> Where darkness was before, when tapers come.
>
> (lines 216–18)

Yet, however dark to earthly sight the 'holy room' may be, Donne is sure that it *is* a 'place', and a spiritual 'home'; as in the *Progress*, where the soul rises through a chaotic post-Ptolemaic universe with a sure homing instinct, arriving at an interior not an exterior. In both poems, then, the soul's revelation is a knowledge of home.

The geographical conceit of the second stanza of the *Hymn* is introduced as a mimesis of this process of 'homing': of higher discovery, higher emplacement. Mimetic distance is marked out by a distinction between thinking and doing: 'And what I must do then, think here before'.[70] Thinking begins with the map image in which the promise of discovery is mitigated by an ominous sense of illness, death and (literally) disorientation. At first, the sole fruits of the hard-won 'south-west discovery' through the remorseless straits of fever (the Strait of Magellan) appears to be a featureless vision of the 'west', the sole redeeming aspect of which is the theorem that west (the direction of decay and occlusion) eventually becomes east (the direction of birth and rising). By the end of the third stanza, the related theorem that 'death doth touch the resurrection' is but tenuously established; an abstraction rather than an experience.

The fourth stanza is more than an extension of the previous two; nor is it an untroubled illustration of a position already reached. Where the third stanza is focused on the idea of direction, this is focused on the all-important idea of emplacement, of 'my home'. Far from being rhetorical, the questions of lines 16 and 17 shock us by their incongruity, their impossibility. 'Is the Pacific Sea my home?' addresses the ominous note of disorientation in the previous two stanzas: the feeling of being swallowed in a featureless immensity, of being 'lost in space' rather than found in place. The idea that the Pacific might represent 'home' is a poetic incongruity reminiscent of the Ortelian world map, the focal energy of which is concentrated on a 'nowhere' point in the Atlantic Ocean. The second question ('Or are / The Easterne riches?') – while not as incongruous – is frustratingly vague, and also resistant to the homing instinct, the expectation of arrival and emplacement. At best, it suggests the oriental shores of the Pacific, Ptolemy's 'Golden Chersonese' (or 'the Far East') perhaps. But it is straining credibility to claim with Helen Gardner that the 'Easterne riches' corresponds geographically with 'Jerusalem' because of a contemporary belief that Paradise and Jerusalem were both in the *Near* East (Mesopotamia).[71] What, then, is the point of these three questions? While admitting that the Pacific, the East and Jerusalem might all be concorded in the ways suggested by Gardner and Hunt, I disagree that the questions simply answer themselves in these terms. They *might* so unpack themselves to a complacently patristic reader like Hugh Broughton. But this is just the point. Donne's use of the new geography is not complacently patristic. The questions are real questions. They are designed to shock and disorientate before they reassure; to provoke the anxiety of placelessness before they assuage it. Like the Ortelian map, they haunt the mind with the ghost of a concentred, emplaced and sacralised geography, at the same time as denying focus and forcing the eye to wander. The ceremonious, almost ritualistic, rhythm suggests that Jerusalem is somehow present in the Pacific and the East. But 'answers' are not immediately forthcoming. The incommensurabilities seem too great.

A curious effect of this stanza (so far unremarked) is the contrast between the solemn assertiveness of the verse with its richly ceremonious intonation of place names, and the ambiguity of the geographic construction: an effect of what seems a deliberate underdevelopment of syntax. How exactly can the three great straits all be 'ways to them', when 'them' has the sense not merely of the Pacific or the East, but also of Jerusalem? Is Donne thinking of completing a westward circumnavigation by re-entering the strait of Gibraltar, after already having left it (presumably on falling ill)? Or is he now thinking of Gibraltar in medieval terms, where it occupied a remote and terminal position in relation to the Jerusalem-centred world, roughly equivalent to the remoteness of Anian and Magellan in the new geography? The syntax refuses closure. Ambiguity also seems essential to the last line ('Whether where Japhet dwelt, or Cham, or Shem'). Does this refer merely to the old world?[72] Or, bearing in mind the extension of the Noah theory to the New World, might it not include America as well? Are these domains being imagined as a point of departure, as way-stations, or even as a destination?[73] The imprecision of the syntax, and the powerful rhyme between 'them' and 'Shem', makes the third alternative a real possibility. So, too, does the chiastic shape of the stanza as a whole; with the possible destinations followed by the names of the straits, followed by a repeated emphasis on the straits as 'ways to them', followed by the three Noachides. Characteristically (as in the Bible of which Donne's usage is reminiscent) the *chiasmus* creates an effect of gravity, weight and equivalence between its first and last terms.

At this point, however, one begins to wonder whether fixing the meaning and sharpening the geographic focus is germane to the poetic effect. Central to that effect is the need for emplacement. But to read the stanza without forcing the places into a rigid itinerary, is suddenly to become more aware of pattern and play; and in particular, of a kind of game Donne plays with the 'homing instinct'. We want to arrive, to find 'home', but Donne deliberately defers this expectation beyond the stanza. Thus place is continually confounded in space, centres in edges, definition in the indefinable, somewhere in everywhere. On this voyage, one finds oneself precisely in being lost. It is no accident that the 'south-west discovery' ends in a dispersal myth. Discovery and diaspora, dispersal and return, are mystically related. This is not just a regression into the old geography, with its infantile certainties and *omphalos*-fixation. The real and original achievement of the stanza is to have entertained two incommensurate geographies at the same time – the old geography of emplacement and the new geography of extension – and to have turned the resulting *aporia* into a kind of revelation: the sound of one hand clapping.

Few texts better illustrate or better entertain the paradox of the new geography as I have defined it throughout this book: the paradox of a geography conscious of its novelty, confident of its superiority to the ancient geography, energetically generating a new poetry to make sense of its radically incongruous world-image, yet still enthralled to the imagery of the past.

Notes

I MAPPING THE OTHER: VICO, SHAKESPEARE AND THE GEOGRAPHY OF
DIFFERENCE

1 J. D. Rogers, 'Voyages and Exploration: Geography: Maps', ch. 6 of *Shake-speare's England: An Account of the Life and Manners of his Age* (2 vols., Clarendon Press, Oxford, 1932) vol. 1, pp. 170–72.
2 I shall dispense with inverted commas from this point on, though I am not entirely comfortable in doing so.
3 The question is immediately complicated by the fact that the word 'miscege-nation' is anachronistic and positively misleading when applied to an Eliza-bethan context. According to *A New Dictionary of Sociology*, G. Duncan Mitchell, ed. (Routledge, London, 1979): 'This word was coined by two journalists working as the contemporary equivalent of the dirty tricks depart-ment of the Democratic Party in connection with the U.S. Presidential election of 1864. Under this title they published a little book suggesting that mating between persons of different stock was to be encouraged since it would produce a superior stock. They implied that this was the policy of the Republi-can Party. Appropriately, the word is of irregular derivation (it should have been 'miscegeneration'). Use of the word is to be avoided since, apart from its disreputable origins, it reinforces a pre-Darwinian theory of human variation' (p. 127) Unfortunately, Mitchell fails to supply an alternative. Even if one were available, however, the notion of a value-free terminology is rather utopian. For this reason, and because I wish to emphasise rather than deny the problems of historicity, I will continue to use 'miscegenation', though with caution.
4 This and all subsequent Shakespeare citations are from William Shakespeare, *The Complete Works*, Stanley Wells, Gary Taylor, John Jowett and William Montgomery, eds. (Clarendon Press, Oxford, 1986).
5 Fascinating analyses of 'sacred' constructions of space in traditional or ancient cultures can be found in the following: William Arthur Heidel, *The Frame of the Ancient Greek Maps* (Arno Press, New York, 1976); J. B. Harley and David Woodward, eds. *The History of Cartography: Volume One: Car-tography in Prehistoric, Ancient, and Medieval Europe and the Mediterranean* (University of Chicago Press, Chicago and London, 1987); Samuel Y. Edger-ton, 'From Mental Matrix to *Mappamundi* to Christian Empire: The Heritage of Ptolemaic Cartography in the Renaissance', in David Woodward, ed., *Art & Cartography: Six Historical Essays* (University of Chicago Press, Chicago and

London, 1987), pp. 10–50; J. Oliver Thomson, 'Orbis Terrarum: Some Reflections on the Roman Empire', *University of Birmingham Historical Journal*, 1 (1947), 1–12; Mircea Eliade, 'Sacred Space and Making the World Sacred', in *The Sacred and the Profane: The Nature of Religion*, Willard R. Trask, tr. (Harcourt, Brace & World, Inc., New York, 1959), pp. 20–65; 'Symbolism of the "Centre", in *Images and Symbols: Studies in Religious Symbolism*, Philip Mairet, tr. (Sheed & Ward, New York, 1969), pp. 27–56; Jonathan Z. Smith, *Map is not Territory* (E. J. Brill, Leiden, 1978); B. L. Gordon, 'Sacred Directions, Orientation, and the Top of the Map', *History of Religions*, 10 (1970), 211–27.

6 Edward Said, *Orientalism* (Routledge & Kegan Paul, London and Henley, 1978); Robert Harbison, *Eccentric Spaces* (Alfred A. Knopf, New York, 1977), p. 124.

7 Michel Foucault, 'Of Other Spaces', *Diacritics*, Spring (1986) 22–7; Gaston Bachelard, *The Poetics of Space*, Maria Jolas tr. (Beacon Press, Boston, 1969).

8 Thomas Goddard Bergin and Max Harold Fisch, eds., *The New Science of Giambattista Vico: Revised Translation of the Third Edition (1744)* (Cornell University Press, Ithaca, New York, 1968), p. 285. All further references in the text are to this edition.

9 The construction *terras domibus negata* (*Odes*, 1.22.22) suggests lands which are not merely inhospitable, but actively hostile to human habitation. See R. G. M. Nisbet and Margaret Hubbard, *A Commentary on Horace: Odes, Book 1* (Clarendon Press, Oxford, 1970), pp. 272–3, note 22.

10 Aelius Aristides, *Panathenaic Discourse* in J. H. Oliver, 'The Civilizing Power: A Study of *The Panathenaic Discourse* of Aelius Aristides Against the Background of Literature and Cultural Conflict, with Text, Translation, and Commentary', *Transactions of the American Philosophical Society*, new series, vol. 58, part 1 (1968), 47.

11 J. P. Vernant, 'Hestia-Hermes: The Religious Expression of Space and Movement in Ancient Greece', in *Myth and Thought among the Greeks* (Routledge & Kegan Paul, London, Boston, Melbourne and Henley, 1983), pp. 127–75.

12 According to Plutarch, Theseus marked the birth of Athens as a city-state by setting up a boundary *Herm*: 'After this he joined Megara to Attica, and erected that famous pillar on the Isthmus, which bears an inscription of two lines, showing the bounds of the two countries that meet there. On the east side, the inscription is, "Peloponnesus there, Ionia here", and on the west side, "Peloponnesus here, Ionia there".' (*Plutarch, The Lives of the Noble Grecians and Romans*, John Dryden, tr. revised by Arthur Hugh Clough, Modern Library, New York, p. 16). All further citations are from this edition (hereafter, '*Lives*'), barring those in Chapter 4, below, in which the 1579 translation of Sir Thomas North is preferred.

13 Heidel, *Greek Maps*.

14 See the discussion of *eschatia* in François Hartog, *The Mirror of Herodotus: The Representation of the Other in the Writing of History*, Janet Lloyd, tr. (University of California Press, Berkeley and London, 1988), pp. 12–14.

15 *Herodotus*, A. D. Godley, ed., tr., The Loeb Classical Library (4 vols., Harvard University Press, Cambridge, Mass.; Heinemann, London, 1921).

16 Hartog, *The Mirror of Herodotus*, p. 212.

17 Edith Hall, *Inventing the Barbarian: Greek Self-Definition through Tragedy* (Clarendon Press, Oxford, 1989).

18 *Ibid.* In ch. 4, 'An Athenian Rhetoric', Hall explains how the invention of the barbarian was tied to the invention of *Hellas*, both of which were driven by Athenian politics.

19 The analogy of Amazons and Persians is discussed by Page duBois, *Centaurs and Amazons: Woman and the Pre-History of the Great Chain of Being* (University of Michigan Press, Ann Arbor, 1982), p. 56. For an account of how the Persians required the invention of a specifically 'Oriental' variety of barbarism, see Hall, *Inventing the Barbarian*, ch. 2, 'Inventing Persia', especially p. 99. See also Said, *Orientalism*, pp. 56–8.

20 See duBois, *Centaurs and Amazons*, ch. 2, 'Centauromachy/ Amazonomachy'.

21 Aristides, *Panathenaic Discourse*, 47. Aristides draws a strict equation between geographic centrality and ethnic purity: 'as in the case of a shield where circles fall within circles, there is a fifth which constitutes the central boss, if indeed Hellas lies in the middle of the whole earth, Attica in that of Hellas, in that of the country the polis, again in that of the polis the Polis [i.e. the Acropolis]'.

22 'The notion of the barbarian in his developed form as the "other", the generically hostile outsider just beyond the gates, appears at a similar stage in the history of other ancient cultures. In Egypt it was certainly the experience of founding an empire which created the sense of a unified Egyptian identity, and its corollary, the barbarians of the periphery. In ancient China the process is even clearer. During the Chou dynasty ... there was no clear-cut antithesis ... no collective identity. But in 221 BC, at a time when the threat from the north was becoming acute ... Shih Huang-ti's response was to clarify the boundaries of China and to order the building of the great wall ... An absolute distinction now appeared between the "inner" Chinese agriculturalists and the "outer" barbarians ... the word for "people" (*min*) which had been used for both Chinese and non-Chinese tribes ... now ... came to refer exclusively to the privileged Chinese "hundred clans". The distinction between Chinese and non ... had acquired for the first time a political dimension.' (Hall, *Inventing the Barbarian*, pp. 60–1).

23 Hartog, *The Mirror of Herodotus*, pp. 14–18.

24 'Furthermore, the principle of symmetry is so evident that it has a certain heuristic value, for, knowing the course taken by the Ister, I can, by analogy, infer that taken by the Nile. Just as the Ister ... "cuts clean across Europe ... thus I suppose the source of the Nile in its passage through Libya to be like the course of the Ister"'. See Hartog, *The Mirror of Herodotus*, p. 14; see also *Herodotus*, 2.33–4.

25 Edward Gibbon, *The History of the Decline and Fall of the Roman Empire*, J. B. Bury, ed. (7 vols., Methuen, London, 1900), vol. 1, pp. 2–3. In a note on this passage, Bury cites various classical sources for Gibbon's assertion: Tacitus, Dion Cassius and Augustus himself.

26 Sir James George Frazer, ed., *Ovid's Fasti*, The Loeb Classical Library (Harvard University Press, Cambridge, Mass.; Heinemann, London, 1951), pp. 106–7.

27 For a representative sample of other proverbs of this sort, see Thomson, 'Orbis Terrarum', 2.

28 Thomson, 'Orbis Terrarum', 2–5 especially.
29 Plutarch, *Lives*, p. 3. The rest of this passage (introducing the *Life of Theseus*) suggests that Plutarch anticipates Vico in perceiving an analogy between the depiction of remote geographic regions and remote or mythological history: 'so in this work of mine . . . after passing through those periods which probable reasoning can reach to and real history find a footing in, I might very well say of those that are farther off: "Beyond this there is nothing but prodigies and fictions, the only inhabitants are the poets and inventors of fables; there is no credit, or certainty any farther"'.
30 Nisbet and Hubbard, *A Commentary on Horace*, p. 268.
31 Sir William Smith and Sir John Lockwood, eds., *Chambers Murray Latin-English Dictionary* (Chambers, Edinburgh; John Murray, London, 1988), p. 275. Jonson makes systematic use of the moralised Roman imagery of boundaries in *Sejanus* and *Catiline*. But see his meditation on 'Tyranni': 'There is nothing with some princes sacred above their majesty; or profane but what violates their sceptres. But a prince with such counsel is like the God Terminus, of stone, his own landmark' (*Discoveries*, lines 1227–300, in Ian Donaldson, ed., *Ben Jonson*, Oxford University Press, Oxford and New York, 1985, p. 554).
32 According to Plutarch, Remus was killed as punishment for leaping over 'a ditch where he [Romulus] designed the foundation of the city-wall' (*Lives*, p. 30). The equivalence of the estate boundary and the orbic margin is nicely figured in Horace's ode, *Integer Vitae*. My citation of Nisbet and Hubbard on the sacralisation of the *terminus* is taken from their commentary on this ode. The first lines are cited in *Titus Andronicus* (4.2.20–21), which registers their full poetic geographic force throughout (see Chapter 4, below).
33 Lucan, *Pharsalia*, 2.381, in *Lucan: The Civil War, Books I–X*, J. D. Duff, ed., tr., The Loeb Classical Library (Putnam, New York; Heinemann, London, 1928), pp. 84–5.
34 Velleius Paterculus, *The History of Rome*, 2.46, in *Compendium of Roman History: Res Gestae Divi Augusti*, Frederick W. Shipley, ed., The Loeb Classical Library (Harvard University Press, Cambridge, Mass.; Heinemann, London, 1961), p. 151. See also Thomson, 'Orbis Terrarum', 4.
35 See Gail Kern Paster, *The Idea of the City in the Age of Shakespeare* (The University of Georgia Press, Athens, 1985), p. 15.
36 Virgil, *Georgics*, 2.114–54, in *Virgil: With an English Translation*, H. Rushton Fairclough, ed., The Loeb Classical Library (2 vols., Harvard University Press, Cambridge, Mass.; Heinemann, London, 1967), vol. 1, pp. 122–25. All further citations from Virgil are to this edition.
37 For a discussion of this tradition, see the index entries under 'temperies' and 'climate' in Richard F. Thomas, *Lands and Peoples in Roman Poetry: The Ethnographical Tradition*, The Cambridge Philological Society (The Cambridge University Library, 1982), especially pp. 11–12. See also Hippocrates, *Airs, Waters, Places*, in *Hippocrates*, W. H. S. Jones, ed., The Loeb Classical Library (6 vols., Putnam, New York; Heinemann, London, 1923), vol. 1, pp. 65–137.
38 Lidia Storoni Mazzolani, *The Idea of the City in Roman Thought: From Walled City to Spiritual Commonwealth*, S. O'Donnell, tr. (Hollis & Carter, London,

1970). See especially ch. 3, 'Cultural Factors and the Ecumenical Idea' and ch. 6, 'The Precedent of Alexander'.

39 Mary Douglas, *Purity and Danger: An Analysis of the Concepts of Pollution and Taboo* (Ark Paperbacks, London, Boston, Melbourne and Henley, 1984), p. 114. See also ch. 7, 'External Lines', and ch. 8, 'Internal Lines'.

40 *Contributions to Indian Sociology*, 3 (July 1959), 37. Cited in Douglas, *Purity and Danger*, p. 126.

41 Lucan, *Pharsalia*, 7.405. The imagery of orbic margins figures powerfully in the *Pharsalia*. Caesar's victory over the Republic is imagined as an implosion of the whole Roman world, a reversal of the control which Rome, as centre, had exercised over the geographical margins of the empire. The implosion can happen only because the centre has already been corrupted by the morals of the hinterland. The idea is treated as a commonplace in the satires of Juvenal. See particularly Satire 3, lines 62ff.: 'Long has Syrian Orontes flowed down into the Tiber / With its language and its morals'.

42 The Elder Seneca, *Declamations in Two Volumes, vol. 2: Controversiae, Books 7–10, Suasoriae*, M. Winterbottom, ed., The Loeb Classical Library (Harvard University Press, Cambridge Mass.; Heinemann, London, 1974), pp. 485–507, paras 4 and 11.

43 Caius Julius Solinus, *The Excellent and Pleasant Worke, Collectanea Rerum Memorabilium, of Caius Julius Solinus*, Arthur Golding, tr. (1587), George Kish, ed. (Scholars' Facsimiles & Reprints, Florida, 1955).

44 See, for example, George Abbot, *A Briefe Description of the Whole World (London, 1599)*, The English Experience, no. 213 (Da Capo Press, Theatrum Orbis Terrarum, Amsterdam and New York, 1970), p. C; also Andrewe Thevet, *The New Found Worlde or Antarctike (London: 1568)*, The English Experience, no. 417 (Da Capo Press, Theatrum Orbis Terrarum, Amsterdam and New York, 1971), p. 5.

45 John Noble Wilford (*The Mapmakers*, Junction Books, London, 1981) finds evidence of the ancient theory as late as 1761, in this legend on a map of Africa: 'It is true that the centre of the continent is filled with burning sands, savage beasts, and almost uninhabitable deserts. The scarcity of water forces the different animals to come together to the same place to drink. Finding themselves together at a time when they are in heat, they have intercourse with one another, without paying regard to the differences between species. Thus are produced those monsters which are to be found there in greater numbers than in any other part of the world' (p. 35).

46 Euripides, *Andromache*, lines 170–8, in *Euripides: Orestes and Other Plays*, Philip Vellacott, ed., tr. (Penguin, Harmondsworth, 1972), p. 151.

47 Euripides, *Iphigenia in Aulis* in *Orestes and Other Plays*, p. 412.

48 Aristotle, *The Politics*, T. A. Sinclair tr., Trevor J. Saunders, ed. (Penguin, Harmondsworth, 1986). It is quite possible that Aristotle's interpretation of Iphigenia's words was closer to Euripides's meaning than our own ironic reading. John Ferguson (*A Companion to Greek Tragedy*, University of Texas Press, Austin and London, 1972) finds no irony in the passage: 'It is tempting to suppose irony in view of the pretentious Hellenism of the Macedonian court. Yet Iphigeneia is no tongue-in-cheek creation ... There is no irony there' (p. 463).

49 Barbarous promiscuity has a concealed significance in Aristotle, being not only a link between several varieties of barbarian, but also a universal marker of an inferiority for which – Aristotle acknowledges (*Politics*, 1254b32) – there is no unambiguous physical sign.

50 Claude Lévi-Strauss, *The Elementary Structures of Kinship*, James Harle Bell, John Richard von Sturmer and Rodney Needham, trs., Rodney Needham, ed. (Eyre & Spottiswoode, London, 1969), p. 10.

51 Hall, *Inventing the Barbarian*, ch. 3, 'The Barbarian Enters Myth'; also ch. 4, 'An Athenian Rhetoric'. In 451–450 BC, Pericles passed a law whereby 'all but those who could prove that both parents were Athenians, and of the citizen class, were now excluded from its priveleges' (p. 175). See also John K. Davies, 'Athenian Citizenship: The Descent Group and the Alternatives', *The Classical Journal*, 73, 2 (1977–8), 105–21.

52 Hall supposes that Medea 'probably began as the Peloponnesian Agamede of the *Iliad*, who was the granddaughter of the sun and knew "all the drugs ... which the wide earth nourishes". Eumelus, the Corinthian poet whose name is associated with the earliest known Argonautic epic, made a conscious attempt to link the story of the Argo with a Corinthian cult. In doing so he turned Aeetes, father of Medea, into a Corinthian hero who emigrated to the Black Sea; later in the poem Medea was recalled to Hellas to rule the Corinthians. Her pharmaceutical skills were an old element in the story, but her conversion into a barbarian was almost certainly an invention of tragedy, probably of Euripides himself' (*Inventing the Barbarian*, p. 35).

53 Ovid, *Ovid In Six Volumes: III Metamorphoses*, Frank Justus Miller, tr., G. P. Gould, ed., The Loeb Classical Library (Harvard University Press, Cambridge, Mass.; Heinemann, London, 1977), pp. 316–37.

54 For a discussion of the lost Sophoclean tragedy, see Hall, *Inventing the Barbarian*, pp. 103–5.

55 The Latin text is: '*radix micat ultima linguae, / ipsa iacet terraeque tremens inmurmurat atrae*'.

56 Versions of this gory witticism appear in Seneca's *Thyestes* and Shakespeare's *Titus Andronicus*.

57 The Holy Bible, The Revised Version (Cambridge University Press, Cambridge, 1898).

58 Edmund Leach, *Genesis as Myth and Other Essays* (Jonathan Cape, London, 1969): 'the theme of homosexual incest in the Cain and Abel story recurs in the Noah saga when drunken Noah is seduced by his own son Ham ([Genesis] ix. 21–5). The Canaanites, descendants of Ham, are for this reason accursed. (That a homosexual act is intended is evident from the language "Ham saw the nakedness of his father". Compare Leviticus xviii. 6–19, where "to uncover the nakedness of" consistently means to have sexual relations with.)' (p. 19).

59 Though the root ('*Euxinos*', or 'hospitable') for the Greek name, 'Euxine Sea', is anything but 'black' in its suggestion, Greek authors were liable to invert the Greek name, as in *Iphigenia in Tauris*, where Euripides plays on the similarity of *Euxinos* to *axeinos* or 'unfriendly'. See Euripides, *Alcestis / Hippolytus / Iphigenia in Tauris*, Philip Vellacott, tr., ed. (Penguin, London, 1974), p. 185, note 7.

60 Arthur O. Lovejoy and George Boas, *Primitivism and Related Ideas in Antiq-*

uity (With Supplementary Essays by W. F. Albright and P.E. Dumont)(The Johns Hopkins University Press, Baltimore, 1935).

61 The phrase *'non sufficit orbis'* is a commonplace, used by Juvenal (*Satires*, 10.168) and Lucan (*Pharsalia*, 5.356) among many others. In the Renaissance, the phrase contributes towards the iconography of the New World. For the first *Suasoria*, see above, note 42.

62 Plutarch, *Lives*, p. 849; Lucan, *Pharsalia*, 10.40–43.

63 Quintilian, *The Institutio Oratoria of Quintilian*, H. E. Butler, ed., tr., The Loeb Classical Library (4 vols., Harvard University Press, Cambridge, Mass.; Heinemann, London, 1964), vol. 3, p. 105, 7.4, 1–2.

64 Velleius Paterculus, *The History of Rome*, 2.46, in *Compendium of Roman History*, p. 151; Lucius Annaeus Florus, *Epitome of Roman History*, Cornelius Nepos, ed., tr., The Loeb Classical Library (Heinemann, London; Putnam, New York, 1929), I.45.16, p. 205.

65 Ben Jonson, *Sejanus his Fall* (1.1,145–46), W. F. Bolton, ed. (Ernest Benn, London, 1966). Compare Lucan, *Pharsalia*, 10.22–4: 'the mad son of Macedonian Philip, that fortunate free-booter'.

66 Thomas, *Lands and Peoples*, p. 15. Remarking that 'examples are plentiful enough and hardly need mention', Thomas cites some in note 30.

67 Plutarch, *Lives*, p. 874. The themes of incest and invasion are linked in various earlier legends, both Greek and Latin, mythological and historical. In Aeschylus's *Seven Against Thebes*, the *Polis* is assailed by a horde of savage outsiders as a direct result of a feud between Oedipus's incestuously begotten sons, Eteocles and Polyneices. While the feud is the efficient cause of the invasion, the deeper cause is what two modern editors call 'the miasma of violated *Dike*' (a term representing 'the sanctity of the basic relationships between god and man, host and guest, parent and child, brother and brother, relationships which Laios and his descendents defied' (Anthony Hecht and Helen H. Bacon, eds., *Aeschylus: Seven Against Thebes*, Oxford University Press, London, 1974, pp. 5–6). Eventually, the pollution is cleansed and the city's integrity assured only by the deaths of the two brothers. Hecht and Bacon point out that an Athenian audience might have recognised a reference to the attempted invasion of Athens some twenty-three years earlier by Hippias, exiled son of Peisistratos (p. 6). In Herodotus (6.107), Hippias dreams of sleeping with his mother the night before landing at Marathon. Hecht and Bacon suggest that Herodotus's account may have been influenced by Aeschylus. An early Roman example of what we might call the 'incestuous invader' theme is provided by the historical legend of Coriolanus. Like Caesar and Hippias, Coriolanus is confronted by a violable mother. Here, however, the mother is no phantasm, and her pleas prevent both the invasion and the violation from taking place.

68 See *Plutarch's Lives*, Bernadotte Perin, ed., The Loeb Classical Library (10 vols., Heinemann, London; Macmillan, New York, 1914), vol. 7, p. 523, note 2.

69 Christopher Marlowe, 'Lucan's First Book Translated Line for Line', in *Christopher Marlowe: The Complete Poems and Translations*, Stephen Orgel, ed. (Penguin, Harmondsworth, 1971), pp. 185–207.

70 Euripides, *Medea and Other Plays*, Philip Vellacott, ed., tr. (Penguin, Harmondsworth, 1963).

71 Seneca the Younger, *The Tenne Tragedies of Seneca Translated into English*, The Spenser Society, 43 (Burt Franklin, New York, 1967), second chorus, p. 260.

72 Joseph de Acosta, *The Natural and Moral History of the Indies ... Reprinted from the English Translated Edition of Edward Grimstone 1604*, Clements R. Markham, ed. (2 vols., Burt Franklin, New York, 1970), vol. 1, p. 35.

73 This type of 'voyager' river-pollution may be compared with the more sanguinary river-pollution of the conqueror. Lucan's Alexander 'defiled distant rivers, the Euphrates and the Ganges, with Persian and Indian blood' (*Pharsalia*, 10.36–8).

74 George Best, 'Experiences and reasons of the Sphere, to proove all partes of the worlde habitable, and thereby to confute the position of the five Zones', in Richard Hakluyt, *The Principal Navigations Voyages Traffiques & Discoveries of the English nation: Made by Sea or Over-land to the Remote and Farthest Distant Quarters of the Earth at any time within the compasse of these 1600 Yeeres* (8 vols., James MacLehose & Sons, Glasgow, 1903), vol. 5, p. 182. Remarking on the birth of a black English child to 'an Ethiopian as blacke as a cole' and 'a faire English woman', Best concludes that 'this blacknes proceedeth rather of some natural infection of that man, which was so strong, that neither the nature of the Clime, neither the good complexion of the mother concurring, coulde anything alter' (p. 180). Regardless, then, of where they may be or with whom they may copulate, moors will continue to beget offspring 'polluted with the same blot of infection' (p. 181).

75 *The Oxford English Dictionary*, second edition, prepared by J. A. Simpson and E. S. C. Weiner (Clarendon Press, Oxford, 1979) offers this definition as appropriate to later seventeenth-century usages. However, it suits Ben Jonson's 1599 usage ('Magick, Witchcraft, or other such exotick arts') as well or better.

76 *Oroonoko* first appeared in the form of Aphra Behn's novel, *Oroonoko: Or, The Royal Slave* (1688). In 1695 it was adapted for the stage by Thomas Southerne under the title, *Oroonoko: A Tragedy*, being performed at Drury Lane *c.* 1695.

77 The circumstantial character of Othello's generalship is not only suggested by the extraordinary circumstance posed by the Turkish threat, but by the Duke's mention of 'Marcus Luccicos', who (from the context) would appear to be his first choice as general:

> *Duke.*   'Tis certain then for Cyprus.
>   Marcus Luccicos, is not he in town?
> *First Senator.* He's now in Florence.
> *Duke.*   Write from us, wish him post post-haste, dispatch.
>
>   (1.3.43–46).

As no more is heard of this mysterious person, it is reasonable to conclude that his absence from Venice in its hour of need was more meaningful in some earlier version of the text. The only possible inference we can draw from the hint as we have it, is that Othello's appointment hinges on Luccicos's absence.

78 The first definition can be found in the *Shorter OED on Historical Principles*. For the second, see 'A Sermon Against Whoredom and Uncleanness', in *Sermons or Homilies Appointed to be Read in Churches in the Time of Queen*

Elizabeth of Famous Memory (Clarendon Press, Oxford, 1816), p. 99. For the Virginian law on miscegenation (1691), see Winthrop D. Jordan, *White Over Black: American Attitudes Toward the Negro, 1550–1812* (University of North Carolina Press, Williamsburg, Virginia, 1968), p. 80.

79 Mary Douglas remarks how, in some societies, the pollution resulting from adultery lights on the offended party as well as (or rather than) on the offender. Elizabethan society is a case in point. In the rural institution of the 'skimmington', the cuckolded husband incurs the pollution of the adulterous wife and is ritually mocked for it. Othello clearly thinks in these terms, imagining himself as an object of ritual mockery (*Purity and Danger*, pp. 144ff.).

80 See Hugh Honour's discussion of how the more decorous and decorative exoticism the later seventeenth century evolves from the more uncompromising exoticism of the sixteenth century, particularly in relation to the tapestries, 'Les Indes' (1687) and 'Les Nouvelles Indes' (1737), and in relation to Rameau's opera 'Les Indes Galantes' (1735). (*The New Golden Land*, Pantheon Books, New York, 1978, pp. 97–102).

81 See note 75, above.

82 See 'The Measure of *Thoma*', in Hartog, *The Mirror of Herodotus*, pp. 230–37.

83 G. Wilson Knight, *The Wheel of Fire: Interpretations of Shakespearean Tragedy* (Methuen, London, 1972), pp. 97–8.

84 For *The Indian Queen*, see *The Works of John Dryden*, James Harrington Smith and Douglas MacMillan, eds. (20 vols., University of California Press, Berkeley and Los Angeles, 1967), vol. 8, pp. 180–304. For *The Indian Emperor*, see *Works*, vol. 9 (1966), John Loftis, ed., pp. 1–112. Behn's depiction of Oroonoko and Dryden's depiction of Amerindians appear to owe more to Spanish literary example than to English colonial experience. See John Van Horne, 'The Attitude Toward the Enemy in Sixteenth Century Spanish Narrative Poetry', *The Romanic Review*, 16 (1925), 341–61; also Martin Hume, *Spanish Influence on English Literature* (Haskell House, New York, 1964), ch. 7, 'The Literature of Travel and of War', pp. 184–213.

85 Mandeville was dropped from the second edition of 1599 (the text on which the 1903 Glasgow edition, cited in note 74, above, is based). This is fully in keeping with a collapse in his prestige among the more serious geographers at the turn of the century (see *The Travels of Sir John Mandeville*, C. W. R. D. Moseley, ed. (Penguin, Harmondsworth, 1983, p. 32). Mandeville's continued influence over less serious geographers, however, is suggested by the fact that Samuel Purchas reinstated him ('albeit heavily cut') into the travel archive which he inherited from Hakluyt (p. 31).

86 Pliny, *The History of the World, Commonly Called the Natural History of C. Plinius Secundus, or Pliny*, Philemon Holland, tr., Paul Turner ed. (McGraw-Hill, New York, Toronto and London, 1964), pp. 312–13.

87 I attribute this opinion to Mandeville for the sake of convenience. It is found in the text of *The Travels* included in the first edition of *The Principal Navigations* (*The Principall Navigations Voiages and Discoveries of the English Nation*, London, 1589, D. B. Quinn, R. A. Skelton and A. Quinn, eds., The Hakluyt Society and The Peabody Museum of Salem, Cambridge University Press, 1965, p. 45). The whole chapter in which it appears ('Caput 24: *Persuasio ad non credentes terrarum diversitates per orbem terrae*', pp. 45–6), is

thought to be the interpolation of a sixteenth-century editor (*The Travels*, C. W. R. D. Moseley, ed., pp. 45ff.). My citation has been translated from the Latin of Hakluyt's text by Colin Mayrhoffer.

88 'The Metamorphoses of Sir John Mandeville' in *The Yearbook of English Studies*, 4 (1974), 5–25, *passim*.

89 *Ibid.*, 6.

90 Margaret T. Hodgen, *Early Anthropology in the Sixteenth and Seventeenth Centuries* (University of Pennsylvania Press, Philadelphia, 1964). See especially ch. 6, 'The Ark of Noah and the Problem of Cultural Diversity'.

91 See Hogden, *Early Anthropology*, ch. 7, 'Diffusion, Degeneration, and Environmentalism'.

92 If the Folio's reading of 'base Iudean' is preferred, then we should assume that Othello is being telescoped with Jews rather than Indians.

93 Emrys Jones ('"Othello", "Lepanto" and the Cyprus Wars', *Shakespeare Survey*, 21 (1968), 47–52), points out that a 'Cypriot setting' would have had 'an ominous character' for Elizabethans of 1602–4, the years when *Othello* was first acted, because by then 'Cyprus had been in Turkish hands for over thirty years' (49). Iago's reference to the 'Cyprus wars' suggests the eventually successful 'Turkish attack on Cyprus' in 1570 (49).

94 Christopher Marlowe, *The Jew of Malta* (2.3.134), in *Christopher Marlowe: The Complete Plays*, J. B. Steane, ed. (Penguin, Harmondsworth, 1975). Interestingly, Ithamore is also referred to as a Turk (see, for example, 4.1.130 and 4.2.46). Shakespeare's Aaron is also Thracian (or Scythian) in being compared to a tiger (*Titus Andronicus*, 5.3.5) – like Tamora, his gothic mentor. The harsh educational regimen that Aaron proposes for his son (4.2.177–80) closely resembles what classical authorities reported of the martial upbringing of the Thracians (see, for example, a passage of Sidonius cited by George Sandys in *Ovid's Metamorphoses Englished: Oxford, 1632*, Garland, New York and London, 1976, p. 228).

95 Thomas Coryat, *Coryats Crudities, 1611*, William M. Schutte, ed. (Scolar Press, London, 1978), pp. 171–3. There is a fuller citation of this passage, and a more detailed discussion in Chapter 4, below.

96 Gerard Mercator, *Mercator-Hondius-Janssonius: Atlas, Or a Geographicke Description of the World*, R. A. Skelton, ed. (2 vols., Theatrum Orbis Terrarum, Amsterdam, 1968), vol. 1, frontispiece.

97 Cited in Ruth Cowhig, 'Blacks in English Renaissance drama and the role of Shakespeare's Othello' in *The Black Presence in English Literature*, David Dabydeen, ed. (Manchester University Press, 1985), p. 17.

98 *Ibid.*, p. 16.

99 Winthrop D. Jordan, *White Over Black*, pp. 85–91.

100 Thomas Rymer, 'A Short View of Tragedy' (1693) in *Critical Essays of the Seventeenth Century*, J. E. Springarn, ed. (3 vols., Indiana University Press, Bloomington, 1957), vol. 2., pp. 221–2.

101 The terminology of 'racial prejudice' is used more or less unproblematically by Ruth Cowhig (see note 97, above) and in G. K. Hunter, 'Othello and Colour Prejudice', *Proceedings of the British Academy*, 53 (1967), pp. 139–63.

102 Steven Mullaney, *The Place of the Stage: License, Play, and Power in Renaissance England* (University of Chicago Press, Chicago and London, 1988), pp. 63, 60.

103 Mercator, *Atlas*, vol. 1, p. 31.
104 Bachelard, *The Poetics of Space*, p. 47.
105 Stephen Greenblatt, *The Power of Forms in the English Renaissance* (Pilgrim Books, Norman, Oklahoma, 1982).
106 Wilford, *The Mapmakers*, p. 40.
107 Mikhail Bakhtin, 'The Problem of Speech Genres' in *Speech Genres and Other Late Essays*, Caryl Emerson and Michael Holquist, eds., Vern W. McGee, tr. (University of Texas Press, Austin, 1986), pp. 60–102.
108 The quote is from the Folio's *The Tragedy of King Lear* as distinct from the Quarto's *The History of King Lear*. The texts are printed separately in the Oxford *Complete Works*. As the Quarto text lacks act divisions, all following *Lear* citations that show only scene and line divisions will be from the Quarto text. All citations showing act, scene and line divisions will be from the Folio text.
109 For Columbus's reading, see Felipe Fernández-Armesto, *Columbus* (Oxford University Press, 1991), ch. 2, '"The Secrets of this World": The Formation of Plans and Tastes, *c.* 1480–1492'.
110 For Columbus's obsession with finding Amazons, see Fernández-Armesto *Columbus*, pp. 34, 40, 84, 174. The citations are from: *The First Three English Books on America: Being chiefly Translations, Compilations, &c., by Richard Eden*, Edward Arber, ed. (Kraus Reprint Co., New York, 1971), pp. 30, 69. The obsession persists: *The Australian* (9 March 1991) reported the departure of an Indonesian expedition to Brazil for the purpose of finding Amazons.

2 OF 'VOYAGES AND EXPLORATION: GEOGRAPHY: MAPS'

1 R. H. Coote, 'Shakspere's "New Map"', *New Shakspere Society Transactions*, 1877–9, Part 1, 1878, 88–100; R. H. Coote, 'Note on The "New Map"', in *The Voyages and Works of John Davis the Navigator*, A. H. Markham, ed. (Burt Franklin Reprints, New York, 1970), pp. lxxxv–xcv.
2 In his note on Wright's map (Entry 221) in his *The Mapping Of The World: Early Printed World Maps 1472–1700* (The Holland Press, London, 1987), Rodney W. Shirley observes: 'The Wright-Molyneux map certainly delineates the East Indies and Japan fully, but in no greater detail than maps by others such as Plancius, Ortelius or Mercator in circulation during the previous decade' (p. 239).
3 Alden T. Vaughan ('Shakespeare's Indian: The Americanization of Caliban', *Shakespeare Quarterly*, Vol. 39, 1988, 137–53), remarks that 'Lee's advocacy went a long way toward popularizing ... [the] ... new interpretation and making it acceptable among Shakespearean specialists' (145).
4 This and the following citation from Lee are given in Vaughan, 'Shakespeare's Indian', 140.
5 Sir Sidney Lee, 'The American Indian in Elizabethan England' in *Elizabethan and Other Essays by Sir Sidney Lee*, Frederick S. Boas, ed. (Clarendon Press, Oxford, 1929), pp. 263–301.
6 C. M. Gayley, *Shakespeare and the Founders of Liberty in America* (Macmillan, New York, 1917).
7 Sir A. W. Ward, 'Shakespeare and the Makers of Virginia', *Proceedings of the British Academy*, 9 (1919–20), pp. 141–85.

8 R. R. Cawley, 'Shakespeare's Use of the Voyagers in *The Tempest*', *Proceedings of the Modern Languages Association of America*, 41 (1926), 688–726.

9 E. E. Stoll, *Poets and Playwrights: Shakespeare, Milton, Spenser, Jonson* (University of Minnesota Press, Minneapolis, 1930), pp. 212–13.

10 William Shakespeare, *The Tempest*, Frank Kermode, ed., The Arden Shakespeare (Methuen, London, 1962), p. xxv.

11 Leo Marx, 'Shakespeare's American Fable' in *The Machine in the Garden: Technology and the Pastoral Ideal in America* (Oxford University Press, New York, 1964), pp. 34–72; Leslie Fiedler, 'The New World Savage as Stranger; or, "'Tis new to thee."' in *The Stranger in Shakespeare* (Croom Helm, London, 1973), pp. 199–253.

12 Paul Frey, '*The Tempest* and the New World', *Shakespeare Quarterly*, 30, 1 (Winter 1979), 29–41.

13 William Shakespeare, *The Tempest*, Stephen Orgel, ed., The Oxford Shakespeare (Oxford University Press, Oxford and New York, 1987).

14 Vaughan, 'Shakespeare's Indian'; Meredith Anne Skura, 'Discourse and the Individual: The Case of Colonialism in *The Tempest*', *Shakespeare Quarterly*, 40, 1 (Spring 1989), 42–69.

15 Paul A. Jorgensen, 'Shakespeare's Brave New World' in *First Images of America: The Impact of the New World on The Old*, Fredi Chiapelli, ed. (2 vols., University of California Press, Berkeley, Los Angeles, London, 1976), vol. 1, pp. 86–7.

16 Hayden White, 'The Forms of Wildness: Archaeology of an Idea' in *Tropics of Discourse: Essays in Cultural Criticism* (Johns Hopkins University Press, Baltimore and London, 1978), pp. 150–82.

17 See the entry under 'stranger' in *The New Bible Dictionary*, J. D. Douglas, ed. (Inter-Varsity Press, London, 1970), p. 1219.

18 In all, sixteen references to 'map', 'maps', 'mapp'd' and 'mapp'ry' appear in Martin Spevack, *The Harvard Concordance to Shakespeare* (The Belknap Press of Harvard University Press, Cambridge, Mass., 1973), p. 788.

19 According to Svetlana Alpers ('The Mapping Impulse in Dutch Art', in David Woodward, ed., *Art & Cartography*, pp. 51–96), the rhetorical figure of *ecphrasis* was the conceptual basis of the Renaissance idea of cartographic 'description': 'To call a picture descriptive at the time was unusual, since description was a term commonly applied to texts. From antiquity on, the Greek term for description *ekphrasis*, was a rhetorical term used to refer to a verbal evocation of people, places, buildings, or works of art. As a rhetorical device *ekphrasis* depended specifically on the power of words. It was this verbal power that Italian artists in the Renaissance strove to equal in paint when they rivalled the poets. But when the word "description" is used by Renaissance geographers it calls attention not to the power of words but to a mode of pictorial representation. The graphic implication of the term is distinguished from the rhetorical one. If we look back on Ptolemy now, we would have to say that his term *grapho* was opened up to suggest both picture and writing' (p. 69).

20 See Catherine Delano Smith, 'Cartographic Signs on European Maps and their Explanation before 1700', *Imago Mundi*, 37 (1985), 9–29.

21 The political symbolism of the maps in Saxton's *Atlas* is well discussed in Richard Helgerson, 'The Land Speaks: Cartography, Chorography, and Sub-

version in Renaissance England' in *Representing the English Renaissance*, Stephen Greenblatt, ed. (University of California Press, Berkeley, 1988), pp. 327–61.

22 *The Mariner's Mirrour* (London, 1588) is an English translation of the first of such atlases: Lucas Janszoon Waghenaer's *Spieghel der Zeevaerdt* (Leiden, 1584–5). The roots of the sixteenth-century maritime map are deep. In medieval cartography, the genre is represented by the 'Portolan Chart', which bears something of the same relationship to the highly moralised *Mappamundi* as the Renaissance maritime map bears to the monumental 'Cosmographic' genre of Ortelius and Mercator. In Roman times, the maritime map is represented by the *Periplus*, which again is strictly functional by comparison with the more 'poetic' official maps of the Roman world.

23 Two facts strongly suggest the utilitarian character of this cartographic genre relative to the general atlases of Ortelius and Mercator. First, the original edition of Waghenaer appeared in the Dutch vernacular rather than in Latin (a Latin edition would follow). The original edition of Ortelius, on the other hand, is in Latin, the learned and international language. Second, the gap between the appearance of the English translation of Waghenaer in 1588 and the Dutch version (1584–5) is considerably shorter than the gap between the original Latin edition of Ortelius (1570) and the English translation in 1606.

24 The quotation is from 'A True Description of the Sea Coastes Betweene Laredo and Sentillana' in *The Mariner's Mirrour* (London, 1588), R. A. Skelton, ed. (Theatrum Orbis Terrarum, Amsterdam, 1966).

25 The symbolism of Milford is discussed in Emrys Jones, 'Stuart *Cymbeline*' in *Shakespeare's Later Comedies*, D. J. Palmer, ed. (Penguin, Harmondsworth, 1971), pp. 248–63.

26 Two modern editors of *The Tempest* differ over the meaning of this exchange. Frank Kermode thinks that Gonzalo's identification of Tunis and Carthage is simply bad geography (*The Tempest*, Arden, p. 47, note to line 78). Stephen Orgel, however, helpfully suggests that Gonzalo is wrong only if judged by a 'technical' geographic standard. Yet this 'need not be narrowly topographical' (*The Tempest*, Oxford, p. 42, note 2). A map of 'The Haven of Carthage' in the *Parergon*, the section of Ortelius's atlas devoted to historical geography, shows both cities in the same inset-view, but with Carthage just to the south of the peninsula of Tunis. See Abraham Ortelius, *The Theatre of the Whole World* (London, 1606), R. A. Skelton, ed. (Theatrum Orbis Terrarum, Amsterdam, 1968), pp. 112–13.

27 The miscegenation of Aaron and Tamora in *Titus Andronicus* represents a yet more ominous and elaborate recapitulation of the Dido legend. See the discussion of this play, in Chapter 4, below.

28 The scientific originality of Wright's map is rarer than it might seem. Most supposedly 'new geographical' maps of the period are simply copied from existing plates. For this reason, the genuine discoveries displayed by Wright had to wait thirty years or more to find their way on to the more popular world maps of the Flemish and Dutch printing houses which tended to replicate the originals of Ortelius and Mercator.

29 Rogers cites this passage (presumably in his own translation) in *Shakespeare's England*, p. 171.

30 The full account can be found in *Fonti Ricciane: Edizione nazionale delle opere*

202 Notes to pages 51–5

edite e inedite di Matteo Ricci, Pasquale D'Elia, ed. (2 vols., Rome, 1942), vol. 1, pp. 207–12, vol. 2, pp. 58–62. Discussions of Ricci's cartographic contributions to Chinese culture can be found in: Samuel Y. Edgerton, 'From Mental Matrix to *Mappamundi* to Christian Empire: The Heritage of Ptolemaic Cartography in the Renaissance' in Woodward, ed., *Art & Cartography*, pp. 10–50; Helen Wallis, 'The influence of Father Ricci on Far Eastern Cartography', *Imago Mundi*, 19 (1965), 38–45; Helen Wallis, 'Missionary Cartographers to China', *The Geographical Magazine*, 47, 12 (September 1975), 751–9; J. F. Baddeley, 'Father Matteo Ricci's Chinese World-Maps, 1584–1608', *The Geographical Journal*, 50 (1917), 254–76; *Une Rencontre de l'Occident et de la Chine: Matteo Ricci, Travaux et Conférences du Centre Sèvres* (Centre Sèvres, 1983).

31 Reproductions of various editions of Ricci's map can be found in D'Elia, ed., *Fonti Ricciani*, vol. 2, Tavola VIII; Woodward, ed., *Art & Cartography*, pp. 25–6. Reproductions also appear in the article by J. F. Baddeley, and both articles by Helen Wallis cited in note 30, above.

32 Ortelius's *Typus Orbis Terrarum* was by far the most popular world map for some forty years (1570–c. 1612). In this period, the *Theatrum* went through some forty-two Folio editions in Latin and the major European languages including English, into which it was translated as *The Theatre of the Whole World* in 1606. A list of all Folio editions is supplied in R. V. Tooley, *Maps and Map-Makers* (Batsford, London, 1949), pp. 30–31. To the list of Folio editions, should be added the thirty-one pocket editions which were published throughout Europe from 1576–1697. This makes a total of seventy-three editions, the bulk of which occur between 1576–1612 (Tooley, p. 30). To obtain a true measure of the popularity of Ortelius's world map, however, we would have to include all the imitations and variants to be found not just in other atlases, geographic books and wall-maps, but also in the great number of non-geographic works which include versions of the *Typus* (many of which are reproduced in Shirley's *The Mapping of the World*). The *Typus* was by far the most widely imitated map of the period.

33 Ethel Seaton, 'Fresh Sources for Marlowe', *Review of English Studies*, 5, 20 (1929), 385–401; Alan H. Gilbert, *A Geographical Dictionary of Milton* (Russell & Russell, New York, 1968).

34 Gilbert argues that Milton's major geographical source was Peter Heylyn's *Microcosmus: Or a Little Description of the Great World* (Oxford,1621). See also R. R. Cawley, *Milton and the Literature of Travel* (Gordian Press, New York, 1970).

35 The best study of Donne's relationship with contemporary 'cosmography' is Marjorie Hope Nicholson's *The Breaking of the Circle: Studies in the Effect of the 'New Science' upon Seventeenth Century Poetry*, revised edition (Columbia University Press: New York and London, 1960).

36 Harley and Woodward, eds., *The History of Cartography, Volume 1*. Volume 1 is the first of a projected six volumes.

37 The linguistic model is taken by Harley and Woodward from Arthur H. Robinson and Barbara Bartz Petchenik, *The Nature of Maps: Essays Toward Understanding Maps and Mapping* (Chicago University Press, 1986).

38 Woodward here cites from Wilbur Zelinsky, 'The First and Last Frontier of

Communication: The Map as Mystery', *Bulletin of the Geography and Map Division, Special Libraries Association*, 94 (1973), 2–8.

39 For a survey of medieval cartography, see Harley and Woodward, eds., *The History of Cartography*, vol. 1; C. Raymond Beazley, *The Dawn of Modern Geography, Volume 2: A History of Exploration and Geographical Science from the Close of the Ninth to the Middle of the Thirteenth Century (c. AD900–1260)* (3 vols., Peter Smith, New York, 1949), ch. 7. Sixteenth-century cartography is too widely discussed to be covered here, but see the complete cartobibliography of Renaissance maps in Shirley, *The Mapping of the World*; also R. A. Skelton, *Decorative Printed Maps of the 15th to 18th Centuries: A Revised edition of Old Decorative Maps and Charts by A. L. Humphreys* (Staples Press, London and New York, 1952).

40 Christopher Marlowe, *Tamburlaine the Great*, J. S. Cunningham, ed. (Manchester University Press, 1981), p. 190.

41 Had Marlowe meant 'the initial meridian of longitude', exclusively of any other meaning, why would he not use the word 'meridian'? It is the more precise cartographic usage, and moreover, Marlowe so uses it earlier in the same act. Curiously, however, Marlowe's use of 'meridian' actually has the sense of 'perpendicular':

> Smile, stars that reigned at my nativity
> And dim the brightness of their neighbour lamps –
> Disdain to borrow light of Cynthia,
> For I, the chiefest lamp of all the earth,
> First rising in the east with mild aspect
> But fixed now in the meridian line,
> Will send up fire to your burning spheres
> And cause the sun to borrow light of you.
>
> (I:4.2.33–40)

The 'meridian line' is the longitudinal coordinate of any place on earth, which, because the terrestrial poles are assumed to coincide with the celestial poles, also implies a coincidence with the celestial meridian. If the sun is in the 'meridian line', then it is directly overhead or *perpendicular* to the plane of the earth's surface. When, therefore, Marlowe speaks of beginning 'the perpendicular' from a point at Damascus, he may indeed mean that he is calculating the meridian on a modern map or drawing the vertical axis of the TO map.

42 Donne also aims at effects of this kind. See the discussion of the 'Hymn to God my God in my Sickness' in Chapter 5, below.

43 Robert Lloyd, 'A Look at Images', *Annals of the Association of American Geographers*, 72, 4 (1982), 536.

44 Eugene Waith, *The Herculean Hero in Marlowe, Chapman, Shakespeare and Dryden* (Chatto & Windus, London, 1962), p. 121.

45 The map, entitled *Romani Imperii Imago*, is preceded by a lengthy introduction, itself entitled (in the English version): 'The Romane World, Or The Romane Empire'. Ortelius cites a number of tropical versions of the *Orbis Terrarum*, including Ovid's '*Romanae spacium est urbis et orbis idem*' and Tertullian's '*Revera Orbis cultissimum huius Imperii rus est*' ('The whole world is nothing else but a farme well stocked and stored, belonging to this empire').

Interestingly, the imperial spirit of these tropes finds its way on to the map itself. Two matching cartouches to the left and right of the map suggest the symbolism of imperial city (*Urbs*) and world empire (*Orb*). The left-hand cartouche frames a military head with the legend: *Roma Tuum Nomen Terris Fatale Regendis*. The right-hand cartouche frames a bardic head with the legend: *Romulo Urbis Aeternae Conditori*. See Ortelius, *The Theatre of the Whole World, Parergon*, pp. vii–viii. Ortelius's map of the Roman Empire was evidently known to John Speed, who copied it into his own world atlas, *A Prospect of The Most Famous Parts of the World* (London, 1627).

46 Harbison, *Eccentric Spaces*, ch. 7, 'The Mind's Miniatures: Maps'.

47 For a discussion of this type of map, see George Kish, 'The Cosmographic Heart: Cordiform Maps of the 16th Century', *Imago Mundi*, 19 (1965), 13–21. Ortelius's first world map (1564) was on a cordiform projection (Shirley, *The Mapping of the World*, entry 114, plate 97). Mercator's first world map (1538) was also of this type (*The Mapping of The World*, entry 74).

48 My suggestion owes much to the pioneering discussion of the 'teleological' and 'ontological' dimensions of the New World by Edmundo O'Gorman, *The Invention of America: An Inquiry into the Historical Nature of the New World and the Meaning of its History* (Indiana University Press, Bloomington, 1961), especially 'Part Four: The Structure of America's Being, and the Meaning of American History', pp. 125–45.

49 Edgerton, 'From Mental Matrix to *Mappamundi* to Christian Empire' in Woodward, ed., *Art & Cartography*, pp. 10–50.

50 Foucault, 'Of Other Spaces', 22–7.

51 John Donne, 'Elegies, 19: To his Mistress Going to Bed' (*John Donne, The Complete English Poems*, A. J. Smith, ed., Penguin, Harmondsworth, 1980, p. 125).

52 William G. Niederland, 'The Naming of America' in *The Unconscious Today: Essays in Honor of Max Schur*, Mark Kanzer, ed. (International Universities Press, New York, 1971), p. 461.

53 Mercator, *Atlas*, vol. 1, p. 39.

54 This choice of plays raises the possibility of a subsidiary question: Does genre affect geography? Will the geography of a tragedy function differently from what is essentially the same geography in a comedy? The discussion of *The Merchant of Venice* and *Othello* in Chapter 4, below, suggests otherwise.

55 Maurice Charney, *Shakespeare's Roman Plays: The Function of Imagery in the Drama* (Harvard University Press, Cambridge, Mass., 1961), p. 80.

56 Shakespeare clearly associates the trope with the consciously Alexandrian legend of Julius Caesar. Thus, in *Cymbeline*, the trope is used in relation to Caesar: 'Caesar's ambition / Which swelled so much that it did almost stretch / The sides o' th' world' (3.1.48–50).

57 See the discussion of Agrippa's map in O. A. W. Dilke, *Greek and Roman Maps* (Thames & Hudson, London, 1985), pp. 39–54; also, Harley and Woodward, eds., *The History of Cartography*, vol. 1, pp. 207–9.

58 According to J. Oliver Thomson, the Romans deliberately suppressed knowledge of the 'Seres' in order to make the eastern boundary of the 'world' more approximate to the eastern boundary of the Roman Empire ('Orbis Terrarum', 3–4).

59 Fernand Braudel, *The Perspective of the World (Volume 3: Civilization and Capitalism 15th–18th Century)*, Sian Reynolds, tr. (Fontana, London, 1984), p. 127, map 15: 'The Voyages of The Gallere da Mercato'. Braudel offers four sketches of Venetian maritime trade routes in the years: 1482, 1495, 1521 and 1534. By the last two dates, the Italian, North African, Iberian, English and North European trade routes have all disappeared, leaving only the Levantine trade to the Middle East. Braudel supposes that 'the system was probably operating at peak capacity in about 1460' (p. 127).

60 Braudel provides a dramatic illustration of the disastrous effect of the Portuguese discoveries on the Venetian spice trade: 'in 1504, when the Venetian galleys arrived in Alexandria in Egypt, they found not a single sack of pepper waiting for them' (*The Perspective of the World*, p. 143). Thus, even the Levantine routes which were all that remained of Venetian maritime trade in the sixteenth century, were badly affected. What had become of the pepper? 'The unexpected arrival on the Antwerp scene of pepper, which was shipped in directly once the Portuguese had opened up the Indies route, entirely changed the terms of trade there. The first spice ship dropped anchor in 1501; in 1508, the king of Lisbon founded the *Feitoria de Flandres*, the Antwerp branch of the *Casa da India* in Lisbon' (p. 149). Braudel supplies a graphic illustration of the very different pattern of maritime trade required to command the Iberian dominated trade of 'India', 'The Indies' and 'Mexico' in Map 16: 'The Principal Trade Routes to and from Antwerp' (p. 144). Even here, however, it is clear that Antwerp herself did not trade directly with either Indies. It acted simply as a clearing house for goods supplied from 'Indian' destinations by the Spanish and the Portuguese. It was, in other words, a world maritime capital only by proxy. Spain and Portugal were too busy commanding the trade of the West and East Indies respectively, to be able to develop a world trading centre of their own.

61 Lewes Roberts's *The Marchants Mapp of Commerce* (London, 1638) expresses a seventeenth-century English merchant's contempt for the decline of Venice from a city of sailors into a city of money-changers. G. D. Ramsay (*The City of London in International Politics at the Accession of Elizabeth Tudor*, Manchester University Press, Manchester, 1975) describes the importance of Antwerp (the commercial successor of Venice) as a model for London, especially in ch. 1: 'Antwerp: The Metropolis at its Zenith', pp. 1–32.

62 See the discussion of 'wind-heads' in Chapter 5, below.

63 The First Folio's 'Colchos strond' is a direct verbal echo of Golding's translation of Ovid. See *Shakespeare's Ovid Being Arthur Golding's Translation of the Metamorphoses*, W. H. D. Rouse, ed. (Centaur Press, London, 1961), Book 7, p. 200, line 219.

64 Plutarch, *Shakespeare's Plutarch: The Lives of Julius Caesar, Brutus, Marcus Antonius and Coriolanus in the Translation of Sir Thomas North*, T. J. B. Spencer, ed. (Penguin, Harmondsworth, 1964), p. 204.

65 Plutarch, *Shakespeare's Plutarch*, p. 263. Because this attempted voyage to other worlds is actually a response to defeat – corresponding with Antonius's self-exile to the house he builds over the sea in memory of Timon the misanthrope – the possibility that it is present in the opening words of Shakespeare's Antony, is quite remote.

66 J. M. Cohen, ed., *The Four Voyages of Christopher Columbus* (The Cresset Library, London, 1988), p. 265.
67 The wider 'poetic' significance of this Renaissance geographic inspiration, then, is that Antony's love of Cleopatra can never be accounted for in the ledger of folly. Monstrous follies are indeed committed, but when all are duly weighed, the sum of folly is about as close to the *plenum* of love as Gibraltar is to the Caribbean. They are 'worlds' apart.

3 THEATRES OF THE WORLD

1 In 'English Maps and Mapmakers of the Sixteenth Century', Edward Lynam describes the spectacular advance in English cartographic techniques after 1586 as a result of the influx of Flemish cartographers after the fall of Antwerp (*The Mapmaker's Art: Essays on the History of Maps*, Batchworth Press, London, 1953, pp. 55–78).
2 Svetlana Alpers finds terms such as '*Speculum*' and 'glass', 'in about every geographic text' of the later sixteenth and early seventeenth century (Woodward, ed., *Art & Cartography*, p. 88).
3 'Abraham Ortelius Citizen of Antwerpe, and Geographer to Philip The Second, King of Spaine, to the courteous Reader'. All the Ortelian apologies cited on this page and the next are from the English edition of 1606, *The Theatre of the Whole World*, R. A. Skelton, ed. (Theatrum Orbis Terrarum: Amsterdam, 1968). Edward Lynam suggests that Saxton's atlas (a notable beneficiary of Flemish influence) was likewise conceived in a 'historical' spirit; that it was originally designed as 'a companion volume to Holinshed's *Chronicles*' on the principle that 'the national history and the national atlas were intended to illustrate each other' (*The Mapmaker's Art*, pp. 64–5).
4 This commonplace point is also made by a character in William Cunningham's *The Cosmographicall Glasse (London: 1559)*, The English Experience, no. 44 (Da Capo Press, Theatrum Orbis Terrarum, Amsterdam and New York, 1968): 'Although by your wordes, I have received more commoditie at this present, then by all my readyng touching the true difference of these three names: yet if it may please you to geve me the figures of every of them, I shall so stedfastly printe it in my mynde, as I truste not to forget them, for it is truly said, thinges sene have longer impression then only harde.' (fol. 7).
5 This does not include non-standard geographic works. By 1553, Antonio Lafreri had issued a generic frontispiece depicting 'a symbolic figure of Atlas supporting the world on his shoulders' for binding with individually custom-ised map-collections (R. V. Tooley, Charles Bricker and G. R. Crone, *Land-marks of Mapmaking: An Illustrated Survey of Maps and Mapmaking*, Words-worth: Ware, Hertfordshire, 1989, p. 59).
6 A Greek text of Ptolemy's 'Geography' (composed at Alexandria, *c.* AD 160) was brought from Byzantium to Florence in 1400. In 1406, it was translated into Latin, the language of all sixteenth-century editions. In 1415, maps were drawn to illustrate the text, the first printed edition of which appeared in 1475. The first printed edition with maps appeared in 1477. See the introduction to R. A. Skelton, ed., *Claudius Ptolemaeus Cosmographia (Bologna: 1477)* (Theatrum Orbis Terrarum: Amsterdam, 1963), pp. v–vi. Reading the 'Geog-

raphy' through the more familiar *Almagest*, Ptolemy's book on cosmology, and conceiving of the earth in cosmographic terms through their reading of Macrobius, Renaissance geographers renamed the 'Geography' as the 'Cosmography' or *Cosmographia*.

7 Quoted in Juergen Schulz, 'Maps as Metaphors: Mural Map Cycles of the Italian Renaissance', in Woodward, *Art & Cartography*, p. 99. I should mention that my reading of the Ortelian title-page differs from that of R. A. Skelton, who insists that 'no such symbolic or figurative intention need be assumed', because 'it is simply a variation on a decorative theme which had, since about 1550, been in vogue for engraved titlepages ... since the antiquary Enea Vico introduced the fashion in his first book printed at Venice in 1548' (Ortelius, *Theatrum Orbis Terrarum*, Antwerp, 1570, p. viii).

8 Schultz writes: 'The treatise on the Cardinalate by Paolo Cortesi, published in 1510, includes an entire chapter on the kind of residence appropriate to the cardinal's office and the sort of decorations it should contain. In the reception room of the cardinal's summer apartment, Cortesi prescribes representation of what he calls "learned" matter. He instances paintings of engineering works ... and ... geographical subjects'. (Woodward, ed., *Art & Cartography*, p. 117. See also p. 228, note 45).

9 For Ortelius's use of Anverian 'Ornament Print Cycles', see: James A. Welu 'The Sources and Development of Cartographic Ornamentation in the Netherlands' in Woodward, ed., *Art & Cartography*, pp. 147–173. For his map frames and cartouches, Ortelius borrowed prints 'designed specifically to be used by craftsmen for decorating objects' (p. 149). A painting might be such an object. Among many examples of Ortelius's use of Ornament Prints, Welu cites Ortelius's borrowing an ornamental frame intended for a mythological painting, for use as a cartouche (pp. 149, 150, Fig. 5.4). The frame in question contains a notional image of Apollo and Daphne. Another, below it, contains a notional image of the rape of Europa. Such subjects, framed by these very 'ornament prints' could be found adorning the edge of a map, or a wall or ceiling or cornice of a Renaissance map-room. Schultz, for example, has an illustration of the *Sala del Mappamondo* of the *Palazzo Farnese* which shows maps surmounted by mythological paintings, one of which is the rape of Europa (pp. 100–101, Fig. 3.3).

10 John Donne, 'The Canonisation', line 32, *Poems*, p. 14.

11 Lynam, *The Mapmaker's Art*, p. 93. Lynam continues: 'In the rather too elaborate form given it by the Dutch after the fall of Antwerp it prevailed all over Europe right down to about 1700'.

12 See Clare Le Corbeiller, 'Miss America and her Sisters: Personifications of the Four Parts of the World', *The Metropolitan Museum of Art Bulletin*, 19 (April 1961), 209–223. Le Corbeiller thinks 'it is quite possible that the Renaissance acquired its first visual ideas about the Four Continents through a love of parades', and notes that 'by the end of the century, the Four Continents were familiar attendants of royal entries, and nowhere were they more popular than in Antwerp ... largest and most active port city in Europe' (209–10). She observes, 'it is not surprising that personifications of the four parts of the world in the sixteenth century should occur principally in Flemish art' (210). Le Corbeiller also links the 'Continents' with the characteristic pageant archi-

tecture of stage and arch. Noting how, 'triumphal arches . . . sometimes simply painted with allegorical figures and coats of arms, but more often . . . fitted with a stage, set in above the opening of the arch, for tableaux vivants in which "living allegories" were unveiled at each turn of the royal route', she remarks how 'the Four Continents regularly acknowledged the supremacy of the visiting prince' (209).

13 Translated from the Latin of Adolph Mekerch (*Theatrum Orbis Terrarum*, Antwerp, 1570, p. B) by Douglas Kelly. The versified explication does not appear in the 1606 English translation of Ortelius, nor elsewhere to my knowledge.

14 Preparation of cannibal meals by roasting and boiling is a classical topos. Compare Mekerch's '*Corpora, quae discissa in frustra trementia lentis / Vel torret flammis, calido vel lixat aheno*' ('She cuts them up into quivering pieces and either roasts them over a slow fire or boils them in a steaming cauldron') with *Thyestes* (765–67), '*haec veribus haerent viscera et lentis data / stillant caminis, illa fammatus latex / candenet aeno iactat*' ('And soon the meat is on the spits, the fat / Drips over a slow fire, while other parts / Are tossed to boil in singing copper pans' (Seneca the Younger, *Four Tragedies and Octavia*, E. F. Watling, tr., Penguin: Harmondsworth, 1985). Of this passage, R. J. Tarrant remarks that 'the division of parts into those roasted and those boiled in a cauldron is a fixed element in ancient descriptions of cannibal meals' (*Seneca's Thyestes*, R. J. Tarrant, ed., Scholars Press: Atlanta, Georgia, 1985, p. 200). Compare also, *Metamorphoses* (6.645–6), dealing with Procne's preparation of the body of Itys. The detail of body-pieces which continue to 'quiver' is also a topos. Compare *Thyestes* (755–6): '*erepta vivis exta pectoribus tremunt / spirantque venae corque adhuc pavidum salit*' ('The entrails torn from the warm bodies lay, / Quivering, veins still throbbing, shocked hearts beating', Watling tr.). Compare too, *Metamorphoses* (6.558, 644–5), dealing with the quivering of Philomel's severed tongue and that of Itys's body. Mekerch's *aposopiesio* (rhetorical interruption) on America's 'barbarous irreligion' ('*impietas . . . barbara*') is generally reminiscent of the use of this tactic by Seneca's *Nuntius* in announcing the murder and cooking of Thyestes's children by Atreus.

15 In his introduction to *The Theatre of the Whole World* (London, 1606), Skelton writes: 'By 1606 . . . the long career of Ortelius's atlas-works had spent its impetus . . . The *Theatrum* was, in conception and development, essentially a creation of the sixteenth century. Its maps (in the perceptive judgement of Koeman 1964) have the "characteristic mark of external perfection, but lack the internal quality of critical regeneration", while those of Mercator, "likewise externally perfect, result from a complete cartographic reshaping of carefully examined critical data". Unlike Mercator's *Atlas*, the *Theatrum* did not contain the seeds of further growth' (p. xvii).

16 According to Lloyd A. Brown, the figure of Atlas makes its first appearance in an Italian atlas of 1575: 'The Lafreri or Roman Atlas as it is sometimes called . . . is interesting because of its title page. In addition to a conventional border design, the artist used, apparently for the first time, the figure of Atlas with the terrestrial globe on his shoulders as a symbol of the contents of the volume. No one knows whether it was this figure, used hundreds of times by later publishers, or Mercator's running title beginning with the word Atlas, that was

responsible for the use of the word as a synonym for a map collection' (*The Story Of Maps*, Cresset Press: London, 1951, p. 166).

17 Whether or not the emblem was actually displayed in the Globe Theatre, the figure is treated as emblematic of the 'tragedians of the city' by Shakespeare himself in *Hamlet*, in the context of the phrase 'Hercules and his load'. See: Ernst Schanzer, 'Hercules and his Load', *Review of English Studies*, new series, 19, 51–3.

18 E. K. Chambers, *The Elizabethan Stage* (4 vols., Clarendon Press: Oxford, 1923), vol. 2, p. 419.

19 *Ibid.*, pp. 420–23.

20 E. R. Curtius, *European Literature and the Latin Middle Ages*, Willard R. Trask, tr. (Routledge & Kegan Paul, London and Henley, 1979), pp. 138–9.

21 Joseph B. Pike, *Frivolities of Courtiers and Footprints of Philosophers: Being a Translation of the First, Second, and Third Books and Selections from the Seventh and Eighth Books of the* Policraticus *of John of Salisbury* (Octagon Books, New York, 1972) p. 171.

22 Macrobius: *Commentary on the Dream of Scipio*, William Harris Stahl, ed. (Columbia University Press, New York, 1952), p. 142. The analogy between the spheres and the form of the classical temple or theatre was a topos. Stahl points out that Macrobius's cosmography has much in common with that of Vitruvius (p. 16).

23 Thomas Heywood, *An Apology for Actors with 'A Refutation of the Apology for Actors' by I. G.* (Garland Publishing Inc, New York and London, 1973) pp. 24–5.

24 The consonance between Boissard and Heywood is noted by Harriet Bloker Hawkins, '"All The World's A Stage" Some Illustrations of the *Theatrum Mundi*', *Shakespeare Quarterly*, 17 (1966), 175. Another example of the genre is Pierre Boiastuau's *Théatre du Monde* (1587), translated by John Alday as *Theatrum Mundi, The Theatre or Rule of the World* (1603).

25 Macrobius notes Cicero's use of the word *circus* to describe 'the great circles that girdle the outermost sphere' (*Commentary*, p. 148).

26 Frances A. Yates, *Theatre of the World* (Routledge & Kegan Paul, London and New York, 1987), p. 166.

27 Pike, ed., *Policraticus*, p. 180. The whole of ch. 9 is devoted to explaining the role of such men in the *theatrum mundi*.

28 Greene's use of the topos in the play *A Looking Glass for London and England* (*c.* 1590) is described in Anne Righter, *Shakespeare and the Idea of the Play* (Penguin: Harmondsworth, 1967), pp. 69–70. Jonson made his own précis (headed: *De piis & probis*) of John's chapter on the virtuous sages, along with several other key passages from the *theatrum mundi* chapters of the *Policraticus*, in his *Discoveries*. See Margaret Clayton, 'Ben Jonson, "In Travaile with Expression of Another": His Use of John of Salisbury's *Policraticus* in *Timber*', *Review of English Studies*, new series, 30 (1979), 397–408. In his prologue to the *Epigrams*, Jonson alludes to an episode from Martial in which Cato's entry to a theatre shames the audience and performers alike into suspending their lewd revelry and staging something more uplifting. See Donaldson, Ian, *Ben Jonson*, pp. 221–2, and the notes on p. 647. Shakespeare has no one corresponding to these metatheatrical exemplars at all, unless we

think of disillusioned but unreformed 'comedians' such as the melancholy Jacques and Macbeth. For the influence of the topos on the thought of Montaigne, see Jean Starobinski, 'Montaigne on Illusion: The Denunciation of Untruth' *Daedalus*, 108, Summer 1979, 85–101.

29 See Chapter 2, note 32.

30 The 'necessary fiction' of a heavenly viewpoint of the earth is used and acknowledged by Ptolemy in his discussion of how to express or project the relationship of the *oikumene* to the spherical globe as a conic section. (Woodward, *Art & Cartography*, p. 37). This presents us with the paradox that Ortelius was more self-consciously classical (in the sense of his moralising stoicism) than Ptolemy, for whom the fiction of the heavenly viewpoint is merely a geometrical convenience.

31 Marcus Tullius Cicero, *Tusculan Disputations*, IV, 37. Ortelius has slightly altered Cicero's text. For that and the translation, see the Loeb edition by J. E. King, *Cicero: Tusculan Disputations* (Heinemann: London; Harvard University Press: Cambridge, Mass., 1950) p. 367.

32 Shirley, *The Mapping of the World*, entry 158, plate 130.

33 Rodney Shirley remarks: 'The oval world map used previously has been updated in two major respects: South America now assumes the more correct shape ... and the Solomon isles are marked for the first time' (*The Mapping of the World*, p. 181). At the same time, Shirley remarks that the map includes none of the truly major cartographic advances to have occurred over the last thirty-six years. The scientifically rigorous Hakluyt actually apologised for including the *Typus* in the *Principal Navigations* of 1592.

34 Shirley, *The Mapping of the World*, entry 119, plate 102.

35 The translation is from: C. W. Keyes, ed., *Cicero: De Re Publica De Legibus*, The Loeb Classical Library (Heinemann, London; Harvard University Press, Cambridge, Mass., 1948) pp. 266, 267.

36 Smith and Lockwood, eds., *Latin-English Dictionary*, p. 745.

37 Mercator explains that '*Numa Pompilius* ... dedicated to the Goddess *Vesta*, a Temple of a round forme' for the reason that the spherical form linked the earth to the heavens (*Atlas*, vol. 1, p. 40). In the *Apology for Actors*, Heywood describes at some length the elaborate cosmographic symbolism (complete with mechanical effects) of Caesar's amphitheatre in Rome: 'the coverings of the stage, which wee call the heavens ... were Geometrically supported by a Giant-like *Atlas*, whom the poets for his Astrology, feigne to beare heaven on his shoulders, in which an artificiall Sunne and Moone of extraordinary aspect and brightnesse had their diurnall, and nocturnall motions; so had the starres their true and coelestiall course; so had the spheares, which in their continuall motion made a most sweet and ravishing harmony' (p. D3).

38 For the differing character of the pre- and post-Baconian cosmological discourses, see Nicholson, *The Breaking of the Circle*, ch. 4.

39 See Stahl's introduction to the *Commentary*, p. 10.

40 Macrobius reads '*Hoc Templo*' (Cicero's phrase for 'sky') as: 'appropriate ... for the edification of those who think there is no other god except the sky itself and the celestial bodies we are able to see. In order to show, therefore, that the omnipotence of the Supreme God can hardly ever be comprehended and never witnessed, he called whatever is visible to our eyes the temple of that God who

is apprehended only in the mind, so that those who worship these visible objects as temples might still owe the greatest reverence to the Creator, and that whoever is inducted into the privileges of the temple might know that he has to live in the manner of a priest' (*Commentary*, p. 142). The earth, on the other hand, is taken literally (and physically) as the sink of the universe: 'Of all the matter that went into the creation of the universe, that which was purest and clearest took the highest position and was called ether ... lastly, as a result of the downward rush of matter, there was that vast impenetrable solid, the dregs and off-scourings of the purified elements, which had settled at the bottom, plunged in continual and oppressing chill, relegated to the last position in the universe, far from the sun. Because this became so hardened it received the name terra' (*Commentary*, p. 182).

41 Chaucer makes extensive allusion to 'The Dream of Scipio' in the first 112 lines of 'The Parliament of Fowls' (F. N. Robinson, ed., *The Works of Geoffrey Chaucer*, Oxford University Press, London, 1974, pp. 311–12).

42 The translation is in: T. H. Corcoran, ed., *Seneca in Ten Volumes*, vol. 7, *Naturales Quaestiones I*, The Loeb Classical Library (Heinemann, London; Harvard University Press: Cambridge, Mass., 1971) p. 6.

43 A *stadium* is approximately a furlong. For the influence of Aristotle's calculation on Posidonius and other authors, see Heidel, *The Frame of the Ancient Greek Maps*, pp. 87–8. For Aristotle's influence on Macrobius, see Stahl's remarks in his introduction to the *Commentary*, p. 21.

44 The other two citations are as follows: '*Equus Vehendi Causa, Arandi Bos, Venandi Et Custodieni Canis, Homo Autem Ortus Ad Mundum Contemplandum*' (The horse for riding, the ox for ploughing, the dog for hunting and keeping guard, man himself however came into existence for the purpose of contemplating and imitating the world) (Cicero, *De Natura Deorum*, 2, 37, in H. Rackham, ed., *De Natura Deorum Academica*, The Loeb Classical Library, Heinemann, London; Harvard University Press, Cambridge, Mass., 1961, pp. 158–9); '*Utinam Quemadmodum Universa Mundi Facies In Conspectum Venit, Ita Philosophia Tota Nobis Posset Occurrere* (I only wish that philosophy might come before our eyes in all her unity, just as the whole firmament is spread out for us to gaze upon) (Seneca, *Epistle LXXXIX* in R. M. Gummere, ed., tr., *Seneca: Ad Lucilium, Epistolae Morales*, The Loeb Classical Library, 2 vols., Heinemann, London; Harvard University Press, Cambridge, Mass., 1953, vol. 2, pp. 378–9).

45 It is no accident that the medieval and Renaissance word 'cosmography' (meaning both 'geography' and 'astronomy') would begin to give way to the essentially modern word 'cosmology' (meaning 'astronomy' only) in the course of the seventeenth century. *The Shorter O.E.D. on Historical Principles* dates 'cosmology' from 1656.

46 The reversal is perhaps explained by the fact that this Atlas is not the Titan of Greek mythology, but the cosmographer 'king of Mauretania' supposed to have given his name to the Atlas mountains (Tooley, Bricker and Crone, *Landmarks of Mapmaking*, p. 72).

47 See the discussion of generic iconography in Chapter 5, below.

48 Mercator, *Atlas* (1636), vol. 1, between pp. 40 and 41.

49 'Geographie is differing from Cosmographie, as the part from the whole, and

is also distinguished from corographie, as the whole from the part: for Cosmographie is the discription of all the world ... when one speaks of the whole world, we understand the world, as well Elementary, as Celestiall.' (Mercator, *Atlas*, 1636, vol. 1, p. 31). The definition is a direct echo of that in Ptolemy's first chapter, '*In quo differt Cosmographia a Corographia*'.

50 The contents of the posthumous *Atlas* were originally published in three parts: in 1585, 1589 and 1595. Thus Shakespeare could easily have been familiar with Mercator in Latin by *c.* 1600, the date of *Hamlet*.

51 *Hamlet, Prince of Denmark*, Philip Edwards, ed., The New Cambridge Shakespeare (Cambridge University Press, 1985) p. 47. See too, Edwards's note to the speech: 'This famous speech, so often quoted as an example of the world-weariness not only of Hamlet but of a whole age, is part of Hamlet's campaign to mislead Rosencrantz and Guildenstern and keep them off the true scent. Its plausibility is not meant to deceive the audience who, having been permitted to share Hamlet's deepest feelings, and to know the cause of them, can distinguish a parade of fashionable melancholy from the real thing' (p. 130).

52 Neville Coghill, *Shakespeare's Professional Skills* (Cambridge University Press, 1964), pp. 8–9.

53 My use of the word 'utter' acknowledges Bakhtin's notion of the 'utterance', whereby meaning is defined not merely by the words themselves, but by the total environment of the speech-act. In 'The Problem of Speech Genres' (ch. 1, note 106), Bakhtin argues that words vehiculate the intentions of the listener as well as of the speaker ('the speaker listens and the listener speaks'). If this is so, then the effective 'context' of any speech-act must include whatever 'horizon' is brought to bear by the listener as well as by the speaker, and also the physical environment of the utterance.

54 Juergen Schulz, 'Maps as Metaphors: Mural Map Cycles of the Italian Renaissance' in Woodward, ed., *Art & Cartography*, p. 112.

55 Yates, *Theatre of the World*, p. 116. See, too, the preliminary and partial version of the case in Frances Yates, *The Art of Memory* (Routledge & Kegan Paul, London and Chicago, 1966), chs. 15 and 16; also the reply by I. A. Shapiro, 'Robert Fludd's Stage Illustration', *Shakespeare Studies*, 2, 1966, 192–209; and also Yates's reply to Shapiro, 'The Stage in Robert Fludd's Memory System', *Shakespeare Studies*, 3, 1967, 138–66.

56 This is quite consistent with the general case Yates presents for Vitruvian architecture as a functional analogue and possible source of the 'idea' of an Elizabethan theatre, which was also designed to function as a machine for what Alberti called 'the orb of the voice'. Sixteenth-century cosmographers such as Mercator and Ortelius certainly understood the cosmic connotations of the rotundity of the ancient temples. It is plausible that Elizabethan dramatists were equally aware that the cosmic symbolism of their own rotund theatres had a precedent in the rotundity of ancient temples and theatres. Yates rightly remarks the suggestive fact that the sole surviving image of the interior of an Elizabethan playhouse (a copy of a drawing of 'The Swan' by a Dutch tourist, Johannes de Witt) construed the Elizabethan features in terms of ancient theatrical architecture. It is also suggestive to find illustrations of

ancient theatrical buildings in non-architectural contemporary sources such as Boissard's *Theatrum Omnium Miseriarum.*

57 I am indebted to the useful discussion of this passage in Righter, *Shakespeare and the Idea of the Play*, p. 67.

58 *Vitruvius: On Architecture*, Frank Granger, ed., tr., The Loeb Classical Library (2 vols., Heinemann, London, 1955), vol. 1, p. 289.

59 I am indebted to the discussion of this passage in Samuel Y. Edgerton, *The Renaissance Discovery of Linear Perspective* (Harper & Rowe, New York, Evanston, San Francisco and London, 1976), ch. 7, 'Enter Cartography', p. 92.

60 Because of the rich visual legacy of Inigo Jones's drawings of masque-designs, it is possible to be more definite about the ethnographic inspiration of exotic costume in the masque. Stephen Orgel and Roy Strong (*Inigo Jones: The Theatre of the Stuart Court*, 2 vols., University of California Press, Berkeley and Los Angeles; Sotheby Park Bernet, London, 1973), have conclusively demonstrated Jones's reliance on ethnographically informed costume manuals such as Cesare Vecellio's *Habiti Antichi et Moderni*. Ethnographic costumes might simply be copied (vol. 2, catalogue nos. 211, 212) or thrown together in spectacularly bizarre combinations (vol. 1, p. 43). See also Frances A. Yates, 'Boissard's Costume-Book and Two Portraits', *Journal of the Warburg and Courtauld Institutes*, 22–3 (1959–60), 365–6. The same volume includes E. E. Veevers, 'Sources of Inigo Jones's Masquing Designs', 373–4. The ethnographic inspiration of elements of Amerindian costuming and accoutrements in Chapman's *Memorable Masque* is obvious.

61 See Martin Holmes, 'An Unrecorded Portrait of Edward Alleyn', *Theatre Notebook*, 1950–1952, pp. 11–13.

62 Jews with theatrical noses are depicted in David Kunzle, *The Early Comic Strip: Narrative Strips and Picture Stories in the European Broadsheet from c.1450 to 1825, History of the Comic Strip*, vol. 1 (University of California Press, Berkeley, Los Angeles and London, 1973), 'The Jewish Criminal', pp. 179–86.

63 My definition is indebted to Stephen Orgel, *The Tempest*, Oxford, p. 145, note to line 37.

64 It is just possible that the inspiration of this stage may have been Elizabethan. Jodocus Hondius, father to Henry, had spent ten years in London as an exile, after the fall of Antwerp. He appears to have had enough to do with the design of this edition for *his* picture (rather than Henry's) to be featured on the decorative border of the world map.

65 A good account of the tradition from Johannes Boemus is given in Hodgen's *Early Anthropology in the Sixteenth and Seventeenth Centuries*, chs. 4 and 5, pp. 111–206.

66 The *Great Voyages* represents a series of reprintings – with illustrations by Theodore de Bry and his sons – of major works of discovery and ethnography concerning the New World. Bernadette Bucher provides a list of these publications in Appendix 2 of her *Icon and Conquest: A Structural Analysis of the Illustrations of de Bry's 'Great Voyages'*, Basia Miller Gulati, tr. (University of Chicago Press, Chicago and London, 1981). Bucher also provides a list of the

'Plates in the *Great Voyages*' in Appendix 1. A detailed bibliographical description of the *Great Voyages* is provided in Henry Stevens, 'The de Bry Collector's Painful Peregrination Along the Pleasant Pathway to Perfection' in *Bibliographical Essays: A Tribute to Wilberforce Eames* (Books For Libraries Press, Freeport, New York, 1976), pp. 269–76.

67 While the union between geographic and chorographic imagery represented by the *carte à figures* is not generally found in the sixteenth century, the *figures*, as such, are. They can be found as far back as the *Civitates Orbis Terrarum* (1572) of Braun and Hogenberg – the city atlas which was designed as a kind of complement to the *Theatrum*. As the scope of the city atlas was *chorographic* by definition, the representation of local inhabitants was entirely logical. The representation of local inhabitants on the border of a geographic map was not automatic. It required a step of the imagination.

68 John Speed: *A Prospect of the Most Famous Parts of the World* (London, 1627), R. A. Skelton, ed. (Theatrum Orbis Terrarum, Amsterdam, 1966), pp. 10–11. Significantly, an equivalently accoutred figure (described as wearing the 'habit of cape of good hope') is found adjoining the Cape on the ornamental border of Speed's map of Africa, pp. 6–7. Speed seems to have concorded the two figures on the basis of the perceived primitivism of the bushman and the Fuegian. This powerfully suggests that the skin-cloak thrown over the back operates as an indicator of the ultimate primitivism.

69 The iconographic transformations and the unconscious 'mythological' significance of this figure are fascinatingly discussed in Bucher, *Icon and Conquest*, chs. 7, 8 and 9, pp. 86–131, Plates 10–16.

4 'THE OPEN WORLDE': THE EXOTIC IN SHAKESPEARE

1 We are not told of the fate of Claribel's marriage to the 'African' king of Tunis in *The Tempest*, but it seems ominous enough, and neither appears on-stage in any case.

2 Strictly speaking, there is no reason to suppose that an earlier source-document is presupposed by the eighteenth-century chapbook *History of Titus Andronicus*. See G. K. Hunter, 'Sources and Meanings in *Titus Andronicus*' in *The Mirror up to Shakespeare*, J. C. Grey, ed. (Toronto University Press, 1983), pp. 171–88; 'The "Sources" of *Titus Andronicus* – Once Again', *Notes and Queries*, 228 (1983), 114–16. My point, however, is unaffected. If the *History* is entirely discounted, as Hunter argues it should be, then the role of Aaron is not just remade but entirely new, and strikingly gratuitous to the story in the remaining source material.

3 See Geoffrey Bullough, ed., *Narrative and Dramatic Sources of Shakespeare* (8 vols., Routledge & Kegan Paul, London; Columbia University Press, New York, 1966), vol. 1, pp. 445–514. In the earliest extant European version of the bond story in the *Gesta Romanorum* the villain is a merchant, not a Jew (p. 448). The Jewish stereotype is present in the first English version of the story in the late-thirteenth-century *Cursor Mundi*, and also in the Renaissance Italian version, *Il Pecorone* (pp. 448–9). Shylock, however, defies the stereotype in important ways. There is no moor in pre-Shakespearean versions of the caskets story (pp. 457–62).

4 See *Titus Andronicus*, Eugene M. Waith, ed., The Oxford Shakespeare (Oxford University Press, Oxford and New York, 1984), p. 90, note 136.

5 Kinship is the explicit context of Ovid's *omnia turbasti* ('you have confused all natural relations'). Thus, Philomel bewails becoming the mistress of her brother-in-law and the erotic rival of her own sister. Implicitly, however, the expression 'all natural relations' has a political resonance in Aristotle's derivation of the state from the family, and the political bond from the marital bond.

6 The properties are clearly indicated in the dialogue:

> ... look for thy reward
> Among the nettles at the elder tree
> Which overshades the mouth of that same pit ...
> This is the pit, and this the elder tree ...
>
> (2.3.271–3, 277)

7 The Ovidian parallel is insisted on in several ways. Tigers are commonly associated with Thrace and Scythia in classical literature. And, both Titus and Aaron describe the forest in Ovidian terms. Titus finds the 'place ... where we did hunt' as 'Patterned by that the poet here describes, / By nature made for murders and for rapes' (4.1.54–7). Aaron anticipates him: 'The woods are ruthless, dreadful, deaf, and dull' (2.1.129); 'And many unfrequented plots there are, / Fitted by kind for rape and villainy' (2.1.116–17).

8 For the original, see *Aeneid* 4, 129–72 (*Virgil*, H. Rushton Fairclough, ed., vol. 1, pp. 404–7).

9 The translation is by E. F. Watling in *Seneca: Four Tragedies and Octavia*, E. F. Watling, ed. (Penguin, Harmondsworth, 1985).

10 See also Albert H. Tricomi, 'The Aesthetics of Mutilation in *Titus Andronicus*', *Shakespeare Survey*, 27 (1974), 18.

11 See, for example, Earl G. Schreiber and Thomas Maresca, eds., *Commentary on the First Six Books of Virgil's Aeneid by Bernardus Silvestris* (University of Nebraska Press, Lincoln and London, 1979): 'Having buried his father, Aeneas goes hunting. Driven by storms into a cave, he dallies with Dido and there commits adultery ... Aeneas is driven to a cave by storms and rain, that is, he is led to impurity of the flesh and of desire by excitement of the flesh and by the abundance of humors coming from a superfluity of food and drink. This impurity of the flesh is called a cave, since it beclouds the clarity of mind and of discretion' (p. 25).

12 *Aeneid* 4, 110–12 (*Virgil*, H. Rushton Fairclough, ed., vol. 1, pp. 402–3).

13 Sandys, *Ovid's Metamorphoses Englished*, p. 228.

14 The terminology is René Girard's. See *Violence and the Sacred*, Patrick Gregory, tr. (Johns Hopkins University Press, Baltimore and London, 1986), p. 74.

15 See Douglas, *Purity and Danger*, ch. 8, 'Internal Lines'. Douglas argues that where moral rules characteristically distinguish between the perpetrator of a polluting crime and the victim, pollution rules tend not to. Thus the innocent partner to a marriage will tend to share the pollution of the adulterous party, and the victim of rape will share the pollution of the rapist. The stage cuckold would be a common example of how adultery-pollution can affect the innocent partner, particularly if male. But adultery-pollution can also fall on the

virtuous wife in Shakespeare. Thus Adriana in *The Comedy of Errors* imagines herself catching adultery-pollution like a blood-disease through her 'undividable, incorporate' (2.2.125) bond with an adulterous husband:

> I am possessed with an adulterate blot;
> My blood is mingled with the crime of lust.
> For if we two be one, and thou play false,
> I do digest the poison of thy flesh,
> Being strumpeted with thy contagion.
>
> (2.2.143–7)

As in Tamora's 'Rome and I are now incorporate', Shakespeare characteristically uses the word 'incorporate' with a Pauline resonance. If husband and wife 'shall become one flesh', then 'he that is joined to a harlot is one body' (1 Corinthians 6.16).

16 Watling, ed., *Seneca: Four Tragedies*, p. 126. Not only does the monster recapitulate the minotaur in form, being half bull, but its very apparition is a form of monstrous birth: 'the ocean, big-bellied with a monster', throws the creature on to the shore (p. 139). The connection between the idea of a monstrous (hybrid) birth and the death of Hyppolytus by dismemberment is not random. It re-echoes in Phaedra's anguished cry: 'What creature ... Cretan bull / Bellowing in a Daedalian labyrinth, / Horned hybrid – can have torn you in pieces?' (p. 139)

17 See Ian Donaldson, *The Rapes of Lucretia* (Clarendon Press, Oxford, 1982). Donaldson finds that the heroine's suicide becomes problematic from the time of Augustine (for whom it was vain and impious). Interestingly, Shakespeare – though expressing this critical view (in the person of Junius Brutus) – effectively endorses the ancient pollution view.

18 With a glance in the direction of the principle of social 'reciprocity' in Lévi-Strauss (see note 54, below), Girard coins this term to describe the counter-economy of violence in ancient and traditional societies, also in Greek Tragedy. (See the index entry under 'Reciprocity, violent' in Girard, *Violence and the Sacred*, p. 330.)

19 The sole difference between the legend of Coriolanus and that of the 'incestuous invader' mentioned earlier (Chapter 1, note 67), is that Coriolanus finally recoils from perpetrating the twin outrages of invading the mother-city and raping the mother. The cost of avoiding the ultimate pollution, however, is his own quasi-sacrificial, quasi-suicidal death.

20 See Lovejoy and Boas, *Primitivism and Related Ideas in Antiquity*, ch. 11, 'The Noble Savage in Antiquity'; also Thomas, *Lands and Peoples*, chs. 4 and 6.

21 Aaron's indifference to pain and fear is in stark contrast to the craven behaviour of his moorish counterpart in the prose *History of Titus Andronicus*.

22 For the primitivism of Shakespeare's Goths, see Ronald Broude, 'Roman and Goth in *Titus Andronicus*', *Shakespeare Studies*, 6 (1970), 27–34. The same kind of opposition that Broude finds between 'Roman and Goth' can be found between Roman and Briton in *Cymbeline*.

23 For the impact on Roman opinion of Julius Caesar's flirtation both with Cleopatra and the idea of eastern despotism, and its consequences for the Roman view of Antony, see M. P. Charlesworth, 'The Fear of the Orient in the Roman Empire', *The Cambridge Historical Journal*, 2, 1 (1926), 9–16, 10–11.

24 Mazzolani, *The Idea of the City in Roman Thought*, p. 149.
25 *Ibid.*, especially ch. 3, 'Cultural Factors and the Ecumenical Idea'.
26 Plutarch (in North's translation) describes the investitures as follows: 'he called the sons he had by her "the Kings of Kings": and gave Alexander for his portion, Armenia, Media, and Parthia (when he had conquered the country); and unto Ptolemy for his portion, Phoenicia, Syria, and Cilicia. And therewithal he brought out Alexander in a long gown after the fashion of the Medes, with a high copped-tank hat on his head ... and Ptolemy apparelled in a cloak after the Macedonian manner, with slippers on his feet, and a broad hat with a royal band or diadem ... such was the apparel and old attire of the ancient kings and successors of Alexander the Great' (*Shakespeare's Plutarch*, p. 242).
27 Plutarch offers a précis of Antonius's position: 'Roman nobility was multiplied amongst men by the posterity of kings when they left their seed in divers places; and by this means his ancestor was begotten by Hercules, who had not left the hope and continuance of his line and posterity in the womb of one only woman, fearing Solon's laws or regarding the ordinance of men touching the procreation of children; but that he gave it unto Nature, and established the foundation of many noble races and families in divers places' (*Shakespeare's Plutarch*, p. 222).
28 For the Renaissance legend of Antonius, see Howard Erskine-Hill, 'Antony and Octavius: The Theme of Temperance in Shakespeare's *Antony and Cleopatra*', *Renaissance and Modern Studies*, 14, 1970, 26–47.
29 *Aeneid* 8, 685–8 (*Virgil*, H. Rushton Fairclough, ed., vol. 2, pp. 106–7).
30 Mazzolani suggests that: 'for Augustus to complete the overthrow of his late rival on the ideological plane, he would have to stress the anti-Hellenic, anti-barbarian character of Actium' (*The Idea of the City in Roman Thought*, p. 139). Commenting upon the passage from Virgil, C. J. Fordyce (*P. Virgili Maronis Aeneidos: Libri VII-VIII*, Oxford University Press, 1977) stresses the calculated overstatement of Antony's 'triumphs in the East' (*victor ab Aurorae populis*): 'Designed to enhance the glory of Octavian, the description which makes Antony into another Alexander, has little or no foundation ... he had never been near the shores of the Indian Ocean' (p. 280). Similarly, 'Virgil leaves entirely out of sight the fact that a large part of Antony's strength consisted of legionary troops ... that his commanders were Roman, and that he had a large following of Roman senators' (p. 280).
31 Mazzolani, *The Idea of the City in Roman Thought*, p. 159. Mazzolani points out that such propaganda is also to be found in other major poets of the Augustan settlement, such as Propertius and Ovid.
32 *Ibid.*, p. 136.
33 *Ibid.*, p. 131.
34 In his *On the Fortune of Alexander*, Plutarch credits Alexander with 'a clear-cut programme of universal brotherhood' (Mazzolani, *The Idea of the City in Roman Thought*, p. 82).
35 Unlike Virgil who depicts a conflict between Rome and the East (see note 29, above), Plutarch stresses the cosmopolitan composition of both armies and the international character of the conflict (*Shakespeare's Plutarch*, p. 250).
36 *Shakespeare's Plutarch*, p. 180.
37 *Ibid.*, p. 204.

38 Maurice Charney, *Shakespeare's Roman Plays: The Function of Imagery in the Drama* (Harvard University Press, Cambridge, Mass., 1961), p. 81.

39 Lucan portrays Cato as savage-looking: with unkempt beard and hair – which is exactly how Plutarch portrays Antonius after his journey on the Alps: 'since the overthrow he . . . suffered his beard to grow at length . . . and the hair of his head also without combing' (*Shakespeare's Plutarch*, p. 193).

40 Juvenal, Third Satire, lines 62–3, in *Sixteen Satires upon the Ancient Harlot*, Steven Robinson, ed., tr. (Carcanet New Press, Manchester, 1983), p. 91.

41 A. D. Godley, ed., tr., *Herodotus*, vol. 1, Books 1 and 2. All further citations of the Egyptian *logos* from this edition.

42 Hartog, *The Mirror of Herodotus*, pp. 225–30.

43 This motive is also found in Horace, *Odes*, 1.37, lines 29–32. Joseph P. Clancy (*The Odes and Epodes of Horace*, University of Chicago Press, Chicago, 1960) translates the passage as follows:

    so highly she dared, her mind set on death.
    Not for her the enemy ship, the crownless
    voyage, her role in the grand
    parade: she was no weak-kneed woman.

44 In terms of its internal political organisation, Venice was a model of republicanism. In terms of its external reach, however, Venice was a model of empire, aping the Roman imperial style and in turn copied by English colonialists such as William Alexander (*An Encouragement to Colonies*, London, 1624, The English Experience, no. 63, Da Capo Press, Theatrum Orbis Terrarum, Amsterdam and New York, 1968).

45 *The Commonwealth and Government of Venice. Written by the Cardinall Gasper Contareno, and translated out of Italian into English, by Lewes Lewkenor . . . Esquire With Sundry Other Collections* (London, 1599), The English Experience, no. 101 (Da Capo Press, Theatrum Orbis Terrarum, Amsterdam and New York, 1969), pp. A2–A3. Further references are given in the text.

46 According to Douglas, ed., *The New Bible Dictionary*: 'the name Babel is explained by popular etymology based on a similar Hebrew root *balal*, as "confusion" or "mixing"' (p. 116).

47 The earliest date for 'cosmopolitan' in the *OED* is 1844. 'Cosmopolite', however, is dated to 1645. For Renaissance uses of the Babel myth, see Chapter 1, above, section 5, also notes 89 and 90. It follows from the close link between the ideas of 'dispersal', 'diversity' and 'degeneration' that any new 'Babel' – any attempt to concentrate cultural diversity in one place (particularly a city) – would be regarded as an abomination. Several 'Babelesque' accounts of St Paul's church market in London are cited by Jean-Christophe Agnew (*Worlds Apart: The Market and the Theater in Anglo-American Thought, 1550–1750*, Cambridge University Press, 1986, pp. 86–8), including this one by Thomas Dekker: 'What damnable bargaines of vnmercifull Brokery, and of vnmeasurable Vsury are there clapt up? . . . and such humming (every mans lippes making a noise, yet not a word to be vnderstoode,) I verily beleeve that I am the Tower of *Babell* newly to be builded up, but presentlie despaire of euer beeing finished because there is such a confusion of languages. Thus am I like a common Mart where all Commodities (both the good and the bad) are to be bought and solde' (*The Dead Tearme*, 1608).

48 Coryat, *Coryats Crudities*, pp. 171–3. Further references to Coryat are in the text.

49 Earlier, Coryat speaks of 'Albania' as being 'a city of the greater Armenia', in the context of expounding another Venetian legend associated with another statue of 'a grave old Venetian Gentleman ... who was flea'd amongst the Turks' (p. 223). The Albanian brothers are, then, Turks, which is consistent with the fact that they are depicted 'with their fawchions by their sides' (p. 188).

50 Plutarch, *Lives*, p. 921.

51 Ugo Tucci, 'The Psychology of the Venetian Merchant in the Sixteenth Century', in J. R. Hale, ed., *Renaissance Venice* (Faber & Faber, London, 1973), p. 347.

52 Aristotle, *Politics*, Book 1, chs. 8–10.

53 Marcel Mauss, *The Gift: Forms and Functions of Exchange in Archaic Societies*, Ian Cunnison, tr. (Cohen & West, London, 1966), pp. 76–7.

54 Lévi-Strauss, *The Elementary Structures of Kinship*, p. 52. Lévi-Strauss is heavily reliant on Mauss for the concept of 'reciprocity' within kinship systems.

55 'The Intercourse' is described in G. D. Ramsay, *The City of London*, p. 22.

56 John C. Rolfe, ed., tr., *The Attic Nights of Aulus Gellius*, The Loeb Classical Library (3 vols., Harvard University Press, Cambridge, Mass.; Heinemann, London, 1967), vol. 3, 20.1, p. 425.

57 W. R. Smith, *Marriage in Early Arabia* (Cambridge, 1885), pp. 56–9, as paraphrased by Hartog in *The Mirror of Herodotus*, pp. 113–14.

58 See, for example, 3.1.32–7.

59 For the homily, see *Sermons or Homilies Appointed to be Read in Churches in the Time of Queen Elizabeth of Famous Memory*, fourth edition (Clarendon Press, Oxford, 1816), p. 102. The reference to 1 Corinthians 6 is given in the margin. The homily's 'For ye are dearly bought: Glorify God in your bodies' directly echoes 1 Corinthians 6.20, 'For ye were bought with a price: glorify God therefore in your body'.

60 When asked whether 'the allies of the Romans' might be 'made free citizens of Rome', the youthful Cato 'made no answer, only he looked steadfastly and fiercely on the strangers' (Plutarch: *Lives*, p. 919).

61 'English law forbade its citizens from becoming private money-changers, just as it required alien merchants to obtain hosts or sponsors for their trade' (Agnew, *Worlds Apart*, p. 45). Fairs were one way of circumventing such prohibitions: 'the entire "mercantile estate" ... ventured to the fair where the usual tolls and prohibitions against foreigners and usury were suspended' (p. 47).

62 Stationer's Register entry, cited in C. L. Barber, 'The Merchants and the Jew of Venice', in John Wilders, ed., *Shakespeare: 'The Merchant of Venice': A Casebook* (Macmillan, Basingstoke, 1989), p. 177.

63 See the note on this passage in *Measure for Measure*, J. W. Lever, ed., The Arden Shakespeare (Methuen, London, 1976), p. 111.

64 Bacon summarises contemporary opinion on usury in the opening paragraphs of 'Of Usury' in *Francis Bacon: The Essays*, John Pitcher, ed. (Penguin, Harmondsworth, 1985), pp. 183–6.

65 That Antwerp saw itself in the imperial tradition of Venice, seems evident from the 'saucy monogram SPQA – *Senatus Populusque Antwerpiensis* – with its Roman and even Republican overtones', emblazoned on the façade of the classically styled exchange (the 'Bourse') completed in 1546. See Ramsay, *The City of London*, pp. 14–15. After its recapture by the Spanish in 1585, however, such pretensions must have seemed hubristic, and are likely to have confirmed longstanding English suspicions of Anverian 'openness'.

66 Elizabeth McGrath, 'Rubens's *Arch of the Mint*', *Journal of the Warburg and Courtauld Institutes*, 37 (1974), 203–4. G. D. Ramsay explains that 'the Merchants Adventurers were not themselves a City company but a national trading organization, with a headquarters outside England' (*The City of London*, p. 41). Paradoxically, therefore, their immense prestige and 'almost total predominance' found no direct outlet 'in the ancient constitution' of the City which 'rested on the established City companies' (p. 41). However, 'the Merchants Adventurers had ... a special connection with the Mercers' Company, which ... had become the outstanding livery company of the City' (p. 42).

67 McGrath, 'Rubens's *Arch of the Mint*', 192. Further references to McGrath's article, which I follow closely, are given in the text.

68 Fiedler, *The Stranger in Shakespeare*, pp. 139–45ff.

69 See Chapter 1, note 77, above.

70 Leslie Fiedler suggests that in dreaming of miscegenation, Brabanzio is actually dreaming of incest because of his prior wish-dream identification with Othello (*The Stranger in Shakespeare*, p. 142).

71 Hayden White, *Tropics of Discourse*, p. 187.

72 In her *Icon and Conquest: A Structural Analysis of the Illustrations of de Bry's 'Great Voyages'* (Basia Miller Gulati, tr., University of Chicago Press, Chicago and London, 1981), Bernadette Bucher finds a similar duality between attraction and repulsion in de Bry's standard visual depiction of the Amerindian. On the one hand, the normative Indian was 'physically healthy and well proportioned' and 'endowed with eternal youth' (p. 37). On the other hand, 'some types, appearing sporadically, stand apart from these norms. We see giants and dwarfs; headless men; others, wild-looking, disheveled ... and above all, a type of woman who appears more frequently as the series advances and whose portrayal runs against the canon of proportions observed in the pictures of the other Indian women. She is afflicted with an uncomely appearance and sagging breasts: sometimes this trait combines with the robust youth of the other women; sometimes, on the contrary, with hideous, emaciated, old women' (p. 38).

73 Karen Newman, '"And wash the Ethiop white": Femininity and the Monstrous in *Othello*', in Jean E. Howard and Marion F. O'Connor, eds., *Shakespeare Reproduced: The Text in History and Ideology* (Methuen, New York and London, 1987), p. 152.

74 Coryat remarks that Venice accommodated 'at least twenty thousand' prostitutes or 'courtezans', observing that the 'tolleration of such licentious wantons in so glorious, so potent, so renowned a City' should be 'an occasion to draw down upon them Gods curses and vengeance from heaven, and to consume their city with fire and brimstone, as in times past he did Sodome and

Gomorrha' (*Coryats Crudities*, p. 264). According to Coryat, there is a kind of symbiotic relationship between Venetian wives and Venetian courtesans, in as much as 'the chastity of their wives would be the sooner assaulted ... were it not for these places of evacuation' (pp. 264–5). A less excusable reason for the presence of so many courtesans is that 'the revenues which they pay unto the Senate for their tolleration, doe maintaine a dozen of their galleys' (p. 265). Venice's popular reputation for venery is remarked in *Much Ado About Nothing* (1.1.253–4).

75 For some traditional examples of 'the shipwreck' as an emblem of tragic hubris, see Guy de Tervarent, *Attributs et Symboles dans l'Art Profane 1450–1600* (Librairie E. Droz, Genève, 1958), especially 'Naufrage', p. 282, and 'Tronc Brisé dont une Branche Reverdit', p. 389. The polemical attitude of the 'Bermuda Pamphlets' – with their shrill celebration of God's mercy in preserving the company of the *Sea Venture*, which was earlier supposed to have sunk with all hands in a storm off the Bermudas – indicates that the wreck had been represented by the opponents of the Virginia Company as a divine judgement on the hubris of its activities.

76 In addition to its specifically dramatic effects – confused outcries, sounds – and its emblematic point (the argument between Gonzalo and the boatswain), the wreck has a precise technical logic. As the ship is driven towards a lee shore, the sailors strike the topsail and set the foresail in an attempt to increase the ship's stiffness in the water and improve its ability to point into the wind. (See *The Tempest*, Stephen Orgel, ed., The Oxford Shakespeare, Oxford University Press, Oxford and New York, 1987, Appendix A.)

77 The phrase would have been familiar from what was perhaps the most famous late-sixteenth-century account of the New World, *The Natural and Moral History of the Indies* by Joseph de Acosta. It was translated by Edward Grimston in 1604.

78 Orgel, ed., *The Tempest*, Oxford, pp. 19–20; also p. 115, note to line 258. Orgel notes Kermode's theory that Sycorax 'is strongly influenced by the Circe legend' because of a suggestion in Conti's *Mythologiae* that Circe 'was born in Colchis, in the district of the Coraxi tribe' (p. 19). But he points out that no mention of the Coraxi is found in Conti.

79 Speed, 'The Description of Europe' in *A Prospect of the Most Famous Parts of the World*, between pp. 7 and 8. Speed's map provides the missing documentary link between Sycorax and Scythia.

80 Sandys, *Ovid's Metamorphoses Englished*, p. 253. On the Herodotean assumption that the 'marvelous' (in the sense of the precious or rare) would always be associated with the 'monstrous', Sandys supposes that the mythological monsters which guard the golden fleece must have been real animals such as the 'Alergatoes' which threaten the 'Divers for Pearle in the inland Lakes' of America.

81 For the motif of 'Temperance' in the play, see my 'Shakespeare's Virginian Masque', *English Literary History*, 1986, 673–707.

82 *Ibid.*, 678–82.

83 See Chapter 1, above, section 2 and note 37.

84 Setebos is described as a 'great deuyll' in Antonio Pigafetta's *A Briefe Declaration of the Voyage or Navigation Made Abowte the Worlde*, in Edward

Arber, ed., *The First Three English books on America, [?1511]–1555 A.D.*, p. 252. Caliban's description of Setebos as 'my dam's god' (1.2.376) is fully consistent with Pigafetta's account of Setebos as a devil, in view of Prospero's repeated references to Caliban as a devil.

85 Antonello Gerbi ('The Earliest Accounts on the New World', in Fredi Chiapelli, ed., *First Images of America: The Impact of the New World on the Old* (2 vols., University of California Press, Berkeley, Los Angeles and London, 1976, vol. 1, 37–43), points out that Pigafetta's grotesquely primitive portrait of giant-like Patagonians, 'remained a legend for several centuries – a cliché and a stimulus for the inquisitive European mind. No less a philosopher than Vico made the *Patacones* the prototypes of a barbaric and heroic humanity' (p. 42). Well before Vico, however, the Patagonian is routinely depicted as the most primitive Amerindian type on the early seventeenth-century *carte à figures* (see Chapter 3, above, notes 68 and 69).

86 Julia Kristeva, *Powers of Horror: An Essay on Abjection*, Leon S. Roudiez, tr. (Columbia University Press, New York, 1982), p. 8. The passage is particularly suggestive of Prospero and Caliban: 'The one by whom the abject exists is thus a *deject* who places (himself), *separates* (himself), situates (himself) ... Situationist in a sense, and not without laughter – since laughing is a way of placing or displacing abjection. Necessarily dichotomous, somewhat Manichaean, he divides, excludes, and without, properly speaking, wishing to know his abjections is not at all unaware of them.'

87 'Husks wherein the acorn cradled' would represent a dystopian version of human diet in the golden age – a diet of acorns.

88 Francis Bacon, 'Of Vicissitude of Things' in *Essays*, p. 229. Further references to this essay appear in the text.

89 Francis Bacon, *The Advancement of Learning*, G. W. Kitchin, ed. (Dent, London, 1976), pp. 70–71. The fact that Gonzalo makes detailed reference to two types of Mandevillian monster – bull-headed men and 'such men / Whose heads stood in their breasts' – strongly suggests that each one of the 'shapes' originally represented *a specific type* of Mandevillian monster. This would exactly account for the wording of Prospero's compliment to his spirit-actors. These 'meaner ministers' perform '*their several kinds*' with 'good life'.

90 Gillies, 'Shakespeare's Virginian Masque'.

91 Robert Johnson, *The New Life of Virginea* (London, 1612), The English Experience, no. 332 (Da Capo Press, Theatrum Orbis Terrarum, Amsterdam and New York, 1971), 'The Epistle Dedicatorie'. Further citations from this work are given in the text.

92 Louis B. Wright and Virginia Freund, eds., *The Historie of Travell into Virginia Britania (1612) By William Strachey, gent.* (Hakluyt Society, London, 1953). See ch. 3, 'De origine, Populi', pp. 53–62, especially pp. 54–5.

93 As the illustration does not appear in modern reprintings of the pamphlet with which I am familiar, it is necessary to consult an original or a microfilm.

94 See Louis B. Wright, *Religion and Empire: The Alliance between Piety and Commerce in English Expansion, 1558–1625* (University of North Carolina Press, Chapel Hill, 1943), ch. 4, 'A Western Canaan Reserved for England', pp. 84–114, especially pp. 89–110.

95 Skura, 'Discourse and the Individual'.

96 Lewis Hanke, *Aristotle and the American Indians: A Study in Race Prejudice in the Modern World* (Hollis & Carter, London, 1959), p. 10. See also Lewis Hanke, *All Mankind is One: A Study of the Disputation between Bartolome de las Casas and Juan Gines de Sepulveda in 1550 on the Intellectual and Religious Capacity of the American Indians* (Northern Illinois University Press, DeKalb, 1974).

97 Hanke writes: 'on the eve of the battle with Las Casas, he had just completed and published at Paris in 1548 his Latin translation of Aristotle's *Politics*, which he considered his principal contribution to knowledge. It was the best translation that had appeared, and was recognized for centuries as an indispensable work' (*Aristotle and the American Indians*, p. 31).

98 The metaphoric contest between the 'library' and the 'road' is described in Francis Bacon, *The New Organon and Related Writings*, Fulton H. Anderson, ed. (The Liberal Arts Press, New York, 1960), pp. 78–84. Wayne Franklin (*Discoverers, Explorers, Settlers: The Diligent Writers of Early America*, University of Chicago Press, Chicago and London, 1979) compellingly argues that the title *Novum Organum* was deliberately intended to recall both *Mundus Novus* and *Novus Orbis Terrarum*, and to be 'the scientific equivalent of Columbus's arguments prior to 1492' (p. 8). Bacon fully recognised the importance of the voyager myth to his age and made a concerted effort to transform it into a metaphoric vehicle of the experimental method. The frontispiece to the *Instauratio Magna* (1620) shows a ship sailing out through the Pillars of Hercules.

99 Hanke rehearses the argument in detail (*All Mankind is One*, p. 83).

100 The irony is not entirely inadvertent: 'Early in his career Las Casas proposed the introduction of Negro slaves to the islands, in order to spare the Indians the heavy labour which was destroying them ... Spaniards never fought ... as hard or as consistently against Negro slavery as they did on behalf of the Indians, not even Las Casas. Despite his final rejection of Negro slavery, as late as 1544 he owned several Negro slaves and no document has come to light which reveals any concerted opposition to Negro slavery during the sixteenth century' (Hanke, *Aristotle and the American Indians*, p. 9).

101 On the immediate impact of *The Spanish Colonie*, see John Parker, *Books to Build an Empire: A Bibliographical History of English Overseas Interests to 1620* (N. Israel, Amsterdam, 1965), p. 116. For 'the black legend', see Colin Steele, *English Interpreters of the Iberian New World from Purchas to Stevens: A Bibliographical Study. 1603–1726* (The Dolphin Book Co, Oxford, 1975), pp. 133–4.

102 William Crashaw's *A Sermon Preached in London Before the Right Honorable the Lord Lawarre, Lord Governour and Captaine Generall of Virginia, and Others of his Maiesties Counsell* (London, 1610), otherwise known as *A New-Yeere's Gift to Virginea*, is actually built on the conceit that the sermon represents a parental 'New Year's Gift' to a foster-daughter. Virginia is also referred to as an 'adopted and legall Daughter' of England in Purchas's 'Virginias Verger: Or a Discourse Shewing the Benefits which may Grow to this Kingdome from American English Plantations, and Specially those of Virginia and Summer Ilands' (1625), in *Hakluytus Posthumus or Purchas His Pilgrimes: Contayning a History of the World in Sea Voyages and Lande*

Travells by Englishmen and others (20 vols., James MacLehose and Sons, Glasgow, 1905), vol. 19, p. 239. In his *Virginia Reviewed* (1638), George Donne cites from the introduction to *Purchas His Pilgrimes* (1625), in remarking how Virginia's 'virgin-soile ... was never yet polluted by any Spaniards lust' (T. H. Breen, 'Notes and Documents: George Donne's "Virginia Reviewed": A 1638 Plan to Reform Colonial Society', *William and Mary Quarterly*, third series, 30, 3, July 1973, 454). The figurative origin of this protestant colonial topos would appear to have been the myth of Vespucci raping 'America', as in the *Frontispicci Explicatio* of the 1570 *Theatrum*.

103 Purchas, *Virginias Verger*, p. 229. Leviticus is cited in the margins of John-son's *The New Life of Virginea*, and Crashaw's *A New-Yeere's Gift to Virginea*.

104 It is arguable that Caliban is finally 'included' to the extent of his resolving to 'be wise hereafter / And seek for grace' (5.1.294–5). Yet this, like the question of whether or not he is to accompany Prospero back to 'civilisation', is pointedly unresolved.

105 Arber, ed., *The First Three English Books on America*, p. 78.

106 See Niederland, 'The Naming of America', 459–72; also the discussion of Niederland's ideas in Chapter 3, above. See also White, *Tropics of Discourse*, p.187.

107 John Keats, 'On First Looking Into Chapman's Homer', lines 9–14 in *The Poetical Works of John Keats*, H. W. Garrod, ed. (Oxford University Press, London, New York and Toronto, 1959), p. 38.

5 THE FRAME OF THE NEW GEOGRAPHY

1 This phrase represents the title of Chapter 4 in John Noble Wilford's *The Mapmakers*.

2 Brown, *The Story of Maps*, p. 171.

3 Such a map was Fra Mauro's *mappamundi* of 1459–60, intended '*a contem-plation de questa illustrissima signoria*'. See Juergen Schulz, 'Jacopo de' Barba-ri's View of Venice: Map Making, City Views, and Moralized Geography Before the Year 1500', *Art Bulletin*, 60 (1978), 453.

4 It is, in fact, peculiar that this striking omission was not remarked by Shake-speare. If the *Hydrographiae Descriptio* was indeed the 'new map' of *Twelfth Night*, it is odd that Maria should remark on its 'augmentation of the Indies' when the 'augmentation' on the map is not remarkable and when any of a dozen or more maps of the period could claim as much. (See Shirley, *The Mapping of the World*, p. 239.) The omission of the southern continent was far more striking, and was what makes the map truly remarkable. It is, moreover, *this* feature that the copious legends within large cartouches advertise as the map's chief novelty.

5 If Ortelius was the first to introduce personified continents to the Renaissance map (see Chapter 3, above), the elements and seasons made their entry with Mercator's *Atlas*. Lynam notes that, 'the maps in the *Theatrum* may be taken as models of the Flemish style of cartography which ousted the Italian and was

rapidly adopted in every country' (*The Mapmaker's Art*, p. 93). See also Tooley, *Maps and Mapmakers*, p. 30.

6 Shirley, *The Mapping of the World*, Entry 114, Plate 97.

7 William Salmon, *Poligraphice, or the Arts of Drawing, Engraving* (London, 1675).

8 This and the other quoted advice on drawing wind-heads in this paragraph are from Salmon. The source is Brown, *The Story of Maps*, pp. 177–8.

9 Shirley, *The Mapping of the World*, Entry 100, Plate 86.

10 See, for example, the world map in Peter Apian's *Cosmographia* of 1524, where the three southern-most 'African' wind-heads are skull-like (Shirley, *The Mapping of the World*, Entry 82, Plate 70).

11 Under 'The interpretacion of certeyne woordes', below the table of contents of Eden's translation of Peter Martyr's *Decades of the Newe Worlde*, London, 1555 (Arber, ed., *The First Three English Books on America*, p. 45).

12 From 'The Description of the Whole World', in the English translation of the *Theatrum*: *The Theatre of the Whole World* (London, 1606), R. A. Skelton, ed., p. 1.

13 Though 'Magellanica' is included along with Europe, Africa, Asia and America on the title-page of the *Theatrum*, it is only as a bust. See Plate 9.

14 The *Aevi Veteris Typus Geographicus* (1590), or 'A Draught and Shadow of the Ancient Geography' (Shirley, *The Mapping of the World*, Entry 176, Plate 143).

15 See, for example, Arnold van Langren's world map (*c.* 1594) designed 'with Ortelius's current world map in mind' (Shirley, *The Mapping of the World*, Entry 186, Plate 151). Van Langren has removed the classical citations from the circular cartouches of the third state of the *Typus Orbis Terrarum* and replaced them with 'small maps of the four continents' (p. 205).

16 Shirley, *The Mapping of the World*, Entry 187, Plate 152, p. 207.

17 *Ibid.*, Entry 208, Plate 167.

18 *Ibid.*, Entry 294, Plate 229, p. 317.

19 The fashion for showing 'imperially mounted riders' seems to begin with Blaeu in 1606 (Shirley, *The Mapping of the World*, Entry 258, Plate 203, p. 276). Three of Visscher's beasts are chimeric. The fourth, a bear, is natural, but dangerous.

20 Heidel, *The Frame of the Ancient Greek Maps*, pp. 19–20.

21 Samuel Y. Edgerton ('From Mental Matrix to *Mappamundi* to Christian Empire', pp. 12–15) points to the profound effect on Renaissance readers of Ptolemy's insistence that the shape of the cartographic image owed more to point of view than to the immanence of the geographic object.

22 This effect was not possible on the cordiform projection commonly used before the oval projection of Ortelius and the stereographic projection of Mercator. It is notable that Ortelius's 1564 world map was cordiform.

23 See J. Enterline, 'The Southern Continent and the False Strait of Magellan', *Imago Mundi*, 26 (1972), 48–59, 53.

24 As in van den Ende's world map of 1604 (Shirley, *The Mapping of the World*, Entry 243, Plate 190).

25 Brown, *The Story of Maps*, p. 164.

26 Tzvetan Todorov, *The Conquest of America: The Question of the Other*, Richard Howard, tr. (Harper & Row, New York, 1984), p. 30.

27 Cited in Mark Kanzer, 'The Self-Analytic Literature of Robert Louis Stevenson', in George B. Wilbur and Warner Muensterberger, eds., *Psychoanalysis and Culture*, p. 425. Further reference is given in the text.

28 John Donne, 'Elegies, 19: To his Mistress Going to Bed', line 26, in John Donne, *The Complete English Poems*, A. J. Smith, ed. (Penguin, Harmondsworth, 1980), p. 125.

29 Shirley, *The Mapping of the World*, Entry 158, p. 181.

30 It is curious that Ortelius should have seen it as his duty to reject both Cicero's geography and his moralisation in the *Aevi Veteris Typus*, while piously asserting it in the *Typus Orbis Terrarum*.

31 Earl Rosenthal argues that Charles V adopted the emblem of the Herculean columns in the summer of 1516 in the course of 'the meeting of the eighteenth chapter of the Burgundian Order of the Golden Fleece' ('The Invention of the Columnar Device of Emperor Charles V at the Court of Burgundy in Flanders in 1516', *Journal of the Warburg and Courtauld Institutes*, 36, 1973, 201). The original panel used on that occasion no longer exists, but it is likely that it included the earlier Burgundian form of the imperial motto (*Plus Oultre*) along with maritime imagery (203–4).

32 Rosenthal argues in compelling detail that *Non Plus Ultra* was in fact a back-formation from the imperial motto, rather than its antecedent ('*Plus Ultra, Non Plus Ultra*, and the Columnar Device of Emperor Charles V', *Journal of the Warburg and Courtauld Institutes*, 34, 1971, 204–28). What the imperial motto inverted, therefore, was not *Non Plus Ultra* as such, but an extensive ancient tradition combining the Herculean columns with prohibitions on sailing further.

33 Dante, *The Divine Comedy of Dante Alighieri*, John D. Sinclair, ed. (3 vols., Oxford University Press, London, Oxford and New York, 1975), vol. 1, Canto XXVI, lines 107–9, pp. 324–7.

34 The hero of this fifteenth-century epic wants to explore the world 'as Ulysses had aspired to do', and is encouraged by an advisor who rejects 'the admonition *non passar più oltre*' (Rosenthal, '*Plus Ultra, Non Plus Ultra*, and the Columnar Device of Emperor Charles V', 220). Rosenthal remarks: 'It is Luigi Pulci who provides the clearest statement of the intellectual ambience that prepared for not only the daring adventure of Columbus but also Charles's choice of the motto and the columns' (221).

35 For the use of the golden fleece as a maritime emblem, see the discussion of Rubens's *Arch of the Mint* pageant in Chapter 4, above. See also the *Typus Cosmographicus Universalis* (Basle, 1532), Plate 18, on which Jason, Medea and the golden fleece function as code for the spice trade. For England's adoption of the imperial mythology, see Frances Yates, *Astraea: The Imperial Theme in the Sixteenth Century* (Penguin, Harmondsworth, 1977), pp. 22–3, 48–55; also, Roy Strong, *Gloriana: The Portraits of Queen Elizabeth I* (Thames & Hudson, GDR, 1987), pp. 95–107.

36 Elizabeth McGrath mentions that 'it had been a commonplace among humanist writers of the sixteenth century to liken the venturesome *conquistadores*, on the trail of Spanish gold, to the intrepid band of ancient Argonauts' ('Rubens's

Arch of the Mint', 196). Caspar Gevaerts, author of the commemorative *Pompa Introitus Ferdinandi*, preferred Cortés and Pizarro to Jason because 'they have brought to Spain not one, but an annually repeated Golden Fleece of treasure' (196).

37 See Chapter 4, note 98, above.

38 The *OED* backdates this word to 1582. Marlowe used it *c.* 1590 in *The Jew of Malta*, 4.2.17.

39 As Ptolemy's *Geographia* seems to have been read through his astronomical treatise, the *Almagest*, he was incorporated into and made to authorise the entire macrocosm/microcosm mania of the sixteenth century (a phenomenon which has led to his being held responsible for 'world views' with labels such as 'Ptolemaic universe' and 'Elizabethan world picture'). It is not unlikely, therefore, that he would also be read *through* rather than *against* pre-Ptolemaic formulations of the *Orbis Terrarum*.

40 Shirley, *The Mapping of the World*, Entry 19, Plate 25.

41 This and the following translation of the German text is by Roger Hilman.

42 Shirley, *The Mapping of the World*, Entry 67, Plate 61.

43 See the discussion of the spice trade, above, Chapter 2, note 60.

44 Shirley, *The Mapping of the World*, Entry 173, Plate 140. According to Shirley, the engraver was probably Jodocus Hondius. This seems likely. The biblical 'theme' of Broughton's map is consistent with other 'Christian' maps by Hondius, such as the celebrated 'Christian Knight Map of the World' of *c.* 1597 (Plate 20), and a map entitled 'Iehova' of 1592 (*The Mapping of the World*, Entry 182, Plate 147).

45 Robert Thorne's *Septentrio Orbis Universalis Descriptio*, in Richard Hakluyt, *Divers voyages touching the discoverie of America, and the Ilands adiacent unto the same* ... (London, 1582), facsimile edition (Theatrum Orbis Terrarum, Amsterdam, 1967) pp. 43–5.

46 Ben Jonson, *The Alchemist*, Alvin B. Kernan, ed. (Yale University Press, New Haven and London, 1974).

47 Jonson is scathingly funny on Broughton's apocalyptic commentary on Gog and Magog from the Northern 'end' of the biblical earth. See 4.5.1–36.

48 Ortelius, *Parergon: Geographia Sacra*, insert map: *Haec notula locum Ophirae designat*. Latin text within a nearby cartouche summarises the position as follows: 'Because this map is not able to identify the region of Ophir, we have indicated this worldwide area and noted thereupon the judgements of writers of differing views. But if anyone should desire my opinion on this matter, let him consult my *Thesaurus Geographicus* and his own opinion'. (Translated by Greg Horsley.)

49 Douglas, ed., *New Bible Dictionary*, p. 1239. 'Tarshish' was Jonah's destination. It is also the name of a son of Javan, grandson of Noah.

50 Heidel supposes that Aristotle's 'Tartessus' is 'unquestionably the biblical Tarshish' (*The Frame of the Ancient Greek Maps*, p. 39). In theorising about the northern border of the Greek frame, Aristotle had supposed the existence of a river called 'Tartessus' on the same latitude as the 'Ister'. He supposed both to rise in the Pyrenees, with the Ister flowing East into the Euxine and the Tartessus flowing west into the ocean.

51 Shirley, *The Mapping of the World*, Entry 198, Plate 161, p. 219.

52 *Ibid.*, p. 219.
53 In his manuscript *Volume of Great and Rich Discoveries* (1577), John Dee proposed that: 'the ultimate goal of British enterprise should be that part of the reputed rich mainland lying south of Java which was prominently shown on the recent maps of Mercator and Ortelius as Locach or Beach' (E. G. R. Taylor, 'John Dee and the map of North-East Asia', *Imago Mundi*, 12, 1955, repr. 1970, 103). Dee also argued that *Terra Australis* could be reached via the north-east passage shown in his own Asian map and the world maps of Ortelius and Mercator (104–5). In 1580, such a voyage was actually attempted, but was blocked by ice at the Kara Sea (105). Francis Drake also had instructions to explore the Beach peninsula to latitude 30° S on his circumnavigation, but wisely seems to have ignored them (105).
54 Shirley, *The Mapping of the World*, Entry 260, Plate 205.
55 *Ibid.*, Entry 273, Plate 215.
56 See, too, Günter Schilder, 'Willem Jansz. Blaeu's Wall Map of the World, on Mercator's Projection, 1606–07 and its Influence' *Imago Mundi*, 31 (second series, vol. 4, 1979), 36–54. Several of Schilder's illustrations contain continental group-portraits similar to Visscher's, apart from the fact that, like Hondius's *Christian Knight Map*, the continental group is located against the backdrop of *Terra Australis Incognita*.
57 In Renaissance mythography, Ceres is regarded as the donatrix of civilisation as well as of agriculture. See Boccaccio's account of her in *De Claris Mulieribus* (*Forty Six Lives, Translated From Boccaccio's 'De Claris Mulieribus' by Henry Parker, Lord Morley*, Early English Text Society, Oxford University Press, London, 1943, p. 23).
58 According to Bernadette Bucher, de Bry's images of the Amerindians unconsciously fused two commonplace protestant perspectives: that the Indians were on the one hand Adamic, and on the other hand in an advanced state of 'natural decay' (*Icon and Conquest*, pp. 53–7).
59 Sepúlveda used the gospels in a similar way in the course of his debate with Las Casas. Thus, the parable of the wedding feast, in which the Lord commands his servants to go out into the highways and byways to bring passers-by into the feast by 'force' if necessary, was cited in support of an argument that 'war may be waged against infidels in order to prepare the way for preaching the faith'. See Lewis Hanke, *All Mankind is One*, p. 95.
60 John Donne, *The Complete English Poems*, pp. 347–8.
61 Clay Hunt, *Donne's Poetry: Essays in Literary Analysis* (Yale University Press, New Haven and London, 1962), p. 101. Hunt's comprehensive, influential and generally excellent reading of the poem occupies the whole of his fourth chapter, pp. 96–117. In an apparent echo of Hunt, Louis B. Martz notes that 'the flat map is only an illusory diagram' (*The Poem of the Mind: Essays on Poetry, English and American*, Oxford University Press, Oxford and New York, 1969, p. 41).
62 Hunt, *Donne's Poetry*, p. 104.
63 Hunt and Martz both proceed on this assumption. See also Helen Gardner's untroubled commentary in *John Donne: The Divine Poems* (Clarendon Press, Oxford, 1952), pp. 107–9. David Novarr (*The Disinterred Muse: Donne's Texts and Contexts*, Cornell University Press, Ithaca and London, 1980), suggests

that the *Hymn* is controlled by 'an attitude which is more entirely unilateral' than in the Holy Sonnets (p. 177).

64 From the 1475 letter which Toscanelli wrote to accompany the map which Columbus would use as a guide on his first trans-Atlantic voyage (*The Life of the Admiral Christopher Columbus by His Son Ferdinand*, Benjamin Keen, ed., tr., The Folio Society, London, 1960, p. 45).

65 A. J. Smith, ed., *John Donne: The Critical Heritage* (Routledge & Kegan Paul, London and Boston, 1975), p. 460. The citation is from George MacDonald's 1868 essay on the *Hymn*, pp. 458–62.

66 Hunt, *Donne's Poetry*, p. 241.

67 The first reading is Gardner's (*The Divine Poems*, p. 108); the second is Hunt's (*Donne's Poetry*, p. 105).

68 Martz, *The Poem of the Mind*, p. 41.

69 Louis B. Martz, *The Poetry of Meditation: A Study in English Religious Literature of the Seventeenth Century* (Yale University Press, New Haven and London, 1978), pp. 221–35.

70 The same kind of distinction is made in *The Progress of the Soul*. The soul's imagined flight up through the cosmos is continually marked by the use of the word 'think', and ends at the soul's arrival at the 'room': a kind of knowing that merges thought and action.

71 Gardner, *The Divine Poems*, p. 108.

72 Gardner cites from a sermon to suggest that this is what Donne had in mind: '"Anian, Magellan and Gibraltar, ways to the East, the Pacific and to Jerusalem, are all straits, and however we travel to them – from Europe, Africa or Asia – we must travel by hard and difficult ways"' (*The Divine Poems*, p. 109). Hunt and Martz also construe the line in this way. See Hunt, *Donne's Poetry*, pp. 104–5, also Martz, *The Poem of the Mind*, p. 42.

73 Where Gardner chooses the first alternative (see previous note), Louis Martz allows for the second as well: 'But however one goes, the voyage is full of pain and difficulty. And this is true whatever regions of the earth he may sail from or sail between, "Whether where *Japhet* dwelt, or *Cham*, or *Sem*." In thus recalling the ancient division of the earth into the inheritance given to the three sons of Noah, Donne suggests the universality and the inevitability of those straits which face every man who seeks his ultimate home' (*The Poem of the Mind*, p. 42).

Bibliography

PRIMARY SOURCES

Abbot, George, *A Briefe Description of the Whole Worlde* (London, 1599), The English Experience, no. 213, Da Capo Press, Theatrum Orbis Terrarum, Amsterdam and New York, 1970.

Acosta, Joseph de, *The Natural and Moral History of the Indies ... Reprinted from the English Translated Edition of Edward Grimstone 1604*, Clements R. Markham (ed.), 2 vols., Burt Franklin, New York, 1970.

Aeschylus, *Seven Against Thebes*, Anthony Hecht and Helen Bacon (eds.), Oxford University Press, 1974.

    Aeschylus: Prometheus Bound, Mark Griffith (ed.), Cambridge University Press, Cambridge, 1983.

Alday, John, *Theatrum Mundi: The Theator or Rule of the World*, London, 1603.

Alexander, William, *An Encouragement to Colonies* (London, 1624), The English Experience, no. 63, Da Capo Press, Theatrum Orbis Terrarum, Amsterdam and New York, 1968.

Anderson, Fulton H. (ed.), *Francis Bacon: The New Organon and Related Writings*, The Liberal Arts Press, New York, 1960.

Arber, Edward. (ed.), *The First Three English books on America [?1511]–1555 AD. Being chiefly Translations, Compilations, &c., by Richard Eden*, Kraus Reprint Co., New York, 1971.

Aristides, Aelius, *Panathenaic Discourse* in J. H. Oliver, 'The Civilizing Power: A Study of *The Panathenaic Discourse* of Aelius Aristides Against the Background of Literature and Cultural Conflict, with Text, Translation, and Commentary', *Transactions of the American Philosophical Society*, new series, vol. 58, part 1 (1968), 45–90.

Aristotle, *The Politics*, Trevor J. Saunders (ed.), T. A. Sinclair (tr.), Penguin, Harmondsworth, 1986.

Bacon, Francis, *The Advancement of Learning*, G. W. Kitchin (ed.), Dent, London, 1976.

    The Essays, John Pitcher (ed.), Penguin, Harmondsworth, 1985.

Bakhtin, Mikhail, *The Dialogic Imagination: Four Essays by M. M. Bakhtin*, Michael Holquist and Caryl Emerson (eds., trs.), University of Texas Press, Austin, 1981.

    'The Problem of Speech Genres' in *Speech Genres and Other Late Essays*, Michael Holquist and Caryl Emerson (eds.), Vern W. McGee (tr.), University of Texas Press, Austin, 1986.

Behn, Aphra, *Oroonoko: or, The History of the Royal Slave*, K. A. Sey (ed.), Ghana Publishing Corporation, Tema, Ghana, 1977.

'Bermuda Pamphlets', see Bullough, Geoffrey, *Narrative and Dramatic Sources of Shakespeare*.

Best, George, 'Experiences and reasons of the Sphere, to proove all partes of the worlde habitable, and thereby to confute the position of the five Zones' in Hakluyt, Richard, *The Principal Navigations Voyages Traffiques & Discoveries of the English nation: Made by Sea or Over-land to the Remote and Farthest Distant Quarters of the Earth at any time within the compasse of these 1600 Yeeres*, 8 vols., James MacLehose & Sons, Glasgow, 1903, vol. 5, pp. 171–220.

The Holy Bible, The Revised Version, Cambridge University Press, 1898.

Boccaccio, Giovanni, *Forty Six Lives, Translated from Boccaccio's 'De Claris Mulieribus' by Henry Parker, Lord Morley*, Early English Text Society, Oxford University Press, London, 1943.

Bodin, Jean, *The Six Bookes of a Commonweale: A Facsimile reprint of the English translation of 1606, corrected and supplemented in the light of a new comparison with the French and Latin texts*, Kenneth Douglas McRae (ed.), Harvard University Press, Cambridge, Mass., 1962.

Boemus, Johannes, *The Fardle of Façions* (London, 1555), The English Experience, no. 227, Da Capo Press, Theatrum Orbis Terrarum, Amsterdam and New York, 1970.

Botero, Giovanni, *The Travellers Breviat* (London, 1601), The English Experience, no. 143, Da Capo Press, Theatrum Orbis Terrarum, Amsterdam and New York, 1969.

Braun & Hogenberg: Civitates Orbis Terrarum: 'The Towns of the World', 1572–1618, R. A. Skelton (ed.), 3 vols., The World Publishing Company, Cleveland and New York, 1966.

Breen, T. H., 'George Donne's *"Virginia Reviewed"*: A 1638 Plan to Reform Colonial Society', *William and Mary Quarterly*, third series, vol. 30, no. 3 (July 1973), 449–66.

Broughton, Hugh, *A Concent of Scripture* (London, 1588–9).

Bullough, Geoffrey (ed.), *Narrative and Dramatic Sources of Shakespeare*, 8 vols., Routledge & Kegan Paul, London; Columbia University Press, New York, 1966.

Carpenter, Nathanael, *Geography Delineated Forth in Two Bookes* (Oxford, 1625), The English Experience, no. 787, Walter J. Johnson, Amsterdam and New York, 1976.

Chaucer, Geoffrey, *The Works of Geoffrey Chaucer*, F. N. Robinson (ed.), Oxford University Press, London, 1974.

Cicero, Marcus Tullius, *De Natura Deorum Academica*, H. Rackham (ed.), The Loeb Classical Library, Harvard University Press, Cambridge, Mass.; Heinemann, London, 1961.

'Scipio's Dream' in *De Re Publica De Legibus*, C. W. Keyes (ed.), The Loeb Classical Library, Harvard University Press, Cambridge, Mass.; Heinemann, London, 1948, pp. 260–83.

Tusculan Disputations, J. E. King (ed.), The Loeb Classical Library, Harvard University Press, Cambridge, Mass.; Heinemann, London, 1950.

Cohen, J. M. (ed.), *The Four Voyages of Christopher Columbus*, The Cresset Library, London, 1988.

Columbus, Ferdinand, *The Life of the Admiral Christopher Columbus*, Benjamin Keen (ed., tr.), The Folio Society, London, 1960.

Contarini, Gasparo, *The Commonwealth and Government of Venice. Written by the Cardinall Gasper Contareno, and Translated out of Italian into English, by Lewes Lewkenor Esquire ... With Sundry Other Collections* (London, 1599), The English Experience, no. 101, Da Capo Press, Theatrum Orbis Terrarum, Amsterdam and New York, 1969.

Coryat, Thomas, *Coryats Crudities, 1611*, William M. Schutte (ed.), Scolar Press, London, 1978.

Crashaw, William, *A Sermon Preached in London Before the Right Honorable the Lord Lawarre, Lord Governour and Captaine Generall of Virginia, and Others of his Maiesties Counsell* (London, 1610).

Cunningham, William, *The Cosmographicall Glasse* (London, 1559), The English Experience, no. 44, Da Capo Press, Theatrum Orbis Terrarum, Amsterdam and New York, 1968.

Dante, *The Divine Comedy of Dante Alighieri*, John D. Sinclair (ed., tr.), 3 vols., Oxford University Press, London, Oxford and New York, 1975.

D'Elia, Pasquale (ed., tr.), *Fonti Ricciane: Edizione nazionale delle opere edite e inedite di Matteo Ricci* (Rome, 1942).

De Jode, Gerard, *De Jode: Speculum Orbis Terrarum* (Antwerp, 1578), R. A. Skelton (ed.), Theatrum Orbis Terrarum, Amsterdam, 1965.

Donne, John, *John Donne: The Complete English Poems*, A. J. Smith (ed.), Penguin, Harmondsworth, 1980.

Dryden, John, *The Indian Queen* in *The Works of John Dryden*, James Harrington Smith and Douglas MacMillan (eds.), 20 vols., University of California Press, Berkeley and Los Angeles, 1967, vol. 8, pp. 180–304.

The Indian Emperor in *Works*, vol. 9, 1966, John Loftis (ed.), pp. 1–112.

Eden, Richard, see Arber, Edward (ed.), *The First Three English Books on America*.

Euripides, *Orestes and Other Plays*, Philip Vellacott (ed., tr.), Penguin, Harmondsworth, 1972.

Medea and Other Plays, Philip Vellacott (ed., tr.), Penguin, Harmondsworth, 1963.

Alcestis / Hippolytus / Iphigenia in Tauris, Philip Vellacott (ed., tr.), Penguin, London, 1974.

Fairholt, Frederick W., *Lord Mayors' Pageants*, Percy Society, London, 1943.

Federici, Cesare, *The Voyage and Travaile into the East India* (London, 1588), The English Experience, no. 340, Da Capo Press, Theatrum Orbis Terrarum, Amsterdam and New York, 1971.

Florus, Lucius Annaeus, *Epitome of Roman History*, Cornelius Nepos (ed., tr.), The Loeb Classical Library, Heinemann, London; Putnam, New York, 1929.

Gellius, Aulus, *The Attic Nights*, John C. Rolfe (ed., tr.), The Loeb Classical Library, 3 vols., Harvard University Press, Cambridge, Mass.; Heinemann, London, 1967.

Gibbon, Edward, *The History of the Decline and Fall of the Roman Empire*, J. B. Bury (ed.), 7 vols., Methuen, London, 1900.

Hakluyt, Richard, *The Principal Navigations Voyages Traffiques & Discoveries of the English nation: Made by Sea or Over-land to the Remote and Farthest Distant Quarters of the Earth at any time within the compasse of these 1600 Yeeres*, 8 vols., James MacLehose and Sons, Glasgow, 1903.

The Principall Navigations Voiages and Discoveries of the English Nation (London, 1589), facsimile reprint, D. B. Quinn, R. A. Skelton and A. Quinn (eds.), 2 vols., The Hakluyt Society and The Peabody Museum of Salem, at The Cambridge University Press, 1965.

Divers voyages touching the discoverie of America, and the Ilands adiacent unto the same ... (London, 1582), facsimile edition, Theatrum Orbis Terrarum, Amsterdam, 1967.

Hall, Joseph, *The Discovery of a New World (Mundus Alter Et Idem): Written Originally in Latin by Joseph Hall, CA. 1605; Englished By John Healey, CA. 1609*, Huntington Brown (ed.), Harvard University Press, Cambridge, Mass., 1937.

Herodotus, A. D. Godley (ed.), The Loeb Classical Library, 4 vols., Harvard University Press, Cambridge, Mass.; Heinemann, London, 1921.

Heylyn, Peter, *Microcosmus: Or a Little Description of the Great World* (Oxford, 1621), The English Experience, no. 743, Da Capo Press, Theatrum Orbis Terrarum, Amsterdam and New York, 1975.

Heywood, Thomas, *An Apology for Actors with 'A Refutation of the Apology for Actors', by I.G.*, Garland, New York and London, 1973.

Hippocrates, *Airs, Waters, Places* in *Hippocrates*, W. H. S. Jones (ed.), The Loeb Classical Library, 6 vols., Heinemann, London; Putnam, New York, 1923.

Horace, *The Odes and Epodes of Horace*, Joseph P. Clancy (ed., tr.), University of Chicago Press, 1960.

Johnson, Robert, *The New Life of Virginea* (London, 1612), The English Experience, no. 332, Da Capo Press, Theatrum Orbis Terrarum, Amsterdam and New York, 1971.

Jonson, Ben, *Discoveries* in *Ben Jonson*, Ian Donaldson (ed.), Oxford University Press, Oxford and New York, 1985.

The Alchemist, Alvin B. Kernan (ed.), Yale University Press, New Haven and London, 1974.

Sejanus his Fall, W. F. Bolton (ed.), Ernest Benn, London, 1966.

Juvenal, *Sixteen Satires upon the Ancient Harlot*, Steven Robinson (ed., tr.), Carcanet New Press, Manchester, 1983.

Keats, John, *The Poetical Works of John Keats*, H. W. Garrod (ed.), Oxford University Press, London, New York and Toronto, 1959.

Knolles, Edward, *The General Historie of the Turkes* (London, 1603).

Las Casas, Bartolomé de, *History of the Indies*, Andrée Collard (ed., tr.), Harper & Row, New York, Evanston and London, 1971.

In Defense of the Indians: The Defense of the Most Reverend Lord, Don Fray Bartolomé de Las Casas, of the Order of Preachers, Late Bishop of Chiapa, Against the Persecutors and Slanderers of the Peoples of the New World Discovered Across the Seas, Stafford Poole (ed., tr.), Northern Illinois University Press, De Kalb, 1974.

Livy, Book 36, 17, *Livy in Fourteen Volumes*, Evan T. Sage (ed., tr.), The Loeb Classical Library, Harvard University Press, Cambridge, Mass.; Heinemann, London, 1968.

Lucan, *Pharsalia* in *The Civil War Books I–X*, J. D. Duff (ed., tr.), The Loeb Classical Library, Heinemann, London; Putnam, New York, 1928.

Lynche, Richard, *An Historical Treatise of the Travels of Noah into Europe: Containing the first inhabitation and peopling thereof* (London, 1601).

Macrobius, *Commentary on the Dream of Scipio*, William Harris Stahl (ed., tr.), Columbia University Press, New York, 1952.

Mandeville, Sir John, *The Travels of Sir John Mandeville*, C. W. R. D. Moseley (ed.), Penguin, Harmondsworth, 1983.

'The voyage of Ion Mandevil knight in Latin', Hakluyt, Richard, *The Principal Navigations* (London, 1589).

Marlowe, Christopher, *The Complete Poems and Translations*, Stephen Orgel (ed.), Penguin, Harmondsworth, 1971.

The Complete Plays, J. B. Steane (ed.), Penguin, Harmondsworth, 1975.

Mercator, Gerard, *Mercator-Hondius-Janssonius: Atlas, Or a Geographicke Description of the World* (Amsterdam, 1636), R. A. Skelton (ed.), 2 vols., Theatrum Orbis Terrarum, Amsterdam, 1968.

Morton, Thomas, *The New English Canaan* (Amsterdam, 1637), The English Experience, no. 140, Da Capo Press, Theatrum Orbis Terrarum, Amsterdam and New York, 1969.

Mun, Thomas, *England's Treasure by Forraign Trade* (London, 1664), Blackwell, Oxford, 1959.

Nichols, John, *The Progresses and Public Processions of Queen Elizabeth*, 3 vols., John Nichols & Son, London, 1823.

The Progresses, Processions . . . of James the First, 4 vols., Burt Franklin, New York, 1967.

Oliver, J. H., 'The Civilizing Power: A Study of the Panathenaic Discourse of Aelius Aristides Against the Background of Literature and Cultural Conflict', *Transactions of the American Philological Society*, new series, no. 58, pt. 1 (1968), 45–90.

Orgel, Stephen and Strong, Roy, *Inigo Jones: The Theatre of the Stuart Court*, 2 vols., Sotheby Parke Bernet, London; University of California Press, Berkeley, 1973.

Ortelius, Abraham, *Theatrum Orbis Terrarum* (Antwerp, 1570), R. A. Skelton (ed.), Theatrum Orbis Terrarum, Antwerp, 1964.

The Theatre of the Whole World (London, 1606), R. A. Skelton (ed.), Theatrum Orbis Terrarum, Amsterdam, 1968.

Ovid, *Ovid's Fasti*, Sir James George Frazer (ed., tr.), The Loeb Classical Library, Harvard University Press, Cambridge, Mass.; Heinemann, London, 1951.

Ovid In Six Volumes: III Metamorphoses, G. P. Gould (ed.), Frank Justus Miller (tr.), The Loeb Classical Library, Harvard University Press, Cambridge, Mass.; Heinemann, London, 1977.

The Metamorphoses of Ovid, Mary M. Innes (ed., tr.), Penguin Books, Harmondsworth, 1953.

Shakespeare's Ovid Being Arthur Golding's Translation of the Metamorphoses, W. H. D. Rouse (ed.), Centaur Press, London, 1961.

Ovid's Metamorphoses Englished (Oxford, 1632), George Sandys (ed., tr.), Garland, New York and London, 1976.

Paterculus, Velleius, *The History of Rome*, 2. 46, in *Compendium of Roman*

History: Res Gestae Divi Augusti, Frederick W. Shipley (ed.), The Loeb Classical Library, Harvard University Press, Cambridge, Mass.; Heinemann, London, 1961.

Pigafetta, Antonio, 'A Briefe Declaration of the Voyage or Navigation Made Abowte the Worlde', Arber, Edward (ed.), *The First Three English Books on America*, pp. 249–62.

Pike, Joseph B., *Frivolities of Courtiers and Footprints of Philosophers: Being a Translation of the First, Second, and Third Books and Selections from the Seventh and Eighth Books of the 'Policraticus' of John of Salisbury*, Octagon Books, New York, 1972.

Pliny, *The History of the World, Commonly Called the Natural History of C. Plinius Secundus, or Pliny, Translated by Philemon Holland*, Paul Turner (ed.), McGraw Hill, New York, Toronto and London, 1964.

Plutarch, *The Lives of the Noble Grecians and Romans*, John Dryden (tr.), revised by Arthur Hugh Clough, Modern Library, New York.

Plutarch's Lives, Bernadotte Perin (ed.), The Loeb Classical Library, 10 vols., Heinemann, London; Macmillan, New York, 1914.

Shakespeare's Plutarch: The Lives of Julius Caesar, Brutus, Marcus Antonius, and Coriolanus in the translation of Sir Thomas North, T. J. B. Spencer (ed.), Penguin, Harmondsworth, 1964.

Ptolemy, Claudius, *Cosmographia* (Roma, 1478), R. A. Skelton (ed.), Theatrum Orbis Terrarum, Amsterdam, 1966.

Cosmographia (Bologna, 1477), R. A. Skelton (ed.), Theatrum Orbis Terrarum, Amsterdam, 1963.

Pulci, Luigi, *Il Morgante*, Giuseppe Fatini (ed.), Unione Tipografico, Torino, 1984.

Purchas, Samuel, 'Virginias Verger: Or a Discourse Shewing the Benefits which may Grow to this Kingdome from American English Plantations, and especially those of Virginia and Summer Ilands' (1625), in *Hakluytus Posthumus or Purchas His Pilgrimes: Contayning a History of the World in Sea Voyages and Lande Travells by Englishmen and Others*, 20 vols., James MacLehose and Sons, Glasgow, 1905, vol. 19, pp. 218–67.

Quintilian, *The Institutio Oratoria of Quintilian*, H. E. Butler (ed., tr.), The Loeb Classical Library, 4 vols., Harvard University Press, Cambridge, Mass.; Heinemann, London, 1964.

Roberts, Lewes, *The Marchants Mapp of Commerce* (London, 1638), The English Experience, no. 689, Walter Johnson Inc., Theatrum Orbis Terrarum, Amsterdam and Norwood, NJ, 1974.

Salmon, William, *Poligraphice, or the Arts of Drawing, Engraving* (London, 1675).

Seneca, *The Tenne Tragedies of Seneca Translated into English* (London, 1581), The Spenser Society, no. 43, Burt Franklin, New York, 1967.

Seneca: Four Tragedies and Octavia, E. F. Watling (ed., tr.), Penguin, Harmondsworth, 1985.

Seneca: Medea, C. D. N. Costa (ed.), Clarendon Press, Oxford, 1973.

Seneca's Thyestes, R. J. Tarrant (ed.), Scholars Press, Atlanta, Georgia, 1985.

'Lights in the Sky (De Ignibus In Aere)' in *Seneca in Ten Volumes, vol. 7: Naturales Quaestiones I*, T. H. Corcoran (ed., tr.), The Loeb Classical

Library, Harvard University Press, Cambridge, Mass.; Heinemann, London, 1971.

'Epistle LXXXIX: On the Parts of Philosophy', *Seneca: Ad Lucilium, Epistolae Morales*, R. M. Gummere (ed., tr.), The Loeb Classical Library, Harvard University Press, Cambridge, Mass.; Heinemann, London, 1953.

Seneca The Elder, *The Elder Seneca Declamations* in Two Volumes, vol. 2: *Controversiae, Books 7–10, Suasoriae*, M. Winterbottom (ed., tr.), The Loeb Classical Library, Harvard University Press, Cambridge, Mass.; Heinemann, London, 1974.

Sermons or Homilies Appointed to be Read in Churches in the Time of Queen Elizabeth of Famous Memory, fourth edition, Clarendon Press, Oxford, 1816.

Servius, *Servianorum In Vergilii Carmina Commentarium Vol. 3 (Aeneid, Books 3–5)*, Oxford University Press, 1965.

Shakespeare, William, *The Complete Works*, Stanley Wells, Gary Taylor, John Jowett and William Montgomery (eds.), Clarendon Press, Oxford, 1986.

   Mr. William Shakespeares Comedies, Histories, & Tragedies: A facsimile edition, Helge Kökeritz and Charles Tyler Prouty (eds.), Yale University Press, New Haven and London, 1968.

Silvestris, Bernardus, *Commentary on the First Six Books of Virgil's Aeneid by Bernardus Silvestris*, Earl G. Schrieber and Thomas Maresca (eds., trs.), University of Nebraska Press, Lincoln and London, 1979.

   The Commentary on the First Six Books of the 'Aeneid' of Vergil Commonly Attributed to Bernardus Silvestris, Julian Ward Jones and Elizabeth Frances Jones (eds.), University of Nebraska Press, Lincoln and London, 1977.

Solinus, Caius Julius, *The Excellent and Pleasant Worke, Collectanea Rerum Memorabilium, of Caius Julius Solinus*, Arthur Golding (tr., 1587), George Kish (ed.), Scholars Facsimiles & Reprints, Gainesville, Florida, 1955.

Southerne, Thomas, *Oroonoko: A Tragedy* (London, 1695) in *Restoration Tragedies*, James Southerland (ed.), Oxford University Press, London, Oxford and New York, 1977, pp. 355–438.

Speed, John, *A Prospect of the Most Famous Parts of the World* (London, 1627), R. A. Skelton (ed.), Theatrum Orbis Terrarum, Amsterdam, 1966.

Strachey, William, *The Historie of Travell into Virginia Britania* (1612), Louis B. Wright and Virginia Freund (eds.), Hakluyt Society, London, 1953.

Thevet, Andrewe, *The New Found Worlde or Antarctike* (London, 1568), The English Experience, no. 417, Da Capo Press, Theatrum Orbis Terrarum, Amsterdam and New York, 1971.

Vico, Giambattista, *The New Science of Giambattista Vico: Revised Translation of the Third Edition (1744)*, Thomas Goddard Bergin and Max Harold Fisch (eds.), Cornell University Press, Ithaca, New York, 1968.

Virgil, *Virgil with an English Translation*, H. Rushton Fairclough (ed.), The Loeb Classical Library, 2 vols., Harvard University Press, Cambridge, Mass.; Heinemann, London, 1967.

   Virgil: Aeneid Book VIII, K. W. Gransden (ed.), Cambridge University Press, Cambridge, New York and Melbourne, 1976.

   P. Vergili Maronis Aeneidos: Libri VII–VIII, C. J. Fordyce (ed.), Oxford University Press, 1977.

The Eclogues, Georgics and Aeneid of Virgil, C. Day Lewis (ed., tr.), Oxford University Press, London, 1974.

Vitruvius, *Vitruvius on Architecture*, Frank Granger (ed., tr.), The Loeb Classical Library, 2 vols., Harvard University Press, Cambridge, Mass.; Heinemann, London, 1955.

Waghenaer, Lucas Janszoon, *Spieghel Der Zeevaerdt* (Leyden, 1584–5), R. A. Skelton (ed.), N. Israel, Meridian Publishing Co., Amsterdam, 1964.

The Mariners Mirrour (London, 1588), R. A. Skelton (ed.), Theatrum Orbis Terrarum, Amsterdam, 1966.

Withington, Robert, *English Pageantry: An Historical Outline*, 2 vols., Benjamin Blom, New York and London, 1918.

SECONDARY SOURCES

Agnew, Jean-Christophe, *Worlds Apart: The Market and the Theater in Anglo-American Thought, 1550–1750*, Cambridge University Press, Cambridge, London, New York, New Rochelle, Melbourne and Sydney, 1986.

Ahl, Frederick M., *Lucan: An Introduction*, Cornell University Press, Ithaca and London, 1976.

Alpers, Svetlana, 'The Mapping Impulse in Dutch Art' in Woodward, David (ed.), *Art & Cartography*, pp. 51–96.

The Art of Describing, John Murray, London, 1983.

Aurousseau, M., *The Rendering of Geographical Names*, Hutchinson University Library, London, 1957.

Bachelard, Gaston, *The Poetics of Space*, Maria Jolas (tr.), Beacon Press, Boston, 1969.

Baddeley, J. F., 'Father Matteo Ricci's Chinese World-Maps, 1584–1608', *The Geographical Journal*, vol. 50 (1917), 254–76.

Badian, E., 'Alexander the Great and the Unity of Mankind', *Historia*, 7 (1958), 425–44.

Bagrow, Leo, *History of Cartography: Revised and Enlarged by R. A. Skelton*, Watts & Co, London, 1964.

Barker, Francis, Hulme, Peter and Iverson, Margaret (eds.), *Europe and its Others: Proceedings of the Essex Conference on the Sociology of Literature, July 1984*, University of Essex, Colchester, 1985.

Baron, Hans, *From Petrarch to Leonardo Bruni: Studies in Humanistic and Political Literature*, Chicago University Press, 1968.

Beardwood, Alice, *Alien Merchants in England, 1350–1377: The Legal and Economic Position*, The Medieval Academy of America, Cambridge, Mass., 1931.

Beazley, C. Raymond, *The Dawn of Modern Geography, 3 Vols. Vol. 1: A History of Exploration and Geographical Science from the Conversion of the Roman Empire to A.D. 900*, Peter Smith, New York, 1949.

The Dawn of Modern Geography, Vol. 2: A History of Exploration and Geographical Science from the Close of the Ninth to the Middle of the Thirteenth Century (c. A.D. 900–1260), 3 vols., Peter Smith, New York, 1949.

The Dawn of Modern Geography, Vol. 3: A History of Exploration and Geographical Science from the Middle of the Thirteenth to the Early Years of the Fifteenth Century (c. 1260–1420), 3 vols., Clarendon Press, Oxford, 1906.

Bennett, J. W., *The Rediscovery of Sir John Mandeville*, The Modern Languages Association of America, New York, 1954.

Bloker Hawkins, Harriet, '"All the World's a Stage" Some Illustrations of the Theatrum Mundi', *Shakespeare Quarterly*, 17 (1966), 174–88.

Boas, Frederick S., *Elizabethan and Other Essays by Sir Sidney Lee*, Clarendon Press, Oxford, 1929.

Boose, Lynda E., 'Othello's Handkerchief: "The Recognizance and Pledge of Love"', *English Literary Renaissance*, 5 (1975), 360–74.

Bradner, Leicester, 'Columbus in Sixteenth Century Poetry' in *Essays Honouring Lawrence C. Wroth*, Portland, Maine, 1951, pp. 15–30.

Braudel, Fernand, *The Perspective of the World (Volume 3, Civilization and Capitalism 15th–18th Century)*, Sian Reynolds (tr.), Fontana, London, 1984.

Brody, Paula, 'Shylock's Omophagia: A Ritual Approach to *The Merchant Of Venice*', *Literature and Psychology* 17 (1967), 229–34.

Broude, Ronald, 'Roman and Goth in *Titus Andronicus*', *Shakespeare Studies*, 6 (1970), 27–34.

Brower, Reuben A., *Hero & Saint: Shakespeare and the Graeco-Roman Heroic Tradition*, Clarendon Press, Oxford, 1971.

Brown, Lloyd A., *The Story of Maps*, Cresset Press, London, 1951.

Bucher, Bernadette, *Icon and Conquest: A Structural Analysis of the Illustrations of de Bry's Great Voyages*, Basia Miller Gulati (tr.), University of Chicago Press, Chicago and London, 1981.

Bueler, Lois E., 'The Structural Uses of Incest in English Renaissance Drama.' *Renaissance Drama*, new series, 15 (1984), 115–45.

Burgin, Victor, 'Geometry and Abjection' in *Psychoanalysis and Cultural Theory: Thresholds*, James Donald (ed.), MacMillan, London, 1991, pp. 11–26.

Butcher, Philip, 'Othello's Racial Identity', *Shakespeare Quarterly*, 3 (1952), 243–7.

Cary, M. and Warmington, E. H., *The Ancient Explorers*, Penguin, Harmondsworth, 1963.

Cawley, R. R., 'Shakespeare's Use of the Voyagers in *The Tempest*', *Proceedings of the Modern Languages Association of America*, 41 (1926), 688–726.

   Unpathed Waters: Studies in the Influence of the Voyagers on Elizabethan Literature, Octagon Books, New York, 1967.

   Milton and the Literature of Travel, Gordian Press, New York, 1970.

Chambers, E. K., *The Elizabethan Stage*, 4 vols., Clarendon Press, Oxford, 1923.

Charlesworth, M. P., 'The Fear of the Orient in the Roman Empire', *Cambridge Historical Journal*, 2, 1 (1926), 1–16.

Charney, Maurice, *Shakespeare's Roman Plays: The Function of Imagery in the Drama*, Harvard University Press, Cambridge, Mass., 1961.

Chiapelli, Fredi. (ed.), *First Images of America. The Impact of the New World on the Old*, 2 vols., University of California Press, Berkeley, Los Angeles and London, 1976.

Chisholm, Michael and Smith, David M., *Shared Space: Divided Space, Essays on Conflict and Territorial Organization*, Unwin Hyman, London, Boston, Sydney and Wellington, 1990.

Chitty, C. W., 'Aliens in England in the Sixteenth Century', *Race*, 8 (1966–7), 129–45.

Clayton, Margaret, 'Ben Jonson, "In Travaile With Expression Of Another": His Use of John of Salisbury's Policraticus In Timber', *Review of English Studies*, new series, 30 (1979), 397–408.

Coffin, Charles Monroe, *John Donne and The New Philosophy*, The Humanities Press, New York, 1958.

Coghill, Nevill, *Shakespeare's Professional Skills*, Cambridge University Press, 1964.

Conacher, D. J., *Aeschylus' Prometheus Bound: A Literary Commentary*, University of Toronto Press, Toronto, Buffalo and London, 1980.

Coote, C. H., 'Shakspere's "New Map"', *New Shakspere Society's Transactions*, 1877–9, Part 1 (1878), 88–100.

'Note On The "New Map"', in *The Voyages and Works of John Davis the Navigator*, A. H. Markham (ed.), Burt Franklin Reprints, New York, 1970, lxxxv–xcv.

Cowhig, Ruth, 'Blacks in English Renaissance drama and the role of Shakespeare's Othello' in Dabydeen, David (ed.), *The Black Presence in English Literature*, Manchester University Press, 1985, pp. 1–25.

'Actors, Black and Tawny in the Role of Othello – and their Critics', *Theatre Research International*, Glasgow, 4 (1979), 133–46.

Crone, G. R., *Maps and Their Makers: An Introduction to the History of Cartography*, Hutchinson's University Library, London, 1953.

Cunningham, J. S. (ed.), *Tamburlaine The Great: Christopher Marlowe*, Manchester University Press, 1981.

Curtius, Ernst Robert, *European Literature and the Latin Middle Ages*, Willard R. Trask (tr.), Routledge & Kegan Paul, London and Henley, 1979.

D'Amico, Jack, *The Moor in English Renaissance Drama*, University of South Florida Press, Tampa, 1991.

Davies, John K., 'Athenian Citizenship: The Descent Group and the Alternatives', *The Classical Journal*, vol. 73, no. 2 (1977–8), 105–21.

Davis, David Brion, *The Problem of Slavery in Western Culture*, Cornell University Press, Ithaca, New York, 1966.

de Certau, Michel, *The Writing of History*, Tom Conley (tr.), Columbia University Press, New York, 1988.

Heterologies: Discourse on the Other, Brian Massumi (tr.), *Theory and History of Literature, Volume 17*, Manchester University Press, Manchester, 1986.

de Tervarent, Guy, *Attributs et Symboles dans L'Art Profane 1450–600*, Librairie E. Droz, Genève, 1958.

Dilke, O. A. W., 'Illustrations from Roman surveyors' manuals', *Imago Mundi*, 21 (1967), 9–29.

Greek and Roman Maps, Thames & Hudson, London, 1985.

Donaldson, Ian, *The Rapes of Lucretia*, Clarendon Press, Oxford, 1982.

Australia and The European Imagination: Papers from a Conference held at the Humanities Research Centre, Australian National University, May 1981, Humanities Research Centre, Australian National University, 1982.

Douglas, J. D. (ed.), *The New Bible Dictionary*, Inter-Varsity Press, London, 1970.

Douglas, Mary, *Purity and Danger: An analysis of the concepts of pollution and taboo*, Routledge & Kegan Paul, London and Henley, 1979.

duBois, Page, *Centaurs and Amazons: Woman and the Pre-History of the Great Chain of Being*, University of Michigan Press, Ann Arbor, 1982.

Edgerton, Samuel Y., 'From Mental Matrix to *Mappamundi* to Christian Empire: The Heritage of Ptolemaic Cartography in the Renaissance' in Woodward, David (ed.), *Art & Cartography*.

The Renaissance Discovery of Linear Perspective, Harper & Row, New York, Evanston, San Francisco and London, 1976.

Edwards, Philip (ed.), *Hamlet, Prince of Denmark*, The New Cambridge Shakespeare, Cambridge University Press, Cambridge, New York, Melbourne, New Rochelle and Sydney, 1985.

Eliade, Mircea, 'Sacred Space and Making the World Sacred', *The Sacred and the Profane: The Nature of Religion*, Willard R. Trask (tr.), Harcourt, Brace & World Inc., New York, 1959.

'Symbolism of the "Centre"', *Images and Symbols: Studies in Religious Symbolism*, Philip Mairet (tr.), Sheed & Ward, New York, 1969.

Elliot, J. H., *The Old World and the New, 1492–1650*, Cambridge University Press, 1970.

'Renaissance Europe and America: A Blunted Impact?' in Chiapelli, Fredi (ed.), *First Images of America*, vol. 1, pp. 11–23.

'The Discovery of America and the Discovery of Man', *Proceedings of the British Academy*, 58 (1974), 101–25.

Enterline, J., 'The Southern Continent and the False Strait of Magellan', *Imago Mundi*, 26 (1972), 48–59.

Erskine-Hill, Howard, 'Antony and Octavius: The Theme of Temperance in Shakespeare's *Antony and Cleopatra*', *Renaissance and Modern Studies*, 14 (1970), 26–47.

Evans, K. W., 'The Racial Factor in Othello', *Shakespeare Survey*, 5 (1970), 124–40.

Ferguson, John, *A Companion to Greek Tragedy*, University of Texas Press, Austin and London, 1972.

Fernández-Armesto, Felipe, *Columbus*, Oxford University Press, 1991.

Fiedler, Leslie, *The Stranger in Shakespeare*, Croom Helm, London, 1973.

Flemming, E. McClung, 'The American Image as Indian Princess, 1765–1783', *Winterthur Portfolio*, 2 (1965), 65–81.

'From Indian Princess to Greek Goddess: The American Image, 1783–1815', *Winterthur Portfolio*, 3 (1967), 37–66.

'Symbols of the United States: From Indian Queen to Uncle Sam', Browne, Ray B., Crowder, Richard H., Lokke, Virgil L. and Stafford, William T. (eds.), *Frontiers of American Culture*, Purdue University Studies, 1968, pp. 1–24.

Foss, Paul, 'Theatrum Nondum Cognitorum', Bostman, Peter, Burns, Chris and Hutchings, Paul (eds.), *The Foreign Bodies Papers*, Local Consumption Publications, Sydney, 1981, pp. 15–38.

Foucault, Michel, 'Of Other Spaces', *Diacritics*, Spring (1986), 22–7.

Franklin, Wayne, *Discoverers, Explorers, Settlers: The Diligent Writers of Early America*, University of Chicago Press, Chicago and London, 1979.

Frey, Paul, 'The Tempest and the New World', *Shakespeare Quarterly*, 30, 1 (Winter 1979), 29–41.

Garber, Marjorie (ed.), *Cannibals, Witches, and Divorce: Estranging the Renaissance*, Johns Hopkins University Press, Baltimore and London, 1987.

Gardner, Helen, *John Donne: The Divine Poems*, Clarendon Press, Oxford, 1952.

Gates, Henry Louis, Jr. (ed.), *'Race,' Writing, and Difference*, University of Chicago Press, Chicago and London, 1986.

Gayley, C. M., *Shakespeare and the Founders of Liberty in America*, Macmillan, New York, 1917.

Geertz, Clifford, *The Interpretation of Cultures*, Basic Books Inc., New York, 1973.

Gerbi, Antonello, *Nature in the New World: From Christopher Columbus to Gonzalo Fernández de Oviedo*, Jeremy Moyle (tr.), University of Pittsburgh Press, Pittsburgh, 1985.

'The Earliest Accounts on the New World', Chiapelli, Fredi (ed.), *First Images of America*, vol. 1, pp. 37–43.

Gilbert, Alan H., *A Geographical Dictionary of Milton*, Russell & Russell, New York, 1968.

Gillies, John, 'Shakespeare's Virginian Masque', *English Literary History* (Winter 1986), 673–707.

Girard, René, *Violence and the Sacred*, Patrick Gregory (tr.), Johns Hopkins University Press, Baltimore and London, 1986.

'Myth and Ritual in Shakespeare's *A Midsummer Night's Dream*', Harari, Josué V. (ed.), *Textual Strategies: Perspectives in Post-Structuralist Criticism*, Methuen, London, 1980, pp. 189–212.

Goldberg, S. L., 'The Tragedy of the Imagination: A Reading of *Antony and Cleopatra*', *Melbourne Critical Review*, 4 (1961), 41–64.

Goody, Jack (ed.), *Kinship*, Penguin, Harmondsworth, 1971.

Gordon, B. L., 'Sacred Directions, Orientation, and the Top of the Map', *History of Religions*, 10 (1970), 211–27.

Greenblatt, Stephen Jay, *Renaissance Self Fashioning: From More to Shakespeare*, University of Chicago Press, Chicago and London, 1980.

'Learning to Curse: Aspects of Linguistic Colonialism in the Sixteenth Century' in Chiapelli, Fredi (ed.), *First Images of America*, vol. 2, pp. 564–80.

'Invisible Bullets: Renaissance Authority and its Subversion', *Glyph*, 8 (1981), 40–61.

The Power of Forms in the English Renaissance, Pilgrim Books, Norman, Oklahoma, 1982.

(ed.), *Representing the English Renaissance*, University of California Press, Berkeley, 1988.

Marvellous Possessions: The Wonder of the New World. The Clarendon Lectures and the Carpenter Lectures, 1988, University of Chicago Press, Chicago, Illinois, 1991.

Hale, J. R. (ed.), *Renaissance Venice*, Faber & Faber, London, 1973.

Hall, Edith, *Inventing the Barbarian: Greek Self-Definition through Tragedy*, Clarendon Press, Oxford, 1989.

Hand, Wayland D., 'The Effect of the Discovery on Ethnological and Folklore Studies in Europe' in Chiapelli, Fredi (ed.), *First Images of America*, vol. 1, pp. 45–55.

Hanke, Lewis, *Aristotle and the American Indians: A Study in Race Prejudice in the Modern World*, Hollis & Carter, London, 1959.

All Mankind is One: A Study of the Disputation between Bartolomé de Las Casas and Juan Ginés de Sepúlveda in 1550 on the Intellectual and Religious Capacity of the American Indians, Northern Illinois University Press, DeKalb, 1974.

Harbison, Robert, *Eccentric Spaces*, Alfred Knopf, New York, 1977.

Hardie, Philip, *Vergil's Aeneid: Cosmos and Imperium*, Clarendon Press, Oxford, 1986.

Harley, J. B. and Woodward, David, *The History of Cartography, vol. 1: Cartography in Prehistoric, Ancient and Medieval Europe and the Mediterranean*, University of Chicago Press, Chicago and London, 1987.

Hartog, François, *The Mirror of Herodotus: The Representation of the Other in the Writing of History*, Janet Lloyd (tr.), University of California Press, Berkeley and London, 1988.

Harvey, David, *The Condition of Postmodernity: An Enquiry into the Origins of Cultural Change*, Blackwell, Oxford, 1989.

Heidel, William Arthur, *The Frame of the Ancient Greek Maps*, Arno Press, New York, 1976.

Helgerson, Richard, 'The Land Speaks: Cartography, Chorography, and Subversion in Renaissance England' in *Representing the English Renaissance*, Greenblatt, Stephen (ed.), pp. 327–61.

Hodgen, Margaret T., *Early Anthropology in the Sixteenth and Seventeenth Centuries*, University of Pennsylvania Press, Philadelphia, 1964.

Holmes, Martin, 'An Unrecorded Portrait of Edward Alleyn', *Theatre Notebook*, 1950–52, 11–13.

Holquist, Michael and Clark, Katerina, *Mikhail Bakhtin*, Bellknap Press, Cambridge, Mass., and London, 1984.

Honour, Hugh, *The New Golden Land*, Pantheon Books, New York, 1978.

How, W. W. and Wells, J., *A Commentary on Herodotus*, 2 vols., Clarendon Press, Oxford, 1912.

Howard, D. R., 'The World of "Mandeville's Travels"', *Yearbook of English Studies*, 1 (1971), 1–17.

Hulme, Peter, *Colonial Encounters: Europe and the Native Caribbean, 1492–1797*, Methuen, London and New York, 1986.

Hulme, Peter and Whitehead, Neil L. (eds.)., *Wild Majesty: Encounters with Caribs from Columbus to the Present Day. An Anthology*, Clarendon Press, Oxford, 1992.

Hume, Martin, *Spanish Influence on English Literature*, Haskell House, New York, 1964.

Hunt, Clay, *Donne's Poetry: Essays in Literary Analysis*, Yale University Press, New Haven and London, 1962.

Hunter, G. K., 'Othello and Colour Prejudice', *Proceedings of the British Academy*, 53 (1967), 139–63.

'Sources and Meanings in *Titus Andronicus*' J. C. Grey (ed.), *The Mirror up to Shakespeare*, Toronto University Press, 1983, pp. 171–88.

'The "Sources" of *Titus Andronicus* – Once Again', *Notes and Queries*, 228 (1983), 114–16.

Hyde, James Hazen, 'L'Iconographie des Quatre Parties du Monde dans les Tapisseries', *Gazette des Beaux-Arts*, Paris (1924), 253–72.

Immerwahr, Henry R., *Form and Thought in Herodotus*, Press of Western Reserve University, Cleveland, 1966.

Israel, Jonathan I., *European Jewry in the Age of Mercantilism, 1550–1750*, Clarendon Press, Oxford, 1989.

Jauss, Hans Robert, *Toward an Aesthetic of Reception*, Timothy Bahti (tr.), University of Minnesota Press, Minneapolis, 1982.

Johnson, Hildegard Binder, 'New Geographical Horizons: Concepts' in *First Images of America*, Fredi Chiapelli (ed.), vol. 2, pp. 615–33.

Jones, Eldred, *Othello's Countrymen; the African in English Renaissance Drama*, Oxford University Press, 1965.

    The Elizabethan Image of Africa, University of Virginia Press, Charlottesville, 1971.

Jones, Emrys, '"Othello", "Lepanto" and the Cyprus Wars', *Shakespeare Survey*, 21 (1968), 47–52.

    'Stuart *Cymbeline*' in *Shakespeare's Later Comedies*, Palmer, D. J. (ed.), Penguin, Harmondsworth, 1971, pp. 248–63.

Jordan, Constance, *Pulci's Morgante: Poetry and History in Fifteenth-Century Florence*, Folger Shakespeare Library, Washington; Associated University Press, London and Toronto, 1986.

Jordan, Winthrop D., *White Over Black: American Attitudes Toward the Negro, 1550–1812*, University of North Carolina Press, Williamsburg, Virginia, 1968.

    The White Man's Burden: Historical Origins of Racism in the United States, Oxford University Press, New York, 1974.

Jorgensen, Paul A., 'Shakespeare's Brave New World' in Chiapelli, Fredi (ed.), *First Images of America*, vol. 1, pp. 83–9.

Kanzer, Mark, 'The Self-Analytic Literature of Robert Louis Stevenson' in *Psychoanalysis and Culture: Essays in Honour Of Géza Róheim*, George B. Wilbur and Warner Muensterberger (eds.), International Universities Press, New York, 1951, pp. 425–35.

Kaplan, Paul H. D., 'The Earliest Images of Othello', *Shakespeare Quarterly*, 39 (1988), 171–86.

Kermode, Frank (ed.), *The Tempest*, The Arden Shakespeare, Methuen, London, 1962.

Kimble, G. H. T., *Geography in the Middle Ages*, London, 1938.

Kish, George, 'The Cosmographic Heart: Cordiform Maps of the 16th Century', *Imago Mundi*, 19 (1965), 13–21.

Knight, G. Wilson, *The Wheel of Fire: Interpretations of Shakespearean Tragedy*, Methuen, London, 1972.

Kristeva, Julia, *Powers of Horror: An Essay on Abjection*, Leon S. Roudiez (tr.), Columbia University Press, New York, 1982.

Kunzle, David, *The Early Comic Strip: Narrative Strips and Picture Stories in the European Broadsheet from c.1450 to 1825*, History of the Comic Strip, vol. 1, University of California Press, Berkeley, Los Angeles and London, 1973.

Lane, Frederic C., *Venice: A Maritime Republic*, Johns Hopkins University Press, Baltimore and London, 1973.

Law, Robert A., 'The Roman Background of *Titus Andronicus*', *Studies in Philology*, 40 (1943), 145–53.

Lawall, Gilbert, 'Apollonius' Argonautica: Jason as Anti-Hero', *Yale Classical Studies*, vol. 19 (1966), 121–69.

Leach, Edmund, *Genesis as Myth and Other Essays*, Jonathan Cape, London, 1969.

Leach, Edmund and Aycock, Alan D., *Structuralist Interpretations of Biblical Myth*, Cambridge University Press, Cambridge, London and New York, 1983.

Le Corbeiller, Clare, 'Miss America and Her Sisters: Personifications of the Four Parts of the World', *The Metropolitan Museum of Art Bulletin*, 19 (April 1961), 209–23.

LeFebvre, Henri, *The Production of Space*, Donald Nicholson-Smith (tr.), Blackwell, Oxford, 1991.

Lever, J. W (ed.), *Measure for Measure*, The Arden Shakespeare, Methuen, London, 1976.

Lévi-Strauss, Claude, *The Elementary Structures of Kinship*, James Harle Bell, John Richard von Sturmer and Rodney Needham (trs.), Rodney Needham (ed.), Eyre & Spottiswoode, London, 1969.

Lloyd, G. E. R., *Polarity and Analogy: Two Types of Argument in Early Greek Thought*, Cambridge University Press, Cambridge, London, New York and Melbourne, 1966.

Lloyd, Robert, 'A Look at Images', *Annals of the Association of American Geographers*, 72, 4 (1982), 532–48.

Lloyd, T. H., *Alien Merchants in England in the High Middle Ages*, Harvester, Brighton, 1982.

Logan, Oliver, *Culture and Society in Venice: 1470–1790: The Renaissance and its Heritage*, Batsford, London, 1972.

Lovejoy, Arthur O. and Boas, George, *Primitivism and Related Ideas in Antiquity (With Supplementary Essays by W. F. Albright and P. E. Dumont)*, The Johns Hopkins Press, Baltimore, 1935.

Lynam, Edward, *The Mapmaker's Art: Essays on the History of Maps*, Batchworth Press, London, 1953.

Malouf, David, 'A First Place: The Mapping of a World', *Southerly*, 45, 1 (1985), 3–10.

Manguel, Alberto and Guadalupi, Gianni, *The Dictionary of Imaginary Places*, Harcourt Brace Jovanovich, San Diego, New York and London, 1987.

Martz, Louis B, *The Poem of the Mind: Essays on Poetry, English and American*, Oxford University Press, Oxford and New York, 1969.

The Poetry of Meditation: A Study in English Religious Literature of the Seventeenth Century, Yale University Press, New Haven and London, 1978.

Marx, Leo, *The Machine in the Garden: Technology and the pastoral ideal in America*, Oxford University Press, New York, 1964.

Mauss, Marcel, *The Gift: Forms and Functions of Exchange in Archaic Societies*, Ian Cunningham (tr.), Cohen & West, London, 1966.

Mazzolani, Lidia Storoni, *The Idea of the City in Roman Thought: From Walled City to Spiritual Commonwealth*, S. O'Donnell (tr.), Hollis & Carter, London, 1970.

McCann, Franklin T., *English Discovery of America to 1585*, Octagon Books, New York, 1969.

McGrane, Bernard, *Beyond Anthropology: Society and the Other*, Columbia University Press, New York, 1989.

McGrath, Elizabeth, 'Rubens's *Arch of the Mint*', *Journal of the Warburg and Courtauld Institutes*, 37 (1974), 191–217.

McPherson, David C., *Shakespeare, Jonson, and the Myth of Venice*, Associated University Presses, London and Toronto, 1990.

Miola, Robert S., '*Titus Andronicus* and the Mythos of Shakespeare's Rome', *Shakespeare Studies*, 14 (1981), 85–98.

Mitchell, G. Duncan (ed.), *A New Dictionary of Sociology*, Routledge, London, 1979.

Moseley, C. W. R. D., 'The Metamorphosis of Sir John Mandeville', *The Yearbook of English Studies*, 4 (1974), 5–25.

Mullaney, Steven, *The Place of the Stage: License, Play, and Power in Renaissance England*, University of Chicago Press, Chicago and London, 1988.

'Brothers and Others, or the Art of Alienation', in Garber, Marjorie (ed.), *Cannibals, Witches, and Divorce*, pp. 67–89.

Newman, Karen, '"... And wash the Ethiop white ...": Femininity and the monstrous in *Othello*' in Howard, Jean E. and O'Connor, Marion F. (eds.), *Shakespeare Reproduced: The Text in History and Ideology*, Methuen, New York and London, 1987, pp. 143–62.

Nicholson, Marjorie Hope, *The Breaking of the Circle: Studies in the Effect of the 'New Science' upon Seventeenth Century Poetry (Revised Edition)*, Columbia University Press, New York and London, 1960.

Niederland, William G., 'The Naming of America' in Kanzer, M. (ed.), *The Unconscious Today: Essays in Honour of Max Schur*, International Universities Press, New York, 1971, pp. 459–72.

Nisbet, R. G. M. and Hubbard, Margaret, *A Commentary on Horace: Odes, Book 1*, Clarendon Press, Oxford, 1970.

A Commentary on Horace: Odes, Book II, Clarendon Press, Oxford, 1978.

North, Martin (ed.), *Leviticus: A Commentary*, SCM Press, London, 1965.

Novarr, David, *The Disinterred Muse: Donne's Texts and Contexts*, Cornell University Press, Ithaca and London, 1980.

O'Gorman, Edmundo, *The Invention of America: An Inquiry into the Historical Nature of the New World and the Meaning of its History*, Indiana University Press, Bloomington, 1961.

Orgel, Stephen (ed.), *The Tempest*, The Oxford Shakespeare, Oxford University Press, Oxford and New York, 1987.

'Shakespeare and the Cannibals', Garber, Marjorie (ed.), *Cannibals, Witches, and Divorce*, pp. 40–66.

Orgel, Stephen and Strong, Roy, *Inigo Jones: The Theatre of the Stuart Court*. See 'Primary Sources'.

Orkin, Martin, 'Othello and the "plain face" of Racism', *Shakespeare Quarterly*, 38 (1987), 166–88.

The Oxford English Dictionary, second edition, prepared by J. A. Simpson and E. S. C. Weiner, Clarendon Press, Oxford, 1989.

Palmer, D. J. (ed.), *Shakespeare's Later Comedies*, Penguin, Harmondsworth, 1971.

Parker, John, *Books to Build an Empire: A Bibliographical History of English Overseas Interests to 1620*, N. Israel, Amsterdam, 1965.

Paster, Gail Kern, *The Idea of the City in the Age of Shakespeare*, University of Georgia Press, Athens, 1985.

Pennington, Loren E., 'The Amerindian in English Promotional Literature, 1575–1625' in *The Westward Enterprise: English activities in Ireland, the Atlantic and America, 1480–1650*, K. R. Andrews, N. P. Canny, P. E. H. Hair (eds.), Liverpool University Press, 1978, pp. 175–94.

Pitt-Rivers, Julian, *The Fate of Shechem or The Politics of Sex: Essays in the Anthropology of the Mediterranean*, Cambridge University Press, Cambridge, London, New York and Melbourne, 1977.

Pullan, Brian S., *The Jews of Europe and the Inquisition of Venice, 1550–1670*, Blackwell, Oxford, 1983.

Quinn, David Beers, 'New Geographical Horizons: Literature' in *First Images of America*, Fredi Chiapelli (ed.), vol. 2, pp. 635–58.

Ramsay, G. D., *The City of London, in International Politics at the Accession of Elizabeth Tudor*, Manchester University Press, 1975.

Righter, Anne, *Shakespeare and the Idea of the Play*, Penguin, Harmondsworth, 1967.

Robinson, Arthur H. and Petchenik, Barbara Bartz, *The Nature of Maps: Essays toward Understanding Maps and Mapping*, Chicago University Press, 1986.

Rogers, J. D., 'Voyages and Exploration: Geography: Maps' in *Shakespeare's England: An Account of the Life and Manners of his Age*, 2 vols., Clarendon Press, Oxford, 1932.

Rosenthal, Earl, '*Plus Ultra, Non Plus Ultra*, and the Columnar Device of Charles V', *Journal of the Warburg and Courtauld Institutes*, 34 (1971), 204–28.

'The Invention of the Columnar Device of Emperor Charles V at the Court of Burgundy in Flanders in 1516', *Journal of the Warburg and Courtauld Institutes*, 36 (1973), 198–230.

Rymer, Thomas, 'A Short View of Tragedy' (1693), in J. E. Springarn (ed.), *Critical Essays of the Seventeenth Century*, 3 vols., Indiana University Press, Bloomington, 1957, vol. 2, pp. 208–55.

Said, Edward, *Orientalism*, Routledge & Kegan Paul, London and Henley, 1978.

Schanzer, Ernst, 'Hercules and his Load', *Review of English Studies*, new series, 19, 51–3.

Schilder, Günter, 'Willem Jansz. Blaeu's Wall Map of the World, on Mercator's Projection 1606–07 and its Influence', *Imago Mundi*, 31 (second series, vol. 4, 1979), 36–54.

Schultz, Juergen, 'Jacopo de'Barbari's View of Venice: Map Making, City Views, and Moralized Geography Before the Year 1500', *Art Bulletin*, 60 (1978), 425–74.

'Maps as Metaphors: Mural Map Cycles of the Italian Renaissance', in Woodward, David (ed.), *Art & Cartography*, pp. 97–122.

Schwartz, Murray M. and Kahn, Coppélia (eds.), *Representing Shakespeare: New Psychoanalytic Essays*, Johns Hopkins University Press, Baltimore and London, 1980.

Seaton, Ethel, 'Fresh Sources for Marlowe', *Review of English Studies*, 5, 20 (1929,) 385–401.

Shapiro, I. A., 'Robert Fludd's Stage Illustration', *Shakespeare Studies*, 2 (1966), 192–209.

Shirley, Rodney W., *The Mapping of the World: Early Printed World Maps, 1472–1700*, The Holland Press, London, 1987.

Skelton, R. A., *Decorative Printed Maps of the 15th to 18th Centuries: A Revised Edition of Old Decorative Maps and Charts by A. L. Humphreys*, Staples Press, London and New York, 1952.

Skura, Meredith Anne, 'Discourse and the individual: The Case of Colonialism in *The Tempest*', *Shakespeare Quarterly*, 40 (1989), 42–69.

Smith, A. J. (ed.), *John Donne: The Critical Heritage*, Routledge & Kegan Paul, London and Boston, 1975.

Smith, Catherine Delano, 'Cartographic Signs on European Maps and their Explanation before 1700', *Imago Mundi*, 37 (1985), 9–29.

Smith, David M., 'Introduction: the Sharing and Dividing of Geographical Space' in *Shared Space: Divided Space*, Michael Chisholm and David M. Smith (eds.), pp. 1–21.

Smith, Jonathan Z., *Map is not Territory*, E. J. Brill, Leiden, 1978.

Smith, Sir William and Lockwood, Sir John, *Chambers Murray Latin-English Dictionary*, Chambers, Edinburgh; John Murray, London, 1988.

Smith, W. (ed.), *A Dictionary of Greek and Roman Geography*, 2 vols., John Murray, London, 1873.

Sommers, Alan, ' "Wilderness of Tigers": Structure and Symbolism in *Titus Andronicus*', *Essays in Criticism*, 10 (1960), 275–89.

Spevack, Martin, *The Harvard Concordance to Shakespeare*, The Belknap Press of Harvard University Press, Cambridge, Mass., 1973.

Stallybrass, Peter and White, Allon, *The Politics and Poetics of Transgression*, Methuen, London, 1986.

Starobinski, Jean, 'Montaigne on Illusion: The Denunciation of Untruth', *Daedalus*, 108 (Summer 1979), 85–101.

Steele, Colin, *English Interpreters of the Iberian New World from Purchas to Stevens: A Bibliographical Study. 1603–1726*, The Dolphin Book Co., Oxford, 1975.

Stevens, Henry, 'The de Bry Collector's Painful Peregrination Along the Pleasant Pathway to Perfection' in *Bibliographical Essays: A Tribute to Wilberforce Eames*, Books For Libraries Press, Freeport, New York, 1967, pp. 269–76.

Stevenson, Edward Luther, *Terrestrial and Celestial Globes: Their History and Construction Including a Consideration of their Value as Aids in the Study of Geography and Astronomy*, 2 vols., Yale University Press, New Haven, 1921.

Stoll, E. E., *Poets and Playwrights: Shakespeare, Milton, Spenser, Jonson*, University of Minnesota Press, Minneapolis, 1930.

Strong, Roy, *Gloriana: The Portraits of Queen Elizabeth I*, Thames & Hudson, GDR, 1987.

Sugden, Edward H., *A Topographical Dictionary to the Works of Shakespeare and his Fellow Dramatists*, Manchester University Press, London and New York, 1925.

Szczesniak, Boleslaw, 'Matteo Ricci's Maps of China', *Imago Mundi*, 11 (1967), 127–36.

Taylor, E. G. R., *Tudor Geography: 1485–1583*, Methuen, London, 1930.

Late Tudor and Early Stuart Geography: 1583–1650, Methuen, London, 1934.
'John Dee and the Map of North-East Asia', *Imago Mundi*, 12 (1955), 103–6.
Tennenhouse, Leonard, 'The Counterfeit Order of *The Merchant of Venice*' in Schwartz, Murray M. and Kahn, Coppélia (eds.), *Representing Shakespeare*, pp. 54–69.
Thomas, Richard F., *Lands and Peoples in Roman Poetry. The Ethnographical Tradition*, Cambridge Philological Society, The Cambridge University Library, 1982.
Thomson, J. Oliver, 'Orbis Terrarum: Some Reflections on the Roman Empire', *University of Birmingham Historical Journal*, 1 (1947), 1–12.
Thrower, Norman J. W., *Maps & Man: An Examination of Cartography in Relation to Culture and Civilization*, Prentice-Hall, Englewood Cliffs, New Jersey, 1972.
'New Geographical Horizons: Maps' in *First Images of America*, Fredi Chiapelli (ed.), vol. 2, pp. 659–74.
Todorov, Tzvetan, *The Conquest of America: The Question of the Other*, Richard Howard (tr.), Harper & Row, New York, 1984.
Tokson, Elliot H., *The Popular Image of the Black Man in English Drama 1550–1688*, Hall & Co., Boston, Mass., 1982.
Tooley, R. V., *Maps and Map-Makers*, Batsford, London, New York, Toronto and Sydney, 1949.
Tooley, R. V. and Bricker, Charles, *Landmarks of Mapmaking: An Illustrated Survey of Maps and Mapmaking*, Wordsworth, Ware, Hertfordshire, 1976.
Tretiak, Andrew, '*The Merchant of Venice* and the "Alien" Question', *Review of English Studies*, 5 (1929), 402–9.
Tricomi, Albert H., 'The Mutilated Garden in *Titus Andronicus*', *Shakespeare Studies*, 9 (1976), 89–105.
'The Aesthetics of Mutilation in *Titus Andronicus*', *Shakespeare Survey*, 27 (1974), 11–19.
Tucci, Ugo, 'The Psychology of the Venetian Merchant in the Sixteenth Century' in Hale, J. R. (ed.), *Renaissance Venice*, pp. 346–78.
Une Rencontre de l'Occident et de la Chine: Matteo Ricci, Travaux et Conférences du Centre Sèvres, Centre Sèvres, 1983.
van den Berg, Kent, *Playhouse and Cosmos: Shakespearean Theater as Metaphor*, University of Delaware Press, Newark; Associated University Press, London and Toronto, 1985.
Van Horne, John, 'The Attitude Toward the Enemy in Sixteenth Century Spanish Narrative Poetry', *The Romanic Review*, 16 (1925), 341–61.
Vaughan, Alden T., 'Shakespeare's Indian: The Americanization of Caliban', *Shakespeare Quarterly*, 39 (1988), 137–53.
'"Expulsion of the Salvages": English Policy and the Virginia Massacre of 1622', *William and Mary Quarterly*, third series, 35, 1 (1978), 57–84.
Veevers, E. E., 'Sources of Inigo Jones's Masquing Designs', *Journal of the Warburg and Courtauld Institutes*, 22–3 (1959–60), 373–74.
Vernant, Jean Pierre, *Myth and Thought among the Greeks*, Routledge & Kegan Paul, London, Boston, Melbourne and Henley, 1983.
Waith, Eugene M., *Titus Andronicus*, The Oxford Shakespeare, Oxford University Press, Oxford and New York, 1984.

The Herculean Hero in Marlowe, Chapman, Shakespeare and Dryden, Chatto & Windus, London, 1962.

Wallis, Helen, 'Missionary Cartographers to China', *The Geographical Magazine*, 47 (1975), 751–59.

'The influence of Father Ricci on Far Eastern cartography', *Imago Mundi*, 19 (1965), 38–45.

Ward, Sir A. W., *Shakespeare and the Founders of Liberty in America*, Macmillan, New York, 1917.

'Shakespeare and the Makers of Virginia', *Proceedings of the British Academy*, 9 (1919–20), pp. 141–85.

Washburn, Wilcomb E., 'The Meaning of "Discovery" in the Fifteenth and Sixteenth Centuries', *The American Historical Review*, 68, 1 (October 1962), 1–21.

Welu, James A., 'The Sources and Development of Cartographic Ornamentation in the Netherlands' in *Art & Cartography*, David Woodward (ed.), pp. 147–73.

White, Hayden, *Tropics of Discourse: Essays in Cultural Criticism*, Johns Hopkins University Press, Baltimore and London, 1978.

Wilders, John (ed.), *Shakespeare: 'The Merchant of Venice': A Casebook*, Macmillan, Basingstoke, 1989.

Wilford, John Noble, *The Mapmakers*, Junction Books, London, 1981.

Woodward, David (ed.), *Art & Cartography: Six Historical Essays*, University of Chicago Press, Chicago and London, 1987.

Wright, Louis B., *Religion and Empire: The Alliance between Piety and Commerce in English Expansion 1558–1625*, University of North Carolina Press, Chapel Hill, 1943.

Yates, Frances, *Theatre of the World*, Routledge & Kegan Paul, London and New York, 1987.

Astraea: The Imperial Theme In The Sixteenth Century, Penguin, Harmondsworth, 1977.

The Art of Memory, Routledge & Kegan Paul, London and Chicago, 1966.

'The Stage in Robert Fludd's Memory System', *Shakespeare Studies*, 3 (1967), 138–66.

'Boissard's Costume-Book and Two Portraits', *Journal of the Warburg and Courtauld Institutes*, 22–3 (1959–60), 365–6.

Zelinsky, Wilbur, 'The First and Last Frontier of Communication: The Map as Mystery', *Bulletin of the Geography and Map Division, Special Libraries Association*, 94 (1973), 2–8.

Index